A HISTORY OF TODMORDEN

Freda Heywood   Malcolm Heywood

Bernard Jennings

LIST OF SUBSCRIBERS
to the hardback edition

Mrs A Adams
Mrs S R Anderton
Mr & Mrs C Anker
Mr D J Armitage
Mr & Mrs R Ashworth
Mr G & Mrs J Astley

Mr & Mrs D M Badger
Mr & Mrs G B Badger
Joyce L Banks
Mrs W Banks
Mr C Bardgett
Mrs A Barker (Toronto)
Mr N D Barker
Mr & Mrs R Barker
Mr & Mrs S Barker
Mr Vincent Barker
Dr W H Barker
Mr H Barnes
Mr & Mrs M Barnes
Mr J M D Bateman
Mr & Mrs G M Batts
Mr & Mrs G Batty
Mr & Mrs F Best
Mr & Mrs F A Beswick
Mr & Mrs B B Binns
Mr R A Birch
Mrs M Birkby
Mrs S P & Mr D Black
Mr & Mrs J A Boon
Mr D G Bowe
Mrs Dorothy Bramley
Mr & Mrs J Bregazzi
Mr R Brennend
Mr & Mrs C B Brown
Mr & Mrs Philip Brown
Mrs A Bulcock
Mr & Mrs T Bullas
Mr E Butler
Mrs P A Butterworth

Mr P Caine
Revd Canon P N Calvert
Mrs A Carey
Mr T Carlton
Mrs C V Carty
Mrs M J Catlin
Mrs D Chopping

Mr L Chopping
Mr & Mrs N Clark
Mr & Mrs V G Clark
Mr & Mrs A Clarke
Mr B J Clarke
Mr D A Clarke
Mr & Mrs G T Clarke
Mr Roy Anthony Claxton
Mr & Mrs G Clegg
Mr & Mrs C C Coates
Miss C E Cockcroft
Mr & Mrs J M Cockcroft
D Collins
Mr J D Connolly
Mr D Cook
Mrs A Cooper
Mr L R Cordingley
Mr & Mrs J Cox
Mrs Avis Crabtree
Mrs B Crabtree
Elizabeth & Keith Crabtree
Mr & Mrs F W Crabtree
Mr & Mrs I J Crabtree
Mr & Mrs I J Crabtree
Mr R Crabtree
Mr & Mrs R S Crabtree
Mr & Mrs S F Cridge
Mr D Crossley
Mr P K & Mrs K Crossley
Dr & Mrs J V Crowther
Miss M J Crowther
Mr R & Mrs S A Curtis
Mr & Mrs P Curzon

Mr & Mrs H Dann
Mr D G & Mrs P Davies
Mr & Mrs J G Davies
N B & M Davies
Mr N J & Mrs A Davies
Mr & Mrs G B Davy-Day
Mr D Dawson
Mr A J Dean
Mrs F Dean
Mr G Dean
Mr S G Dean
Mr S P Dearden
Mrs J Dennett
Mr P H L Devereux

Mr & Mrs R I Dibble
Mrs Berenice Dixon
Mr P & Mrs J Dobson
Miss R A Dolan
Mr S J & Mrs C A Dolan
Mr E Dowling
Mrs M Driver
Miss S J Duerden
Mrs A Duffield
Mrs Elsie Duffield
Miss H C Duffield
Mr I L & Mrs F G Duffield
Mr H A & Mrs J A Duffy
Dennis & Ruby Duke
Mr K Duxbury
Mr & Mrs M Dyson

Mrs Earnshaw
H Edmead
Mr David Elliott
Mr & Mrs S J Emmott
Mr & Mrs M Endley
Sarah Endley
Mrs Sheila Endley
Mrs B L Epton
Mr K & Mrs M Evans
Ms S J Evans

Mr & Mrs B S Farrell
Mr & Mrs A Fawthrop
Mr D R Few
Mr & Mrs A Fiddling
Mr D Field
Mr R Fielden
Mr & Mrs R E Fielden
Miss S Fielden
Mr S Fielden
Mr & Mrs M Fielder
Dr W Mary Findon
Mr R E Finnerty
Mr & Mrs B M Fitzsimmons
Mrs H M Ford MBE

Keith J Gavaghan
Mrs M Gesh
Mr & Mrs P J Gibson
Mr & Mrs L Gilsenan
Miss M Gledhill
Mr S M Godden
P Godfrey
Mr & Mrs T Goldie
Mr & Mrs R W J Goldthorpe

The Reverend S Goodall
Mrs J Green
Mr & Mrs J Green
Mr & Mrs K W Green
Mr & Mrs K C Greenman
Mrs Annie Greenwood
Mr D Greenwood
Mr & Mrs E Greenwood
Mr M Greenwood
Mr P & Mrs B Greenwood
P M Greenwood
Mr R Greenwood
Miss S Greenwood
James Hans Gregory
Dr & Mrs J M S Grieve
Mr Peter James Grieve
Mrs A Grundy
Mr J & Mrs S Gulaiczuk
Mr R C Guthrie

Mrs L Hall
Mr & Mrs R Halliwell
Mrs G Ham
Mr G H Hammersley
Dr S C Hardy
Mr D M Hargreaves
Mr D Hartley
Mr Harold Hartley
Mr J Hartley
Mr & Mrs J Hatton
Mrs E Hawthorn
Mr & Mrs B J Heal
Mr J C Heap
Mr M Hearne
Mr & Mrs C H Helliwell
Mr & Mrs F Helliwell (2 copies)
Mr & Mrs J D Helliwell
Mr & Mrs N A Helliwell
Mr & Mrs S Helliwell
Mrs M Henstock
Mr D Hesling
Mr & Mrs R Hewitt
Mr & Mrs G Hey
Mr Gerald & Mrs Nora Hey
Miss Rita Highley
Mr L & Mrs J Higson
Miss W M Hindle
The Grammar School, Hipperholme
Mr E & Mrs L Hirst
Mr & Mrs S Hirst
Mr & Mrs W E Hodkinson
Mr P S & Mrs L Holland

Mary Hollinrake
Margareta Holmstedt
Mr & Mrs R D C Holt-Pearson
Mrs M Hopkins (Lytham)
Mr Harry & Mrs Kathleen Horsfall
Mr U C Horsfall
Mrs M A Hoskinson
Mrs B Howarth
Mr K Howarth
Mr M & Mrs S E Howarth
Mr & Mrs P Howarth
Mr D Howorth
Mr H Howorth
Mr D & Mrs A Hudders
Mr & Mrs A G Hudson
Mr & Mrs D Hudson
Mrs Mary Hunt

Mr R S Ingham

Mr & Mrs D Jackson
Mr & Mrs I Jarman
Mr & Mrs T Jarman
Mr & Mrs A H Jewell
Mrs E Johnson
Mr & Mrs E L Jones
Mr M L Jones

Mr John G Keegan
Ruth Kelly
Mrs D Kenworthy
Mr J Kershaw
Mr & Mrs John Kershaw
Mrs N Kershaw
Mr & Mrs W Kershaw
Mrs H Kidd
Mr & Mrs J Kidd
Mr B King
Ms S M King
Mr & Mrs J A Kobus

Mr W Lassey
Mr B R Law (2 copies)
Mr & Mrs M Law
Mr & Mrs R Leah
Mrs L N Levick
Barry Lister
Mr & Mrs P M Lister
Dr S A & Mrs M Little
Mr S Loach
Mr & Mrs K Lobley

Mr D Longbottom
Mr & Mrs H Lord
Mr & Mrs K Lord
Leon & Eileen Lovett
Mr D Ludlam
Mr & Mrs K Lumb

Mr & Mrs P McLoughlin
Mr & Mrs E McQuaid
Mr & Mrs K Makin
Mrs E Mamwell
Miss A F Markwell
Professor H & Mrs S M Marsh
Mr A S Marshall JP
Mr I Marshall
Mr & Mrs J Marshall
Miss J E Marshall
Mr & Mrs J P Marshall
Mr K Marshall
Mr & Mrs C J May
Mr K Maynard
Mr & Mrs J M Midgley
Mr A F Mills
Mrs S K Mills
Mr & Mrs B W Mitchell
Mr M W Mitchell
Mrs M Moorhead
Mr & Mrs B Morris
Mrs A J Murray
Mr & Mrs T A Mycock

Mr T & Mrs R C Newell
Mr & Mrs C Nichol
Mr K Nichol
Mr & Mrs G Noble
Mrs M Noble
Mrs G Normington
Ms L A Nutt
Mr & Mrs K Nuttall
Mrs J Nyári

Mr M Ormerod
Mr & Mrs R Ormerod
Mr T Ormerod

D Paish
Mr & Mrs S Parker
Mr & Mrs B Partington
Mr Michael Paul
Mr A H Pendleton MBE
Mr & Mrs J S Perrin

Mrs G Phillips
Mr & Mrs B Pickles
Mr & Mrs H W Platford
Mr & Mrs K Puttock

Mrs D Rawnsley
Mr & Mrs K E Rawson
Mr A Read
Miss E Read
Mr G Ribchester
Mr M Rigg
Mrs L Rimmington
R Robinson
Mr B Rogers
Mr A Roscoe

Dr Joseph Sacco
Mr R G Salkeld
Mrs E M Savage
Mr M J & Mrs C J Savage
Mrs J Saville
Mr & Mrs P Sayer
Mrs J H Scholfield
Mr F & Mrs F Sharp
Alan & Janet Shaw
Mr P K Shaw
Miss R D Y Sheehan
Mrs Laura M Shepherd
Mr & Mrs G Shorrock
Miss M Slack
Mr & Mrs F Slater
A E Smith
Mr M Smith
Mrs D Spencer
Mrs N Stainton
Mr I C Stansfield
Mrs M Stansfield
Mr & Mrs M Stansfield
Mr & Mrs M J Stansfield
Mr N Stansfield
Mr & Mrs F Stanyer
Michael Steed
Mr & Mrs R Steventon
Mr & Mrs M Stone
Mr C & Mrs H J Studd
Eleanor Sunderland
Mr & Mrs W G Sunderland
Mrs B Sutcliffe
Mr & Mrs B G Sutcliffe
Mr C & Mrs J E Sutcliffe
Mrs D Sutcliffe (2 copies)

Mr & Mrs D Sutcliffe
Mr & Mrs D A Sutcliffe
Professor H Sutcliffe
Miss H M Sutcliffe
Miss K J Sutcliffe
Mr & Mrs N Sutcliffe
Mr & Mrs R Sutcliffe
Mrs V Sutcliffe
Mr W Sutcliffe
Mr & Mrs W R Swift

Mr J T Tattersall
Mr & Mrs J Taylor
Mr J & Mrs S Taylor
Mr & Mrs John R Taylor
Mr M Taylor
Robert Taylor
Mr & Mrs D K Tempest
Mr & Mrs W Thewlis
Mr & Mrs D J Thomas
Mr & Mrs P J Thornton
Todmorden C of E School
Ms D J Tokariuk
Mr & Mrs W G Townley
Mr & Mrs P Travis
Mr E & Mrs R Tregonning
Mrs Florence Turner
Mr J M Turner
Mr & Mrs M Twist

Mr J Umpleby
Mr A & Mrs M Unsworth
Mr & Mrs G T Uren
David & Jean Uttley
Mr & Mrs W Uttley

Mr & Mrs R Vernon

Mr & Mrs J F Wade
Mrs Annis Wadsworth
Mr & Mrs B Wadsworth
Mr A K Waller
Mr J D Waller
Mr C J Ward
Mr K Ward
Mr & Mrs R A Ward
Mrs N C Warner
Mr & Mrs D Warren
Mrs J W Wattis
Mr & Mrs A P Wear
Mr & Mrs W Welsh

Ms A West
Mrs Georgina Whalley
John White
Mrs Maud White
Mr C Whitehead
Mr N K Whitehead
Mrs H Whitlock
Frank Whittaker
Mr B Wild
Mrs Mary E Wild
Mr Colin Wilkinson
Mr D E Wilkinson
Mr E J Williams
Mrs I P Williams

Mrs P Williams
Mr R & Mrs S Wilson
Mr C F & Mrs J Windross
Mr & Mrs D Winslow
Mr & Mrs A J Wiszniewski
Mr & Mrs C H Woodall
Mr A P Worsley
Mr L E Wright
Mr & Mrs S Wynne

Jackie Yates
Mr A L Young
Mrs E M Young

LIST OF SUBSCRIBERS

to the paperback edition

Ms J Appleton MBE
Prof & Mrs D A Armstrong
Mr & Mrs F Armstrong
Mr C Aspin
Mr & Mrs T G Ayres

Mr & Mrs G B Badger
David Ball
Mrs E Barker
Mr J Barnes
Mrs P Barrass
Mr D Bates
Ms M A Beaumont
Mr & Mrs M Beet
Mark Binns
Mr & Mrs W Birch
Mrs A Blomeley
Mr & Mrs D A Blood
Mr & Mrs S Boddy
Mrs K M Bradley
Mrs E Brennan
Mrs E Brennan
Mr & Mrs J D Bromley
Gordon Bryant
Mr I G & Mrs A Buglass
Mr & Mrs E J Bunn
Rev Dr L Burton (2 copies)

Mr & Mrs A E Cale

Miss B Callin
Ms A Carling
Mr D J & Mrs B Carpenter
Mr & Mrs W A Caulfield
Cllr D M Chaytor & Ms S N Whittingham
Mrs E Clegg
Ms P J Colbran
Miss I Cooke
Mr & Mrs K C Craven
Mrs M Cropper
Mr P Cross
Miss M J Crowther

Mr & Mrs E Dawson
Mr & Mrs G Dawson
Mr J B & Mrs J M Dawson
Dr V A Dearden (2 copies)
Mrs Barbara Diggle
Mr N Dixon
Ms S M Dodd
Mrs D Dugdale

J C Elliott

Mr D Fielden
Mrs E M Fielden
Mr J Fielden
Mrs J E Fielden
Mr & Mrs R D S Fielden

Mr & Mrs Sam Fielden
Mrs K Fincham
Mr & Mrs R H Ford
Mrs N Fox
Mr & Mrs B M Frain
Mr & Mrs A Fruin

Mr & Mrs J Goldie
Mr J R & Mrs E M Gore
Mr A Greenwood
Mr & Mrs D G Greenwood
Mr J & Mrs P Greenwood
Mrs N Greenwood
Mr & Mrs T Greenwood
Mr & Mrs J Guest

Mrs D Haffner
Mr & Mrs J Hardman
Mr R Harling
Mr & Mrs A Hayes
Mr & Mrs W Healey
Mrs E Heath
Mrs M Helliwell
Mr B Hewson
Mr & Mrs A J Heywood
Mr & Mrs A W Heywood
Mr P D Heywood
Mr R J Heywood
Mrs E Hibbert
Mr & Mrs M Hinks
Mr & Mrs C Hodges
Mr J R Hodgson
Mr G A Holden
Mr J D Holdsworth
Mrs S M Hopkinson (4 copies)
Mr & Mrs C R Horsfall
Mr L Horsfall
Miss P Horsfall
Mr J M Horsford
Mrs M Hudson
Mr C G Hunt
Miss R D Hustler

Mr & Mrs T Isherwood

Terry & Margaret Jones

Mr S P Keane
Mr & Mrs L Kershaw
Mr R B Knights

Mr & Mrs J E Landon-Harrison
Miss D Langfield
Mrs Annie Laughton
Mrs D M Lee
Mrs C Lever
Mr & Mrs H Lever
Mr & Mrs A Lord
Mr P Lucak
Helen C Lunt

Mr & Mrs R F McCormick
Mr & Mrs K McGuire
Mrs E B McLaren
Mrs J McLean
Mrs E A Makin
Mr & Mrs K G Marshall
Mr & Mrs M Marshall
Mrs W Marshall
Mr & Mrs J T Martin
Mrs M Mayson
Mrs S Mellis
Mr A R Mews
Mr & Mrs K Milligan
Mr J Mitchell
Mr K Moss
Miss B J Moyer

Mrs A Louise Nixon

Mr & Mrs R Ogden
Mr J L Oldham
Mr & Mrs A Osborn
Dr V Ozaki

Mrs D M Parker
Mr & Mrs J R Perry
Mr & Mrs R Perry
Mrs L Pickles
Cllr C Pinder
Mrs Joyce Pratt
Mrs S J Provis
Sylvia Pryor

Mrs M J Ratcliff
Mrs H G H Ridley
Miss A Riley
Mrs Carrie Rogers

Mr M Saunders
Mr W Savage
Mrs D Scott

Mrs E Scott
Mr & Mrs B Searson
Mrs M Sefton
Mrs M Sharp
Mr & Mrs M Sheard
Miss L Shenton
Mrs M Simpson
Charlotte V Sleap
Mr F & Mrs M A Slick
Mrs J C Smith
Mr D & Mrs S Stockwell
M Stölting
Mr & Mrs Eric Stuttard
Mr & Mrs K Stuttard
Mr R & Mrs E J Sutcliffe
Mrs S Sutcliffe
Mrs V M Sutcliffe JP

Mr J S Taylor
Mrs G Timewell
Mrs K M Tomlinson
Miss S F. Townend
M Vanda Trotman

Mrs J L Vasey

Mrs B Wadsworth
Mr & Mrs J Walsh
Mr & Mrs K Ward
Mr & Mrs P Ward
Mr J Whitehead
Mrs M B Wilde
Miss A Williams (2 copies)
Mr & Mrs A Wilson
Mr & Mrs B Windle

LIST OF SUBSCRIBERS
to the deluxe edition

1	Todmorden Borough Council	27	Mrs J Crowther
2	Denise and Ken Smith	28	Mr G & Mrs C Davies
3	Freda Heywood	29	Mr Douglas Wilson
4	Malcolm Heywood	30	Mr & Mrs W Speight
5	Bernard Jennings	31	Mr & Mrs P Crossley
6	Lawrence and Lillian Greenwood	32	Mr Roy Steele
7	Mark Whitley	33	Mr & Mrs B Hodgkinson
8	Subscribed	34	Mr N S Beck
9	Subscribed	35	G Williams
10	Subscribed	36	Mr J A Davey
11	Mr B & Mrs P Edwards	37	Mr & Mrs J F Southern
12	Mr D J Clark	38	Mrs K S Kerr
13	Mrs E Firth	39	James Hans Gregory
14	Mr P & Mrs S A Guest	40	Mrs D E Paolozzi
15	Mr J & Mrs R Greenwood	41	Mrs A M Ormerod
16	Mr P Greenwood	42	Mr J D Ratcliff
17	Mr A E & Mrs A Blackburn	43	Mrs M Waller
18	Mrs C Parr	44	Mr & Mrs J Daniels
19	Mrs T J Armitage MCOptom	45	Mr & Mrs M G Hubbard
20	Mr & Mrs Philip Brown	46	Steven & Helena Corder
21	Master H E Whitehead	47	Miss L R Pickles
22	Master J D Whitehead	48	Mr A G Pickles
23	Mr & Mrs A Coote	49	Mr M S Butcher
24	Mr & Mrs G French	50	Mr & Mrs K Marshall
25	Mr C R & Mrs M Parkes	51	Mr R D Uttley
26	Mr & Mrs W Veevers	52	Mrs A Sutcliffe

53	Mr N Crossley	85	Mr & Mrs B Walker
54	Councillor & Mrs C Walton	86	Mr & Mrs R Fielding
55	Mr & Mrs R Fielden	87	Mrs Anne Hill
56	Mr & Mrs D A Hoyle	88	Mr Ivor & Mrs Pat Dower
57	Mr & Mrs I J Grant	89	Mr R M Walker
58	Mr & Mrs M Hollows	90	Mr & Mrs Harry Kershaw
59	Mr B & Mrs J Crowder	91	Mrs A Howorth
60	Mr Harold Clegg	92	Mr & Mrs N A Helliwell
61	Mr A R Smith	93	Mr & Mrs B Moorhouse
62	Mr D Jowett	94	Mr R S Crowther
63	Mr I & Mrs J Wright	95	Mrs P Walker
64	Mr M R Heath	96	Warburtons Funeral Service
65	Mr & Mrs A J Harvey	97	Mrs M Wilson
66	Mr Alan Uttley	98	Mr K W & Mrs J Butler
67	Mr A P Wilson	99	Mr & Mrs H S Gordon
68	Mr & Mrs J Horsfall	100	Ms V C Spedding
69	Mr & Mrs B Radcliffe	101	Mr D J Lemon
70	Mr N Sutcliffe	102	Nathan J Heywood
71	Miss J Bentley	103	Jessica L Heywood
72	Mrs V N Bunn	104	Melanie J Heywood
73	Mrs J Scott	105	Brian E Heywood
74	Mr M L Warner	106	Mr D & Mrs A Roberts
75	Mrs M R Varnam	107	Mr P & Mrs J Stansfield
76	John Stuart Chadwick	108	Peter Marshall
77	Border Bookshop	109	Mr J M & Mrs S Uttley
78	Border Bookshop	110	Mrs C R McMillan
79	Mr & Mrs K Ward	111	Cryers News Centre
80	Ms D Rose	112	Cryers News Centre
81	Mr & Mrs F J Boocock	113	Mr & Mrs D J Pilling
82	Mr J & Mrs B Stansfield	114	Cryers News Centre
83	Mr P & Mrs A Thomas-Ideson	115	Cryers News Centre
84	Mr R A Birch	116	Mrs M M Galdies

A HISTORY OF
TODMORDEN

Malcolm & Freda Heywood
and Bernard Jennings

Special illustrations by
Lawrence Greenwood

Smith
Settle

First published in 1996 by
Smith Settle Ltd
Ilkley Road
Otley
West Yorkshire
LS21 3JP

ISBN   Paperback   1 85825 057 9
        Hardback   1 85825 058 7

British Library Cataloguing-in-Publication data:
A catalogue record for this book is available from the British Library.

Set in Montype Plantin.

Designed, printed and bound by
SMITH SETTLE
Ilkley Road, Otley, West Yorkshire LS21 3JP

Contents

Preface and Acknowledgements

Pennine Valley: A History of Upper Calderdale was published in 1992, the first comprehensive social and economic history of the area. It was the product of many years of research by the Hebden Bridge WEA Local History Group (originally a Leeds University tutorial class). To make it possible to bring out the book at a reasonable price, a good deal of compression was necessary. It was agreed, therefore, that more detailed studies would be produced at a later date, and the royalties from *Pennine Valley* were assigned for this purpose. As *A History of Hebden Bridge* (1991) had already appeared, written by a member of the group, Colin Spencer, it was decided that the next priority should be *A History of Todmorden,* to be published on the occasion of the centenary of the creation of the Borough of Todmorden in 1896.

The text of the present book is the work of Freda and Malcolm Heywood and Bernard Jennings. Lawrence Greenwood has provided his own watercolours and line drawings, some of them reconstructions of ruined buildings and vanished scenes, and with the assistance of Lillian Greenwood has acted as illustrations editor. As the book draws upon the work of the Hebden Bridge Group, as well as new research, we would like to acknowledge the contribution of the other members of the group: Geoffrey Binns, Fred Helliwell, Colin Spencer, Sheila Wade, and the late Leslie Goldthorp, Bella Travis and Edward Watson.

In this book, amounts of money are given in the original pre decimal currency, twelve (old) pence (d) making one shilling (s), with twenty shillings to the pound (£). It seems to us to be less trouble to learn the old system than to be faced with odd figures such as 1.67p as the annual rent of an acre of land, or to wade through a text cluttered by the alternative formulation, eg '4d (1.67p)'.

Brian Law generously made valuable information available to us in advance of the publication of his book *Fieldens of Todmorden:* a *Nineteenth Century Business Dynasty,* which came out in November 1995 shortly before this book went to press. We are grateful to Roger Birch for allowing us to use illustrations selected from his extensive collection. John Chadwick freely provided valuable information, particularly on the early Fieldens and the Greenwoods of Longfield and Stones. Betty Savage was helpful throughout, supplying minute books, township records and other documents and books in her possession. Jack Bednall allowed use of his research into the town's musical heritage and Susan Cockcroft her research into theatre and entertainment. The late William Cross helped with the geological account of the district. Norman Greenwood permitted use of the 'Diary of William Greenwood'. We are grateful for all of this help and for the willingness of local businesses to provide information for the survey summarised in Chapter 13.

We would like to express our thanks to the owners and custodians of the records listed in the Bibliography and References for the use of their material, and to Julian Harber, Chris Aspin, Eric Hebdon, Jenny Cockcroft, Peter Cockcroft, Richard Crabtree, Dennis O'Neill, Kit Hardwick, Ena Marshall, Jack Taylor, Mr and Mrs R Gunton, Dr & Mrs D N Foster, Mr & Mrs D J Pilling, and Edward Riley, editor of the *Halifax Evening Courier*, for their help and support.

We are particularly indebted to the staff of Todmorden, Burnley and Rawtenstall Public Libraries, to the reference librarians in Halifax and Bradford, and to the archivists of Lancashire County, West Yorkshire (Calderdale and Wakefield), Leeds City, the Borthwick Institute of Historical Research and the West Yorkshire Archaeological Society. Ms Pat Sewell, the Calderdale Archivist, made a special effort to supply us with transcripts of some newly-acquired documents in time for them to be used in Chapter 2 on Medieval Todmorden.

Extracts from documents in the Public Record Office and from probate records appear by permission of the Keeper of the Public Records.

We are grateful to David Horsfall for his photography on pages 14, 15(2), 24, 44, 45(2), 54, 66(2), 81, 107, 110, 137, 167, 173, 227, 230, 231, 235(2), and acknowledge with gratitude permission to use photographs as follows: HMSO p 1; Roger Birch pp 9, 41, 55, 63, 123, 126, 147, 158, 178, 180, 196, 200, 201, 202, 203, 206(bottom), 209, 210, 213, 226(2); Geoffrey Boswell p 32; John and Jacqueline Cockcroft p 55; John Chadwick p 100; Todmorden Photographic Society pp 101, 103, 142; Christine Copping p 102; Brian Law pp 153, 156; Todmorden Antiquarian Society p 165; Dennis O'Neill pp 177, 188, 189; *Halifax Evening Courier* pp 29, 186, 187; Todmorden Cricket Club p 201; Peter Roberts p 206(top); *Lancashire Evening Telegraph* p 219; Alan Stuttard p 232; and RCHME (Crown Copyright) p 229. We are also grateful for permission to photograph the interiors of St Mary's Church, Lumbutts Chapel and the Hippodrome Theatre.

The watercolours on pp 7, 11, 59, 120, 139: maps on pp 119, 151: and line drawings on pp 8, 18, 35, 48, 56, 57(2), 64, 86, 96, 97, 98, 99, 108, 109, 111(2), 113, 117, 121, 122, 132, 150, 160, 185, 216: are the work of artist Lawrence Greenwood.

Lawrence Greenwood
Freda Heywood
Malcolm Heywood
Bernard Jennings
January 1996

I

Physical Setting and Prehistoric Evidence

It is impossible to understand the history of an area without taking into account its physical setting. This is especially true of Todmorden and the upper Calder Valley, where the 'bones' of the landscape — the rocks, hills and valleys — together with the abundant water supply and the low watershed between east and west (the lowest Pennine crossing south of the Aire Gap) have all contributed to the development of community life. Before tracing the story of human activity in that part of the upper Calder Valley now known as Todmorden, we need to look in some detail at the physical setting.

The present physical environment has evolved since the beginning of the Carboniferous Period, some 350 million years ago. At this time most of what is now Northern England was covered by sea, deep in the south but shallowing northwards to the shores of the 'Scottish-Scandinavian' continent. In the south, where the water was deeper and clearer, corals and other marine organisms abounded and their remains built up into great thicknesses of limestone. To the north, nearer the shore, sediments from the Scottish-Scandinavian continent masked the formation of limestone in some places, so that only thin beds of limestone are found with sandstone and shales.

In the mid-Carboniferous Period, the sea floor lifted and a great river flowing southwards developed a delta above the limestone. This resulted in the formation of shales, sandstones and gritstones; the latter being called Millstone Grit because it was used to make mill stones. The sea, which was present in the early and middle Carboniferous Periods over the area of Northern England, was becoming shallower, and this shallowing continued into the later Carboniferous Period, resulting in swamps, where there developed forests of tree ferns and other plants growing in a layer of mud

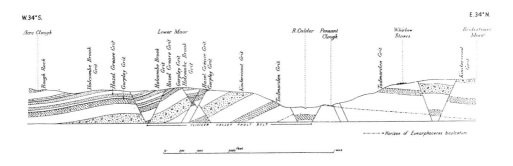

Geological section across the Calder Valley from Bridestones, via Whirlaw Stones and Lower Moor, to Acre Clough in the Dulesgate Valley.

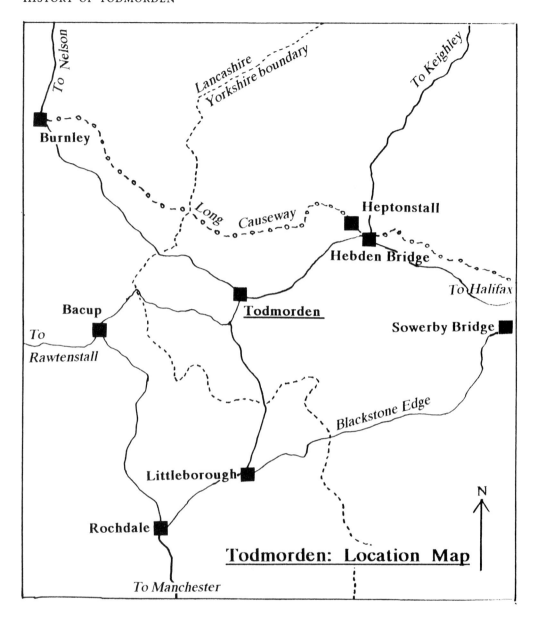

Todmorden: Location Map

and slime. At intervals river deposits submerged these dense forests, compressing them over millions of years to create coal seams interspersed with layers of non-coal bearing river deposits.

At the close of coal measure times, ie the end of the Carboniferous Period (250 million years ago), there began a period of mountain building. Its effect in Northern England was to uplift the Pennines into an anticline along a north-south axis, and it is this formation that is the basic feature of the structure of the area. In the upper Calder Valley the anticline is markedly asymmetrical. West of its axis, which runs from Gorple south to the western edge of Stansfield Moor, and then south-east across Langfield Common to Blackstone Edge, the rock strata dip steeply on the Lancashire side, whilst on the Yorkshire side the beds are nearly horizontal. The geology is further

The Basin Stone, a pre-Ice Age outcrop near Gaddings Dam on Langfield Common.

complicated by a series of faults, resulting in rock strata on opposite sides of some of the valleys being quite different.

After the Pennines were uplifted there followed a long period of erosion or wearing down, when the climate varied from tropical to arctic. The coal measures were worn away from most of Northern England, including the upper Calder Valley, although some are still found in the Burnley Valley and in Dulesgate leading from Todmorden to Bacup. Thus the strata of the upper gritstones have been left to cap the highest hills, and the outcroppings produce well-known local landmarks as at Whirlaw Stones, Bridestones, Buttstones, Orchan Rocks and Basin Stone.

Millions of years of erosion produced a rolling plateau surface at a height of 1,200-1,400 feet, with a valley following a route similar to that of the present Calder Valley, although at a much higher level of between 900 and 1,000 feet. The floor of this prehistoric valley now forms the distinctive geological shelf of the present valley; the prehistoric valley sides are now the slopes rising from the shelf to the moor tops. (The final shape of the present valley sides was sculptured by the subsequent erosion of the prehistoric valley bottom, as outlined below.) This prehistoric valley was joined by tributary valleys, the major one following the line of the present valley from Summit.

Then came the Ice Age, when glaciation considerably modified the local landscape. Two glaciers converged on the area: the Ribble glacier, pushing south along the Burnley Valley and down the Calder Valley to about Eastwood, was reinforced by one which came across South Lancashire from the Irish Sea down the Walsden Valley. Both carried debris which was left behind when the ice melted. Limestone boulders found at a depth of eighteen feet below the valley floor at Lineholme, and blue clay with chert found at Harehill about fifty feet above the valley floor, together with rocks

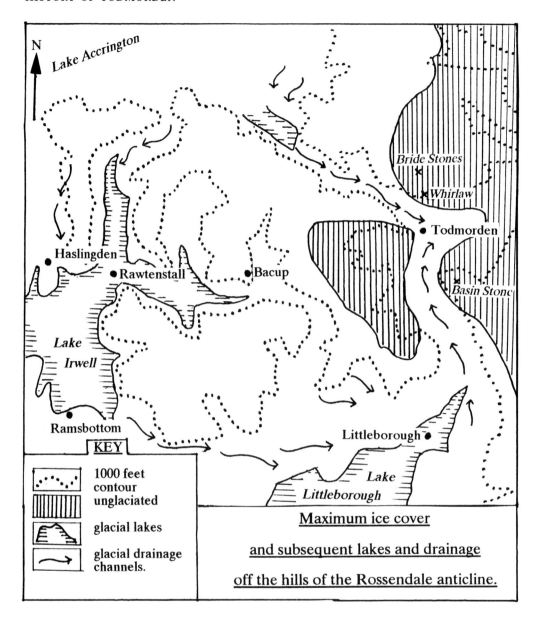

KEY

| | 1000 feet contour unglaciated |
| glacial lakes |
| glacial drainage channels. |

Maximum ice cover

and subsequent lakes and drainage

off the hills of the Rossendale anticline.

from the Lake District (bearing scratches created by the ice) found at Millwood, are evidence enough to establish the existence of ice in the Calder Valley extending at least to the east of Todmorden. It seems likely that the higher land above about 1,000 feet was left uncovered by ice.

The erosive action of the ice deepened the high valleys, already established as the pre-Calder and Walsden valleys, gouging out steep slopes to the valley sides. These slopes now form the upper valley slopes. As the ice melted about 10,000 years ago, a large lake, Lake Littleborough, formed in the Rochdale area and added to the meltwater from the local ice as it drained northward down the Walsden Gorge into the Calder Valley. Later, as the ice retreated to the north of Rossendale, meltwater again formed a vast lake, Lake Accrington, which drained into the Calder Valley through the Cliviger

Gorge. These meltwaters were extremely powerful and deepened the valleys, already established by earlier river erosion and ice, by several hundred feet. The flow along the Cliviger Gorge lasted much longer than that along the Walsden Gorge, hence there was less downcutting in the latter than in the upper Calder Valley. Thus the Walsden tributary has subsequently had to cut a steep descent to the main valley. This steep descent, together with the sharp rise from the old lake floors at Summit and Windy Bridge (Cliviger), has influenced later communications, as witnessed by the numerous locks in the Rochdale Canal, and the tunnels, cuttings, embankments and viaducts which mark the course of the railway on both the Manchester and Burnley lines.

When the meltwater flows ceased, the main rivers re-established themselves, and these have cut the lower part of the valley sides resulting, along the Burnley Valley, in a series of interlocking spurs as the Calder, finding the easiest route, snaked its way to the confluence with Walsden Water at Todmorden. The tributary valleys with their 'cloughs', which fed the main river, were left 'hanging' at the level of the pre-glacial valley, and since then have been actively deepening their valleys as the streams cut down from the old level of the Calder to the new one hundreds of feet below. These cloughs have many spectacular waterfalls or cascades where the cutting-down action has been checked by an outcrop of harder rocks. It is also in the steep sides of these tributary valleys that the geologist can study the varied rock strata which underly the district. The main valleys with their gorge-like character give way at 700-900 feet to broad terraces/shelves, where the land rises relatively gently before sweeping upwards to the moorland plateau, which in places reaches over 1,500 feet.

The moorland surface is bleak, its most striking feature being the outcrops of gritstone, some of which have been carved into weird shapes by the 'sandblasting' action of the constant winds. Drainage on the moorland is poor as rainfall is high, evaporation low and the rocks impermeable. As a result, peat bogs have been formed averaging four feet in depth but attaining fifteen feet in places. Some of these beds have remains of trees, mainly birch, in the lower layers, probably dating from a time when the climate was warmer and drier. Patches of heather and cranberry are found in a few better-drained areas, but generally on these wet acid moorlands it is the cotton grass which prevails.

Below the moors, the terraces are patterned with drystone walls, farmsteads and settlements such as Mankinholes, Bottomley and Shore, with connecting roads and trackways. From the terraces the main Calder Valley is often invisible, whilst it is possible to travel along the valley bottom and remain unaware of the terraces, which are obscured by the gritstone crags overhanging the gorge.

At the time when human activity can first be detected in the district, about 4,500 years ago, the bones of the landscape were much as they are today, with such modifications as man has worked on them since. The Calder Valley, far from being a main artery of communication through the Pennines, was an obstacle to movement, being ill-drained and covered by alder and willow, with a dense undergrowth thriving in the rich silt deposits. The valley slopes and terraces, up to a height of possibly 1,200 feet, were densely wooded, mainly with oak but with birch and pine on the higher ground.

It was on this scene that people of the Middle Stone Age (Mesolithic) made their appearance. Tools used by them have been found on Saltonstall Moor and near Widdop Reservoir. These people were hunters and gatherers, and did not grow crops or domesticate animals as did the New Stone Age (Neolithic) settlers who followed

This view from Tongue Hill, Cornholme, looking towards the Todmorden skyline, shows the 'shelf', the interlocking spurs and other features in the sketch below.

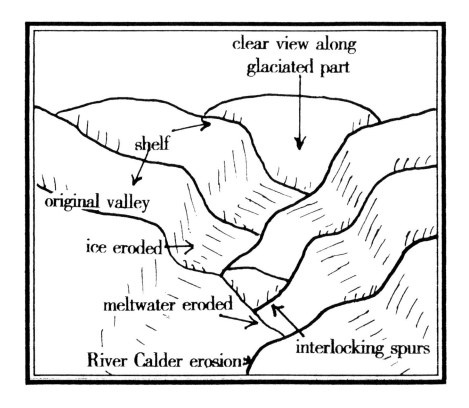

Bottleneck Rock, Bridestones, 1,400 feet above sea level, shows the effect of wind/weather erosion.

This waterfall in Greens Clough, on the south side of the Burnley Valley at Portsmouth, is typical of those on the tributary streams.

them, and the Bronze Age people who came later still. Over the years many implements made by Mesolithic and Neolithic people have been found on the moors surrounding Todmorden, including scrapers, borers, arrow- and spear-heads, knives and thousands of flint chippings, the waste material of these early workers. Flint does not occur locally and must have been brought into the area by travellers, but local hardstone was used for some implements, and chert, found in association with clay brought by glaciers during the Ice Age, was used as a substitute for flint, although it is not as easy to work.

The late Mr Harry Stansfield had a wonderful collection of stone implements, which he had found at various sites around Todmorden, including many from a Neolithic workshop near Widdop Reservoir, where he discovered the anvil stone on which these early workers shaped their tools. Inchfield Moor, Tooter Hills, Todmorden Moor, behind Greens Farm, Portsmouth (where two bombs fell in the Second World War) and Heeley Hill above Lumbutts are all places where Stone Age implements have been found. Many Neolithic flints, stone tools and Bronze Age artefacts have been found at various sites near to the Long Causeway, the ancient trackway which runs high on the hillside avoiding the deep valleys and linking the Halifax and Burnley areas. A Bronze Age site was excavated by Burnley Historical Society at Mosley Height only 150 yards from the Long Causeway, whilst Todmorden's most celebrated find was the Blackheath Barrow, Stansfield, which is now known as the 'Frying Pan' and

These remains are from the Bronze Age Blackheath barrow, near Rive Rocks in Stansfield.

lies on the sixth fairway of the local golf course. The barrow is a Bronze Age burial ground containing the remains, or traces, of large numbers of urns in which the ashes of the dead were interred. The finds are now displayed in Todmorden Public Library.

The Neolithic peoples were the first to establish permanent settlement locally. Although few in numbers, they modified their surroundings with stone and bronze tools as they cleared some of the forest cover to make pastures for their flocks and fields to grow crops. Only the best sites would be colonised, these being the well-drained south-facing slopes and ledges below the summit, where there was a reliable water supply.

From about 500 BC, by which time iron tools were in use, the climate became colder with higher rainfall; this contributed to the creation of large areas of peat and bog on the higher slopes which had been cleared of all woodland. It is likely, that after a few hundred years of these conditions, the higher moors would appear as they do today. Constant grazing and the acid soil would prevent woodland re-establishing itself above about 1,000 feet. As more woodland was cleared on the terraces and the plough and ox-team were introduced, the settlements, which can still be seen today, began to take shape. Stones, cleared from the fields, were utilised in building the dividing walls and the ancient trackways were extended. All activity was still, however, centred on the uplands, the alder jungle in the valley bottom proving too much of an obstacle. There is no evidence, until the twelfth century, of how far development had progressed towards the valley bottom. It was only after the Norman Conquest that the first written evidence of life in the area emerged. Prior to this, place names can point to the influx of different races and where they settled.

Throughout the history of Todmorden the influence of the physical setting is crucial; sometimes offering opportunities, as in the abundant water supply which stimulated the growth of the textile industry; sometimes frustrating development by making transport hazardous, until the valley was opened up. Todmorden has always been a border area, on the edge of extensive medieval lordships and parishes. The boundaries of the latter, and of the counties, did not follow the watershed between the Lancashire and Yorkshire river systems. The watershed between Walsden and Littleborough, only 600 feet above sea level, was no great obstacle to movement. As a result, the authority of whatever tribal group or lordship preceded the manor of Rochdale extended to the middle of modern Todmorden, where the county boundary ran until the 1880s. Further north the same boundary followed Paul Clough down past Stiperden on the Long Causeway, south of which it was found convenient to use Pudsey Clough as a continuation. This left the Brown Birks spur and part of Cornholme, which are geographically on the Yorkshire side, in the Lancashire township of Cliviger. Being on the periphery of affairs, the area had no strategic or economic importance. There were never any powerful, resident lords. Until the fifteenth century, there was no church in the district, the nearest ones being at Heptonstall and Rochdale. The people were not immediately subservient to anyone and became self-sufficient, developing a healthy independence (at times intolerance) of outside authority.

The development of industry saw the underlying geology providing work; lead was mined at Catholes Clough as well as nearby at Thieveley, coal in the Dulesgate and Burnley Valleys, whilst clay, in association with these deposits of Carboniferous times, provided the raw material for brick and pipe works in the same two valleys. When, during the seventeenth century, houses began to be encased or built in stone rather than wood or a rough combination of wood and stone, the local stone was an excellent building material, whether for walls or 'thackstone' roofs, which preceded the use of

Life on the 'shelf' — a view from Stansfield looking south towards Langfield, with Langfield Common behind, across the barely visible Calder Valley, and showing Great House Farm as it appeared in the 1940s.

Welsh slate. Numerous abandoned quarries scar the hillsides as evidence that this excellent building material was delved locally.

As we look over the landscape today, we can understand something of the pressures that have resulted in the fascinating pattern of field, farm and factory, but we now need to look in more detail at the changes brought about since records were first kept and which make up the history of Todmorden.

2

Medieval Todmorden

The social framework within which the medieval inhabitants of the Todmorden area managed their lives was very different from the conventional picture of the lowland village, with its clustered houses surrounded by communal fields, and the manor house and parish church standing as the twin symbols of authority. Settlement was dispersed, most people living in hamlets or on scattered farms. The manorial lords had no arable demesne (private) land, and therefore labour services were either slight or non-existent. What is now the town of Todmorden was made up, in the Middle Ages, of the extremities of three lordships: Wakefield, Rochdale and Clitheroe; and of three parishes: Halifax, Rochdale and Whalley.

The earliest written record of the area is *Domesday Book* (1086). The Yorkshire section reads as follows:

In Wachefeld [Wakefield] with 9 berewicks, Sandala [Sandal Magna], Sorebi [Sowerby], Werlafeslei [Warley], Micleie [Midgley], Wadeswrde [Wadsworth], Crumbetonestun [Cruttonstall in Erringden], Langefelt [Langfield], Stanesfelt [Stansfield], there are for geld 60 carucates of land and 3¹/₃ bovates. 30 ploughs can plough this land. This manor belonged to King Edward. Now they are in the hands of the King [William]. There are 4 villani there, and 3 priests and 2 churches and 7 sokemen and 16 bordarii. Together they have 7 ploughs. Pasturable woodland 6 leagues long and 4 leagues broad. The whole 6 leagues long and 6 leagues broad. In the time of King Edward it was worth £60; now £15.

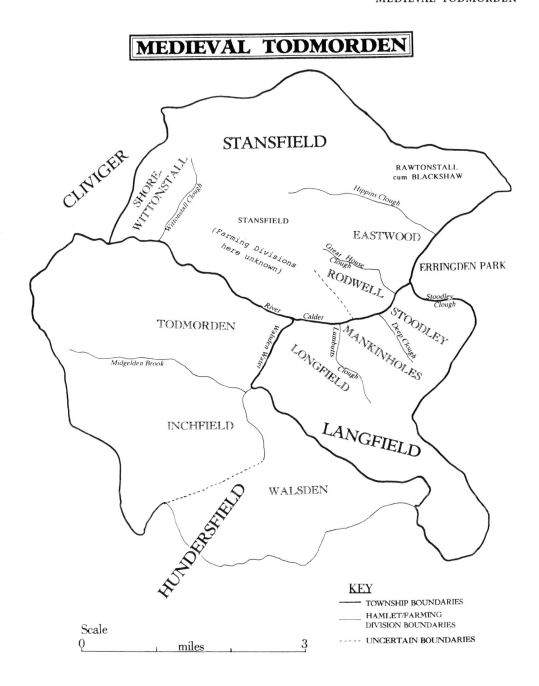

MEDIEVAL TODMORDEN

CLIVIGER

STANSFIELD

RAWTONSTALL
cum BLACKSHAW

SHORE-
WITTONSTALL

Hippins Clough

Wittonstall Clough

STANSFIELD

(Farming Divisions
here unknown)

EASTWOOD

Great House
Clough

ERRINGDEN PARK

RODWELL

Stoodley
Clough

River   Calder

STOODLEY

TODMORDEN

MANKINHOLES

Deep Clough

Lumbutts

Midgelden Brook

Walsden Water

LONGFIELD

Clough

INCHFIELD

LANGFIELD

WALSDEN

HUNDERSFIELD

KEY

——— TOWNSHIP BOUNDARIES

——— HAMLET/FARMING
        DIVISION BOUNDARIES

- - - - UNCERTAIN BOUNDARIES

Scale

0   miles   3

Berewicks, outlying parts of a manor, were integral to it, although often physically separate. The first problem in the interpretation of the local *Domesday* is that only eight berewicks, not nine, are listed. The missing one was formerly conjured up out of a chance occurrence. The name 'Werla/feslie' (Werlaf's clearing, later Warley) is split by the end of the line in the *Domesday* manuscript, leading to the false deduction that 'feslie' means Halifax. If the number nine is correct, the missing berewick must

View southwards from Eastwood Road above Great Rock, showing the farming shelves of the Middle Third of Stansfield and Langfield, areas with common arable fields in medieval times.

Looking south from Cross Stone to Old Royd in Langfield, showing the clearance of 'royd' land below the settlement, with the farming 'shelf' behind.

Looking from the hill behind
Frostholme Mill, Cornholme, towards
Shore and the apron of land which
was a common arable field
in medieval times.

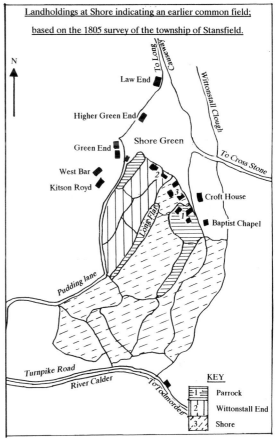

Landholdings at Shore indicating an earlier common field;
based on the 1805 survey of the township of Stansfield.

N

To Long Causeway

Law End

Wittonstall Clough

Higher Green End

Shore Green

Green End

To Cross Stone

West Bar

Kitson Royd

Long Field

Croft House

Baptist Chapel

Pudding lane

Turnpike Road

River Calder

To Todmorder

KEY

Parrock

Wittonstall End

Shore

15

be Halifax cum Heptonstall. In the Middle Ages they formed one unit, as a sub-manor of the manor of Wakefield, and for taxation purposes were recorded simply as 'Halifax'.

'30 ploughs can plough this land'. The amount of land that could be cultivated in one year by an eight-ox plough team was known as a ploughland, made up of eight oxgangs (English term) or bovates (Latin term). A ploughland is conventionally 120 acres, which would mean an oxgang of 15 acres. A survey of 1309 gives the size of the oxgang as 15 acres in Sowerby, 10 in Soyland (which was in Sowerby but separate for this purpose) and 18 in most of Warley. If comparable figures are used in the rest of the manor of Wakefield, the total arable acreage of the lordship would have been of the order of 3-4,000. The term carucate, which can be used interchangeably with ploughland, here denotes the unit for the collection of a tax, the 'geld'. The carucage of the manor was just over twice the measurement of the ploughlands, suggesting that a good deal of its taxable capacity derived from pastoral farming. Two-thirds of the whole area of the manor (54 out of 81 square miles, a league being $1^1/_2$ miles) was classed as pasturable woodland.

The landholders listed in the manor including its berewicks were sokemen, free peasants who owed certain payments or services to the lord, and two classes of servile tenants. 'Bordarii' are smallholders, 'villani' held more land but owed more rents and services. Three priests took care of two churches. One of the latter may have been at Halifax, the centre of a huge parish.[1]

The most striking feature of the local *Domesday* record is the reduction, by three-quarters, in the value and agricultural activity of the manor and its berewicks since 1066. In addition only three of the fourteen dependent townships, which made up the soke of Wakefield (around Wakefield and to the south-west, along the Holme Valley), had any tenants and plough teams in 1086, all three lying close to Wakefield. A comparative study of other large lordships, which include Pennine tracts, suggests, that if fuller details had been given, most of the seven plough teams mentioned would have been found to be in Wakefield and Sandal Magna.

The value of Yorkshire as a whole showed a fall of about two-thirds between 1066 and 1086, with half of the townships in *Domesday* described as wholly or partly 'waste'. The main cause of this situation was the Norman devastation of Yorkshire in the winter of 1069-70, after a rebellion against William the Conqueror. Nearly all of the upper valleys and moor-edge settlements of the Yorkshire Pennines were completely 'waste' seventeen years later. It is, however, most unlikely that the Norman armies could have made a clean sweep of this extensive hill country, destroying all the farms and stock, in a midwinter campaign lasting for two or three months. None of the theories put forward to explain the distribution of 'waste' in 1086 is wholly convincing, but one partial explanation may be offered. Large 'waste' areas in the upland tracts of the great Yorkshire lordships were administered by the new Norman lords as hunting forests, some of which were extensions of pre-Conquest hunting grounds. It is possible that for some townships in these forests, the description 'waste' meant that the people no longer had to contribute to the geld or provide labour services, not that the area was totally depopulated.

All but one of the berewicks of Wakefield formed a compact block in upper Calderdale, up to twenty-five miles distant from the headquarters of the manor. These were Stansfield, Wadsworth, Midgley and Warley on the north side of the River Calder, and Langfield, Cruttonstall and Sowerby on the south side. Although we have to wait until the thirteenth century for the documentary evidence of what was then the Forest of Sowerbyshire, it is probable that the valley was used as a royal hunting forest and for the pasture of the king's livestock both before and after the Conquest.[2]

Todmorden and Walsden are not mentioned in the sparse *Domesday* account of the Lancashire side. They were part of the manor of Rochdale, within the Hundred of Salford. (A Hundred was a sub-division of a county.) In 1066 the Hundred was held as a series of manors by twenty-one thegns (minor lords), one of whom was selected for special mention — Gamel, who held the extensive manor of Rochdale. He was still there in 1086, under the new Norman overlord Roger de Poitou, although he may have lost part of his estates. Neither Cliviger nor Clitheroe is mentioned in the brief *Domesday* survey of Blackburn Hundred, held by King Edward in 1066 and Roger de Poitou in 1086.[3]

A few years after *Domesday* Robert de Lacy, lord of the Honour of Pontefract, was granted Blackburn Hundred, in its new incarnation as the Honour of Clitheroe, to hold under Roger de Poitou. (An Honour was a large lordship, often administered as a collection of manors.) From 1102, when Roger's lands were forfeit to King Henry I, the Lacy family held Clitheroe, together with the manor of Rochdale, directly from the king. At some date before 1121 the manor of Wakefield was granted to the Warenne family, earls of Surrey. All of the Todmorden area was therefore, in the early Middle Ages, under the ultimate control of two of the leading barons of the country. In the fourteenth century the Lacy estates passed to the house of Lancaster, and the Warenne interest to the house of York (not to be confused with the counties of the same names). The duchies of Lancaster and York became Crown property in 1399 and 1461 respectively.[4]

Great lords such as the Lacys and the Warennes held their estates from the Crown for a certain number of knight's fees (sixty in the Lacy case in 1166), in other words the obligation to provide that number of armed knights for the king's service and pay the associated financial dues. They in turn let parts of their lands, as manors or sub-manors, carrying a proportion of the overlord's burdens. There were two such sub-manors in Stansfield.[5]

Leading Landholding Families

The origins of the larger sub-manor are bound up with the mysterious figure of Asulfr, otherwise Essulf, Assulf, Asolf and variants, an English or Anglo-Scandinavian man who, at some time in the first half of the twelfth century, acquired a substantial number of subordinate lordships within the great manor of Wakefield, which he eventually divided between his sons. Two of the latter, John and Jordan, held land in Sowerbyshire. They both became known as 'of Thornhill' (near Dewsbury), and from them descended the Thornhill family who were prominent in the affairs of the upper Calder Valley. In the late twelfth century John granted some land in Stansfield, together with an interest in the corn mill there, to his daughter Amabel on the occasion of her marriage. When this grant was later confirmed by Amabel's brother William, the land was said to measure five bovates, and provision was made for the sharing out of woodland in the neighbourhood if it should be sold or cleared for cultivation.[6]

According to Watson, 'Jordan son of Askolf' granted part of his Sowerbyshire estate, including seven bovates of land in Stansfield and Rawtonstall, to another brother Elias. We next hear of Rawtonstall in 1238 when John de Sothill (Soothill near Dewsbury) granted a twenty-year lease of half an acre of land in the 'township of Ructunstal' to Henry son of Gamel of Ructunstal. The annual rent was 4d, and the

Stansfield Corn Mill, circa 1870, showing the tail goit leading into the River Calder. Demolished in 1953, it was probably on the site of a manorial mill referred to below.

charge for the lease 1s. When John de Sothill died in 1266, his inquisition post mortem showed him to be in receipt of the following annual payments and profits:

> In Stanesfelde and Routonstale he had from free men yearly £4 6s; in meadow and pasture one marc [13s 4d]; from one small meadow in Stanesfelde 12d; and from one water mill there half a marc.

He held the above, together with estates in Soothill and Ovenden, from Sir Richard Thornhill, who answered in turn for the upper Calderdale properties to the lords of Wakefield.[7]

The Soothill estate in Rawtonstall operated as a sub-manor, being described on some occasions as the manor of Rawtonstall with Blackshaw. It stretched from 'Coldeynmythom' (Mytholm, on the west side of Hebden Bridge) to Blackshaw Head. Its precise limits are not recorded, but as Eastwood was in the sub-manor of Stansfield, the boundary between the two jurisdictions was almost certainly Hippins Clough. Although the Soothills held land within the sub-manor of Stansfield, the latter remained under the direct control of the Thornhills. The two sub-manors made up the township of Stansfield.[8]

The Thornhill male line failed on the death of Sir Simon Thornhill in 1369-70, and the property passed by marriage to Sir Henry Savile. A later Sir Henry Savile acquired

Rawtonstall-Blackshaw and the other Soothill interests in Stansfield, by marrying the Soothill heiress in 1533-34. The Saviles, who had a flair for judicious marriages, merged the two sub-manors.[9]

The family surnamed Langfield held by socage (free tenure not involving knight's service) thirteen bovates of land in Langfield, which represented a substantial part of the township. They had under-tenants, including the family of Stoodley, but there is no evidence of a sub-manor — the test being the holding of manorial courts, the authority of which was recognised both locally and by the superior manor. Furthermore the lords of Wakefield retained control of Mankinholes Moor, which was used as one of the summer pastures for the stock on their vaccary (cattle farm) at Withens. In the 1330s the pastures of 'Withnes, Turmleemosse and Mankanhuls' were let on lease, as the lords of Wakefield were withdrawing from pastoral farming in upper Calderdale.[10]

The same lords enjoyed hunting rights in Langfield, claiming in 1276 to have had from time immemorial free chase in their Forest of Sowerbyshire. In the 1230s they had granted limited rights to the Thornhill family to hunt deer under supervision within their sub-manors. By the late thirteenth century their own hunting interest was concentrated mainly in 'the forest of Arikdene' (Erringden), a bleak tract on the south side of the main valley between Sowerby and Mankinholes, where they had four vaccaries — Withens, Cruttonstall, Hathershelf and 'Nettletonstall', the latter being somewhere near Baitings. The Wakefield court rolls for 1277 (the earliest surviving roll is dated 1274) record fines imposed on several men, including some from Langfield, for allowing their cattle to stray into 'Ayrikdene forest'. In 1304, John Earl Warenne prosecuted some men who had illegally hunted his deer in 'Sourby and Langefeld'. When the palings were erected around what then became Erringden Park — the earliest reference to them occurs in 1330 — Mankinholes Moor was left outside, probably because it was also used as common pasture by the farmers of Langfield township.[11]

According to Watson, the Langfield family estate passed by marriage in the fifteenth century to Sir Richard Hamerton. On the death of the latter's grandson in 1515 the property was described as a manor, although there is no evidence that it actually was. The next heir, Sir Stephen Hamerton, was executed for his part in the Pilgrimage of Grace in 1536-37.[12]

In the early Middle Ages the manor of Rochdale was divided into four townships, one of which was 'Huneworthefelde', later known as Hundersfield. It was very large, including Wardle, Littleborough, Walsden and Todmorden. Land in these places was often referred to in deeds and other records as simply being in Hundersfield, which creates problems in tracing the early history of Todmorden and Walsden. A survey of the manor in 1626 described Walsden and Todmorden as separate 'hamlets', and in the Middle Ages they seem to have operated as distinct units for the management of communal aspects of farming.[13]

In the second half of the twelfth century the manor of Rochdale was held, under the Lacy overlords, by the brothers Hugh and Henry de Elland, apparently grandsons of Gamel. On the death of Henry his interest was divided amongst three daughters, and this property, which included land in Walsden, was further fragmented in later generations. Part at least of Todmorden and Walsden lay within Hugh de Elland's estate. This descended in the Elland family until the late fourteenth century, when it passed by marriage to Sir John Savile, father of the Henry Savile who married the Thornhill heiress. Inchfield was presumably part of this property, as it was held in the early fifteenth century by the Saviles, who described it as their manor of Inchfield.[14]

The Radcliffe family began the piecemeal acquisition of land in both Todmorden and Walsden in 1293-94, and by the late fifteenth century had built up the substantial Todmorden Hall estate. They claimed the lordship of 'the manor of Todmorden', but there is no evidence that this, or Inchfield, ever had manor courts.[15]

In the twelfth century Henry de Elland held land in Cliviger, under his elder brother Hugh, who held it in turn from the Lacy lords of the Honour of Clitheroe. Late in the century Henry granted to Kirkstall Abbey, which had been founded by the Lacy family, 'all the land which I have in Cliveschre, namely one carucate'. He executed a second charter which included 'all the men whom I have in the same township with all their progeny and chattels'. The latter wording suggests that they were bondmen. The abbey may have asked for this additional provision to give it a stronger hold over Henry's tenants. Cistercian abbeys sometimes evicted or moved peasant families to make way for a grange. Kirkstall established a grange in Cliviger, but before long it was transferred to Accrington, and the abbey land in Cliviger was let off to rent-paying free tenants. In 1287, as part of a larger deal, the abbey returned Cliviger to the Honour of Clitheroe.[16]

The administrative structure in the later Middle Ages was therefore as follows: Todmorden and Walsden lay in the township of Hundersfield and the manor of Rochdale; Cornholme and Brown Birks in the township of Cliviger and the Honour of Clitheroe. The township of Stansfield was divided into two sub-manors, Rawtonstall/Blackshaw and Stansfield. Most of the land in Langfield was held by or under the Langfield/Hamerton family, but not as a sub-manor.

Social Organisation

The townships of Stansfield and Langfield were still answerable to the courts of the manor of Wakefield for matters of civil administration and criminal jurisdiction. The latter was exercised at the twice-yearly major court meetings, called tourns, held at four different centres in the manor, including Halifax. Routine business, much of it in the form of land transfers (which did not involve the sub-manors), was dealt with at the courts held every three weeks at Wakefield. Township constables were chosen locally, but formally appointed at the tourns. Stansfield was in trouble in 1337 for having no constable. The work was unpaid, and sometimes men paid a small sum to avoid the duty. William Milner, constable of Stansfield, was fined in 1351 for failing to attend the Halifax tourn.[17]

In 1315 Stansfield township was collectively fined £4 for failing to 'raise the hue', that is, to pursue criminals who had burgled the houses of Amery of Hartley and Richard son of Roger of Stansfield. Adam of Swineshead in Langfield was hanged by order of the court in 1336 for the theft of cattle at Heptonstall. At the other end of the scale of criminality, the wife of Richard Clarkson of Langfield was fined 4d in 1337 for offences against the Assize of Ale — probably selling weak beer or overcharging.[18]

A man accused of theft could be brought before the ordinary court to find sureties for his appearance at the next tourn as an alternative to being committed to prison. In May 1277 Richard son of the smith of Stansfield, who was taken on suspicion of theft, gave 13s 4d at the Wakefield court to be under the surety of Alkoc of the Frith, Richard son of Ralph Stansfield, William the carpenter of the same place and John the smith until the Steward's Tourn at Halifax.[19]

When in 1307 five thieves, all named, broke into the house of William de Stodelay and stole goods worth £20, ten local townships, including Langfield and Stansfield, presented the case at court where the arrest of the thieves was ordered. Numerous cases of personal violence appear in the court rolls:

> In December 1308 John of Hertlay was fined 12d for drawing blood from William of Stansfield.
> In January 1352 Nicholas del Grenhirst was fined 12d for drawing blood from William del Shee.
> Adam Peresson del Crosseligh [Cross Lee] had a similar fine for drawing blood from William del Brig.
> Peter Swerd, in July 1286, was convicted of unjustly ejecting Alice del Croft from her land in Mancanholes and of casting down her house (which suggests a small wooden cruck cottage). He was fined 12d with 10s 6d damages.

Not only the men were given to occasional violence:

> In 1337 Isabel, wife of Geoffrey of Stansfeld, was fined 1s for shedding the blood of Constance of Assynghirst.

Sometimes the action of an individual affected the whole township:

> In July 1286 when Peter Swerd, mentioned above, 'unrightfully stopped up a certain footpath between Standfeud [Stansfield] and Mankanholes', he was ordered to remove the obstruction and fined 12d.
> In 1315 Richard del Ker, for a similar offence in 'Stanesfeld', was also fined 12d.
> Richard Lorimar of 'Stanesfeud', in November 1296, encroached on the highway by building a hedge and a ditch (presumably to extend his land). He was ordered to make the road up again and was fined 6d.

Trespass on the lord's land was a common offence:

> In 1275, Thomas, son of John son of Hugh de Mankanholes, was fined 6d for letting his pigs escape into the forest.
> William de Stodley, in 1277, was fined 6s 8d for allowing 6 cows and 8 calves escape into Ayrekedene [Erringden] forest.
> Henry de Stodley was fined the same for allowing 8 cows and 8 calves to escape.
> Wymark de Manckaneholes was fined 6d for his mare and her foal escaping into the forest.
> In 1332/3 Geoffrey de Stodeley and Richard de Northland were fined 40d for depasturing their cattle on the lord's grass in Ayrigdene.

These were relatively minor offences — poaching the lord's deer was much more serious:

> In 1307, Michael de la Schawe, who was caught in 'the Earl's free chase in Sourebyschyre', was fined 10 marks (£6 13s 4d) 'to go quit thereof'.
> At the same time the vicar of Rochdale was fined £20 for a similar offence.[20]

Where land in upper Calderdale was held directly from the manor of Wakefield, that is, in the townships of Warley, Sowerby and Soyland, nearly all the occupiers were bondmen or women, but the restrictions on their freedom were few. They were not allowed to live outside the manor without licence, or hold free land within it. A free man, on the other hand, could hold bondage land, performing the duties attached to it, without compromising his status. Bondmen could not sue their own lord, and therefore had no legal redress if he demanded increased rents or services; nor could they take action in the king's court against a fellow tenant on a matter which fell within the jurisdiction of the manor court. However, several of the normal obligations of bondage, including merchet, a payment to the lord on the marriage of a bondman's daughter, and lecherwit, a fine for the loss of chastity by a bond girl, did not apply in Sowerbyshire, although they did in the rest of the manor of Wakefield.

All of the medieval records of land tenure in Todmorden, Walsden, Stansfield and, with one minor exception, Langfield relate to free tenancies. When William of Stoodley in Langfield died in 1315, his daughters paid 'relief', the death duty due from free land, for all but one acre of his estate. For that acre a 'heriot', the death duty for bondhold land, was charged. The most likely explanation is that the acre had been cleared from the edge of Mankinholes Moor, under the direct control of the lords of Wakefield, and let on standard bondhold conditions.

John the blacksmith of Stansfield was in trouble in 1275. The earl claimed that he was a bondman, who had broken the rules by holding free land in Stansfield. He had probably moved from one of the predominantly bondage townships in the manor of Wakefield and bought a free-holding in Stansfield.

The overall position is clear. In the Todmorden area all, or nearly all, of the people were free. As there was no arable demesne, and hence no labour services, one of the motives for maintaining bondage was absent. The latter system probably operated in Warley and Sowerby because they were part of a large, bureaucratic manor, in some sectors of which bondage was important to the lord.[21]

Topography and Place Names

The documentary sources for medieval settlement patterns and farming systems in the Todmorden area are fragmentary, but two valuable supplements are available — the records etched on the landscape itself, and the evidence of place names. The main limitation in the latter case is that, apart from the *Domesday* references to Stansfield and Langfield, none of the local names appears in written records until the thirteenth century.[22]

The broad outlines of settlement history are clear. Upper Calderdale remained in British hands until the English (Anglo-Saxon) conquest of the British kingdom of Elmet in the AD 630s. Nearly all of the early place names in the Todmorden area are English. The River Calder has a British name, meaning 'violent stream', and Walsden is an English name describing British neighbours — the dene (valley) of the 'Walhs', the English word for foreigner, from which Wales and the second part of Cornwall are derived. Shore in Stansfield has a triangular green on the edge of the settlement, a feature thought to be characteristic of British hamlets. It is, however, impossible to say how many of the hamlets or farms with English names had been renamed, and how many created by English colonisation.

The English place names have a distinctive pattern. There are no examples of 'ham' or 'tun', typical English words for farm or village. Instead 'tonstall' (farmstead) occurs twice — Rawtonstall (rough farmstead) and Wittonstall, the first element of which is apparently 'withig', meaning willow. Upper Calderdale has altogether eight examples of 'tonstall', by far the largest concentration in Yorkshire. There are at least two more 'denes': the valley of Totta's marsh, Tott-mer-den; and Stiperden, where the first element means a post, and probably relates to its position on the parish and county boundaries. Otherwise the commonest early elements are 'ley', a glade or clearing, and the names for copse or stretch of woodland, 'hirst' and 'shaw'. Stansfield

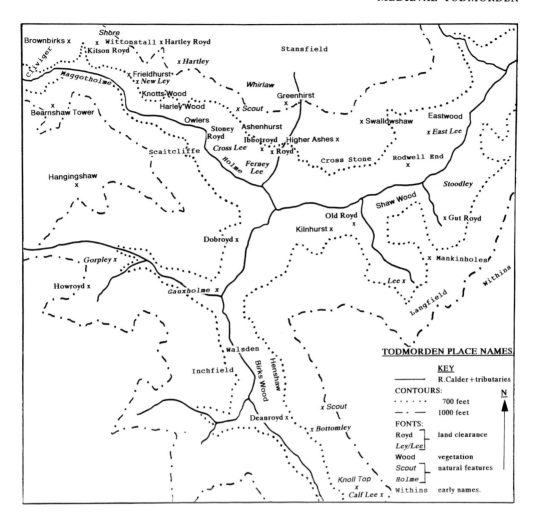

Brownbirks x
Shore
x Wittonstall x Hartley Royd
Kitson Royd
Stansfield
x Hartley
x Frieldhurst
x New Ley
Whirlaw
Maggotholme
Knotts Wood
Greenhirst
x Bearnshaw Tower
Harley Wood
x Scout
Owlers
Eastwood
x Swallowshaw
x East Lee
Stoney Royd
Ashenhurst
Ibbotroyd Higher Ashes x
Cross Lee x x Royd
Scaitcliffe
Ferney Lee
Cross Stone
Rodwell End
Hangingshaw x
Stoodley
Shaw Wood
Old Royd x
x Gut Royd
Kilnhurst x
Dobroyd x
x Mankinholes
Gorpley x
Lee x
Howroyd x
Gauxholme x
Langfield
Withins
Walsden
Inchfield
Henshaw
Birks Wood
x Scout
Deanroyd x
x Bottomley
Knoll Top x
Calf Lee x

TODMORDEN PLACE NAMES

KEY

——— R.Calder + tributaries

CONTOURS: N

· · · · · ·   700 feet

— · —   1000 feet

FONTS:

Royd ⎤ land clearance
Ley/Lee ⎦

Wood   vegetation

Scout ⎤ natural features
Holme ⎦

Withins   early names.

has Hartley, Cross Lee, Ferney Lee, and East Lee; Langfield, Stoodley and Lee; and Todmorden/Walsden, Gorpley and Bottomley. In the second category are Greenhirst, Ashenhurst, Frieldhirst, Kilnhirst, Blackshaw, Swallowshaw, Hangingshaw, Bearnshaw, and Henshaw, together with names including 'wood' (Eastwood, Robinwood, Harleywood, etc), or describing particular trees, eg Birks and Owlers (alder).

The Danish conquest of Yorkshire in 867 does not seem to have had much impact on the Todmorden area. The one distinctive Scandinavian name is Mankinholes — Mancan's hollow. Mancan is an Irish personal name, indicating a penetration, probably in the tenth century, from older Viking colonies in Ireland via north-west England.

The medieval settlement pattern of the Todmorden area was predominantly dispersed. In common with many other areas of the Yorkshire Pennines, Stansfield contained no settlement which bore the township name. Wittonstall/Shore may have formed the largest cluster. Otherwise a map of the earliest recorded names shows a similar distribution to that presented by the seventeenth century yeoman's houses to be seen today, strung out along the broader hillside terraces. Most of Stansfield has the advantage of facing south; aspect is all-important in hilly country.

Celtic heads unearthed locally in the 1960s.

Langfield is on the less favoured northward-facing side of the Calder Valley. The principal medieval settlements, Longfield, Mankinholes and Stoodley, were located on a west-facing terrace sheltered from the east wind by the steep ridge rising to the moors behind. The largest of the three was probably Mankinholes, judging from its situation, the number of old yeomen's houses there and the fact that the moor now labelled Langfield Common on the OS maps was known in the Middle Ages as Mankinholes Moor.

Todmorden and Walsden had the most varied topography. The north-west corner around Bearnshaw Tower, which faced north over Portsmouth and Cornholme, occupied possibly the most inhospitable location in the district. Physical conditions improved south-eastwards as the terrace broadened out from Todmorden Edge and swept round to face south over Dulesgate Valley. In this area most of the scattered farms of the medieval 'hamlet' of Todmorden were to be found. The land on the eastern side of Walsden tumbled down to the valley bottom with no significant shelf, an invitation to the medieval farmers (or their predecessors) to select sites where the curve of the hillside offered a southern aspect. To the west of Walsden Water the valley rises steeply to a relatively broad terrace, but with a mainly northerly aspect at a height of 700-900 feet, where Allescholes and Inchfield are located. Here archaeological evidence of Celtic/British occupation came to light in 1966 when a carved stone head was unearthed on farmland in Walsden. It resembled that of a Celtic god found at Netherby in Cumberland dated the second or third century. Subsequently other heads were discovered locally, some built into field walls; all but one being accepted as genuine.[23]

Farming Systems

In such a wild, mountainous country, with a cool climate and high rainfall (around fifty inches a year in modern times), it might be assumed that farming in the Middle Ages would have been, as it is today, predominantly pastoral. This option was open to monasteries or the lords of great estates, who could locate arable demesne, cattle ranches and sheep pastures in the climatic and soil conditions suitable for each. The vaccaries of the manor of Wakefield have already been mentioned. Over the watershed from upper Calderdale, the Honour of Clitheroe had, circa 1300, about 1,300 head of cattle on twenty-seven vaccaries in the Forests of Trawden, Pendle and Rossendale. (They were, incidentally, still being troubled by wolves, which must have roamed on the Todmorden side as well.) The peasant farmer could not specialise in cattle-rearing. He could not afford to feed his household mainly on meat and dairy produce, and the inadequacies of the marketing system made it impossible to rely on buying grain with the profits of pastoral activities. He therefore had to grow cereals; this meant in practice oats, which could withstand the climatic conditions much better than the other grains. Oats, however, were a low-yielding crop, typically producing two and a half bushels for every one sown. The local 'delicacy', dock pudding, made from the sweet dock leaf (*polygonum bistorta*) picked in early spring, may be a survivor from a range of wild crops culled from the rain-soaked hills to eke out the meagre food supplies.[24]

Taking upper Calderdale as a whole, it is clear from both medieval records and evidence on the ground that much of the arable land lay in unfenced strips in open fields. These were very different from the lowland 'three-field system', with its sequence of winter-sown, spring-sown and fallow. For one thing, there were hardly any winter-sown crops, such as wheat and rye. The management of the open fields in upper Calderdale was decentralised, that is, it was not normal for each township to have one field system. Some villages and hamlets had their own. Otherwise it is probable that the cropping of each 'flatt' or 'furlong' — a block of strips — was independently organised by the occupiers of the flatt.

One physical trace of local open-field organisation is an apron of enclosed fields adjacent to a village or hamlet which has on it no farms, except for a few with significant names such as Westfield or Oldfield, and lacks the network of lanes which criss-cross the terraces and hillsides elsewhere. The 'closes', the name used to distinguish enclosed fields from unfenced 'field' land, were formed by a process of piecemeal enclosure by agreement, which was well advanced by the late fifteenth century. The hamlet of Wittonstall/Shore has such an apron of fields, one of them being called 'Long Flat' in an 1805 survey. Traces of strip layout can be seen on the map of 1805 (see page 15).

Some thirteenth and early fourteenth century deeds describe open-field land in Stansfield, including:

> one plot of land in the township of Stanesfeld as it lies within the fences between the land of Richard de Yrland and the land of a certain John of Holgate called Holegategrene, $1^1/_4$ acres.
> a bovate of land lying within the field of Radewayhalig within the bounds of Stansfeld, namely all the land which Richard Lorimer had of Sir John de Sothill, with a building in a place called Birkinrodesike on the east side.

'Radewayhalig' appears again in 1359 as 'Radowhalgh' and in 1501 as 'Radway-halge', on the former occasion described as lying 'between the highway on one side and the water of Calder on the other'. The closest match of names is with Rodwell Head and Rodwell End, and the 1359 details suggest that the land covered by the 'Rodwell' names extended from the Cross Stone-Blackshaw Head road to the valley bottom.[25]

At Mankinholes, between the settlement and the edge of the valley, is another apron of fields spread on a shelf. Long and narrow, they too resemble medieval strips. Abraham Newell, in a paper on Mankinholes reprinted from a talk he gave on a WEA ramble, comments on these fields:

> These may at one time have been common, for amongst them are three or four which, up to a time early in the last century [19th], were common to as many of the central farms, when by mutual arrangement it was shared among the individuals. A very striking feature of the farms in Mankinholes is the way in which the closes of each farm are scattered among those of the rest. In one case, a man has to travel over his neighbour's land in order to get to his own. When my father gave his paper before your society in 1915 a man was present who had actually had a swathe cut through his grass by a neighbour who wanted to get his hay before the first man was ready ... a plan of Mankinholes and the 'tops' coloured according to occupiers would today (1926), even after these many centuries of individual domination, bargainings and concessions, present a very curious piece of patchwork.[26]

The name 'Lumbutts' is also suggestive of this method of farming, meaning the pool (lumm) abutting the strip of land.[27]

In the north-east corner of Langfield township lay the hamlet of Stoodley, separated from Mankinholes by Deep Clough (now called Shaw Clough) and from Erringden Park by Stoodley Clough. It had its own common arable/meadow field. A conveyance of property in 1346 included both arable and meadow land in 'Stodeleyfeld', namely, 'four selions above Barrellholestuttes' (selions were long, narrow strips); and a piece of meadow lying 'above Dobcrostbent', bounded by a ditch and three 'merestones' (boundary stones).[28]

There are a few references in medieval conveyances of land to one or more open fields in Todmorden, but none for Walsden. The two were separated by Dulesgate Water, except that the occupiers of Gauxholme had the right of common on Inchfield Pasture. 'The field of Todmorden' is mentioned, and land is described as lying between the lands of other occupiers in a way that suggests the existence of strips or blocks of strips. The greatest detail is given in a deed of circa 1300, by which Thomas of the Dean conveyed to his son William all his lands in the 'Mitham' (this appears later as 'les Mithomes' — the word means water-meetings, probably the confluence of

Dulesgate Water and Walsden Water), all his part in Little Royd, all his part in Gauxholme with two selions in Adam Royd, and all his part in the Wetshaw (later Weetshaw) and in 'le hay' (a hey is an enclosure). The words 'all his part in' suggest the existence of shared fields. Adam Royd was on the north side of Scaitcliffe, where the Royd House, now demolished, used to stand.

The most intriguing document, dated 1364, describes lands as lying adjacent to the field of John of Crossley, within the fences of the Ring of Todmorden. Any continuous area of arable and meadow land under communal management would have had a fence, wall or hedge around it, certainly during the growing season. The 'Ring' may have been this fenced area.[29]

Adam Royd, Little Royd, royd land ... royd is a common place-name element in upper Calderdale, usually spelt 'rode' in medieval documents. It means land cleared for cultivation, and was in active use locally in the thirteenth and fourteenth centuries. The earliest documentary evidence of this kind of colonisation, apart from the twelfth century reference to the possible clearance of woodland in Stansfield, appears in a conveyance of land in Walsden in 1235, in which the grantors reserved the right 'to assart the whole of that wood which is on the north side of Lichitheselegh [Light Hazzles, on the east side of the Walsden Valley, just north of Summit] and there to make meadow or arable land at their will'. 'Rode' was the vernacular equivalent of 'assart'.[30]

In the manor of Rochdale, 'rodeland' was charged with an annual payment in lieu of 'puture'. This originally meant the right of the officers of a hunting forest to take food, for themselves and their animals, without payment, from the tenants within the forest. It sometimes evolved into a financial transaction. In the 1320s the 'rodemen' of the manor made a collective payment of 15s a year.[31]

In 1316 Sir John Thornhill granted to William son of Roger of the Eastwood an acre of land from the waste in Stansfield, lying between the land of Richard of the Eastwood and 'a certain place which is called Idderode'; and to William's brother John a plot of land and woods 'lying between Hirperunhirst and the land of Roger del Estwode called Hirperunhirstbank'. The rent in each case was 4d a year. Sir Brian Thornhill, who held the sub-manor of Stansfield from 1322 to 1360, granted to 'Adam son of Henry del Schore a plot of land ... called Wythtunstalbanck' at an annual rent of 12d, therefore probably measuring about three acres.[32]

The Stoodley property (1346), referred to above, included both 'one assart which lies in the common called Hetheknolle', ie a mound on the heath; and a one-sixteenth share of the bank leading down from the Stoodley terrace to the River Calder between Deep Clough and Stoodley Clough. This bank had, for the south side of the main valley, a relatively favourable aspect, facing more to the west than to the north. On the other hand, it was probably too steep for profitable assarting, and is still wooded.[33]

It is not possible to calculate the rate of colonisation in the Todmorden area, but in Sowerby and Warley the area of land under cultivation doubled between the mid-thirteenth and mid-fourteenth centuries. In these townships, as is the case around Todmorden, the 'royd' names are often found on the hillsides below the old terrace settlements. Old Royd in Langfield has a pattern of land tumbling down to the valley which was probably cleared at this time *(see photograph on page 14)*. It is worth noting that two of the above references to clearances refer to 'bank'.[34]

The extension of cultivation did not proceed smoothly. There was a serious check early in the fourteenth century when the disastrously heavy rains of 1315-17 were followed by an outbreak of murrain (cattle plague) in the winter of 1319-20. The

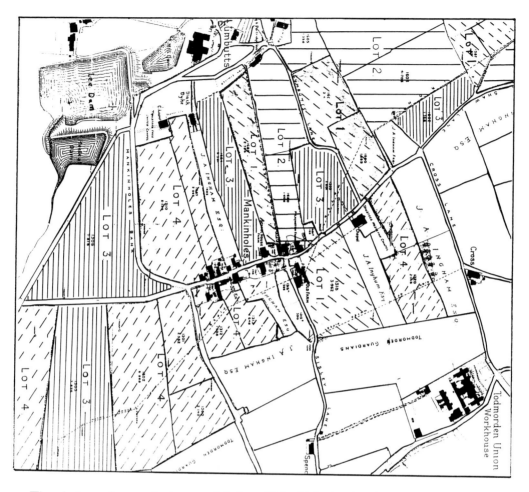

The photograph opposite is an aerial view of Mankinholes showing the field pattern as shown in more detail on the map above. The four dams provided water for the Lumbutts mills.

effects of the latter were still being felt in 1322. The accounts of the manor of Wakefield for the period March-September noted a sharp reduction in rent from the lord's pastures and fines for straying cattle 'because nearly all the animals of that country were destroyed by the murrain'. An attempt had been made to isolate diseased animals: 'from the herbage of Wythnes [Withens] which used to render 10s per year, nothing this year, because it was depastured by the animals of the lord King there with murrain'. (King Edward II had held the manor since the confiscation of the Earl of Lancaster's estates in March 1322.) The accounts of the manor of Rochdale for 1323-24 show that a holding in Walsden for which John Ware had previously paid a rent of 2s a year was in the hands of the lord for want of a tenant.[35]

A much longer halt to colonisation was caused by the Black Death, an outbreak of bubonic plague which reached upper Calderdale in the summer of 1349. There are no figures for the Todmorden area, but conservative estimates of the death rate amongst occupiers of land are 40% for Warley and 33% for Sowerby. Two successive vicars of Halifax died in the plague year, in which the death rate amongst the rectors and vicars of the local deanery (Pontefract) was 40%. The vicar of Rochdale was another victim, and it was eight months before a successor was appointed.[36]

The Black Death caused an acute shortage of labour. The Ordinance of Labourers, issued by the King's Council in June 1349, ordered all wage labourers to continue to work at the old rates and not to move about in search of higher wages. In February 1351, Parliament passed the Statute of Labourers, providing for the fixing of prices and wages by JPs. The township of Stansfield reported to the tourn of the manor of Wakefield in June 1352 that 'John of Otlay, Richard Dykson, Richard Michel, Richard Jakson and Agnes daughter of Matthew Rogerson' were servants who had left the district against the Ordinance. Langfield presented two men for a similar offence.[37]

Assarting was resumed eventually, although on a small scale until about the end of the fifteenth century. The accounts of the manor of Rochdale for 1413-14 include the sum of 12d as the annual rent of a plot called 'Threparr', cleared from the moor by a member of the Radcliffe family in 1374-75. No later clearance was recorded, although nearly forty years had elapsed.[38]

The Beginning of Industry

The corn mill of Stansfield sub-manor has already been mentioned. The sub-manor of Rawtonstall had a corn mill, Hudson Mill on Colden Water, the earliest record of which is 1362-63. Langfield must have had its own mill, but the earliest record is of a mill at Lumbutts near Mankinholes in 1557. In the survey of the manor of Rochdale in 1626, Savile Radcliffe stated that he held property at Gauxholme, including a corn mill on the 'stream parting Walsden and Todmorden', by a deed dated 1430. It is not clear whether the mill was there at that time, but at least one mill for Todmorden and Walsden would have been a practical necessity.[39]

The early records of the textile industry are also fragmentary. There are references to a fuller at Hebden Bridge in 1347 and to the building of a fulling mill in Heptonstall township in 1382. Fulling was done originally by walking on the freshly-woven cloth in a bath of water containing fuller's earth; this thickened and felted the cloth. It was then dried and kept in shape by stretching it on tenters (frames) in the open air (hence Tenterfield Terrace, behind Cinderhill at Castle Street). When it had dried, the nap was raised by teazles and then cropped by shears to give the cloth its smooth finish.[40]

When fulling was mechanised, the walking was done by two heavy wooden hammers alternately raised and dropped to pound the cloth; this worked on a simple trip system powered by a water wheel. Retaining the old terminology, these fulling mills were often referred, to as 'walk' mills. Walk Mill in Cliviger takes its name from one.

In 1498 Sir John Savile granted to John Horsfall land and a licence to build a fulling mill and dam at Keldyz (Callis) in Stansfield. In 1557 Richard Horsfall gave to his daughter Ann 'one walke mylne ... lyenge ... within townshipp of Longfelde'. This seems to be the first record of industry on the Lobb Mill site.[41]

In the 1235 grant of land in Walsden, mentioned above in connection with assarting, the grantors also reserved the right 'to put up forges, and to dig for iron and steel ore to supply those forges, wherever they will on the moors and in the woods which belong to the town(ship) of Hunewithefeld'. A survey of the Forest of Sowerbyshire in 1314 lists an iron-smelting forge worth £9 12s a year, but its location is not given. These forges used the bloomery process, the ore being alternately heated by charcoal to about 1,400 degrees centigrade, and hammered to remove impurities. Slag heaps associated with bloomeries have been found at Bottomley Brook and Birks Wood in Walsden, in Ramsden Clough and Gorpley Clough, and at Birks Wood near Far Hollingworth. The bloomery process produced iron of good quality but was wasteful. One piece of slag at Bottomley Brook was found to contain forty-one per cent iron.[42]

The local bloomeries probably used ore from nearby Ruddle Scout in Cliviger, where several bands of ironstone occur, overlain by a coal seam. The accounts for Cliviger for 1304-05 include 'iron ore sold for 10 weeks, 6s 8d', meaning that someone was licensed to dig for the ore for that period. The 1295-96 accounts for the same township record the sale of 'sea-coals' (mineral coal, so called to distinguish it from charcoal) for 3d. Some coal seams outcrop in Dulesgate but there is no medieval record of mining there.[43]

There were no markets and fairs in medieval Todmorden, the nearest weekly markets being at Halifax, Rochdale and Burnley. Travelling traders would have filled the gap, but hardly at the keenest prices.[44]

Religious Provision and Economic Development

The ecclesiastical map was similarly blank. The parish churches were many miles away, at Rochdale, Whalley and Halifax. The fragment of a cross which survives from the wall of the barn at Bean Hole Head, and gives the name to Cross Stone, may be a link to the eleventh century, when masses were said in the open by travelling priests. (Alternatively, the cross, of Viking age, might have been a grave-marker.) Mount Cross above Shore near the Long Causeway, one of a series along this ancient route, and thought to be of early medieval origin, may also have served as a preaching cross as well as a way-marker. Within the parish of Halifax, a parochial chapel was established at Heptonstall to serve the western end of Calderdale, including Stansfield and Langfield. It can be traced back through architectural evidence to the middle of the thirteenth century, and is mentioned by implication in a document of 1273.[45]

A parochial chapel at Burnley, within the parish of Whalley, was in existence by 1120, but there was no chapel in the Todmorden area until St Mary's Chapel was built, reputedly at the initiative of the Radcliffe family of nearby Todmorden Hall. It was in existence by 1476. Other local chapels were Littleborough, built about 1471, and Holme in Cliviger, which is thought to date from the same period, but neither came early enough to help the Todmorden people. Some fifteenth century chapels

Mount Cross, below the Long
Causeway near Shore in Stansfield.

may have originated as chantries, funded to provide masses for the dead. Both St Mary's and Holme were listed in the sixteenth century chantry surveys.[46]

The local people paid tithes and other dues, including if they were farmers a beast as a 'mortuary' or death duty, to the distant parish church, irrespective of the pastoral care they received. Most of the income of Halifax parish was taken by Lewes Priory, to which the Earls Warenne, founders of the priory, had given the parish church, together with the rectory manor of Halifax cum Heptonstall. The lion's share of the Rochdale tithes went to Whalley Abbey.[47]

It is inconceivable that people from Shore or Mankinholes, however sound in wind and limb, would have been able to travel to Heptonstall, or those from Todmorden and Walsden to either Rochdale or Heptonstall, on fifty-two Sundays and about thirty holy days in the year. It is likely that, apart from the great feasts, their attendance was intermittent and affected by the weather. In such circumstances, irregular attendance was not culpable, but the fear that in the event of sudden illness a priest might not arrive in time to hear the final confession and administer the last rites must have been present in people's minds.

Some indication of the relative economic development of the local townships is given by the taxation returns. From 1290 to 1332 the lay subsidy voted by Parliament was levied upon individuals, in practice the better-off. The only surviving return for our area is for 1332, when the tax was fixed at one fifteenth of the value of assessable crops and stock. The minimum valuation was 10s, therefore the smallest amount payable was 8d. The local details are:

STANSFIELD			LANGFIELD		
Peter of Crosselee	3s		Geoffrey of Stodeley	2s	8d
Michael of Routonstall	2s	8d	Henry of Langfeld	2s	
Adam son of Peter	2s		Richard of Mankanhuls	1s	8d
William of Estwod	1s	6d	Richard of Northland	1s	6d
William son of John	1s		William of the Lane	1s	6d
John of the Ker		8d			
Totals	*10s*	*10d*		*9s*	*4d*

In 1334 the system changed, to a quota fixed for each township. The local figures are given below, with some comparative statistics for other places in the West Riding and Lancashire:

Stansfield	16s	Ripon	£11 6s 8d
Langfield	14s	Sheffield	£7 3s 4d
Wadsworth	16s	Wakefield	£6
Halifax&Heptonstall	11s	Leeds	£3 13s
Midgley	13s	Bradford	£1
Warley	16s	Manchester	£3 7s
Sowerby&Soyland	16s	Oldham	£1
Hundersfield	£1 18s 4d		
Cliviger	£1		

There are no separate figures for Todmorden and Walsden, as they were included in the extensive township of Hundersfield. One third of the quota fixed for the latter is 12s 9d. To put it in another way, it is unlikely that the tax assessment for Todmorden and Walsden was greater than that for Langfield.[48]

Poll taxes were levied in 1377, 1379 and 1381. The local returns for 1377 have been lost. Those for 1379 have been printed; the tax was graduated according to status, with a minimum of 4d per individual or married couple. Beggars and those under the age of sixteen were exempt. Comparisons with the 1377 figures, where available, show that there was widespread evasion in 1379. In the latter year there were in Stansfield 43 taxpayers, of whom 21 were married, giving a total of 64. Langfield had 11 couples and 11 single payers, total 33. Assuming that the married couples had an average of two children under sixteen living at home — some, of course, would have more, but there would also be the recently married and those with children over sixteen or who had left home — the tax-paying population of the two townships would be 161. At three children per couple it would be 193. Making the further assumption that Todmorden and Walsden would have a similar profile to Langfield would give overall figures of 216 and 259. Some addition has to be made for beggars, who would include many of those from the landless, labouring classes who were too old to work or were chronically sick, but it is the problem of evasion which makes further exploration a matter of guesswork rather than calculation.[49]

If the figures were available, we could arrive at the estimated population of the area of the modern borough of Todmorden by adding in the beggars and the evaders, including the population of the Cornholme area of Cliviger township, and excluding the larger population of the lower third of Stansfield (the Hebden Bridge end). An educated guess would give a figure of 300-350 in 1379, and perhaps 450-500 on the eve of the Black Death. As the plague returned, in less severe form, in 1361-62, 1369 and 1375, the population would still be well below the 1348 level. These figures are subject to a wide margin of error, but they can be put into a safer perspective by two comparisons. First, although much of its area was rural, the borough of Todmorden had a population of over 25,000 in 1911. Secondly, we can find in Yorkshire, for example in the Wolds, substantial farming villages which had as many people at the end of the thirteenth century as in the middle of the eighteenth.

In other words, conclusions about the developmental profile of the Todmorden area can safely be drawn. It was thinly populated in the fourteenth century because the people lived predominantly by farming in unfavourable topographical and climatic conditions. Apart possibly from iron, there is no evidence of industrial development beyond small-scale provision for local needs. Commercially, Todmorden was at the end of the line. In 1379 only two men paid more than the minimum 4d, John of Shore and William of Stansfield, who were each charged 1s as merchants. None of the money drawn off by the Church as tithes or other dues was spent locally. The ceiling of economic potential remained low, until the development of a market-orientated textile industry, of which we see the first signs at the end of the fifteenth century.

The countervailing advantages can be summed up in one word — freedom. Not only did the local peasantry enjoy free status and tenure, but there were no resident manorial lords to whom they had to defer. The attitude of Todmorden people to external authority, and the underlying reasons for it, form threads which run through several later chapters.

3

Tudor and Stuart Todmorden

The Tudor period began with the victory of Henry VII over Richard III at the Battle of Bosworth in 1485, but the change of dynasty made no immediate impact on the life of a remote area such as Todmorden. The departures and developments, which can be taken as marking the end of the Middle Ages locally, are dated about half a century later. The Reformation began in the 1530s, by which time the cloth industry was visibly increasing in importance in upper Calderdale. The interaction between religious convictions and the growth of a prosperous textile industry was to shape the social as well as the economic character of the Todmorden area during the next few centuries. The development of the dual economy of farming and textiles is described in Chapter 4.

In the sixteenth century the Savile family held the sub-manors of Stansfield and Rawtonstall (merged in the 1530s) under the manor of Wakefield, which belonged to the Crown, now as part of the Duchy of Lancaster. Langfield belonged to a group of

Todmorden Hall. In 1924 it became the town's main post office, and is now a restaurant.

freeholders, except that the manor of Wakefield had an ill-defined interest in Mankinholes Moor. Todmorden and Walsden formed part of the manor of Rochdale, also Crown property. The leading local landowners were the Radcliffes of Todmorden Hall and a branch of the Savile family holding the Inchfield estate.[1]

In 1625-29 the financial problems of Charles I led to the sale of the manors of Rochdale and Wakefield. The latter had a succession of owners until 1700, when it was bought by the Duke of Leeds. Rochdale was purchased in 1638 by Sir John Byron (whose ancestors had been stewards and lessees of the manor) and descended in his family until it was sold by Lord Byron the poet in 1823.[2]

Landlords, Tenants and Enclosure

The price inflation of the Tudor period, although mild by twentieth century standards — prices trebled between 1540 and 1640 — caused tension and disputes as customary tenants tried to hold on to rents which had long been stable. There are no recorded disputes about rents or tenures in the Todmorden area. Langfield was entirely freehold. Land in Stansfield was either freehold or held on twenty-one year leases from the Saviles.[3] Because of the frequent occurrence of a small number of surnames, eg Greenwood, Sutcliffe, Wadsworth, Ashworth and Horsfall, it is not possible to track the rent levels of particular farms from the estate records. In 1626 Todmorden and Walsden had 3,787 statute acres of enclosed ground, two-thirds of it freehold and the rest copyhold. The latter, otherwise known as customary tenure, derived its name from the form of the title deeds, copies of entries in the manor court rolls. The copyholders of Warley and Sowerby were the successors of the medieval bondmen, but copyhold tenure in Todmorden and Walsden may have originated with the clearance of 'royd' land, or as the process was called from the sixteenth century, 'intaking'. Certainly a fifth of the copyhold land recorded in 1626 can be identified with recent intakes in Walsden. More than half of the land attached to Bearnshaw Tower (near Cornholme), said to have been encroached from the waste by the Radcliffes before 1543, was copyhold.[4]

The Bearnshaw Tower encroachment may in fact go back much further, as an illegal enclosure of a similar size, held by the Radcliffes, was said in 1578 to be about eighty years old. Most of the accusations of encroachment made in the same year related to plots of up to four acres, or the extension of a house on to the common. Richard Crossley of Scaitcliffe was said to have built, earlier in 1578, a house of three bays, 15 yards long and 6 yards wide, of which 'about 3 yards in breadth stand upon the Queen's waste'. Two other Crossley houses involved similar faults. Edmund Lorde of Gorpley, gentleman, had encroached enough land twelve years previously to build a house and barn of four and a half bays.[5]

In 1605 the freeholders of Langfield, twenty-nine in number, who held between them about 500 acres of enclosed ground, brought an action in the Duchy of Lancaster court to prevent an adventurer called John Priestley esquire enclosing part of Mankinholes Moor. An agreement was eventually reached in 1615 that the freeholders would jointly pay to the manor of Wakefield an annual rent of 4d an acre for the best 100 acres of moor, and $^{1}/_{4}$d for the remaining 300 acres, which was very barren. The freeholders at the same time secured the right to divide and enclose the moor by majority agreement.[6]

The freeholders of Inchfield had, before 1626, begun the process of dividing their common pasture, originally between 700 and 800 statute acres in extent. About three-fifths of this had been marked off as the Ox Pasture, of which 107 acres had been enclosed, the rest being a stinted pasture for sixty head of cattle. The Out Pasture was still common land. The Inchfield freeholders claimed exclusive rights to the local commons, but the interest of the lord of the manor in the remaining commons of Todmorden and Walsden had been asserted by 1638, no doubt as a result of the local knowledge of Sir John Byron, who bought the manor in that year. The 420 acres of Walsden Common, known by the names of Salter Rake, Stoney Edge, White Slack and Ramsden, had been divided into sections, giving the lord one third and the occupiers two-thirds. A similar exercise was carried out on 469 acres of Todmorden Common. The intention may have been to facilitate enclosure and improvement, but most of the land concerned is still rough moorland today.[7]

It should be emphasised that at this period 'enclosure' meant intaking from, or dividing up, the common pastures. The former open arable fields had been divided and enclosed by local agreements. A survey of the Savile manor of Stansfield/Rawtonstall in 1604 shows that all of the arable, meadow and improved pasture was enclosed. All of the references to land in Langfield and in Todmorden/Walsden give a similar picture.[8]

In Stansfield township the freeholders and leaseholders were able to intake by securing licences from the Saviles, and paying an entry fine and additional rent. These transactions used the Stansfield customary acre, based on a perch of eight yards. The statute perch was five and a half yards; and four perches multiplied by a furlong of 220 yards gave a statute acre of 4,840 square yards. The local acre was equivalent to almost 2.12 statute acres. (Todmorden and Walsden also used the perch of eight yards, but all the above figures relating to the latter are in statute acres.) Intaking in Stansfield was apparently concentrated in certain years. In the two years 1589-91 only 8 local acres were taken in. In 1597-98 the figure was 16. In 1599-1600, however, sixteen people secured licences for the enclosure of 108 local acres — just over 228 statute acres. It is possible that some of these transactions represent the regularising of encroachments discovered in one of the periodic surveys of the steward.[9]

Manorial and Township Government[10]

The townships of Stansfield and Langfield were still subject to the authority of the twice-yearly tourn of the manor of Wakefield in matters of social regulation. None of the issues involved conflicts between the lord of the manor and local people. Charges were brought by the officers of a township, usually against named individuals, sometimes against neighbouring townships. The officers were the constable and four leading citizens described as 'the four townsmen' or simply 'the four men'. A substantial proportion of the latter, as late as 1737-38 (after which the paper rolls which recorded the preliminary business of the tourns have not been preserved), signed their names with a cross.

Affrays and bloodshed, less frequently reported than in the fourteenth century, were punished in the same way, by a fine. Nuisances dealt with included obstructing or diverting the watercourses which ran in an intricate network down the hillsides. The only farming matters to come before the court were keeping 'scabbed horses' off the commons, and maintaining the walls or fences which prevented stock grazing on the commons from straying into the enclosed lands. In April 1621 Langfield appointed two 'overseares for the mower heggh' (moor edge). Such an arrangement was not normally reported to the tourn, but may have been made informally. The responsibility for maintaining the moor walls rested with the owners of the adjoining lands. In October 1690, for example, those concerned with the stretch between Field Head and Earnshaw Water in Stansfield were ordered to do the necessary repairs by the 1st March 1691, under pain of a fine of 39s.

The largest single item of township business dealt with by the tourns was highway maintenance. The Highways Act of 1555 required each householder to provide, according to his station, one man, or two men with a cart or waggon, to work for four days in the year (later raised to six) on road repairs. The Act was ignored in upper Calderdale, where the older manorial system of making the occupiers of the land responsible for maintaining adjacent stretches of the road was preferred. In an area of dispersed settlement, this system worked reasonably well. The townships appointed 'overseers of the highways' at the tourns, normally two for Langfield and four for Stansfield. When conscience and persuasion failed, the authority of the tourn could be invoked. In October 1660, for example, the occupiers of lands on both sides of the lane between Blackshaw Bridge and Shaw Bridge (this may be Jack Bridge), and those similarly responsible for the road between Cross Stone and Hey Head, were ordered to do the necessary repairs. At the same time the appropriate occupiers were required to clean the sluices which drained the road between High Gate and Blackshawhead. A highway was thought of as a right of passage, rather than as something with a particular surface. Repairs therefore meant scouring ditches and sluices, cutting back overhanging branches and filling holes with stones. Miscreants who dug stones out of the highway could expect a heavy fine, although it might be difficult to determine the line of a road which ran across open moorland. Townships frequently indicted each other for neglect of the main roads or bridges. Langfield charged Erringden, in October 1620, with failure to maintain Marshaw Bridge, and the court ordered the repairs to be done by the 11th November.

The manorial court records show only the tip of the iceberg of township self-government, of which a fuller picture emerges in the eighteenth century through the survival of township records. The responsibilities undertaken by the more substantial inhabitants extended to religious matters. As explained in Chapter 2, there was no church in the Todmorden area until the building of St Mary's Chapel at Todmorden at some date before 1476. Many such chapels were built in places remote from parish churches in the Yorkshire Pennines in the late fifteenth and early sixteenth centuries. No help was forthcoming from the parsons of the parish churches or the monasteries which had appropriated a large share of the tithes. If the people wanted the convenience of a local chapel, they had to build it themselves and find some means of paying the priest. A common method for the latter was an agreement amongst the inhabitants to contribute in proportion to the value of their lands.[11]

In the 1578 lawsuit about encroachments on the common in Todmorden, mentioned above, one witness testified that the thirty or so acres taken in about eighty years previously, and held by Charles Radcliffe, had been charged with the payment of 26s 8d a year to the chantry priest of Todmorden. The intake had presumably been made by community agreement as a painless method of helping to staff the local chapel.[12]

Cross Stone Chapel, founded to serve the townships of Stansfield and Langfield, was in existence by 1537. Thomas Stansfield, of Higgin Chamber in Sowerby, left in his will dated the 3rd April 1537 'to the chapell builded at the Cross Stone' the sum of £5 3s 4d to buy a chalice, to replace one lent by Heptonstall Church. The last Stansfield to live at Stansfield Hall was Thomas's uncle James, who moved away in 1536. It has been suggested that the chapel may have been a parting gift to the district. It was almost certainly built after 1521. In that year John Crossley of Kilnhurst in Langfield left 8s to Todmorden Chapel, as well as 6s 8d to Heptonstall Church where he was buried, and his best beast as a mortuary (death duty) to the vicar of Halifax. His will does not mention Cross Stone.[13]

The Reformation and emergence of Puritanism

The first step in the Reformation, the assertion by Henry VIII of the royal supremacy over the Church in England, may have made only a limited impact on a community to which even the vicars of the parish churches were remote figures. The next act in the drama, the confiscation of monastic lands in 1536-39, also took place on a distant stage. The tithes which had gone to Lewes Priory and Whalley Abbey now belonged to laymen. However, the farmers within the parish of Halifax enjoyed the great good fortune of an agreement made in 1535 to replace the 'great tithes' (corn, hay, wool and lamb) by a fixed annual rent charge on the land. The charge was initially modest, and declined in real terms as prices rose. The Todmorden area played no part in the Pilgrimage of Grace, a rebellion touched off in part by the threat to the monasteries. Sir Stephen Hamerton, who had an estate in Langfield, was executed for his part in the Pilgrimage, but he was not resident locally.[14]

Under Edward VI (1547-53) the Protestant Reformation gathered pace. The Latin mass was replaced by a communion service said in English, and the process began of transforming the sacramental priest into the preaching minister. The doctrine of purgatory was repudiated, which cleared the way for the suppression of the chantries and the confiscation of their endowments. Todmorden Chapel was threatened, but it was spared because it functioned as a general chapel of ease. The inhabitants paid a fee of 6s 8d, but this should be seen as a licence or a bribe rather than the purchase price of the building.[15]

Some of the clergy managed to stay in their posts through all the changes described above. A local 'vicar of Bray' was Robert Turner, appointed as chantry priest at Todmorden Chapel, who continued to serve as curate of the chapel, using in turn the two Edwardian prayer books, the Latin Missal and the Elizabethan Prayer Book, until his death in or about 1564.[16]

After Mary's death in 1558, her successor, Elizabeth I, tried to introduce a religious system which would be acceptable to most people and prevent the country being plunged into religious strife. The Act of Uniformity of 1559 made it compulsory to attend divine service on Sundays and holy days, on pain of a fine of a shilling for each absence, and required people to receive holy communion at least once a year. There was still, however, only one national Church of England; no others were tolerated.[17]

Todmorden and the upper Calder Valley had very few who clung to the Roman Catholic faith, in contrast with the rest of the West Riding, where about a quarter of the nobility and gentry refused to conform. Only two 'recusants', as they were known, were recorded in Heptonstall chapelry in 1580.[18] In east Lancashire, just across the Pennine watershed, recusants were relatively numerous; the Towneleys of Towneley Hall being notable examples.

By contrast, the trend in Todmorden and the upper Calder Valley was, if anything, to favour a more extreme form of Protestantism than that of the Elizabethan church, a form which later became known as Puritanism. There were Protestant vicars in both Halifax and Rochdale, who would encourage priests of similar views in the local chapels of their parishes.

The Vicar of Rochdale for more than thirty years was Richard Midgley, from the township of Midgley. He was trained at Cambridge and was of strongly Puritan views.

Both he and Gilbert Astley, curate of Todmorden, were in trouble for not observing holy days. Richard Midgley was instrumental in the building of Rochdale Grammar School, whose first headmaster was Robert Radcliffe, son of Charles Radcliffe of Todmorden Hall. Joseph Midgley succeeded his father at Rochdale in 1595 and was even more extreme in his Puritanical views.[19]

The Protestant/Puritan religion had a natural appeal to the local self-made clothiers in the wool trade. It went hand in hand with their belief in hard work, thrift and competition. It fitted nicely with the situation in the upper Calder Valley, where five of the six chapels above Halifax, plus St Mary's at Todmorden, had been established and were maintained by the local people — essentially by the local yeomen-clothiers, whose wealth came from both farming and textiles. They hired the ministers who would undoubtedly reflect their own beliefs.

A deed, dated the 3rd December 1572, by which Edward Stansfield conveyed the lands and buildings of Cross Stone Chapel to six feoffees (trustees), illustrates this system. It would appear that the Stansfield family, mentioned before as benefactors to the chapel in 1537, had, until 1572, retained the title to the property. The feoffees were John Horsfall of Rodwell, John Stansfield and Edward Crossley of Shore, William Wilkinson of Crosslee, Richard Horsfall of Mankinholes and John Thomas of Woodhouse. They and their heirs were to choose the 'minister, curate or reader' of the chapel subject to the approval of Edward Stansfield or his heirs. If disagreement persisted, the names of the rival candidates must be submitted to a meeting of the inhabitants of the townships of Stansfield and Langfield, one to be chosen 'by the greatest number of voices'.[20]

When William Laud became Archbishop of Canterbury in 1633, he tried to restore traditional ritual and wearing of vestments. Richard Neile, Archbishop of York, pursued similar policies. In these respects most of the curates of the chapels in the upper Calder Valley were identified as defaulters in the visitations of 1633 and 1635.[21]

The sixteenth century had seen great changes in the religious beliefs of the people in and around Todmorden. Services were now in English, as was the Bible. The days of the chantry priests were gone, and in their place were Puritan ministers preaching to large congregations. The self-made clothiers organised not only the business life of the area but, largely, the religious life as well. In the early seventeenth century, they were able to declare that 'out of their zeal to God's holy religion, they did freely and voluntarily, out of their charges, maintain and give wages to ten preachers, over and above the duties belonging to the Vicar ... and that, by the special grace of God, there was not one Popish Recusant inhabiting in the said great and populous parish of Halifax'.[22]

During the reigns of the first two Stuarts, James I and Charles I, a crisis developed in English public affairs which culminated in the Civil War (1642-1649). One element was constitutional — whether the king could rule despotically or only with the consent of Parliament — and focussed on the issue of taxation. Another was religious, involving the forms of worship and the power of the bishops. Only worship according to the Established Church was allowed.

In the reign of James I, commissioners visited every diocese to check on any irregularities in worship. At Rochdale it was discovered that the vicar, Joseph Midgley, mentioned before, 'refused to observe the order of communion, did not wear a surplice or a cloke with sleeves, did not use the cross in baptism or catechise'. He was also accused of shortening the prayers in order to lengthen his own sermons. He was consequently removed from his post.[23]

The sense of grievance over taxation mounted steadily during the reign of Charles I. He revived an ancient custom by which a man with an annual income from land of

This painting, circa 1912, is from an older illustration of the original sixteenth century Cross Stone Chapel.

£40 or more could be compelled to take a knighthood, or pay a 'composition' or fine to the king. Taking a knighthood was expensive because of the increased taxation and the cost incurred supporting the lifestyle which went with rank. Savile Radcliffe of Todmorden Hall was one who, in 1631, compounded and was fined £25.[24] In 1637, the county of Yorkshire was ordered to share with the port of Hull the cost of providing three ships, needed for the war with France, and a petition of protest was signed by 125 men from the parish of Halifax.[25]

The Civil War

Todmorden and the surrounding districts, being strongly Puritan, sided with Parliament when the Civil War broke out during 1642 and, until the king was executed in January 1649, the country was in turmoil. The woollen trade was badly affected. With the port of Hull closed (occupied for Parliament and besieged by the Royalists), the only market outlet was an awesome overland journey by packhorse to London.

Todmorden seems to have been free from any actual action during the war, although there were plenty of incidents in the neighbourhood. Heptonstall was garrisoned for Parliament and was twice attacked by Royalist forces from Halifax. On the second occasion, in January 1644, discretion ruled and the defenders withdrew, via the Long Causeway to Burnley, leaving Heptonstall to be sacked and burnt. Rochdale was garrisoned for Parliament and Blackstone Edge was defended against Royalist attacks from Halifax, which had been taken for the king along with most of Yorkshire following the Battle of Adwalton near Bradford in June 1643. Before this reversal, Parliamentary forces, under Fairfax, stormed and captured Leeds on the 23rd January 1643. At least two local men took part in this fight, Jonathan Scholefield, minister of Cross Stone Chapel, and Lieutenant Horsfall from Underbank, Eastwood. Leeds was very well fortified but eventually an attack, in which Horsfall performed gallantly, carried the defences and 'Mr Jonathan Scholefield ... in their company begun, and they sang the first verse of the 68th Psalm, "Let God arise, and then His enemies shall be scattered, and those that hate Him flee before Him".'[26]

During 1644 Parliamentary forces began to re-assert their control over Yorkshire, and the Royalists were heavily defeated on the 2nd July at the Battle of Marston Moor, near York. John Crossley of Scaitcliffe Hall and Joshua Radcliffe of Todmorden Hall both fought for the king in this decisive battle. The latter is reported to have fled the field and died in 1676, being buried at Todmorden.[27]

Under Parliamentary rule the church was re-organised. There were no longer any bishops. Lancashire was divided into nine ecclesiastical districts and Todmorden, in the parish of Rochdale, was in the second division known as the 'Bury classis'. This was under the control of a synod or committee of ten clergymen and twenty laymen, who met monthly. Their chief business was to provide ministers for vacant positions and to block unlicensed preachers, who might spread false doctrines. Robert Towne, who was minister of Todmorden Chapel from 1643, was summoned before the 'classis' and accused of Antinomianism, which was an extreme form of Calvinism, believing that salvation was achieved solely by divine grace with no conditions being required of the people who were 'saved'. Towne was driven from his post and the meeting of the classis held on:

> ffebruary ye 10th day 1647/8 [decided] That ye ministr and churchwardens of Todmorden be sent unto and required that they suffer not Mr Robt Towne or any other known Antinomian preacher to preach at Todmorden.[28]

Towne was replaced at Todmorden by a Mr Hill who was ordered to preach at the classis meeting, when he would receive 'approbation' or otherwise if he failed to satisfy them. He was approved in August 1648, but by October was requesting a move from Todmorden 'because of ye uncertainty and incompetency of mainetaynence'.[29]

He obviously left, because by August 1649 Francis Core was minister at Todmorden and was summoned to appear before the classis for preaching without 'approbation of ye classis'. The summons, although repeated at least four times by December 1650, was ignored and, at a commission held in the same year, he was described as 'a man not well qualified but scandalous in lyfe and conversacon'.[30] It seems he was really a Royalist and an Anglican, and he disappears from the records after 1650. By 1658 the minister was one Thomas Somerton, previously of Newchurch in Rossendale. He too had a less than happy time at Todmorden, pleasing some of his parishioners but not others, who besides complaining that he preached strange doctrines, disliked the fact that he had formerly been a blacksmith or farrier. Somerton certainly sympathized with the Quakers, the new religious movement founded by George Fox about 1649. Whilst at Newchurch, he had invited William Dewsbury, a member of the Society of Friends (Quakers), to preach from his pulpit and may well have done the same at Todmorden.[31] The Quakers certainly became well established in the Todmorden area during the 1650s.

One person who, whilst not living in Todmorden, had a lasting effect on the religious life of the district was Oliver Heywood. Born at Little Lever, near Bolton, in 1630, of Puritan parents (he was baptized without the sign of the cross), he graduated from Trinity College, Cambridge, in 1650 and in the same year became the minister at Coley Chapel, near Northowram, Halifax. He was ordained in 1652 by the Bury classis, mentioned earlier.

Growth of Nonconformity

The second half of the seventeenth century saw the gradual development of nonconformity, along with changes in the Established Church. The return of Charles II in 1660 also meant returning to the pre-Civil War forms of worship and church government. Anglican clergy returned to their livings, whilst those who refused to adapt to the restored liturgical forms, by agreeing to the Act of Uniformity, were expelled from theirs. Thus Thomas Somerton left Todmorden to be replaced in 1662 by Henry Krabtree, who remained curate until 1685, and George Stott left Cross Stone to be replaced by the conformist Robert Dewhurst in 1663. More significantly, Oliver Heywood was ejected from Coley Chapel in 1662. When many of the ejected clergymen continued their ministry by preaching in private houses, Parliament passed the Conventicle Act of 1664, which made any religious meeting illegal if there were more than five people present in addition to the household. Ministers who refused to accept the Act of Uniformity had to swear that they would not try to change the system of government of either Church or State. If they refused they were forbidden, by the Five Mile Act of 1666, to go within five miles of their former church or any place where they had illegally preached since they were ejected. The penalty was a £40 fine.[32]

Oliver Heywood considered that this Act, by turning dissenting ministers into itinerant preachers, in fact helped to spread nonconformity. It was certainly true for himself and, along with others, he preached to dissenters in the chapelry of Cross Stone, despite this being officially illegal. On one occasion he preached to a large gathering in a house not far from:

> Crosse Stone Chappel the time pitcht upon was Whitsun — tuesday, (so called) May 29 1683 for several reasons, chiefly because some from whom they feared disturbances would be at Rochedal … I set out from my own house about 5 a clock that morning … I rode about 12 miles, came thither before 10 a clock, begun my work at 11 a clock in the house of one John Helliwell.

During the sermon the constable arrived with a warrant for Heywood's arrest. His name was Major Marshall, deputy constable for John Fielding — a Quaker. He was also 'clark' at Cross Stone Chapel and a friend of the curate, Richard Robinson, 'who hath his meat with this MM'. Heywood dismissed his congregation — his sermon had already lasted nearly two hours — Major Marshall did not seem keen to pursue his mission too rigorously and was perhaps relieved when the official constable, John Fielding, on being shown the warrant, said it was 'no conventicle or unlawful meeting'.

It seems clear that the Heywood meeting was broken up at the instruction of curate Robinson, who had announced a sermon at his chapel on the same day (the king's birthday and anniversary of his coronation), at which, notes Heywood:

> not one person, man or woman came to hear him, wch ceartainly vexed him, for they were generally come to this house.[33]

In November 1683, Heywood preached at Stiperden, a remote spot, significantly just over the border with Lancashire at the extreme western edge of Stansfield on the Long Causeway. His host was Nathaniel Sutcliffe, who lived alone and was obviously very poor, as he could offer Heywood nothing but toasted oat bread and butter, served on the only trencher he possessed, with two pennyworth of ale from the inn next door. Notwithstanding the remoteness of the place:

> God sent abundance of people many miles, tho' it was in the night and very dark and slippery, it did me good to see such a willingness, God affected my

Stiperden Farm in Cliviger lies on the Long Causeway and served seventeenth century travellers as both inn and smithy. The itinerant preacher Oliver Heywood delivered a sermon here in 1683.

heart with poor ignorant soules sad condition in the want of powerfull preaching. I struggled with them in my Lord's name 3 houres that night till I was tired and very hoarse.

He and his companion spent the night next door at the home of William Foster, an innkeeper and blacksmith, who serviced the travellers on the Long Causeway. He refused any payment for his hospitality, but on leaving Heywood 'gave the poor man a shilling where I preach't'.[34]

These examples show the zeal of the early dissenting preachers, the lengths to which they had to go to avoid disturbance by the authorities and their popularity with the local people. Here are the beginnings of nonconformism, which developed into a powerful local influence during the eighteenth and nineteenth centuries.

Heywood continued to preach in Stansfield and was helped by the Rev Matthew Smith, who settled at Mixenden in 1686. The Toleration Act of 1689, passed after William of Orange became king, allowed nonconformists (but not Catholics) to license meeting houses and worship freely. The houses of John Aske (1689) and John Haworth (1690) in Langfield, and of Paul Helliwell in Stansfield were licensed for Presbyterian/Congregationalist groups, similar to those to which Heywood ministered.[35]

In 1699 Heywood's congregation hired a room at Great House, Stansfield, where regular services were conducted by Rev Matthew Smith until 1712, when Mr Joshua Cordingley became the first resident minister. By 1719 the congregation had increased so much that a chapel, seating 200-300, was built at Benthead. The site was purchased in 1717 for £8 2s. This was the first home of Eastwood Congregational Chapel. It was later converted into cottages and is still known as Chapel Houses.[36]

The most severely persecuted from the dissenting groups were the Quakers. In

Hartley Royd in Stansfield, home to John Stansfield in 1580, passed to the Fieldens and was used for Quaker meetings and weddings in the seventeenth century.

Pilkington Farm in Mankinholes was a Quaker meeting house and burial ground.

contrast with the 'quietist' character of later Quakerism, they were quite aggressive in their evangelism and rejected all forms of organised religion, refused to take oaths, bear arms or pay tithes. Thomas Taylor, from Carlton near Skipton, and Thomas Goodaire preached to a Quaker group at Mankinholes in the 1650s.[37] By the early 1660s, the Quakers were organised on a federal basis, consisting of local or Particular Meetings (as at Mankinholes); area or Monthly Meetings (Mankinholes belonged to the Brighouse Meeting until 1707 when it transferred to the Marsden Meeting in Lancashire); and Quarterly Meetings for the whole county.[38]

The Quakers kept careful records, including a book of their 'Sufferings' which detailed the penalties imposed on them for their beliefs. Several local Quakers suffered severely and some repeatedly. John Fielden of Hartley Royd, Stansfield, had goods distrained valued at 18s in 1664 for refusing to pay a 'Church Ley' of 3s 2d. During the same year, along with ten other Friends from Mankinholes Meeting, he was charged at Wakefield Quarter Sessions with holding an illegal religious meeting. Again goods were distrained when he refused to pay the £5 fine. Within the next twenty years, his goods were seized on no fewer than sixteen occasions for non-payment of tithes or fines. In addition, he spent thirty weeks in Halifax gaol in 1688 and, later the same year, eight weeks in Preston House of Correction after being arrested at a Quaker meeting in Padiham. When over seventy years old, he was still being fined for both non-attendance at church and attending Quaker meetings.[39]

Another who suffered was Abraham Stansfield of Shore, who spent fourteen months imprisoned at Halifax for non-payment of tithes in 1668. Shortly after his release, he was re-arrested along with his mother for refusing to pay a mortuary to Heptonstall Church. Imprisoned, this time at York Castle, they both died four months later and were buried there.[40]

In 1670-71 John Sutcliffe, one of the ministers of the Mankinholes Meeting, was fined £50 for holding religious meetings at his house.[41]

On the 3rd May 1684 Henry Krabtree, the curate of Todmorden, surprised a meeting at Daniel Sutcliffe's house at Rodhill Hey. All present were fined 5s and their goods distrained when they refused to pay. The episode was repeated a month later at Henry Kailey's house, Todmorden Edge, when goods valued at £20 plus an ark of oatmeal and a pack of wool were distrained.

The Quakers had their own burial grounds; there was one at Shore, in the grounds of the home of the Stansfield family (now known as Shore Fold), one at Todmorden Edge and one at Mankinholes, where on the 3rd December 1667 half a little croft called Tenter Croft was rented as a burial ground at a yearly rent of 'one twopence of silver' for a term of 900 years. This is now part of Pilkington Farm, where one of the gravestones inscribed 'J.S. 1685' is built into one of the outbuildings.[42]

Following the Toleration Act of 1689, many Quaker houses were licensed for worship: four in Stansfield, including John Fielden's at Hartley Royd, James Stansfield's at Shore and Daniel Sutcliffe's at Rodhill Hey; and five or six in Langfield, including Thomas Sutcliffe's at Studley, Anthony Crossley's at Knowle and Joshua Fielden's, Swineshead. From this evidence, it seeems clear that the Mankinholes Meeting moved around the houses of its leading members until 1695, when a meeting house was built at Shoebroad; after this, meetings, burials and marriages (which had also been conducted in leading members' houses) were held there.[43]

The first Baptist congregations evolved during this period. William Mitchell and his cousin David Crossley became itinerant preachers, building up a large following on both sides of the Pennines, from Rossendale to near Wakefield. Crossley travelled far afield, whilst Mitchell was content to preach to the local groups. After 1689 some twenty houses were licensed by the group which, still unconnected to any sect, became known as 'The Church of Christ in Rossendale'.

By 1692 Crossley, during his travels, had become a Particular (Calvinistic) Baptist. Mitchell joined him in 1693 and gradually their whole group followed suit. In 1703 a meeting house was opened at Rodwell (Rodhill) End in Stansfield 'for the use of Protestant Dissenters known by the name of Baptists or Independents'. In 1717 another chapel was opened in a converted building at Stone Slack in Heptonstall and the community worshipped alternately in the two chapels, formally separating themselves from the Church of Christ in Rossendale in the same year.[44]

So by the end of the seventeenth century three protestant dissenting sects had become established in the Todmorden district — Independents or Congregationalists, Quakers and Baptists. This was not to the liking of the Established Church. In a questionnaire about the state of the Church of England in 1705, Daniel Towne, curate of Heptonstall, complained amongst other things that the 'minister and parish' had been brought to 'a low ebb … by reason of so many Conventicles houses set up in nookes and corners within the said parish'.[45]

Francis Gastrell, Bishop of Chester, in his *Notitia Cestriensis* (circa 1725), estimated that in Todmorden (with Walsden) there were 100 families and amongst them 100 dissenters, comprising 20 Presbyterians, 50 Quakers and 30 Anabaptists.[46] Towne's complaint regarding his parish was echoed at Todmorden in 1706, when Churchwarden Wroe noted: 'The chappelry formerly paid £20 per annum, and thought themselves bound by custom so to doe, but now they are most Quakers.' The outstanding example, noted in 1717, was Todmorden Hall, '… now possessed by a Quaker who has lately bought an Estate of 80l[£80] p[er] an[num] for wch ye Curate used formerly to receive 3l 8s[£3 8s], he now refuses to pay anything, and ye Curate is not able to Sue him'.[47]

This referred to John Fielden, great-uncle to Joshua (founder of the Waterside enterprise), who bought Todmorden Hall from Roger Mainwaring. Roger had married Elizabeth Radcliffe, sole offspring and heiress of Joshua Radcliffe who died in 1676.

Henry Krabtree, the curate of Todmorden mentioned earlier, is worthy of note as being, arguably, the most colourful to occupy the position. He was born in Sowerby and was a contemporary there of John Tillotson, later to become Archbishop of Canterbury. He was the first Todmorden curate to keep a register of baptisms, marriages and burials, which, as he was a keen astrologer, he embellished with astrological details, eg:

> 1685 Nov 1 James s. James Taylor. T. b 2 Oct ♀ near sunsetting and also near a
> full) wch is a sure token of a short life
> [s.=son.   T=Todmorden.   ♀=the sign for Venus.   )=moon.]

He was not averse to penning comments which bordered on the profane, as in 1667, following the double burial of Mary and Anne, the daughter and wife of John Bairstow, he wrote almost a page beginning 'John Bairstow of Hollowpin seeing both his daughter and his wife departed in peace presently began to offer sacrifice unto Bacchus for joy …', and continues cataloguing John's drunken behaviour which culminated in his death and burial less than a month later.

Being of a superstitious nature, Krabtree once closed the service hurriedly, when a mouse ran across the Bible; he went straight home to Stansfield Hall, where he found thieves had been and disturbed his study.

A reconstruction drawing of Rodwell End Chapel, built in 1865 on the site of first local Baptist chapel (1704).

He was also an author and in 1685 published an almanack entitled *Merlinus Rusticus* where for each month he made seasonal comments:

March: For curing and preventing of diseases 'tis good now to take advice of the astrological physician. If you stand in need you may vomit, purge and bleed.

These measures, drastic though they seem to us, were common enough then:

May: Rise early, walk in the fields, where every garden and hedgerow affords food and physic. Walk by running streams of water and feast thy lungs with fresh air. For food, sage and sweet butter make an excellent breakfast. Clarified whey, with sage, scurvy grass, ale and wormwood beer, are now wholesome.
October: The time now requires that you consult with your tailor as well as with your physician. Therefore a good suit of warm cloth is worth 2 purges and one vomit. Keep warm betimes, for cold creeps upon men insensibly and fogs ofttimes beget a whole winter's distemper.
November: The best exercise is hunting or tracing hares, but be sure that the park or Lordship be your own, and then you need not fear an indictment nor a fine at the next sessions.

Krabtree won quite a reputation as a physician in the surrounding districts. Strangely enough his own death is not recorded in the registers, although that of his widow occurs on:

Dec 15 1719 Old Mrs Krabtree, wid. of Mr Krabtree
(Mary wid of Henry Krabtree late curate of T.).[48]

4

The Rise of the Yeoman-Clothier

Forasmuch as the Paryshe of Halyfaxe and other places theronto adjoyning, beyng planted in the grete waste and moores, where ... the inhabitantes ... altogether doo lyve by clothe making ... by means of whiche Industrye the barreyn Gronde in those partes be nowe muche inhabyted, and above fyve hundrethe householdes there newly increased within theis fourtye yeares past ...

The above is part of the preamble to the famous 'Halifax Act' of 1555, which allowed the small producers of the district to buy wool from middlemen, whose activities had been prohibited by an Act of 1552. The provision was necessary because the local wool supply was inadequate in both quantity and quality for market production, as distinct from making a few pieces of cloth a year for household needs.[1]

The boggy, acid moorlands were not very suitable for sheep. In the Todmorden area 41 out of 43 inventories from the years 1564 to 1743 — listing the stock, crops, farm and industrial equipment, furniture and other moveable goods of the deceased — include cattle, but only 16 had sheep. Most of the latter were in Walsden, which suggests that some of its commons provided a rather better feed. It was said in 1588 that upper Calderdale drew its fine wool mainly from Lincolnshire and sold its coarse wool to 'men of Ratchedall'. The Burnley-Rossendale area produced mainly coarse woollen cloths at this time, and the Walsden farms may have been supplying this market.[2]

The emergence of a major textile industry in the Halifax-upper Calderdale area, and particularly its rapid expansion in the early sixteenth century, are at first sight difficult to explain. For access to both raw materials and markets, the area was worse off than the rest of the West Riding except the northwest corner. It had the advantage of soft water for washing and dyeing wool, and plentiful sites for fulling mills, but so too did many parts of West Yorkshire.

The Beginnings of Industrial Growth

A study of the textile regions of Yorkshire and Lancashire reveals two important causes of industrial growth. The first was the common practice amongst farmers, who were either freeholders or copyholders, of leaving some share of their land to a younger son or sons, instead of passing the holding intact to the eldest son. In some copyhold areas this practice had evolved into a manorial custom of equal division, but in upper Calderdale the process remained discretionary. When a farmholding was fragmented, extra resources were needed. Before the Black Death of 1349 these were created by clearing and cultivating waste land. Because of the difficulties of farming in a hilly

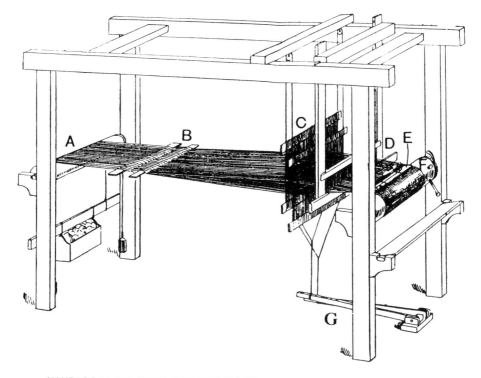

HANDLOOM WITH HAND–THROWN SHUTTLE

A Warp beam   B Lease rods, move as the warp is let off

C Healds (or heddles)   D Reed, which divides the warp
   threads, and Batton, which pushes the weft into place

E Temple, a device to keep the cloth stretched laterally.
   The shuttle can be seen between D and E.

F Cloth beam   G Foot pedal to operate healds.

and wet area, the loom offered a better prospect than the plough. The possibility of developing a dual economy of farming and textiles would have encouraged sub-division, and, to provide additional pasture and land for tenters, it was worthwhile to enclose high-lying land which might have been too bleak for farming alone. Therefore subdivision, industrial development and intaking became inter-active processes.[3]

The second factor was the possibility of building cottages on the commons, and taking in small plots of land, either legally or illegally. Each handloom weaver needed five or six spinners to provide an adequate supply of yarn. Other work done in the cottages by women and children included carding short-staple wool, ie working it into slivers by means of a pair of wire brushes. (Combing long-staple wool for worsted manufacture, using pairs of heavy combs with rows of long metal teeth, and requiring more skill than carding, was a man's job.) The growth of a numerous cottager class was therefore essential for the development of large-scale cloth production. It was not just a matter of the workforce having somewhere to live. Because the flow of work was irregular, a plot of land to cultivate and perhaps a cow pastured on the commons underpinned the cottage economy.

The Dual Economy

The dual economy of farming and textiles seems to have developed rather later in the Todmorden area than lower down the Calder Valley, where there were market centres at Heptonstall and Halifax. The tax assessments of 1545 and 1546, based upon goods as well as land, give a rough indication of relative economic development. Taking Halifax township together with the eight townships which occupy the area between Sowerby Bridge and Shore, we find that Warley and Sowerby together accounted for half of the valuation, Halifax township for 18%, Wadsworth and Heptonstall together for 15%, but Stansfield and Langfield together for only 7%, the remaining 10% being taken up by Erringden and Midgley. There are no separate figures for Todmorden and Walsden.[4]

The yeomen-clothiers of upper Calderdale were always ready with an explanation of their industrial success which linked the loom and the pulpit. In the course of a lawsuit in 1637 they argued that as a result of their:

> trade and of godly and true religion there professed and embraced, manie thousand of his Majestie's subjects are nourished and exercised in Godly labour, manie poore people and theire families honestly mainteyned and vertuously brought up, a great number of impotent and aged persons relieved, manie godly Preachers mainteyned, and his Majestie's Revenues much encreased.

All of this had been achieved by the hard work of the Pennine people, 'the places which they inhabitt being soe mountainous and rough, soe barren and unfruitfull as it will not suffice to yield victualls for the third part of the inhabitants …'[5] Their proposition, that the victory over 'the barren and unfruitful hills' was a product of their moral virtues, may be equally valid in reverse — that their value system, embracing a spirit of enterprise and the 'protestant work ethic', was itself a product of their struggle to survive and prosper in an unfavourable environment.

For a detailed picture of the age of the yeomen-clothiers, we can turn to wills and probate inventories. They throw light upon the work and lifestyles of the few local gentry; of the substantial households with two or three looms alongside farming activities comparable in scale; and of their humbler neighbours with smaller farms and a single loom. The poor cottagers did not leave wills or probate inventories behind. They appear in the written records only through the parish registers, or if they needed poor relief or otherwise came to the attention of the township officers.

Henry Radcliffe, who died in April 1600, is described in his will as 'esquire', the highest rank of any local residents. He owned Todmorden Hall and about 1,100 acres in Todmorden and Walsden, as well as Mereley, on the western slope of Pendle Hill. He farmed the Todmorden Hall estate of 362 freehold acres, including the Dobroyd and Stones areas, and the Hall Ings (meadows) on the west side of the river as far as Gauxholme. He had 148 acres of copyhold land at Priestbooth and South Grain on the north side of the Dulesgate valley, and another 312 acres of pasture, part freehold and part copyhold, reaching to Flower Scarr Hill. He had barley (used for making beer) in both the barn and the gatehouse, and both oats and wheat (a rare local reference) growing in the ground. The stock consisted of about 45 head of cattle, including 10 plough oxen, about 70 sheep and lambs, 2 pigs and a few geese. He owned four horses, apparently used for personal transport or sport. Other interesting items were his white suit of armour, a shirt of mail, a coat of plate armour, halberds, bills, muskets and crossbow, and three fishing nets and other gear for use in the local rivers.

A perfect Inventory of the goods and cattels of Thomas Lord
of over Swinshead in Walsden in hundersfield
in the County of Lancaster husbandman deceased
Apprised the thirttey day of october Ann' Dom 1676
[apparently overwritten 7, possibly meant to be 9]
by Abraham fielden Symeon Lord and Charles
Lord and Joseph Lord

	L	s	d
It[em] his Apparell and money in his purse	02	10	00
It a standingbed and clothes belong ing and a chest	03	04	00
It three bedststeeds and clothes belonging	02	18	00
It an arke and a chist and a glase cobard	00	18	00
It two linnen poakes and a setchel	00	03	00
It in meal and flesh	01	00	00
It in butter and cheese	01	00	00
It a couboard	00	12	00
It in brass and pewther	01	14	06
It in wodden and Earthen vessels	01	05	00
It in fireirne tongs and a spit	00	07	00
It a saltpie two boards and an ower glas	00	06	00
It in cheares and quishines	00	08	00
It a peare of lomes and forneture with wheels and cardes	01	02	00
It a meare and furneture three beasts and fodder and winter pasture	12	05	08
It in cloth woll and yarne	06	17	00
It a bible and other bookes	00	04	00
It in A plough and plowirnes sleds and Lowse boards and other husbandry Instrements	01	15	00
It an arke in the barne	00	09	00
It soles and rakes and all other huselment	00	04	00
The Sum is	39	02	02

Symeon Lorde
Abraham   fielden
his marke
Joseph Lord
Charles Lord

The inventory of Thomas Lord of Over Swinshead, 1676, and a transcript.

At this time Todmorden Hall was a timber-framed structure with, on the ground floor, hall (the main living room), three parlours, kitchen and buttery (wine/provisions store). Upstairs were five chambers, and outbuildings included a milkhouse, stable, 'great barne', ox house and a gatehouse. In the yeoman's house the main bedroom was always a parlour, ie on the ground floor, and often we find at least one chamber (upstairs) used for storage only. In Todmorden Hall two parlours had beds in, as did four chambers, the fifth being a storeroom.

In the early seventeenth century Henry Radcliffe's grandson and heir Savile Radcliffe rebuilt Todmorden Hall in stone. Stone houses were rare at this period, although Croft Gate in Langfield has the datestone 1598, and Rake Farm above Cross Lee in Stansfield, 1560. In the 1626 survey of the manor of Rochdale it was identification enough to refer to Stone House, near Bottomley in Walsden, simply as Stone House. As the century progressed, new houses were built in stone and some existing houses were either rebuilt or encased in stone. There is little surviving evidence of the earlier cruck-framed type of construction in our district. Crucks were pairs of matching curved timbers, made by splitting a tree trunk and its first main branch, which met at

Cruck-framed buildings are uncommon locally — this cottage at Inchfield Fold
is a rare example

the roof to support the ridge-beam. One example is at Inchfield Fold in Walsden, and
some cruck blades have been identified as re-used in later buildings, mainly barns.
The area had perhaps generated enough wealth and acquired the technical expertise
at an early date to build with vertical timber-framing. The main impetus for using
stone came from the continued development and prosperity, locally, of the dual
economy of textiles and farming.

Housing and Domestic Life

The survival of many fine stone houses, built between the late sixteenth and mid-
eighteenth century, is one of the glories of the district. At Mankinholes they are grouped
in one settlement, but usually they are strung out along the hillsides close to the
packhorse road and following the line of the local springs. Their strong millstone grit
walls, low-pitched thacked/slated roofs, mullioned windows and some fine porches
blend as naturally with the landscape as the rocky outcrops that erupt along the edge
of the moors.

The houses of the yeomen-clothiers, and of the small minority of farmers who
were not also involved in the cloth trade or some other craft, fell into two groups.

Two-cell houses ('two up/two down') had a hall/house/housebody, as the living
room was variously known, and a parlour-bedroom on the ground floor; and two
chambers above. Good examples of these are Flailcroft above Scaitcliffe, and Stile
House on the opposite hillside; the latter was originally 'Lower Ibbotroyd' and home
to Paul Halliwell, a one-loom clothier and farmer in 1730. The barn has now dis-

Stile House, Stansfield, known earlier as Lower Ibbotroyd, is a good example of a two-cell house of the seventeenth century.

appeared. Both of these houses had the entrance to the housebody in the gable end, and the service rooms were accommodated in an outshot constructed all along the back of the house and separated from it by a screens passage. Originally, the housebody would be open to the roof, a chamber being created later by putting in a floor. At Oaks, above Sandbed, a roof beam now obstructs and dominates the centre of the chamber.

In the three-cell house, the housebody occupied the middle of the facade, with a parlour on one side and shop or second parlour on the other. Sometimes another parlour was behind the first, making the house two rooms deep, occasionally with a separate kitchen, although this did not preclude cooking in the housebody. The main entrance, on the front of the building next to the housebody, opened on to a cross-passage leading to the back of the house. A door in the cross-passage beyond the fireplace gave access to the housebody, often along a timber screen, which reduced the draught. The parlour or, where there was more than one, at least one of them, had a fireplace in the wall opposite the housebody. On the other side of the cross-passage to the housebody was 'the low end', nearly always consisting of the 'shop' with its industrial equipment. The three-cell yeoman-clothier's house, notwithstanding individual variations in design, was fundamentally two-thirds residential and one third industrial. Virtually every household with more than one loom had such a house. At Great House Clough Farm in Stansfield the shop was a separate entity, and sometimes, as at Higher Kilnhurst in Langfield, Royd Farm in Stansfield and Todmorden Hall, it was reached by an exterior staircase.

This painting of Kilnhurst farm, Langfield, showing the 'takkin' in' steps leading to the 'shop', is by local artist Alfred Bayes (1831-1909).

Both two- and three-cell houses normally had a barn or similar outbuildings for the farming side of the dual economy. The most substantial of these houses was Hartley Royd near Shore in Stansfield, which in 1697 detailed a housebody and shop, each with its chamber, three parlours and three more chambers (one being a wool chamber), a kitchen, milkhouse, barn, sykehouse, wainhouse and stable with stable chamber. Green End at Shore, home of Nicholas Fielden until his death in 1698, had a housebody, parlour and shop at ground level, each with a chamber above, plus a barn and milkhouse. A similar pattern occurs at Cross Gap in Stansfield, home until 1695/6 of Edward Sutcliffe, although here no shop chamber is mentioned. Old Royd in Langfield, where Robert Farrar died in 1701, was another three-cell house, as was Swallowshaw in Stansfield, home until 1730 of William Sutcliffe. At Mankinholes, in what is now Pilkington Farm, lived William's cousin John, whose inventory dated 1701/2 attests to a housebody, upper and lower parlours and shop, all with chambers, plus a cellar and barn.

One of the most impressive of the larger houses is East Lee at Eastwood in Stansfield, with its lovely porch dated 1630 and magnificent twelve-light run of mullioned windows. This was home to another Sutcliffe, Job, who died in 1706/7.

A three-loom clothier would employ journeymen to weave in his shop, handloom weaving being almost always a man's job. In addition he would require carders or combers and spinners, and so might employ twenty or more workers, most of them

East Lee, near Eastwood in Stansfield, is an impressive three-cell yeoman's house which has a fine double-storied porch (with pigeon loft above) dated 1630.

working in their own cottages. These workers very rarely left an inventory or owned property, and were described thus by Daniel Defoe on his tour in the 1720s: 'among the manufacturers' houses are likewise scattered an infinite number of cottages or small dwellings in which dwell the workmen which are employed'.

Looking inside the houses we find very few books (amongst these, only the Bible was named); this is not surprising, as in the seventeenth century many local men of substance were illiterate. Wills and inventories are often signed or witnessed by means of a cross or crudely-shaped initials.

There was not much physical comfort, either. No upholstered furniture is mentioned, hence the importance of the cushions on the long-settles and chairs. Abraham Ormeroyd of Brownbirks (1743), had seven chairs and seven cushions; John Kendall, Hawkstones (1727), had six of each; whilst Michael Clegg of West Bar, Shore (1722), was more comfortable with four chairs and eight cushions. 'Coach' chairs were the most expensive at 15s to £1 3s; 'ceiled' chairs were valued at 2s 6d to 6s; 'joined' chairs at 2s and 'hewn' chairs at under 1s were the cheapest.

The main table was supplied with forms (benches) for family mealtimes. References to 'table and forme' or 'long table and formes thereunto belonging' are found in twenty-two of the inventories. In others, for example, Henry Kirshawe of Inchfield (1628), 'bords and trests' are recorded, and in these cases the table would be erected by laying the 'bords' on top of the 'trestles'. These could be dismantled when not in use. The table was the main work-surface in the housebody, which was the domestic workroom as well as the living room. The fire on which cooking was done was in the

Lower Ashes, Cross Stone, Stansfield, is a fine yeoman's house. This rear view shows the blocked-up doorway of the 'shop'. The 1759 datestone marks a later renovation, whilst that of 1610/14 on the front elevation dates the original building.

This arched fireplace at Lower Ashes is typical of many found locally in yeomen's houses.

housebody and, depending on economic status, was accompanied by a variety of equipment and pans where broths could be cooked or meat roasted. For example, Michael Helliwell of Ashenhurst (1699), had a fire iron, spit and rack, tongs, an old iron pan, a frying pan and a 'backstone'. Edward Sutcliffe, Cross Gap, had similar equipment, together with an oil pan, a brass pot with hooks to suspend it over the fire, and 'one dripen pan with tosting irne'.

The 'backstone' or baking stone was common to most households. When heated it was used to cook oat-cakes, an important element in the staple diet based on oatmeal. The large, flat, thin oat-cakes or haver-cakes, when baked, were hung over the 'breadfleak' (a rack suspended from the ceiling) to be eaten when needed as an alternative to the oatmeal porridge, which was daily food for most people. Thirty-two inventories include amounts of 'meale', James Gibson of Lower Ashes (1735) having fifteen loads (240 lbs=1 load) valued at £15 15s, whilst two others refer simply to 'meale arkes', the large wooden chests in which meal was traditionally stored. Five record 'corn' without specifying the variety of grain, which was probably oats, the predominant local crop, and three refer to 'groates', probably crushed/ground oats. Only three references are made to wheat and two to malt, the latter being used in brewing. Fewer than half the inventories record other kinds of food. There are seven references to bacon, five to beef, nine to unspecified 'flesh', seven to butter and four to cheese, but there is no evidence to suggest that meat formed a regular part of the diet of most of these families, not to mention those lower down the economic ladder.

The 'arke' used for storing grain was only one kind of chest, which was a common piece of domestic furniture used for holding clothes and other possessions. There were no wardrobes then, and only seventeen of the inventories mention cupboards, but chests proliferate. Robert Farrar of Old Royd had ten in various parts of the house, and John Fielden of Hartley Royd (1697) had seven. It is possible that others had as many, but often they are recorded collectively as 'chists' or 'arkes and chists', without giving the number.

The tableware consisted, in order of frequency of reference, of pewter mugs and dishes, wooden trenchers (plates) and bowls, and earthenware vessels. James Gibson, for example, had 73 lbs weight of pewter and four dozen wooden trenchers. Henry Radcliffe had three dozen of the latter, but the superior lifestyle of the gentry was marked by his possession of eighteen silver spoons.

Farming

The limited scale of sheep rearing has already been mentioned. Cattle are listed in forty-one inventories, ranging from Martha Stansfield of Shore (1692/93) with 'one little old cow' to Anthony Crossley's twenty-eight beasts (1707). There are only two references to pigs — two Yorkshire-wide surveys of 1688-89 and 1720-22 show an average of less than one pig per farm, even counting a sow and seven young as eight pigs. Apart from Henry Radcliffe's geese, no poultry are mentioned. Perhaps they were too cheap to mention, or were regarded as the private property of the housewife, but they were clearly unimportant economically.

Twenty-seven of the testators had a horse, including seven with two. In a few cases these animals can be identified as packhorses, but there are thirteen references to packcloths and one to packsaddles. Eight inventories included wheeled vehicles. John Fielden of Hartley Royd had a wain for hay or corn, one cart for dung and two for peat. The favoured device for moving goods across the often steeply-sloping fields

Looking south from Bridestones in Stansfield to Trough Edge, with the unenclosed Inchfield Pasture to the left of Gorpley Reservoir. The only visible farm is Flailcroft, and the cultivated land behind and to its right could be the 'Ring of Todmorden'.

was the sledge, owned by twenty-seven testators. Nineteen had more than one; William Sutcliffe of Swallowshaw had five.

About three-quarters of the farmers were engaged in corn-growing, if references to ploughs, harrows, scythes, seed corn, corn-growing, corn and hay, and hay and straw are included. The scale of arable farming is not easy to quantify; the price of corn varied with the season, higher shortly before the harvest (when stocks were lower) than in spring or early summer; hay and corn were often lumped together with no separate value for each; and finally, there is no way of knowing how much had been grown locally and how much imported. The locality could not have been self-sufficient in corn, and those who could afford it are likely to have bought in supplies at local markets such as Rochdale or Halifax, when prices were at their lowest after the harvest. This would be stored and then taken for grinding as required.

The inventory does not always give a complete picture. That of John Stansfield of Shore (1717), shows no evidence of arable farming, yet in his will he bequeaths the 'tenement where I live with crops growing or reaped at my death'. There are five other references to crops being grown: Nicholas Fielden, Shore (September 1698), had 'corn growing £1'; Paul Halliwell of Lower Ibbotroyd (August 1730) had 'one butt of corn in the meadow £3'; William Sutcliffe of Swallowshaw (July 1730) had '15 days work of hay, grasse and corn £24'. (A 'day's work' was the amount of land that could be ploughed by one plough team in a normal day and was reckoned as seventy per cent of a statute acre.) John Fielden of Inchfield, Walsden (March 1665), had 'for plowing, harrowing and seed sown £5 18s'; whilst Samuel Whiteley of Studley Lee (April 1693) had 'for plowing and sowing £2 8s'. There are four other references made to 'seed corne', which is corn set aside for next year's sowing.

It was usual to describe straw crops simply as 'corn', but the available evidence suggests that, locally, oats predominated. They could survive the cool, damp conditions better than other corn crops, and as a bonus oat straw provided a relatively nutritious feed for stock. Apart from that on the Todmorden Hall estate, wheat is recorded only twice: John Fielden of Shore (1720), had 'oatmeal, wheat, and the chest £3 10s'; and Abraham Ormeroyd of Brownbirks had 'oatmeal and wheat 5s'.

Textiles

The other side of the dual economy was textiles. Thirty-two inventories include looms, usually one or two. Two had more than two looms, and four an unspecified number. The commonest local cloth was kersey, woven from short-staple wool, usually in pieces one yard wide and eighteen long. We can follow the manufacturing process clearly through the inventories.

James Gibson of Lower Ashes had 'swingle trees', hinged rods used for beating the raw wool. It was then picked over to remove burrs, and treated with a mixture of rape oil and butter for easier processing. Several inventories had entries such as Samuel Whiteley's 'oil and butter, oil pot, 2 oil tubs', valued at 16s. The next stage was carding, mentioned on page 50.

The wool was then ready for spinning, the work of the older girls and women, done on a 'great wheel' turned by hand. The spinner first drew out the roving as fine as she could, whilst turning the wheel to put in the 'twist', which gave the thread its strength, the wheel was reversed and the spun thread wound onto the bobbin. A different type of wheel with a foot pedal, called the Saxony wheel or line wheel, was used for spinning flax (known as line) or long-staple wool used as worsted yarn. By freeing both hands the spinner could lay the fibres parallel before the twist was inserted, and by using a bobbin and flyer the twisting and winding processes could be done simultaneously. There are thirty-three references to wheels, most households having more than one. They include four line wheels, three of which are in addition to other wheels in the house. It would seem almost certain that the vast majority of the wheels recorded were 'great wheels'.

As it took five or six spinners and several carders to keep one weaver in work, some of this work was 'put out' to cottager families, it being impossible for even a one-loom household to keep its weaver (the husband or son) supplied with thread.

In order to arrange the warp threads, which were on the beam at the rear of the loom, a frame called a 'warping ough' or 'wough' was used, and fourteen references are made to this equipment and one to a 'warping mill'. For example Thomas Helliwell of Stansfield (1692) had two 'pairs of looms', a spoil wheel, warping wough and rings valued at £1 10s, as well as three spinning wheels (presumably 'great') and a line wheel, thirteen yards of woollen cloth worth £1 7s, and wool and yarn at £11 10s. A more modest operator was Joshua Lord of Ditches (1686), with 'one pair of loomes and warping worke, £1'. A pair of looms was one loom — the usage was similar to a pair of scissors or trousers.

The woven cloth was taken to a local fulling mill to shrink it and matt together the surface fibres. Much of the strength of woollen cloth derived from the fulling process, whereas in worsted and linen it came from the interlacing of stronger and smoother thread. The fulled cloth was stretched on 'tenters', long adjustable wooden frames, to dry in the open air and shrink to a regular shape.

Jonas Clegg of Rodwell End in Stansfield (1720) had cards, three great wheels, a line wheel, two pairs of looms and their equipment, and four tenters, which with other finishing tools were valued at £8. He may well have been finishing other people's cloth as well as his own. Henry Sutcliffe of Langfield, also 1720, was a merchant finisher in a modest way. He had three tenters, a press and dressing tools worth £12, and wool and cloth valued at £75. His inventory included wheels, cards, a tub and oil. Some members of his household were carding and spinning, but he had no loom.

The final process was known as dressing, the nap being raised by teazles, then cropped with heavy shears before the pieces of cloth were interlined with paper and placed in a press.

In the late seventeenth century the Halifax area began to experiment with worsted manufacture. Worsted yarn was made from long-staple wool, which was combed, not carded. The cloth was finished without fulling. For a long time it was thought that the woollen (eg kersey) and worsted industries were organised quite differently, the first being in the hands of independent small masters, the second being controlled by merchant capitalists who employed combers, spinners and weavers. In fact, in upper Calderdale the structure of the two branches was remarkably similar. Some kersey masters were large-scale employers, their money being tied up mainly in materials at different stages of production. At the end of the seventeenth century, one kersey piece would buy a loom. There were also worsted weavers, whose inventories testify to their independence by valuing wool, yarn and cloth as well as equipment.

One interesting feature of the Todmorden area in the early eighteenth century is that several households were producing both woollens and worsteds. Elizabeth Horsfall, Stansfield, had 'cloth' (woollen) and 'worsett' looms, together with wool, a worsted warp, 'cards of all sorts', and three spinning wheels. Michael Clegg of West Bar had looms for both kersey and shalloons, a type of worsted. William Sutcliffe of

Swallowshaw had four looms, four wheels, combs and a warping wough, and both kersey and worsted cloth. Although there are no specific references to worsted cloth in the seventeenth century inventories, there are several references to combs, sometimes alongside cards, as far back as James Fielding of Bottomley in 1602, who had wheels, cards and combs. Bays, a cloth made from a worsted warp and woollen weft, became established in the Rochdale area around 1600, and Todmorden may have become involved in this branch. It made sense to produce worsteds as well as woollens, as the trade in one might be active when the other was depressed.

Wills and Inheritance

Although probate inventories rank about the most informative of local records during the seventeenth and eighteenth centuries, the wills themselves are valuable sources. In particular they show that testators tried to make provision for all of their children. The eldest son might receive the largest share, but he was commonly charged with payments to his sisters.

When John Heap of Stiperden died in 1691, his net estate (excluding land) was worth £27 6s 6d. He left his best hat to his brother-in-law, his best 'shoon' (shoes) and a 'payer lether briches' to his two sons-in-law, and the residue to his wife. His daughters were not mentioned; they had probably been given their portions as a dowry on marriage. Edward Sutcliffe of Cross Gap in Stansfield made complicated arrangements for his four young children when he died in January 1696. His moveable goods were valued at £102 16s 10d, but he had debts of £107 3s 6d. Cross Gap was to be used to maintain the family until the youngest child was twenty-one, at which point the eldest son then living was to inherit the property, paying £2 10s a year for ten years to be divided equally amongst the younger children. At the same time the moveable goods were to be divided, one third going to Edward's wife Ann as her traditional dower, the rest shared by the children. Ann had £50 of her own, and if this passed to the eldest son, he had to share it with the younger children. Finally the latter were to share equally in a piece of land called 'Loynes' at Eastwood on the death of Edward's mother.

John Sutcliffe had ten children to provide for when he died in 1701, obviously older than Edward's family as two of the six daughters were married. The three eldest sons received property, charged with payments to their unmarried sisters. The eldest, John, who inherited the main property at Mankinholes, had to pay money to his two married sisters and £50 to his youngest brother Daniel (who received no real property) at the age of twenty-one. The widow Mary was granted the rent of two of the properties for seven years, and all the rest of her husband's goods.

William Sutcliffe of Swallowshaw had an unusual amount of money to deploy in his testamentary arrangements. His net personal estate was nearly £1,000, much of it money lent on mortgage. His properties at Swallowshaw and Hallstones were divided equally between his eldest sons John and Richard, John also receiving property at Royton, near Oldham. The third son William was to have £5 a year until the age of twenty-three, when he would inherit £300, and a similar plan for fourth son Daniel involved payments of £2 10s a year and £250. On reaching the age of twenty-three, youngest son Abraham was to have £200, and daughters Mary and Elizabeth £120 each. William's wife Grace and her brother Richard were to receive annual allowances, for taking care of the two girls and Abraham until they were twenty-three, of £2 10s,

Scaitcliffe Hall, seen here on an engraving before its rebuilding in 1833, was home to the influential Crossley family.

£2 10s and £5 respectively. Grace was given a choice in respect of her dower — £3 a year for life out of Swallowshaw if she stayed there, or £20 if she moved out.

Anthony Crossley, 1707, owned such a substantial estate that he was able to subdivide it amongst his sons, providing each with a viable inheritance. He married twice, going to live with his second wife, a widow Grace Ramsden, at Broadhalgh, Spotland, Rochdale. Eldest son John inherited Scaitcliffe Hall, Flailcroft, Dike, and Scaitcliffe corn and fulling mills. He was to receive other properties in Scaitcliffe after his sisters Judith and Ann had received £100 each from the profits (rents) of them. Second son Anthony got Further Scaitcliffe, Royd House, and the dwelling house and fulling mill at Robinwood. Luke, his third son, was to have Rodwell End, Matthew Laithe and the Chief House of Eastwood (Great House in Stansfield). Anthony and Luke were also to have Ballingroyd with two cottages there and land called Miles Commons.

One daughter, Susan, received property at Eastwood; another, Mary who had married John Fielden of Hartley Royd, got land at Barewise which would consolidate her husband's estate; whilst the only unmarried daughter, Judith, received Midgelden.

Intriguingly, instead of John his eldest son being his executor (as was customary), his executors were his two youngest sons Anthony and Luke, who were also to receive the rest of his personal estate; there was a proviso that if John attempted to interfere

A rear view of Swallowshaw Farm above Cross Stone, where William Sutcliffe, a substantial yeoman-clothier and farmer, lived in 1730.

in any way in the bequests made to the other children, then his bequests became void and passed to Anthony and Luke.

The dual economy, as evidenced in these wills and inventories, was still flourishing on the eve of the Industrial Revolution. At the apex of the system were families, economically independent, living by a combination of farming and textiles, and owning their own property, equipment and materials. At the base were those who lived by selling their labour; within this group were some skilled workers who owned a little land, and others who lived intermittently in and out of poverty or permanently in it.

The independent group comprised a mixture from the modest one-loom weaver/farmer to the prosperous putters-out and merchant finishers. This 'yeoman' class had a dominant influence on local society, serving as township officers and giving the district its religious and political flavour. In contrast to those living in areas dominated by 'squire and parson', they were subservient to no one. Anthony Crossley described himself in his will as 'yeoman', but was labelled 'gentleman' in his inventory. He was certainly wealthy enough to live in the style of a gentleman, but he may have shared the characteristic yeoman's attitude — that there was nothing wrong with having tin in your buttons if you had gold in your pockets. The only form of ostentation that the prosperous yeomen-clothiers permitted themselves was the embellishment of their fine houses, many of which survive to stand sentinel to their memory.

5

Social Life in the Eighteenth and
Early Nineteenth Centuries

Community Life

The organisations out of which the framework of local community life was constructed were the county, the parish, the manor, the township and the settlement, ie town, village or hamlet. The counties, the West Riding of Yorkshire and Lancashire, were concerned with the administration of justice, through the Quarter Sessions presided over by a group of justices of the peace. The counties provided houses of correction, under Acts of 1576 and 1597, maintained by a county rate. The West Riding House of Correction at Wakefield was in existence by the late 1590s, and the county of Lancashire acquired a building at Preston, for a similar purpose, in 1619. Later, the township of Todmorden and Walsden was using the Manchester House of Correction. These houses were originally intended for the reform of 'idle vagabonds', by a combination of whipping and industrial training. A petition, presented to the Lancashire Quarter Sessions in 1606, praying for the establishment of a house of correction, described vagabonds as people who refused to hire themselves for the year at the wages offered by their masters and demanded, at the same time, the effective regulation of wages by JPs. The Preston house contained woollen cards, kersey looms, shears and shear-boards, and the Wakefield house probably had similar equipment. Over the years, these houses became general county prisons, with the cruder forms of labour, such as the treadmill, surviving as part of the punishment regime. The old-established county jails at York (serving all three Ridings) and Lancaster continued in use, especially for prisoners awaiting trial.[1]

As a social unit, the county mattered only to the gentry — which in descending order of status were, baronets, knights, esquires and gentlemen. There were no baronets or knights resident in the area in the eighteenth century. The Saviles of Thornhill were the leading landowners, lords of three sub-manors, but after the Civil War they made their home at Rufford Abbey in Nottinghamshire. Other branches of the Savile family played a leading role in West Riding affairs and often acted as spokesmen for the clothing interest, but they had no other specific links with the upper Calder Valley. In Todmorden, the Radcliffe family severed its connection with the district when Roger Mainwaring sold Todmorden Hall to John Fielden of Bottomley, Walsden, in 1717.[2] The Stansfields of Stansfield Hall left the district in 1536.[3] The only remaining local gentry were the Crossleys of Scaitcliffe Hall. For good or ill the area lacked the leadership which might have come from a group of resident gentry, influential as both landlords and JPs. Indeed, in the second half of the eighteenth century very few of the local gentry were willing to undertake the responsibility of being a justice. Local constables often had to travel to Bradford or Keighley in search of a West Riding JP, or to Middleton or Oldham for a Lancashire JP, to issue a warrant or

An ancient packhorse route paved with causey stones below Whirlaw in Stansfield.

Packhorse roads cross the cloughs over picturesque bridges like this one at Hudstone on Pudsey Clough, often describing a V as they deviate from the direct route in search of the easiest crossing point.

transact other legal business. Some local gentry, who had been appointed to the commission of the peace, refused to go through the necessary formalities to become active because they were afraid of being overwhelmed with business.[4]

The parish of Halifax, with its twenty-two townships, was much too large to act as an effective focus of local loyalties, except to the extent that it coincided with a natural geographical region which was also dominated by the cloth trade. Even the ancient chapelry of Heptonstall contained five townships, each with its own churchwarden keeping separate township accounts. Stansfield and Langfield were responsible for maintaining Cross Stone Church as well as paying their shares to Heptonstall Church, which was still the parish church. Rochdale parish was also extensive. Todmorden and Walsden were not only the most remote township from Rochdale Church, but were also on the Yorkshire side of the Pennine watershed.

The manor of Wakefield was a much more relevant institution. Manorial admin-istration operated at two levels. The officers of the manor concerned themselves with land tenure and transfers, rents and fines, and any other matters affecting the economic interests of the lord, eg mining. Community affairs were regulated at the twice-yearly tourns at Halifax by juries elected from the copyholders and freeholders. The comm-unity jurisdiction of the tourns covered the whole of the Yorkshire part of the valley, including the sub-manors.[5]

The remaining units were the township and the settlement. The nucleated villages, such as Mankinholes, provided a focus for local loyalties and in some cases were concerned with the regulation of communal aspects of farming. Over most of the area, however, settlement was too dispersed for this kind of identification to be general. The basic unit of social regulation, within the manor, was the township, which had been, from the time of the earliest surviving records, the unit of manorial administration and taxation. The responsibilities created by Tudor legislation were taken on, without at first disturbing the traditional framework of the township operating within the manor. By the eighteenth century the officers of the township were operating within a dual structure of responsibility, to the manor and to the JPs. For example, the appointment of township constables was recorded in the manor court rolls and approved by the justices. The surveyors of the highways were, under the Highway Act of 1691, nominated by the township but formerly appointed by the county justices at special 'Highway Sessions'. However, roads in need of repair were still being 'pained' in the manor court in 1738.[6]

The township offices — constable, churchwarden, overseer of the poor and surveyor of the highways — were shared between the landholders on a rota system. The system allowed for the use of substitutes, who were presumably paid for their trouble by the person whose turn it was, and occasionally for the appointment of deputies, in the sense of assistants. The constables' accounts for Todmorden and Walsden record:

1782. John Greenwood, Deputy Constable for Wm. Sutcliffe for this year, his disbursments are as under …
1783. Jno. Greenwood, Deputy Constable for Job Cockroft …
1784. John Greenwood, Deputy Constable for Wm. Mitchell …

He had also done the job in 1781, so must have taken a liking to it or been well rewarded. There was no training for the work; the rudiments of administrative skills were learned by experience and to some degree were passed on within families which undertook these periodic public duties.[7]

Todmorden and Walsden were, until 1801, part of the extensive township of

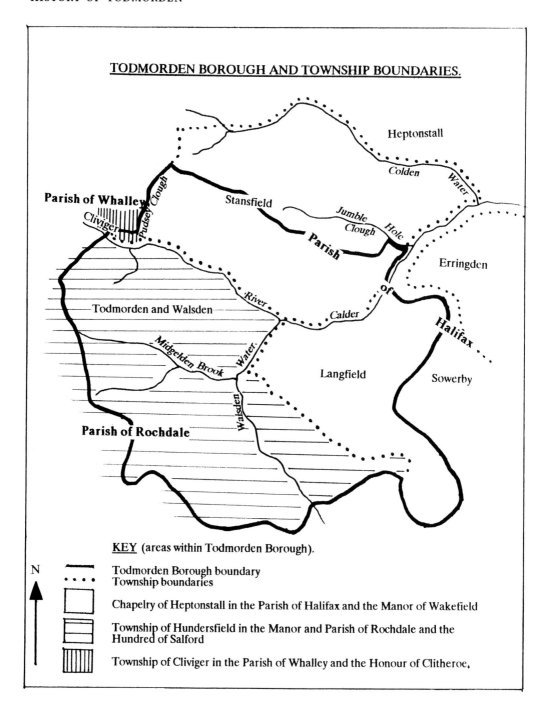

TODMORDEN BOROUGH AND TOWNSHIP BOUNDARIES.

Heptonstall

Colden

Water

Parish of Whalley

Stansfield

Cliviger

Pudsey Clough

Jumble Clough

Hole

Parish

Erringden

of

River

Calder

Halifax

Todmorden and Walsden

Midgelden Brook

Water

Langfield

Sowerby

Walsden

Parish of Rochdale

KEY (areas within Todmorden Borough).

N

Todmorden Borough boundary
Township boundaries

Chapelry of Heptonstall in the Parish of Halifax and the Manor of Wakefield

Township of Hundersfield in the Manor and Parish of Rochdale and the
Hundred of Salford

Township of Cliviger in the Parish of Whalley and the Honour of Clitheroe.

Hundersfield. However, they had their own constable and overseers of the poor, who kept their own accounts, subject to ratification by Hundersfield. As far as the evidence goes, they raised and spent money as though they represented an independent township. As will be explained, there were three separate units for highway management — Todmorden, and the Henshaw and Inchfield areas of Walsden. Todmorden had one churchwarden, who was concerned both with the local St Mary's Church and the mother church at Rochdale. He was in a similar position to the churchwardens of Stansfield and Langfield in relation to Cross Stone Chapel and Heptonstall Church. In other words, in a discussion of community government, Todmorden and Walsden can be treated as a township.

The upper Calder Valley generally is rich in township records. The townships of Stansfield, Langfield and Todmorden with Walsden have various surviving records relating to the eighteenth and nineteenth centuries, now in the care of Calderdale Archives. However, some of the records, available when Joshua Holden wrote his *History of Todmorden* (1912), have since been lost and we are indebted to him for examples which he extracted from various township books. Other records used were copied by Mr G Jackman, late assistant overseer of the Todmorden Union; his son Mr H Jackman; and Mr James Whitehead, late clerk to the Todmorden Education Committee, whose extracts survive where the originals are lost; although most of the constables' accounts from 1738 to 1784 have survived.[8]

The Constable

The constable was both the principal officer of the township and the one with the heaviest and most varied duties. His responsibilities included law and order, weights and measures, the pinfold, turbary (right to cut turf/peat), the militia and tax collection. Periodically — normally four times a year — he was instructed by the chief constable of the county to carry out a 'privy search' for vagrants. The latter were defined by an Act of 1743-44 to include 'idle and disorderly persons', beggars, anyone returning to a parish from which he or she had been removed, fortune tellers, those 'playing at any unlawful game of chance', 'all those … buying, receiving or carrying away any ends of yarn, weft, thrums … or other refuse of cloth', and people sleeping rough 'and not being able to give a good account of themselves'.[9] Vagrancy business occurs frequently in the constables' accounts. The Langfield constables' accounts contain references to a 'Privet Search' costing 1s, which, judging by similar entries in other townships, seems to be the the the customary allowance for ale and food. The Todmorden and Walsden constable spent 3s in 1756 in conveying and lodging 'four vagrants viz. a woman and three children passing from Leeds in Yorkshire, to Rossendale in Lancashire the place of their abode'.

Of the townships' punitive instruments — stocks, whipping post and ducking stool — which were commonly mentioned in earlier times, only the stocks seem to have continued into the eighteenth century. There is no record in the eighteenth century constables' accounts of any whipping, but amongst the inventory of articles in the possession of the Stansfield constable in 1790 are a whip, thumbscrew and two hand-cuffs. Most of the local townships can boast of still possessing at least the remains of their stocks; perhaps the best-preserved example is the one at Cross Stone in Stansfield. There are frequent references to the repair and use of stocks. The length of stay was normally a few hours, but in some cases could run to a few days.

The stocks at Cross Stone, now built into a wall to the east of the former church, were the last remaining form of punishment used by the townships.

Frequently the constable had to undertake journeys to the house of correction. For example:

Langfield: 1777-78 Pd for a warrant for Sabina Sutcliffe 2s; Pd to a Bailiff for going with her to Wakefield House of Correction 9s.
Todmorden and Walsden: Oct 27 1766 For conveying Jas Nuttall and Jas Crossley from Hundersfield to Manchester House of Correction 10s.

Some townships provided their own lock-up, invariably referred to as the 'dungeon', for the custody of prisoners until they could be taken to a JP or to the manor court. Thus for Todmorden and Walsden hamlets in 1751-52 is recorded 'Mar 4. Pd my share of the repairs of the dungeon 2s 4d', and for Langfield in 1797 'A warrant for Betty Greenwood 5s; Her house watching 5s; Lock-up expences 3s 1d'.

The constable also found himself responsible for the custody of animals in the township pinfold, although the detailed task fell upon the pinder, appointed by the township and paid a small wage out of the constable rate. Animals which had strayed on to the highway were impounded until a small fine was paid. The constables' accounts contain frequent references to the repair of pinfolds. In 1822 Langfield resolved 'That the Pinder be ordered to impound any lime or coal horses which may be suffered by their drivers to remain on the Common for the purpose of pasturing'. This is a reminder that the centuries-old method of transporting bulky goods such as lime and coal by packhorse was still in existence. Langfield's pinfold was in Lumbutts, near Lee Farm, until 1814, when Samuel Fielden obtained permission to remove it elsewhere, as he wanted to construct a reservoir for his spinning mill.

In the seventeenth century, particularly during the ascendancy of the Puritans, the constables were kept busy on Sundays pursuing those who profaned the Sabbath by drinking or gambling. Perhaps surprisingly, the Sunday observance laws were still being enforced in the late eighteenth and early nineteenth centuries. Luke Law, the Stansfield constable, was particularly vigilant, for he recorded the following receipts:

1805 Feb 13th of Paul Greenwood for not going to Divine Worship 1s [under an Act of 1559]; of Thomas Cunliffe, Thomas Marshall, Willm Marshall 3s 4d each for Sabbath Breaking 10s 0d; March 15 of Abraham Newell, Eliz and Ebez Greenwood, James Clegg, Abm Clegg, Jno Holt 3s 4d each 16s 8d; Wm Dobson. Oakhill for swearing 1s.

The constable had to collect, in addition to his own and the county rate, various national taxes. The most important of the latter were the window tax, and the land tax, both in operation from 1695 to 1851. The constable was also the unpaid inspector of weights and measures in his township, which necessitated his keeping his own standard weights and measures in good order so that he could check those of innkeepers, shopkeepers and millers etc. There are frequent references in the constables' accounts to his purchasing new weights and measures and to his rounds of inspection. The following are fairly typical:

Stansfield: 1782 Aug 2 My journey to Halifax to bespeak weights and measures 2s; Aug 9 When I received weights and measures, spent on Marks 1s; Aug 9 Pd. for weights and measures 10s 1d; Aug 9 Sometime pd. for stamping a peck and a half 8d; Aug 9 Sometime for tinn measures 1s 1¹/₄d; 1785 Going through town to try weights and measures 12s 0d.

(The 12 shillings would mostly be spent on quenching his thirst at the various inns. One imagines that this would not be the most uncongenial of his many duties!)

It was not only in connection with weights and measures that innkeepers came into contact with the constable. The latter had to accompany them to Brewster Sessions in order that their licences could be renewed. In the case of Todmorden this involved a journey to Rochdale.

Entries relating to travellers with a 'pass' are very common in all the constables' accounts. Licences signed by two JPs might be granted to poor people, whether civilians, soldiers or sailors, enabling them to receive relief in any parish through which they travelled. The constable, or sometimes the overseer of the poor, would deal with these people, and then pass them on to the constable of the next township. The most exotic entry is in the Todmorden and Walsden accounts for February 1748: 'To Eleven Turkey Slaves [? slaves freed by British ships] travelling to Newcastle, 2s'.

The constable was personally involved in military affairs through his responsibility for the militia. The Jacobite Rebellion of 1745, during which the forces of the Young Pretender marched south through Lancashire as far as Derby, caused a great flurry of activity. The Todmorden and Walsden accounts for 1746-47 contain several references to 'Conducting his Majestie's Forces' as well as payments for the relief of Scottish prisoners in Lancaster Castle. The accounts of the same township include: '1757 Jan 12th Paid Rt. Woolfenden for cleaning ye. Halberts 2s' (a halberd consisted of a wooden shaft about six feet long, surmounted by an axe-like instrument balanced on the opposite side by a hook or pick).

The old system of 'watch and ward', especially to guard the key bridges, was revived during the 1745 rebellion, occasioning this entry for Todmorden and Walsden: '1745

1756	Henry Marshall Constable for Todmorden and Walsden in the Year 1756 his Accounts are as under.	£	s	d	
May 21st	For attending the Commissioners of the Land and Window Taxes at Royton	.	2	0	
Augt 16th and 17th	For attending his Majestys Window Viewer thro' my Constablery ———	.	3	0	
7ber 7th	Paid my Share of a Money Warrant	1	3	8	¾
29th	Paid Mr Dearden wth my List of Freeholders	.	1	0	—
Xber 30	Paid my Share of a Money Warrant	.	3	2	
1757 Jan 12th	Paid for two Warrants for the Surveyers of the Highways	.	8	—	
	For attendance of the Justices of the Peace and Commissioners of the Land Tax, at the Boars head in Middleton, five separat Days and Times since the 29th Day of December last	.	10	—	
	Paid my Share of a Money Warrant	.	7	3	
	Spent at laying the Lay	.	2	6	
	For conveying four Vagrants viz. a Woman and three Children passing from Leeds in Yorkshire, to Rossendale in Lancashire the place of their abode, and Charges of one Nights Lodging for them	.	3	0	
	Paid Rt Woolfenden for cleaning ye Halberts	.	2	0	
	Paid Do my Ballance of Accounts ——	.	3	7	
	Total paid ...... £	3	9	2	¾
	Recd by Lay .... £ 1 . 10 . 2 ¾				
	Do from my Predecessor .... 2 . 10 . 5½	4	0	8	¼
	Rem. in hand ... £ — 0 . 11 . 5 ½				

April 5th 1758, Inspected and approved by Us

Jno Fielden
Ely Fielden
The Mark of
Robert Dawson

Wm Greenwood
Joshua Fielden
Samuel Ffielden

An extract from the Todmorden with Walsden constables' accounts for 1756.

9ber 30th Pd 4 Watchmen 4s' (9ber is November, ie the ninth month when the new year started in March).

Partly as a result of the Jacobite scare, and partly because of the outbreak of the 'Seven Years' War' in 1756, an Act was passed in 1757 which revived and reorganised the national militia force. Each township had to supply a certain quota of men, who were chosen by ballot from a list of all the men between the ages of eighteen and sixty. The list had to be submitted by the constable to the Lord Lieutenant of the county (or riding) or his deputy. Todmorden and Walsden recorded:

1760 Jan 2nd For attending Deputy Lieutenants at Manchester with a list of our militia men 2s 6d;
1776 To swearing a Militia Man 1s.

The press-gang was not unknown in this area, and there are two entries for the year 1779, during the War of American Independence:

Langfield: Spent at James Howarth's at Todmorden, when we impressed men 9s.
Stansfield: 1779-80 May 3rd Paid for a new Press Act 2s;
1794 June 15th Journey to Halifax and Press Warrant 3s.

It is highly probable that the press-ganged men would be vagrants, rather than inhabitants of the township.

Recruiting could be time-consuming and expensive as, not unnaturally, during times of war few were keen to be enrolled. In 1796 the Stansfield constable spent the enormous sum of £53 on the recruitment of four men, one of whom was James Crabtree. He had his shoes soled, and was given a waistcoat and a pair of breeches, in addition to subsistence expenses and a bounty — unspecified except for a part payment of £6 6s.

The 1757 Act allowed for substitutes, to be provided by the men who had been balloted. In peacetime, militiamen normally did a month's training and then returned home, but in time of war they were liable, as in the case of Territorials today, to be sent anywhere. It was during wartime that 'listed' men tried hardest to find substitutes, who would have to be paid. During the long French Revolutionary and Napoleonic Wars, men could almost ask their own prices to serve as substitutes. The practice grew up of establishing Militia Clubs; each member paid a certain sum, and if one of their number was balloted to serve, a substitute would be found and paid for out of the club funds. Such a club was set up at Walsden in 1803. There were eighty-eight members and the treasurer was William Fielden of the Sun Inn, near Lanebottom. The substitute need not be of the same parish as the balloted man. In 1809 Langfield paid the overseer of Heptonstall £2 16s to go to the wife of Thomas Sunderland, 'a militiaman serving Langfield'; in 1810 'Pd the overseer of Northowram for Jeremiah Robinson a substitute in the militia for 13 weeks at 4s — £2 12s'; whilst in the same year James Knowles was paid £72 14s 10d for 'hireing militiamen'. The numbers of men serving in the militia swelled enormously, owing to the outbreak of war with France in 1793, and the townships spent increasingly large sums in maintaining their wives and children. By the end of the Napoleonic Wars, wives were usually receiving 2s 6d a week, with 1s 6d for each child. The constable was expected to fill the gaps in the regular army by going on recruiting campaigns. In 1803 the Stansfield constable was looking for recruits in Todmorden, Worsthorne and Heptonstall, and spending his township's money lavishly on a prodigious consumpton of ale!

In 1808 during the Napoleonic invasion scare, the Drums and Fifes of the West Halifax Volunteers were invited to Todmorden to assist in raising volunteers for the local militia. They had bread, cheese and ale at William Patchett's in Hebden Bridge, and slaked their thirst again at Bottoms Inn, Eastwood, on their march to Todmorden. How successful they were is not recorded, but they stayed in the town for at least two days, not without incident it would seem if this entry means anything: 'Pd 8 drummers at the Royal George Inn — Mr Saml Hanson having refused to let the men remain any longer in his house 12s 2d'. In 1813 the township decided to raise its quota of forty-one men by volunteering rather than ballotting, and on the 21st January the civil officers of the township, along with the commissioned officer of the company, met at the White Hart Inn 'to receive the offers of Services of such British youths as are again disposed to fill the ranks of the third company [of the Oldham Regiment of Royal Lancashire Local Militia] the pride of the Valley of Todmorden'. One wonders whether any of those who volunteered took part in the Battle of Waterloo two years later. After 1815 the militia was no longer important, and reference to it in the local records almost cease.

For this great amount and range of unpaid work, the township constable received no formal training, and yet we have seen that in many ways he held together the fabric of local government, being the link with the wider network of county and national agencies. There are numerous references in the Todmorden and Walsden accounts to these wider responsibilities, eg repairing the Manchester House of Correction and paying a share of the governor's wages each half year; and regular attendance at the justices' sessions at Middleton, Heywood, Rochdale, Royton etc. Todmorden and Walsden being part of the larger township of Hundersfield, the constable had to report to central office, as it were, to make account of his year's activities. This is recorded annually:

1768 Mar. 22nd For entering my Disbursments and also my Lay Book into the large folio Book in Rochdale 1s 6d.

The Churchwarden

The office of churchwarden rivals in antiquity that of the constable, and is the only one of the four township offices to survive to the present day. The principal duties were the maintenance of the church building and its furnishings, the upkeep of the churchyard, and the provision of vestments, a Bible, a Book of Common Prayer and a Book of Homilies. The account of St Mary's Chapel prepared by the vicar and churchwardens for the bishop's visitation held at Manchester in 1778 lists the belongings as: 'one bell, a communion table, one cloth, one napkin, one flagon, one cup and salver, all pewter, one surplice, two registers, one Bible, two common prayer books, two forms, one spade, one mattock, one bier, one cloth, two deal planks'.[10] The churchwardens also had certain responsibilities under the Tudor poor laws, and under an Act of 1532-33 (later renewed and amended) they made payments for the destruction of vermin. In the Stansfield accounts during the 1740s are recorded payments of 3d for a foxhead and 1½d for an 'urchin' (hedgehog).[11]

The church at Heptonstall served five townships: Heptonstall, Stansfield, Langfield, Erringden and Wadsworth. Each township had its own churchwardens — Heptonstall always had two — and kept separate accounts. Langfield and Stansfield also had their own 'chapel of ease' at Cross Stone. Amongst some Langfield papers for 1786 it is stated that 'The gift of the said chapel belongs to the Vicar of Halifax for the time being and the chapel is repaired by and at the expense of the inhabitants of Stansfield and Langfield, Stansfield paying two thirds and Langfield one third.' At Todmorden, it was the custom for the inhabitants to nominate three persons for churchwarden at the annual Good Friday Vestry Meeting. The nominations were then laid before the Rochdale Vestry Meeting on Easter Tuesday, when the vicar and warden of Rochdale chose one to serve Todmorden for the ensuing year.[12]

The churchwardens were unpaid, but the clerk at Heptonstall received £1 11s a year 'for ringing Eight o Clock (Matins) and Cleaning Communion plate and Linnen, washing Surplice and winding up Clock'. The sexton received 10s 6d a year plus a new coat every three years for general oversight of the church. The church bells were installed about 1440, when William Brigge of Heptonstall left £6 13s 4d in his will 'to the making of the bells at Heptonstall'. When they were recast in 1749 there were five bells, and Stansfield paid nearly £37 as its share of the cost. There are frequent references to their upkeep. A sixth bell was added in 1788. The ringers received 3s each per quarter for their regular duties, and extra for special peals. One of these was rung on the 5th November, apparently in the evening: '1769 Ringers for Gunpowder Treason 5s; Pint oyl, candles, lamp weaking 5d'. The bells were often rung to mark national events but the only such entry in the Heptonstall accounts, dated the 1st December 1805, relates to the Battle of Trafalgar: 'Ringers for Ringing for the Victory over the French and Spanish Fleets by Lord Nelson on the 21st October 9s'.

The fabric of the churches, whether at Heptonstall, Cross Stone or Todmorden, was in constant need of repair, and the accounts read like those of a careful householder maintaining his dwelling. The following excerpts from the Todmorden and Walsden accounts are typical examples: '1721 glass and glasing of chapel windows 1s 7d'. Windows would be of small panes set in lead — note an entry in '1780 Saml. Fielden for white lead 1s 11d'. Moss was used to pack crevices round the window frames and between the roof slates to make them watertight and draught-proof before the winter, and each year saw this being done. The operation was not always successful, and payments for clearing snow out of the church appear in the Todmorden accounts. The inside of the church was whitewashed and the same accounts record: '1801-2 To church seats cleaning after whitewashing 4s'. Perhaps the 'whitewash splasher' learnt his trade from one Thomas Bibby, who for years previously had maintained the fabric of the church: '1752 To Thomas Bibby for daubing 1s 6d; 1757 To Thomas Bibby for slating & pointing of steeple and other work £1 7s 8½d; 1764 To Bibby for glazing and pointing 2s 3d'. Pointing was done using a mixture of lime and hair. Bibby was something of a character, warranting an article in the local *Comet* (1840) where he is described as five feet six or eight inches in height, usually wearing an old Scotch grey coat of coarse manufacture, with buttons of ample dimensions, stout leather trousers, grey stockings of coarse yarn, and shoes with large buckles, the whole being splashed with lime and paint.[13]

The Todmorden minister's surplice was provided by the churchwardens, and in 1791 Samuel Fielden was paid £1 4s for '12 yards of cloth for surplices'; making them cost 7s 6d each. Todmorden Church purchased a new Bible in 1802 for £3 10s, and in 1748 a 'Flacket for ye sacrament urn' was bought from James Newell for 1s 6d. It was usual to display the Ten Commandments, and in 1724 Todmorden paid for 'commandments, frames and writing and weathercock £4 1s 4d'. In 1740, £2 10s was spent in 'repairing Cross Stone Chapel and writeing ye King's Armes and 10 commandments with Goulden Letters'.

When Caroline, wife of King George II, died in 1737, the Todmorden churchwardens spent 8d on a 'paper of directions for alteration of prayers after queen's death'. Wine had to be purchased for use on the five sacrament days — Michaelmas, Christmas, Palm Sunday, Good Friday and Easter Day, with Whit Sunday taking the place of Palm Sunday from 1751. Stansfield and Langfield paid for their share of the wine used at Heptonstall. Stansfield records 'Wine at Easter [Heptonstall] 5 gallons 1 pint, Good Friday 2 gallon, Easter Day 2 gallon 1 pint and to Cross Stone 1 gallon £1 15s 10½d'. So out of their quota, Heptonstall allowed one gallon for use at Cross Stone Chapel. In April 1819 Todmorden purchased eight bottles of wine from George Eccles (White Hart) for £2 8s.

Throughout the eighteenth century, Todmorden Chapel had one bell which would be rung by the clerk, as part of his general duties, at service times. In 1745, 3s 4d was paid for bell-ringing at Todmorden. When the tower was raised in 1860 and the bell taken for recasting, it was found to be inscribed S.R.A.L. A.D. 1603 and in Latin 'With pleasantness of sound I will make a noise unto thee O Lord. With sweetness of voice I will sing unto Thy Name'.[14] In 1732 the entry '2 oak forms for singers to sit on 4s' is evidence that a choir was in existence by then, but says nothing of what instruments might have accompanied them. No organ was installed until 1805, when one was purchased from Christopher Rawdon of Underbank for £250. The money was raised by subscription and by holding an 'oratorio' in the church, with seat prices varying from 2s to 3s 6d. The organ was placed in the south-west gallery, but damp affected it, and in 1808-9 an entry shows 2s 6d being spent on charcoal to warm the organ.

Prior to this in 1770, Todmorden Chapel had been largely rebuilt; initially the finances were borne by Anthony Crossley of Scaitcliffe Hall, and throughout the accounts are references to repaying him: '1771 To Anthony Crossley towards the disbursements on Todmorden Chapel paid in at Sundry times £60 17s 6d'.

The expenses of the chapelry of Heptonstall were shared by the five townships in a ratio probably determined by some earlier rateable valuation. Wadsworth paid one third of the total, Heptonstall and Erringden together paid one third (in the ratio two to one respectively) and Stansfield and Langfield paid the remaining third, with Stansfield paying three parts to Langfield's one. Having calculated the amount to be met by their own township, the churchwardens then added their personal expenses, and levied a church rate to raise the amount needed. The average annual expenses of the chapelry were about £25 in the period 1750-1800, and the townships could meet this by levying a rate of two pence in the pound (a penny rate yielded about £4 in Wadsworth and £2 12s 6d in Heptonstall).

Todmorden Chapel, as a chapel-of-ease for Rochdale Church, had expenses to pay at Rochdale, and so was in a similar position to Stansfield and Langfield. In 1747 the chapel had 'a house two gardens and a Chappel yard rated at Forty Shillings and a farm in Stansfield ...'. During the eighteenth century, steps were taken to secure the financial position of the chapel by using monies from Queen Anne's Bounty. In 1736 a grant of £200, matched by another £200 raised locally, was used to buy a farm of twenty-five acres, called 'Apple Tree', at Blackshawhead in Stansfield. This farm was let, giving an income of £16 per annum. Further grants of £200 in 1777, 1786 and 1800 bought Black Butt Farm at Heald in Bacup (eight acres, £8 8s per annum), Old Clough Farm, also in Rossendale, and Cold Edge Farm, Luddenden. Payments due for 'services' rendered were as follows for 1747:

Every burial is one Shilling to ye minister. Every Churching is fourpence and a penny to ye Clark. Every Wedding by Banns Eighteen pence and a sixpence to Ye Clark. Every Licensed Wedding five shillings and A Shilling to Ye Clark.

This is St Mary's Church as it appeared from 1770, when it was virtually rebuilt, until the tower was raised to its present height in 1860. A chancel was added in 1896, along with a porch which was removed in the 1989-92 restoration.

In 1778 'chapel dues' remained unchanged, also in 1780 except: 'A Marriage by Licence [cost] £5 [plus 2s 6d for the clerk]' and 'by Banns 4s 6d'. The Clerk earned the following in 1778: 'A Churching 1d. A Publication 6d. For keeping the Registers washing the Linnen, cleaning Pewter and Ringing and sweeping the Chapel 12s', plus 'voluntary contributions from the inhabitants at Midsummer'; whilst the Sexton was paid 'His Wages For digging a Grave for an unbaptised Infant 4d. For baptised Infant 6d. For an Adult 8d.'[15]

The Todmorden churchwardens had problems in collecting the rate or 'lay' which they levied, as a growing number of the inhabitants were members of the 'Society of Friends' or Quakers. In 1779 James Jackson returned the following lays as being owing to him and unpaid by people called Quakers: 'Thos Fielden, Carr Barn, 9d; Jos Fielden, Edge End, 5s 7½d; John & Thos Fielden, Edge, 1s 11½d; Mr.W.Greenwood 8s 5½d; Uriah Brook 2s 5½d; Uriah Brook for mill & cottages, 9d'. It is interesting that ten years later the unpaid lays still included 'Jos Fielden 4s 0d', but by then he was at Waterside.

In 1764 the first mention of postage occurs in the Todmorden accounts when 1s 3d was paid for postage of three letters from Chester (Todmorden was then in the Chester Diocese). Postage was paid by the receiver and not the sender at this time.

In November 1760 the Todmorden constable's accounts included 2s ½d for 'proclaiming the King at Rochdale'. The churchwardens spent £14 in April 1820 'for putting the church in mourning'. Thus was George III's sixty-years reign recorded locally.

Roads and Bridges: the Surveyor of the Highways

The Highways Act of 1555, which provided for the township roads to be repaired by compulsory labour, was ignored locally. The older custom of making the occupiers of land adjoining a stretch of road responsible for keeping it in good order was maintained.

The 'overseer of the highways' inspected the roads and the court of the manor of Wakefield enforced, in a rather leisurely way, the orders for necessary repairs.

By the eighteenth century, most townships had surveyors of the highways, normally two. Some of their accounts survive; Walsden has one volume of surveyors' accounts covering the years 1747-1871. Interestingly, Erringden never appointed surveyors, being content with the system of maintenance 'by reason of tenure'. Partly because the township was a park until the middle of the fifteenth century, no major routeways passed through it. The land was either physically enclosed or allocated in parcels to freeholders, so that every length of road had an occupier or occupiers who accepted responsibility for it. The records of Wakefield manor and of the Quarter Sessions, which could order the repair of highways, show that tenured maintenance continued for minor roads in other townships. In 1738, for example, the Quarter Sessions indicted the occupiers of land along what is now the Hebden Bridge-Todmorden road, then a 'horseway', for neglect of maintenance.

The surveyors concentrated on the upkeep and improvement of the main routeways. Before the turnpike road was made, these ran along the hillside terraces, descending at intervals to cross the steep-sided tributary valleys. The main road from Halifax to Burnley, the Long Causeway, climbed up to Roils Head, went down through Newlands to Luddenden, up the steep Old Gate to Midgley, and along the Heights to Skip. The route descended into the Hebden Valley via Wadsworth Lanes and the present narrow passage, between Stubbings School and the former St John's Church, to the Old Bridge, which gives the name to Hebden Bridge. After crossing into Heptonstall township the route divided, one branch climbing the Buttress to Heptonstall village and then on to Jack Bridge and Blackshawhead; the other turning left along the riverbank, then up 'Mytholm Steeps' to rejoin the first branch at Blackshawhead. From there the Long Causeway led via Keb Bridge and Stiperden to Mereclough and Burnley. From Blackshawhead a road ran south by Great Rock to Rodwell Head and Cross Stone. The steep climbs on these routes made them unsuitable for wheeled vehicles, and goods were carried by trains of packhorses. For the latter a permanent and hardwearing surface was provided by paved causeways, the maintenance of which was the main business of the surveyors in the pre-turnpike period. Causey stones, usually about four feet by eighteen inches, were the usual covering, with smaller stones packed in at the side to give a total width of about two and a half yards.

Each township had its own tools, which were handed on from surveyor to surveyor. At the end of the Walsden accounts for 1777 is the following list: 'Tools Liver'd to the new Surveyors, 2 Ditching Spades, 2 Mattocks, 1 Driving Maul, 2 Picks, 1 Scappling Maul, 1 Iron Crow, 5 Badgering Do, 11 Wedges, 1 Stone Sledge'. Most of the tools have names familiar to present-day builders and 'delvers'. 'Mauls' were hammers of various kinds. The wedges, called 'delfe wedges' in the Heptonstall lists, were driven into the rockface using the driving maul. The 'scappling maul' was used to give the slab of rock its 'causey stone' shape, and the badgering mauls were used to break smaller stones. A mattock is a grubbing tool, with a point at one end and a flat blade at the other. The sledge, used for 'sledding' heavy loads of stone over rough ground, would need frequent attention. Horses were used to pull it.

Some examples of how the money was spent are: '1748 Pd John Dawson for 16 days work 16s; John Butterworth and his nag 3 days 4s 6d; 1749 Pd Jas Turner for 2 stone sledges 7s 6d; To Abram ffielden for repairing Ten Rood of the highway in Alleyscholes Rake 17s 6d; To Saml Jackson for saiting in the Alleyscholes Lane 7s 6d'. Alleysholes Rake is the steep, winding road leading from the valley near Lanebottom

Milestones recording the different phases of local transport — packhorse (above left on Reddyshore Scout Gate, Walsden, and above right near Shurcrack in Langfield), turnpike (bottom right at Copperas House) and canal (bottom left near Bottomley Beck).

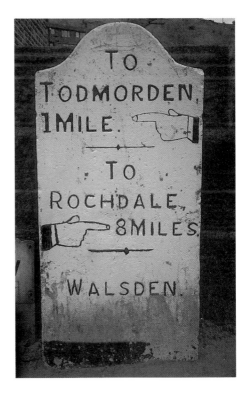

in Walsden up to the 'highway' known as Reddyshore Scout Gate, an ancient route from Todmorden to Rochdale. On the opposite side of the valley it connected with Salter Rake Gate, which led via Bottomley across the moor to Mankinholes, and thence along the farming ledge via Lee Bottom, crossing Stoodley and Beaumont Cloughs, to Horsehold, before dropping down into Hebden Bridge at Hebble End, then joining the old highway to Halifax. 'Saiting' refers to draining the road by inserting stone troughs across the width of the road to lead the surface water off the road to the sides. In 1747 Sam Midgley was paid 2s 2d for 'hewing a trough and setting it'.

When it was necessary to employ labour and buy tools and materials, the money could be raised either by a 'levy' or rate, or by levying 'composition money' in lieu of statute duty (collecting payment in lieu of obligatory labour). In Walsden, which had separate surveyors and accounts for the Inchfield and Henshaw sides of the hamlet, the accounts for 1747-48 show that a rate in Inchfield raised £3 19s 9d. Expenditure came to £2 17s 2d, leaving £1 2s 7d in hand. In 1755, Inchfield paid for 62 days' work and Henshaw for 91. From 1758 to 1769 expenses were very low, indicating that any necessary work was being done by statute labour or by tenurial maintenance. In 1761 the Inchfield surveyor's expenses were only 3s 6d, 1s for 'Riting ye Accounts' and 2s 6d for attending the JPs at Oldham. Occasionally the surveyor had an even easier year, as in 1763 when Todmorden recorded: 'This year the roads were repaired by daywork of the inhabitants, without any lay or assessment, so these accounts may be settled without either pen, ink or paper.'

The involvement of the surveyors with bridges depended upon the status of the latter. The costs for major bridges, regarded as essential to communication within and beyond the county, were met by 'bridge money', part of the county rate. The increase in population and traffic, and the building of new county bridges for turnpike roads, caused a substantial increase in the levies on the townships for bridge money. Those bridges not maintained by the county or wapentake were the responsibility of the township, or more commonly, as township boundaries often followed rivers, of a pair of townships. Heptonstall and Stansfield shared the cost of £21 9s for rebuilding Jack Bridge on Colden Water in 1778; again in 1806 Stansfield contributed £1 15s 10d for 'repairing Jack Brigg'.[16]

The industrial growth of the West Riding and East Lancashire during the first half of the eighteenth century meant extra traffic on the roads, an increasing proportion of which was, as far as the townships were concerned, through traffic rather than local. To deal with this problem, turnpike trusts, which improved and maintained main roads out of the income from tolls, were set up by Acts of Parliament. The earliest trust in the West Riding was established in 1734 for the road from Rochdale, over Blackstone Edge, to Elland and Halifax. Six more Acts for Yorkshire roads were passed in 1741, and by the end of that decade the industrial West Riding had a substantial network of turnpike roads, including Elland-Cleckheaton-Leeds, and Halifax-Leeds-Selby. By 1752 the Halifax-Blackstone Edge-Rochdale road had been improved and widened.[17] It was not until 1760 that an Act of Parliament was secured for the construction of a turnpike road along the Calder Valley from Halifax and Sowerby Bridge to Todmorden, with branches from there to Burnley and Littleborough respectively. This route offers the easiest crossing of the Pennines south of the Aire Gap. On the other hand, most of the early turnpike trusts had taken over and improved existing lines of road. Several stretches of valley-bottom road were already in use for local purposes, but there was no continuous line for the turnpike trust to inherit. This may have been one of the causes of the relatively late date of the enterprise.[18]

About 900 trustees were named in the 1760 Act, although only a few took an active part. The first meeting was held in June 1760, and soon surveyors were appointed and money borrowed at five per cent interest on the security of the tolls. Three members of a wealthy Quaker family — William Greenwood of Stones in Todmorden, gentleman, John Greenwood of Longfield in Langfield, gentleman, and Ambrose Greenwood of Longfield, yeoman — lent between them £2,000. The trustees were empowered to buy the land needed for the new road-works — by compulsion, if necessary. In January 1761, the trustees took over the line of road between Mytholm Bridge and Todmorden, which was in use as a bridleway maintained by the occupiers. Work on this line began later in the year, and the first toll house was built at Charlestown in 1763. New bridges had to be built, and existing ones, unsuitable for wheeled traffic, rebuilt. Mytholm Bridge was rebuilt in 1767 at a total cost of nearly £62, with the county and the townships of Stansfield and Heptonstall each bearing approximately one third. The turnpike trust eventually contributed £15 14s 4d towards the townships' costs. The bridge over Jumble Clough in Stansfield was rebuilt in 1768, and in 1772 Stansfield Bridge was reconstructed, with the trustees, the county and Stansfield sharing the cost.

The slow and piecemeal progress of the turnpike road limited the income from tolls. It was not until 1781 that the whole line was completed and the road could begin to attract through traffic to and from the Rochdale area, away from the hillier Blackstone Edge road. To increase their income, the trustees demanded in 1771 that the surveyors of the townships through which the turnpike passed — including Warley, Midgley, Wadsworth, Heptonstall, Stansfield, Todmorden and Walsden — should each pay over a sum of money equivalent to two days' statute labour. At this time the turnpike was of little use to the people of the hillside settlements, and the demand was both resented and resisted.

In time most of the townships came to terms with the trust, but Midgley, Wadsworth and Stansfield held out. Under a new Act of Parliament in 1777, renewing the life of the trust (originally twenty-one years), two days' duty could be

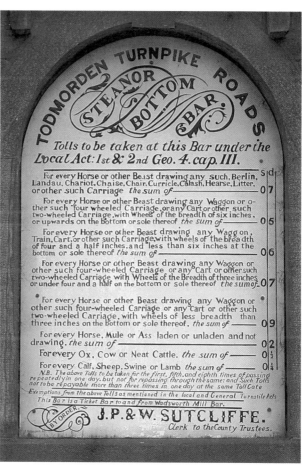

The toll board, dating from 1824, above the door of the Steanorbottom toll house at the junction of the Rochdale and Calderbrook roads, Walsden.

demanded from the other townships, but in the three 'rebel' townships, only those inhabitants living within one quarter of a mile of the new road had to pay two days' statute duty, those within half a mile had to pay one day, and the rest had nothing to pay. It is doubtful if the other townships did pay their levy; Heptonstall certainly did not. After a meeting of the trustees in Todmorden in 1781, 'when the turnpike was compounded for', they paid £5 10s annually for several years, which sum was only about a quarter of what they might have been expected to pay. In the Walsden accounts, from 1780, are annual entries of payments to the 'Surveyor of ye Turnpike Rd', eg in 1782, £4 19s 8d from the Henshaw side and £3 13s from the Inchfield side. (The story is told in detail in the Watson-Gledhill articles.)

Although the local townships were unwilling to make what they saw as excessive contributions towards the cost of the turnpike road, they must have come to appreciate its advantages, as for the first time heavy-wheeled vehicles, carrying coal, cotton, wool and cloth, were able to move freely along the valley bottom. They began to widen their narrow tracks and to make new roads, so that wheeled vehicles could reach the hillside settlements. Road building and widening continued to be an important local industry for the next generation, but 'causeys' were no more. The new vocabulary was 'setting', fitting small rectangular stone setts, and 'boldering', the construction of roads made entirely of small stones to a depth of a foot or even more. The latter used vast quantities of stones, quarried with the aid of gavelocks (large crowbars). The lists of tools in Walsden from 1810 include bouldering mauls. The era of the independent township, its affairs managed by unpaid officers, was coming to an end; in 1860 the Walsden surveyor received '£10 per year of a salary for the next year', including both Henshaw and Inchfield sides.

The Overseers of the Poor

The account books of the overseers of the poor are unrivalled sources of information about the life and condition of the poor during the eighteenth and early nineteenth centuries. From no other documents can such a wealth of detail be gleaned about the paupers and the labouring classes generally, their diet, their clothes, the kind of homes they lived in, and how they fared in times of sickness and other adversity. The office and functions of the overseer were established under the Elizabethan Poor Law Acts of 1572, 1597 and 1601, but no local overseers' records earlier than 1716 have survived. As we have seen with reference to the highways, the upper Calder Valley was in no hurry to follow Tudor legislation on local government, where existing systems were working adequately. In some areas the relief of the poor during the seventeenth century was undertaken, in a desultory way, by the churchwardens. It is possible that the local townships (as distinct from the parish of Halifax and the ancient chapelry of Heptonstall) did not assume responsibility for the poor until after the 1662 Act, which provided for the division of large parishes in the north of England. In effect, this Act made the township the unit for poor law administration, as it already was for law and order and, under the manor of Wakefield, for highways.[19]

The need for an organised system of poor relief was lessened by the operation of private charity. It is noteworthy that of eighteen charities benefiting the Yorkshire section of the valley, which were recorded as still operational by the Charity Commission in 1828, nine had been established in the first half of the seventeenth century. The charities included almshouses, loaves distributed after Sunday morning service to twenty-three poor people at Heptonstall Church, and various allowances in money and kind.[20] Typical of the more modest bequests was that of Henry Pollard, who in his will made in 1608, left 9s a year to the minister of Cross Stone Chapel and 38s a year for the poor of Stansfield. The churchwardens' acounts for 1730 show the money to have been shared amongst thirty-seven paupers.[21]

The overseers levied a poor rate on the annual value of land and buildings, which was used to relieve the impotent poor, apprentice poor children, set the unemployed to work and finance a variety of other tasks. In the first half of the eighteenth century the poor rate was comparatively low, but during the second half, with its growth of industry and population and its frequent wars, together with the setting up of workhouses, there was a sharp increase; for example, the rate in Heptonstall rose from 1s 10d in 1716 to 7s in 1800. The overseers were responsible for orphans and deserted children. When the pauper child was old enough, usually seven, he or she was apprenticed, at the expense of the township, to a master who would agree to teach the child a trade and maintain him or her to the age of twenty-one, or (normally) eighteen in the case of a girl. Children were often apprenticed in another part of the country, so that they would not be a charge on the township in later life. The township also provided a new set of clothes for the apprentice. In 1726 Stansfield spent 19s 1d on apprenticing John Helliwell's son, including 13s 1d for shirts, shoes, stockings, breeches, a coat and a hat.

The following gives the gist of an indenture of apprenticeship:

Entered into 3 May 1748 Between John Sutcliffe & Thos Nowell Churchwarden and overseer of the Poor of Langfield & John Hindson a Poor Child of the said town of the one part and James Marshall a taylor of the other part …

Hindson was put to apprentice until he should reach the age of twenty-four to be taught 'the trade mistery or occupation of a taylor'. James Marshall, in consideration of the sum of £4 10s to be paid in three years time, was:

… to teech Hindson the trade and to provide him with competent meat, drink, washing, lodging and other necessaries meet & fit for an apprentice & provide for him & deliver to his said apprentice two suits of apparole one good & new suit for Sundays or Holy Days and another for working days.

One of the most vexatious problems was bastardy. A woman with an illegitimate child would almost certainly become a charge on the township. The putative father could be ordered by two JPs to pay weekly maintenance, or be committed to the house of correction. The men concerned were often in arrears, and may have absconded, which led the overseers to go to considerable lengths and expense to arrange marriages whenever possible. In 1727-28 the Todmorden and Walsden overseers paid £2 6s for the marriage of John Harrison, including 'his linen'. The 1733 accounts include 1s for a warrant by which Martha Coup named D Robinson as the father of her children, and therefore responsible for their maintenance. The latter was not always easy to collect, as the following entry by Stansfield's overseer shows:

1726 My gate 3 times to Rochdale to entreat of Kershaw to send some money towards maintenance of Sus. Helliwells Bastd child 2s.

On another occasion the Stansfield overseer paid 2s 6d to two men 'for preventing Old Speak marrying a poor woman relieved of the town of Heptonstall'. (Otherwise the woman would have become a charge on the township of Stansfield.)

Under an Act of 1696, the regular paupers had to wear on their shoulders a cloth badge showing the letter 'P' and the initial letter of the township name. There are many references to badging:

> Todmorden and Walsden: 1733 for badging the poor 4d.
> Stansfield 1752: Cloth to badge the poor and to Wm Dearden for badging them 10d.

In 1801 when Todmorden and Walsden became a township in its own right, separate from Hundersfield, it was resolved 'That all persons in future relieved shall be badged according to the statute of the 8 & 9 of Wm Chap 30 Sect 2 with the letters T_PW with either red or blue cloth'.

Allowances made to paupers in money were of two kinds: regular monthly payments, sometimes called 'constants', made to the old and infirm; and irregular payments, or 'inconstants' (called 'emergencies' in Todmorden and Walsden). The regular allowances varied according to need, but were generally in the range 1s 4d to 4s a month in the early eighteenth century, and 3s to 5s 6d (with some receiving as much as 10s a month) by the end of the century. The irregular payments, made mainly to the people who were sick or temporarily in need, take up the greater part of the accounts. Typical entries are:

> Stansfield: 1726 To Haddin wn his wife were sick 1s 6d;
> 1782: James Greenwood, Height — son a coffin 4s 9d;
> Thos Dyneley for attending Ann Crabtree in time of labour and Phisick 7s.
> Todmorden and Walsden: 1747 Pd to Abr Fielden for 7 months when his wife had born him 2 children at a birth £1 1s.

Payments in kind were also very numerous:

> Stansfield: 1726 For a shirt cloth for Martin Butterworth 2s 4½d;
> For 10 yds of kersey to cloath the Poor att 1s 4d per yd 13s 4d;
> To Martha Law for 2 shifts 2s 6d.
> 1782 To Jenny Crabtree 1 pair of clogs 10d.

In Todmorden and Walsden in 1733, woollen cloth was bought at 1s 7d per yard and distributed to the needy:

> Han. Crossley widow having 3 children 2¾ yard 4s 4½d;
> Sam Crossley feeble 4yd 6s 4d.

Linen cloth was also provided:

> 2¼yd for a shirt to John Fielden.

Canvas cloth was distributed to the poor of Stansfield from the 20s a year left by John Greenwood of Hippins in Stansfield (will dated 1705).

Other payments in kind consisted of coal, bedding, furniture and household utensils. In 1728 Stansfield provided John Draper with a bedstead, 3s and two blankets, a rug and a chaff bed, 8s 3d. In 1733 Todmorden provided a 'Caddow [quilt] for Widow Baron 3s'. Sometimes these goods were given outright, but often they were regarded as being on permanent loan until the pauper died, when they would be taken back into the township's stock.

Rents, rates and taxes were often paid by the township on behalf of paupers. In 1722, rents paid for twenty-four poor persons in the hamlets of Todmorden and Walsden amounted to £14, which was about the average for the years 1720-1730.

The homeless poor occasionally had cottages allotted to them, but were usually lodged with other people, many of whom were themselves paupers. These lodgers, known as tablers in the Todmorden and Walsden accounts, were paid small sums by the township. In 1722 three pauper tablers were paid amounts ranging from £1 to £4 10s. The money was disbursed by the churchwarden, showing that the latter office still had a role in poor relief.

In an emergency the overseer provided board and lodging in his own house, as in the case of Alice, wife of Jon Greenwood of Stansfield, 'maintaining her a month at my own house when in the Fever we could place her nowhere else 10s'.

One of the duties of the overseers was to find work for the able-bodied unemployed, and there are many references to the supply of textile equipment, including cards and 'a pair of looms'. A loom cost Stansfield 18s in 1742 and Langfield 30s in 1793.

An Act of 1723 authorised, but did not require, townships to establish workhouses and to refuse poor relief to paupers declining to enter the house. All of the local townships had workhouses at one time or another during the second half of the eighteenth century, but they did not deter applications for outdoor relief. They provided shelter for the homeless poor, part of the cost being covered by the labour of the inmates. According to Holden, Stansfield set up a workhouse about 1738, but gave it up after two years. Later they had one at Blackshawhead. The township of Hundersfield, of which Todmorden and Walsden was a part, opened a workhouse in June 1732 at a place called Stansfield (not to be confused with the local township), 'whereby ye lay was mightily reduced as may apear by comparing the accounts of last year with this':

1732 Total reimburst	£ 60	10s	1¹/₂d	Lays[rates]	£ 50	15s	2d
Previous year	£102	15s	8d	Lays	£106	13s	7d

Immediate use was made of the new poor house:

1732 For carrying John Stansfield's bedding to the Poor house 6d;
For carrying John Lord and his bedding to the Poor house 1s 6d.

The township had to pay towards the upkeep of the workhouse which it shared with the other constituent parts of Hundersfield, viz Wardleworth, Weurdle and Wardle, Blatchinworth and Calderbrook. Its share of the expenses in 1733, which amounted to £105 3s 9d, was £21 9s 6¹/₂d, fractionally more than one fifth.

It was not until 1801 that Todmorden and Walsden acquired their own workhouse. A house belonging to John Sutcliffe and John Shackleton at Gauxholme was rented for eighteen guineas per annum, the owners to make the house suitable for its new purpose. The overseers for the first year were Anthony Crossley, Todmorden Hall, John Crossley, Scaitcliffe, and Joshua Fielden, Waterside, 'being substantial Householders of the Township'. They were to procure ten cast-iron beds at or near two guineas each, these being better than wooden beds. Each bedstead was to have a chaff bed (straw mattress), two blankets, one sheet, one bolster and one woollen quilt, and 'all kinds of furniture proper for a house' was to be provided, as were 'Cloath & linnen & other apparel for cloathing the Poor'.

From 1765 Langfield used a farm at Horsewood as a workhouse, but gave it up in 1772, when an agreement was entered into with the overseers of the township of Newchurch in Rossendale to use their workhouse at Tunstead for a rent of 27s per annum, plus all the cost of keep. The overseers of Langfield were to receive all the benefits of any work performed by the Langfield paupers. Further records about this

The middle floor of this building, Gauxholme (in this reconstruction drawing), was used as the poorhouse by Todmorden with Walsden from 1801 until the union workhouse was built at Stansfield View in 1879.

arrangement are scanty, but in 1786 the township built its own workhouse at Croft Carr Green for a total cost of £164 12s 1d. This would appear to be the only purpose-built workhouse or poorhouse in the area before the 1834 Poor Law Amendment Act.

Judging by the variety and quantity of food supplied to the local workhouses (we know nothing about the quality of the cooking), the inmates were fed much better than they would have been on outdoor relief, and infinitely better than the paupers in the post-1834 Union workhouses. The Stansfield accounts include beef, pork, potatoes, carrots, wheat flour, meal, malt and treacle. The Langfield inmates in 1801 were provided with 26½lbs of bacon (apparently the staple dish), as well as a sheep's head and heart, potatoes, meal, flour, malt and salt; 1 lb of sugar, 1 lb of currants, and 2 lbs of rice were also bought.

The main principle of the 1601 Poor Law was that each parish or township would be responsible for its own poor. Paupers who were not natives of the township could, if they were classified as vagrants, be arrested, punished and sent back to their place of origin, under a series of punitive laws going back to 1388. The position of paupers who were neither local nor vagrant was unclear until the Act of Settlement of 1662. This provided that any stranger could be removed from a parish or township unless he rented a holding of £10 a year or found security to relieve the township of any expense incurred on his behalf. A further Act of 1691 provided that serving a township office, being bound apprentice there, or (if unmarried) being a year in service there, or paying the township rates, gave the right of settlement. The 1696 Act allowed a poor person to enter another parish or township if he or she brought a 'settlement certificate' from the home township, guaranteeing to take responsibility if the migrant became chargeable to the poor rate.[22] Remaining settlement certificates for the local townships, covering the eighteenth and early nineteenth centuries, are deposited in the Calderdale Archives. They were very carefully preserved, because they could prove to be of value after a considerable lapse of time. An extreme example is the case of a man, aged eighty, removed from Sutton to Heptonstall in 1791, because of a settlement certificate granted to his father in 1737, fifty-four years earlier! Until the law was amended in 1794, people without a settlement in a township (and lacking a settlement certificate) could be moved, by order of a JP, at any time, and not only if they applied for poor relief. The receiving township could appeal to the Quarter Sessions against the removal order, and in 1821 Heptonstall, at variance with Stansfield, sent papers to three lawyers asking for separate opinions. Two said the place of legal settlement was Stansfield, and the other considered it was Heptonstall!

The overseers' accounts are very revealing in respect of the prevalent diseases and ailments of the period, and the remedies used. The poor lived mainly on a diet of oatmeal, skimmed milk and potatoes, and the combination of undernourishment, poor hygiene and inadequate medical attention threw a considerable burden on the overseers. Many of the 'emergency' items, in money or kind, relate to illness. The great scourge of the eighteenth century was smallpox. Until vaccination was introduced, it took a heavy toll in epidemic years. Entries such as the following occur frequently at these times:

> Todmorden and Walsden: 1740 Sept. Pd to Robt Hardman when his children had the pox 3s;
> To John Law when his wife and children were in pox 5s;
> 1741 Apr To Abm Feber when his child had smallpox 2s;
> 1747 Pd to Thos Newall when his wife and children were all Bidley of the pox 15s;
> Pd to John Wilde when his children was all badley of the smallpox 5s.

There does not appear to have been a resident doctor in the area during the greater part of the eighteenth century, and in consequence physicians were called in from either Burnley or Halifax, or, occasionally, from Elland. By 1791, however, Dr Heyworth was serving as medical officer for the township of Langfield, and whereas the doctors hitherto called into service submitted separate accounts for each patient, he sent a bill to cover all the paupers he had attended over a given period. From September 1791 to January 1792 he appears to have had an easy passage; during these four months he had administered 'three Blister Plasters, three Stimulating Mixtures, two Pots of Digestive Liniment, a Rubbing Bottle, and some Healing Salve', his total bill amounting to only 12s 10½d.[23]

In addition to paying for midwives and christenings, the overseers paid for pauper funerals, and even for a simple meal at such times, the average total cost to the township being about 10s, the amount paid by Stansfield in 1764 for the burial of George Crowther. Todmorden and Walsden, in 1733, paid for the funeral of the wife and two children of a pauper called Midgley, and for the oldest son and youngest child of James Clayton. One particular Todmorden family's misfortunes, in 1738, can be traced. James Helliwell initially received 17s during illness, but a second payment of £1 19s 6d covered further illness plus his burial. At about the same time 2s was paid for his child's coffin. His widow subsequently received 14s towards her house rent. She was obviously destitute as, after receiving further help in milk, butter and coal, she was moved to the poor house. Her goods were sold and the £4 12s 4d raised was used to offset the money the family had received from the township.

The overseers' accounts can throw light on other aspects of the local economy. For example, in 1740 Stansfield recorded the winnowing, drying in a kiln, and grinding of eight loads of corn, together with 'a quart of ale for dryer, four pounds of beef for our dinners at mill, and 6 quarts of ale at mill'. Apart from indicating that the chance of a quart of ale on the township was never passed up, these entries show clearly that in some years the local crop of 'corn' could not be ripened fully in the field, and had to be artificially dried in a kiln before being taken to the mill. The crop would be oats, as no other grain crop could be grown in the local climatic conditions, and the mill would be either Stansfield Mill (later known as the Old Corn Mill), Halifax Road, or Hudson Mill on the River Colden just below Jack Bridge.

A study of the overseers' accounts leaves the distinct impression that their work, often difficult and tedious, was done very conscientiously, and with compassion. This work was unremunerated, at least until 1814, when Heptonstall began to employ a paid overseer at an annual stipend of £20-£30 a year. At the end of their year of office, the overseers had to submit their accounts to be passed by two JPs, as well as by the township 'vestry'. This was an assembly of the leading men of the community, which took its name from the church vestry in which its meetings were often held, especially where the ecclesiastical parish was also the local government unit. Perhaps in anticipation of this, the Langfield overseer for 1777-78 headed his accounts 'Mistakes are asily made', and at the end of his year of office, they were endorsed 'The accounts examined and allowed by us Errors excepted'! There had probably been some such committee for centuries, to manage the affairs of the township within the manor. Evidence in the court rolls of the 'sworn men' of each township, who presented the business relating to their locality, suggests the existence of some local community organisation.

The operation of poor relief strengthened the identification of local people with their township. The settlement laws did this for the 'labouring poor', not only the regular paupers, but also the many people who might have to turn to the overseers for temporary help in bad times or for a bottle of a patent medicine in sickness. The responsibilities of office did the same for the substantial men of the township. This factor was at the root of the local opposition to the new poor law of 1834 (described in Chapter 8). The autonomy of the township was part of the fabric of community life, and was not going to be surrendered without a struggle.

6

The Evangelical Revival and Quaker Influences

The later years of the seventeenth century saw the emergence of three main groups of Dissenters — the Quakers, the Particular Baptists, and the congregations which were labelled Presbyterians but may in some cases have been Independent. Each sect in the course of time lost its crusading zeal. The Quakers wanted nothing more than to be left in peace, and the other two groups became inhibited by the Calvinist doctrine that salvation was ordained only for the elect.[1]

Archbishop Herring's visitation returns of 1743 give a detailed picture of organised religious life in the area, as reported by the local Church of England clergy.[2] The affiliations of local families were given as follows:

Chapelry	Total no. of families	Presbyt- erian	Baptist	Quaker
Cross Stone (Stansfield, Langfield)	250	14	7	13

(The township of Todmorden with Walsden, being in Lancashire and in the Diocese of Chester, was not included in these returns, but the Quakers are known to have been relatively strong in the township at this time. Branches of the Fielden family lived at Swineshead, Bottomley, Hollingworth, Todmorden Hall and Edge End, and the Greenwoods of similar persuasion held the Longfield estates in Langfield and Stones in Todmorden.[3])

Details of Dissenting meeting houses were given as follows:

Denom	Location	Chapelry	Minister /Leader	Frequency of mtgs	Est nos attdg
Presbyterian	Benthead Stansfield	Cross Stone	Robert Hesketh	Every Sunday	130
Baptist	Rodhill End Stansfield	Cross Stone	Henry Lord	Every Sunday	50
Quaker	Shoebread Langfield	Cross Stone	John Varley	Every Sun & Thur	100
Baptist	Stone Slack Heptonstall	Heptsl	David Crossley & Richard Thomas	Alternate Sundays	30

According to Baptist sources, Richard Thomas was the pastor of both Rodhill End and Stone Slack.[4] David Crossley was pastor of a Baptist chapel in the Rossendale

Valley (where he died in 1744).[5] Henry Lord may have been one of the elders at Rodhill End.

If the above statistics are correct, only about fourteen per cent of the families in the Chapelry of Cross Stone were Dissenters in 1743. This does not mean, however, that the remainder were devout members of the Church of England. The clergy were not asked to give figures of attendances at their own churches, but only about nine per cent of those described as 'communicants' actually received Easter Communion at Cross Stone, when 'communion' was only celebrated twice a year. If the Dissenters are excluded, the figure rises to about eleven per cent; even allowing for the numbers of people, apparently substantial, who had not yet been confirmed, there is no evidence of a great devotion to the sacrament.

Evangelical Revival

The main pioneers of Methodism in the upper Calder Valley were two men markedly different in style and background, William Grimshaw and William Darney. Grimshaw (1708-63) was appointed curate of Todmorden in 1731, shortly after graduating from Cambridge. He was married twice but in both cases only briefly. His first wife (1735) was Sarah Sutcliffe, a young widow and daughter of John Lockwood of Ewood in Midgley township; she died in 1739. His second wife (1741) was Elizabeth, daughter of Henry Cockcroft of Mayroyd in Wadsworth; she died in 1746.

In 1746 Grimshaw became perpetual curate of Haworth. He was already aware of, and had begun to respond to, the stirrings of the Evangelical Revival, and he launched himself enthusiastically into the new movement at Haworth:

> My church began to be crowded, insomuch that many were obliged to stand out of doors. Here, as in other places, it was amazing to hear and see what weeping, roaring and agonies many people were seized with at the apprehension of their sinful state and the wrath of God.[6]

William Darney was described in the mid-1750s as:

> ... a man of prodigious size, and, when he chose, of a terrific countenance ... a man possessing few personal attractions, of a broad Scottish dialect, and, when dwelling on the terrors of the Lord, terrible to behold; but a man of deep piety, strong sense and burning zeal.[7]

Darney's conversion may have resulted from a slightly earlier revivalist movement in Scotland. He became an itinerant preacher in October 1741. In the winter of 1743/44 he was described as often preaching in the Pudsey area, 'a man commonly called Scotch Will, who carrys a Pack, Sells Hankerchers, Stockings, etc ...'.[8]

Darney preached in several places in the upper Calder Valley, and formed his followers into societies. The earliest of these seems to have been one at Gauxholme, near Todmorden, formed with ten members in 1744. Other local societies were established at Walsden, Shore and Cross Stone.[9]

The partnership between Grimshaw and Darney began in 1744. At that time neither had any formal link with John and Charles Wesley, and in 1746 Darney tried to interest Benjamin Ingham in his societies. The latter was another Church of England minister, active in the Evangelical Revival, whose followers in due course formed the Inghamite Connexion. When Ingham declined the invitation, Darney turned to the Wesleys. Charles Wesley visited William Grimshaw and toured Darney's societies in January

1747, and John Wesley followed suit four months later. From this point Grimshaw became an active Methodist, and Darney's societies were drawn into the Methodist fold.[10]

On his visit in May 1747, John Wesley preached at Shore, 'to a loving, simple-hearted people', and then climbed Todmorden Edge, 'where I called a serious people to "repent and believe the Gospel" '.[11] From 1747 William Grimshaw combined his pastoral work at Haworth with the duties of visiting and supervising Methodist societies in Lancashire and the West Riding. Wesley thought very highly of Grimshaw, whom he described as 'an Israelite indeed. A few such as him would make a nation tremble. He carries fire wherever he goes.' John Wesley made Grimshaw the supervisor of the 'Haworth Round', one of the early Methodist circuits which stretched from Todmorden to Whitehaven in Cumberland.[12]

John Wesley returned to the district in August 1748, when as part of his tour he preached at Todmorden Edge where he found, as at other places, 'a large and serious congregation'.[13]

John Wesley's visits, although relatively infrequent, served both to encourage the committed Methodists, and to increase the flow of converts. He did not return for nearly four years, although his brother Charles came in the meantime. The main work of building Methodism in the district was done by Grimshaw, Darney, and other lay preachers such as John Nelson and Thomas Mitchell of Bingley.

The Methodist movement was both spreading and consolidating in the upper Calder Valley, through a combination of both spiritual and organisational factors. The impact of the fervour and devotion of the pioneering preachers, willing to face great hardships and even physical dangers to carry their message to the people, was reinforced by the central doctrinal tenet of Methodism — 'He died to save us all'. John Wesley rejected the twin concepts of high Calvinism — that salvation was reserved to a predestined elect, and that the 'saints' could not fall from grace. The personal struggle to achieve Wesley's ideal of 'Christian perfection' might be hard, but the road to salvation was closed to no one. Charles Wesley's hymns provided powerful emotional support.[14]

John Wesley was not only a great preacher, he was also an organiser of genius; he brought order and discipline to the loosely-knit groups gathered together by men such as Darney. Three levels of organisation developed: the bands or classes which were small groups meeting weekly under a designated leader for guidance and the exchange of spiritual testimony; the Societies, consisting of the Methodists of a particular place, such as Shore; and the Circuits, often known in the early days as the Rounds. The Haworth Round pioneered the system of quarterly circuit meetings which soon became the general practice. The earliest quarterly meeting on record was convened by Grimshaw at Todmorden Edge on the 18th October 1748.[15]

By drawing on the latent capacity of ordinary men to preach, teach and organise — in some cases applying the arts learned in township government — the Methodists were able to bring the gospel to many of the scattered settlements. Two classes of lay preacher emerged: those who preached within their own localities but continued with their normal work; and the full-time preachers, who ranged over a wide area and became known as travelling preachers or itinerants. The latter were supported by the circuits and societies, through the provision of food, clothing, shelter and small money payments.

Lay participation did not, however, mean democracy, which was anathema to John Wesley. He ruled Methodism as an absolute monarch. He and his brother Charles were determined to purge the movement of preachers who were immoral, heretical or grossly incompetent. They wanted to control the appointment of all full-time preachers, and have prospective local preachers examined 'both as to grace and gifts' by 'assistants' (superintendents) such as Grimshaw or by approved full-time preachers.[16]

William Darney caused the Wesleys continuing concern, through his heretical tendencies, preaching style and erratic behavour. He clung stubbornly to some Calvinistic ideas, especially the doctrine of 'the perseverance of the saints'. On one occasion he was standing on a barrel to preach, declaring that the saints could never fall, when the combination of his considerable weight and his physical style of preaching brought him crashing through the top of the barrel.[17]

In January 1749 John Wesley asked two of his leading itinerant preachers in the north, John Bennet and John Nelson, to keep an eye on 'William Darney's Societies'.[18] Two years later Charles Wesley was invited by his brother to tour the country for the purpose of 'purging the preachers' and getting rid of those who were unsatisfactory.

A close look at William Darney convinced Charles Wesley that 'Scotch Will' should be one of the victims of the purge, but Grimshaw argued that Darney's homespun style suited the local people. Charles reluctantly agreed to reprieve him, but on the conditions that he neither abused nor begged from the people, and did not use his doggerel hymns. Darney had annoyed Charles Wesley, the great hymn-writer, by publishing a collection of over 200 hymns.[19] One hymn of 104 verses, intended to be read rather than sung, included the following:

In Heptonstall the Parish through
the Gospel still doth spread;
And here and there there are a few
who on the Saviour fed.

Near Todmorden our blessed Lord
a church hath planted there;
The pillars stand firm to his word,
his goodness they declare.[20]

A few years later Darney was moved from the Pennines, and served in other parts of the country.

John Wesley came twice to the upper Calder Valley in 1752. On his second visit in June he spoke 'on the side of a mountain' at Todmorden 'to a large and earnest congregation'. On this visit he noted that two of his clerical opponents had been brought low, one of whom, Robert Hargreaves, curate of Todmorden, who had denounced the Methodists as 'rogues and knaves and scabbed sheep', was 'slowly recovering from a violent fit of the palsy, with which he was struck immediately after he had been preaching a virulent sermon against the Methodists'. Hargreaves had been on bad terms with Grimshaw and the Methodists for several years, and they had used some uncomplimentary language about him. He resented the irregular evangelism of his predecessor in his own chapelry, especially as it had cost him most of his congregation. Hargreaves had another stroke in 1757, and was still incapacitated seven years later.[21]

At the end of May 1753 Wesley preached at Heptonstall and at General Wood, near Todmorden, where a shade had to be erected for him on 'the hottest afternoon I ever remember in England'. Two years later he was back in action near Todmorden, apparently at Mankinholes. 'The people stood, row above row, on the side of the mountain. They were rough enough in outward appearance; but their hearts were as melting wax.'[22]

The Methodists, growing in strength year by year, occupied an uneasy position in the religious life of the country; John Wesley, and to an even greater extent his brother Charles, insisted that the Methodists were part of the Church of England, in which they were both ordained ministers. Methodist converts were encouraged to attend their parish church. Although buildings were adapted or built for Methodist services, there was to be no clash with the times of local Anglican services. Some Methodist chapels were licensed as Dissenting meeting houses as a legal precaution, because Methodist services could be technically illegal under the Conventicle and Five Mile Acts, which were not repealed until 1812. The Wesleys, however, wanted nothing to do with the Dissenting sects, eg the Baptists and Presbyterians. Charles Wesley told John Nelson, a personal friend, that, rather than see him become a dissenting minister, 'I wish to see thee smiling in thy coffin'.[23]

On the other hand, many of the Anglican clergy rejected Methodism. In the 1764 returns to Archbishop Drummond's visitation enquiry, the vicar of Halifax and the curates of Luddenden and Sowerby Bridge — although not their colleagues at Cross Stone, Heptonstall and Sowerby — included the Methodists with the dissenting sects.[24] There is little doubt that, for most committed Methodists in the upper Calder Valley, their religious life was firmly centred on the local Methodist chapel or meeting house, even if they might occasionally go, singly or in a body, to the Anglican church.

The Evangelical Revival had a powerful impact on the Dissenting churches of the valley. In the above return John Law, curate of Cross Stone, estimated that, of 166 families in his chapelry, one third were Dissenters and that of about 600 communicants only 45 took communion the previous Easter.

From the 1760s the local Baptist cause was stimulated by the work of John Fawcett and Dan Taylor. Fawcett was appointed minister of Wainsgate Particular (ie Calvinist) Baptist Chapel in 1764. Taylor, a coalminer from Northowram, joined the Methodists at the age of twenty and soon became a local preacher. Doubts about doctrinal issues and resentment at John Wesley's authoritarian rule led him to defect in 1762 and establish a small, and at first undenominational, chapel in Wadsworth township.[25]

Dan Taylor became convinced of the propriety of 'believer's baptism', as opposed to the baptism of infants, but could not accept the Calvinist doctrine of predestination. He therefore made contact with the General Baptists, who were not Calvinist, was ordained, and in December 1764 opened a new, small chapel at Birchcliffe, above Hebden Bridge. He did some of the building work himself, but found time to write an *Elegy on the Rev Wm Grimshaw of Haworth*, following the latter's death in 1763.[26]

Taylor formed a warm and lasting friendship with John Fawcett, who was a liberal Calvinist with views on salvation nearer to Taylor's position than was usual with Particular Baptists. They studied together, admonished their followers when doctrinal differences led to squabbling, and combined to form the Heptonstall Book Society, a circulating library, in 1769.

Dan Taylor played an active role in the national affairs of the General Baptists, but soon formed the opinion that he had attached himself to a declining cause. The General Baptists were paralysed by doctrinal controversies, with many of them drifting towards the Unitarian position. Taylor and a few allies decided to form the General Baptist New Connexion, which was launched in London in June 1770. It combined non-Calvinist Baptist orthodoxy with two characteristics of the Methodist movement, evangelical zeal and a strong corporate sense, the latter expressed through an annual delegate meeting and a district conference. Dan Taylor was elected to the chair of the annual meeting in every year except one until his death in 1816.[27]

After a visit to Todmorden in 1756, Charles Wesley wrote less than charitably of the local Baptists as 'a carnal, cavilling, contentious sect, always watching to steal away our children, and make them as dead as themselves'.[28] The Methodists now faced serious competition from the revitalised Dissenting sects — Independents around Halifax and Baptists at the upper end of Calderdale. The Methodists still had some advantages in organisation, not being dependent on either chapels or ordained ministers, and they had a firm grip on some of the smaller settlements. For example, at Gauxholme, near Todmorden, where Wesley had preached in 1757 and 1759, there was in 1763 a society of forty-seven members.[29]

By the 1770s, Wesley was facing much less opposition from the local Anglican clergy, and in 1774 he preached in Heptonstall Church at the invitation of Rev Tobit Sutcliffe. Five years later he preached in the same church again, and in 1780 and 1782 he had the use of both Heptonstall and Todmorden churches. The growth of Methodism had made it expedient, in 1776, to divide the Haworth Round into the Colne Circuit, which included most of the upper Calder Valley, and the Keighley Circuit, including Halifax.[30]

In the meantime Dan Taylor and John Fawcett were continuing their fruitful pastorates in the Baptist cause. Taylor preached at several places away from Birchcliffe, frequently at Shore near Todmorden, described by Adam Taylor as 'a wild, uncultivated and obscure place ... this extremity of the desert ...'. In August/September 1777 a new chapel was opened at Shore.[31]

Meanwhile the oldest Particular Baptist communities in the valley, at Rodhill End and Stone Slack, were in decay. When Rev Richard Thomas died in 1772, it was decided that the congregation at Stone Slack was too small to give any support to a regular minister. John Fawcett agreed to preach there every fourth Sunday. Rodhill End closed in 1783. The Presbyterians of Benthead (Chapelhouses, Eastwood) in Stansfield were also in decline.[32] The Independents, who shared the same doctrines but had different ideas on church government (believing in congregational independence — they later became known as Congregationalists), were greatly influenced by the Evangelical Revival, while Presbyterian ministers were increasingly drawn towards Unitarianism. For the latter reason Rev David Simpson was driven out of Eastwood about 1784. The affiliations of the next few, short-lived, pastorates are unknown, but Rev James Henderson (1792-1804) left a church of only four full members. The life of the chapel was revived by students of the Independent Academy at Idle, near Bradford, one of whom, Rev James Scott, came as minister in 1807 and built a new Independent chapel lower down the hillside at Myrtle Grove.[33]

With the exception of the Quakers, who worshipped at Shoebroad Meeting House in Langfield, all the Dissenting groups existing in the early eighteenth century had been affected by the Evangelical Revival. The Inghamites, who had a society at Todmorden — they built Stansfield New Chapel at the bottom of Ferney Lee Road in 1798 — were, of course, products of the Revival as followers of Benjamin Ingham.[34]

John Wesley paid several visits to the upper Calder Valley in his old age. Persecution had stopped. Local churches were freely offered for his use, although they sometimes had to be declined because of the size of the crowds who gathered to hear him. He still urged Methodists to attend their parish churches, although in 1784 he had signalled the inevitability of a break with the Church of England by ordaining ministers to serve in North America. In the following year he ordained three more men for Scotland.[35]

In 1786 Wesley preached:

at ten in Heptonstall church (the ugliest I know); and in the afternoon at Todmorden church. How changed are both the place and the people since I saw them first! 'Lo, the smiling fields are glad; and the human savages are tame!'.[36]

Wesley came to Todmorden Church again in 1788 and 'found uncommon liberty among those poor mountaineers'. He returned for the last time in the spring of 1790 and died in London on the 2nd March 1791, aged eighty-eight. He had preached over 40,000 sermons and travelled an estimated quarter of a million miles.[37]

The Evangelical Revival had transformed the religious life of the district; the quantitative change in provision was itself impressive. In 1740 Todmorden had two Anglican churches and three Dissenting chapels; at Wesley's death there were — in addition to the two Anglican churches — two Baptist chapels, one Independent chapel, a Quaker meeting house, an Inghamite chapel, a Methodist chapel at Doghouse and other buildings used for Methodist worship. Most of the people were now within relatively easy reach of some place of worship.

Moreover, the prevalence of Dissent and, especially, of Methodism meant that substantial numbers of people were actively involved in the business of their religious societies — as stewards, preachers, class leaders, Sunday school teachers and in other ways — and so had a chance to exercise and to develop their talents. The spiritual temperature had been raised, although it tended to fluctuate according to the abilities and personalities of the leading preachers. Hymn-singing was enjoyable as well as uplifting, and powerful sermons could sweep people up into the exciting, if sometimes frightening, world 'of the aching sorrows of sin, the throbbing joys of salvation'.[38]

The contribution of Methodism and of the Dissenting sects, revitalised by the Evangelical Revival, to the economic achievements of the Industrial Revolution is immeasurable, but undoubtedly considerable. Hard work, persistence, sobriety and thrift were virtues which paid off materially as well as spiritually. The spiritual engine of Methodism was driven by the boundless energy of the reformed individual, his belief in his own potential powerfully enhanced by the pursuit of the Wesleyan ideal of 'Christian perfection'. The same energy could drive the industrial engine on to spectacular business success. John Wesley's compassion, as demonstrated in his attitude to slavery, to prisoners and to the sick, did not extend to any general theory of social obligation. In his writings, economic distress is largely the consequence of individual moral failings, a convenient view of the world for an industrialist who was thrusting ahead with little regard for the well-being of others. In his own lifetime Wesley noticed that Methodists were accumulating wealth, and warned them against its spiritual dangers.[39] It is no coincidence that many of the successful mill-owners in the upper Calder Valley were active nonconformists, to use the term which emerged to embrace Methodism and the older Dissenting sects.

Quaker Influences

The development of Todmorden cannot be appreciated without reference to the part played by some of the families who were members of the Society of Friends or Quakers. Their development as a religious sect has been described earlier. The nature of their faith, under which they refused to take oaths, bear arms or pay tithes, incurred the wrath of the authorities and made them the most severely persecuted of all the Dissenting sects. The universities and professions, such as the law, were closed to them. Therefore they made their way by other means — trade, industry, landholding, banking etc — and it is in these ways that they made an enormous contribution to the life of the district.

By looking in greater detail at two of our local Quaker families, the Fieldens and

Lower Longfield Farm (a reconstuction drawing) was completely rebuilt by Quaker John Greenwood, replacing a previous timber-framed house.

the Greenwoods, we can reveal something of their way of life and their influence locally in the seventeenth and eighteenth centuries.

There have been Fieldens in Todmorden since at least the sixteenth century. In 1561, the earl of Derby sold to James Fielden, Robert Fielden his brother, Edmund Kershaw and Edward Crossley, six messuages and the tenements called Bottomley, which were held in fee of the queen by suit of service to the manor of Rochdale of 10s 2d per year. James Fielden also held other lands at Bottomley by payment of 2s 6d a year to the lord of the manor of Rochdale.[40] James and his wife, Cisley, were settled at Bottomley in Walsden and had two sons, Jeffrie and James. Jeffrie's son, also James, and his wife Isabel had two daughters, Mary and Elizabeth, but James died before Elizabeth was born. When he died in 1594, both his uncle James and grandmother Cisley were still living. In his will he decreed that if his unborn child was a son, he should inherit the full estate when he was of 'full age', ie twenty-one, and at that time pay his sister Mary £20. If the child was a daughter, the two sisters were to share the estate between them. His uncle James died childless in 1602, leaving his estate to his wife Elizabeth, and after her death to be shared equally between his two nieces, the above-mentioned Mary and Elizabeth.[41]

The Fieldens continued to live at Bottomley for many generations and the niece Elizabeth became an important link in the story.

Meanwhile, another Fielden had come into the district. About 1580, Nicholas Fielden of Heyhouses, near Sabden in the Parish of Whalley, purchased a messuage

Middle Longfield Farm (a reconstruction drawing). William Greenwood added the porch in 1700, incorporating his initials with the date.

in Hundersfield from John Stansfield.[42] In 1581 he held fifty acres of freehold land in Hundersfield and Cliviger, together with house and buildings. This estate is described as 'A messuage and three tenements called the Maggott Holme and Cowbanke with several closes adjacent the Common on ye River Calder'.[43] The only place where Todmorden (part of Hundersfield) and Cliviger come together near the Calder is now known as Cornholme, where the southern hillside is still called 'Bonks' and Maggott Holme is known as Bridge End, near the present church.[44] Some of this land, which, as it straddled the river, was part in Stansfield and part in Todmorden and Cliviger, came from John Stansfield at about the same time as Nicholas married Christobel Stansfield, daughter and co-heiress of John Stansfield of Hartley Royd in Stansfield.[45] Later they moved to Inchfield, taking another estate by a deed dated 1612. Judging by its description in the 1626 *Manor Survey*, this would seem to have been Clough Farm, near the site of the original railway station at Walsden. It disappeared when the railway was built, but is clearly marked on a map of 1792 which was drawn up when the Rochdale Canal was being planned (see page 119).

Nicholas and Christobel had five sons and a daughter. The eldest son, John, and younger sons, Joshua and Anthony, inherited their mother's estate in Stansfield, thus introducing the Fieldens into the Shore area, where they were influential for many years. The second son, Abraham, married Elizabeth Fielden of Bottomley mentioned above, thus uniting two branches of the Fielden families, and they inherited Nicholas's

Edge End Farm, Todmorden, was the birthplace in 1748 of Joshua Fielden, founder of the Fielden cotton enterprise at Waterside. A close look at the courses of stonework shows that the building has been extended twice.

estate at Clough in Inchfield. Eventually Elizabeth received her sister Mary's half of the family home at Bottomley, which, with her own half, she wished to leave to her youngest son Joshua, and this was confirmed by his father Abraham's will in 1645.[46]

So the Fieldens were back at Bottomley and the name Joshua had been introduced into this particular line of the family. In 1656 Joshua married Martha Greenwood of North Hollingworth in Walsden. They became Quakers, and suffered the financial penalties incurred in the practice of their faith. In 1685 they and their son had pewter and a Bible, worth together 17s, seized in lieu of the tithes which they refused to pay to the 'steeplehouse', as Quakers called the parish churches. In the previous year, for holding a Quaker meeting, Joshua saw some of the bedding and a brass mortar taken to pay a fine of 5s.[47]

Joshua and Martha had six sons and one daughter, all of whom married within the Quaker faith. The middle son Samuel joined his elder brother Nicholas at Edge End Farm, sharing in the mixed economy of farming with woollen textiles which was predominant in the area. He later lived with his younger brother John at Todmorden Hall, bought from the last branch of the Radcliffe family. Samuel married Elizabeth Veepon of Briercliffe near Burnley in 1703.[48]

When brother John married Tamar Halstead of Erringden in 1707, Samuel and his family moved to Flailcroft Farm where, two months later, their second son Joshua was born. Joshua eventually moved to Edge End, where he and his wife Mary brought up their family, naming their second son, born in 1748, Joshua. In 1771, this son

Joshua married Jenny Greenwood in the Quaker Meeting House at Shoebroad, and was the founder of the Fielden enterprises at Waterside.

He owed some of his substance to his great-uncle, John of Todmorden Hall, who developed a prosperous cloth merchanting business. The steps to his 'takkin-in shop' are still at the rear of the hall. That he was an extremely interesting person can be gleaned from his 'day book' (a diary cum account book) which has survived and covers the years 1723 to 1734. He was a staunch Quaker and served as an itinerant minister, attending meetings in Cheshire, Lancashire and Yorkshire. In October 1698, the minutes of the Brighouse Meeting recorded that the 'ffriends of Mankinhole Meeting ordered to give John ffielden a certificate as to their freedom and unity wth him in his visiting ffriends in ye north for a month or six weeks of time'.[49] He travelled to meetings at York accompanied by his wife Tamar, both on horseback. He frequently ment-

The 'takkin'-in' steps at the rear of Todmorden Hall were constructed when John Fielden (died 1734) owned the hall.

ions meetings at Harod Well (Highroad Well) near Halifax. He was a man of great energy, out on his horse virtually every day. In his prosperous business he dealt directly with John Dorville of Amsterdam, to whom he sold cloth via the port of Hull, to which packhorses carried his cloth, mainly woollen kerseys. They were left in the 'white' (untreated) as Holland was well known for dyeing cloth.

A record of the purchase of some fire irons, cast to his own specification at a cost of 32s, has a distinctively Quaker flavour. 'The 22 MO/12 1723/24 pd at Holm Chapell [Cliviger] to the Clark of the furnace for 2 long piggs for the back of the fire'.[50] Quakers used numbers for the day and the month, to avoid using the names of pagan deities (eg March, from Mars). Until 1752 the new year began on the feast of Annunciation, the 25th March, therefore March was month 12. In Western Europe it began on the 1st January, so businessmen often put dates between January and March in double style, eg 1723/24.

In addition to his own Todmorden Hall estate, John Fielden shared, with his brother Nicholas of Edge End, the ownership of that 'one drying killn, watercorn milln and raising mill, commonly called Gauxholme Milln'.[51] Nicholas's first wife died in 1711, leaving him with three young children, Ann, Nicholas, and William. He married a second time, but died himself soon afterwards in 1714. John then continued to take responsibility for the children, and he and Tamar nursed his nephew Nicholas who died in 1729, which so upset him that he was unable to complete the entry of the death in his day book but left off in mid-sentence. He then took full control of Gauxholme mill, running Nicholas's half for the two remaining children Ann and William. John's sister Hannah had married Quaker Joseph Whalley of Kilnhurst, who inherited his father's house at Southfield, Great Marsden, and nephew William was apprenticed to the cloth trade there with the Whalley family. During a smallpox epidemic, William became a victim. He developed scabs in his hair, which was cut off 'for the best course as his head was scabby', and his uncle John bought him 'a little wig at York to cover his head withal'.

When John Fielden died in 1734, childless, he left his estate to his nephews and nieces on a life interest only. The title to the estate was left to the children of his nephews and nieces. One of these, John's great-nephew Joshua Fielden, was the founder of Waterside. John's will was written by William Greenwood of Longfield, who was his cousin and a member of the second influential Quaker family who had much to contribute to the development of Todmorden.

Mention has already been made of the estate of the Langfield family, which in time transferred to the Radcliffes of Todmorden Hall. During the second half of the seventeenth century this estate, both by purchase and inheritance, came into the possession of the Greenwoods, who already owned other property in the district.

The Greenwoods were staunch Quakers. John Greenwood, the first owner, was brother to Martha Greenwood, mentioned before, who married Joshua Fielden of Bottomley in 1656 and was the mother of John Fielden of Todmorden Hall. By this time there were three separate messuages on the Langfield estate (still in existence) — Further or Higher Longfield, Middle Longfield and Lower Longfield.

John Greenwood rebuilt Lower Longfield as it stands today. As was customary during the seventeenth century, he rebuilt it in stone, replacing the original timber-framed house. Sometimes, when rebuilding, the timber framing was left in place, the plasterwork between the timbers was replaced with stone and then the entire house refaced with stone. This was often a necessary procedure when the family had to live in the house whilst rebuilding was in progress. At Lower Longfield, however, John

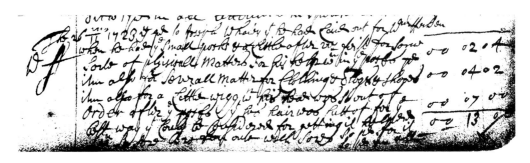

26. 11. 1723. Then paid to Joseph Whaley that he had laid out for Wm ffielden
when he had the small pocks and a little after viz first for some
sorte of phisicall matters for his help when in the pocks.   00   02   04
item also for severall matter for clothing and clogs and shooes   00   04   02
item also for a little wigg when his head was so out of
order after the pocks that his hair was cutt of for the   00   07   00
best way that could be considered for getting it helped
when so sore broken out with sores So paid for it   00   13   06
So paid in all

In this extract from the day book of John Fielden of Todmorden Hall, the William Fielden mentioned was his nephew, who eventually migrated to America, where he founded a branch of the Fielden family.

The White Hart Inn, circa 1880. Rebuilt as the 'New Inn' by John Fielden of Todmorden Hall, it was demolished in 1935 and replaced by the present mock-tudor building. The area in front of the inn was Todmorden's original market place.

and his wife, Ann, were able to move out to other property, so the rebuilding was total. The fine porch with its motif 'I.G.A. 1684' records the date of the new house. The I is for John, the A for Ann and the G for the family name, Greenwood.

John's son William left his mark on Middle Longfield Farm, where he lived as a bachelor before his father's death. He added a porch incorporating the date 1700 and his initials WG. Both Lower and Middle Longfield are typical of the larger houses of the period. The porch gives entry to a cross passage leading to the rear of the house. On one side of the passage are the service rooms, and on the other side the main housebody with parlour beyond. Above all these rooms are the upper rooms, known as chambers. Lower Longfield has a separate barn, whilst Middle Longfield has its original barn attached.

The aisled barn at Middle Longfield is a good example of its type. Constructed in the sixteenth century, it has two parallel rows of vertical wooden posts/pillars, down opposite lengths of the rectangular barn, each row creating an aisle between it and the outer stone wall. These posts, which support the roof beams, were erected upside-down with the root part of the tree at the top and the base mounted on stone. This was done to protect the posts from rotting.

William Greenwood became a wealthy man. Some idea of his wealth in real terms can be gained by comparison with general wage rates of the period. This was the time when John Fielden of Todmorden Hall was rebuilding the New Inn (White Hart) and paying the skilled builder 3s per week and the labourer 2s; William Greenwood's surplus was over 100 shillings per week. Much of his income came from rented property and from loans, on which he usually charged 4½%. For the years 1731 to 1735, his account books show a total profit of £1,322, clear of all living and business expenses. In 1717 he bought the Stones estate from Roger Mainwaring, the last representative of the Radcliffes of Todmorden Hall. He also acted as a lawyer, drafting and writing many of the local Quaker wills.

His second son William inherited Stones, and in 1746 rebuilt it in the Georgian style as it is today. In the Greenwood tradition, his initials and date were carved above the main entrance, but additionally he included a poem of invitation to his guests:

> Friend I dwell here,
> And have in store
> A little worldly pelf,
> Which on my friend
> I keep to spend,
> As well as on myself.
> Whatever fare
> Thou findest here,
> Take welcome for the best.
> That having got,
> Disdain thou not
> For wanting of the rest.

William Greenwood's poem above the door at Stones House.

He and his brothers, John and Ambrose, were chief financial supporters of the turnpike roads.

When William died in 1783, Joshua Fielden, his distant cousin and also a Quaker, had just begun his cotton enterprise at Waterside. Todmorden was poised to develop as an industrial town and, when it did, much of it was built on land which belonged to the Greenwood estate, which by that time comprised Longfield farms and Honey Hole, most of Salford, the White Hart and its lands including the site of Christ Church, vicarage, school and parts of Doghouse, the land between Blind Lane and Wellington Road, Stackhills lands to Halifax Road, Inchfield estate, Stones and Stones Wood estate and part of Sourhall lands. As for the rest of the town, the White Platts estate belonged to the Sutcliffes of Stansfield Hall; a branch of the Fieldens had the Old Shop estate; the Knowles family owned the Kilnhurst estate; whilst the Crossleys of Scaitcliffe owned the upper Burnley Road area along with other estates (see page 63.)

The last Greenwood of Stones, William, who died a bachelor at the age of forty-three in 1864, provides an interesting study. He was the grandson of William the rebuilder of Stones. William was wealthy, but more interested in pursuing his own interests than in running his estates. By the age of twenty-four Greenwood was living the life of a retired gentleman, immersing himself in his scientific studies. He joined many societies both locally and further afield, including the Todmorden Botanical Society, Todmorden Harmonic Society, Todmorden Pastoral Aid Society, Todmorden Cricket Club, Todmorden Reading Society, Todmorden Prosecution Society, the Dalton Club in Todmorden, the Art Union in London and, more significantly, the

In 1866, John Fielden commissioned John Gibson, who was building the Unitarian church, to build Dobroyd Castle, and this photograph was taken shortly after completion in 1869.

Manchester Photographic Society and the British Association for the Advancement of Science.

In his garden at Stones he built an observatory complete with telescope. He had his own gasometer in the grounds, the gas being supplied by Fielden Brothers from their works. He built a hot house in the garden to grow, amongst other things, tobacco plants. Over a period of ten to twelve years he maintained meticulous barometric readings.

He was a keen photographer. The daguerreotype camera, in which photographs were taken using an iodine-sensitized silvered plate and mercury vapour, was invented in 1839. By 1840 Greenwood had bought one and was developing his own plates. Evidence from his accounts shows his health beginning to deteriorate. His purchases included a stick, then a crutch, then two crutches. He bought a lot of wine and aerated water. Along with tobacco, which he bought by the pound and cigars by the bundle, he bought hemp seed. He died in 1864 and although, from this distance in time, nothing can be proved, it is possible that he was an early victim of mercury poisoning from inhaling the vapour during his photographic sessions, and he went on to develop cancer of the bone. Smoking hemp seeds could have helped to relieve the pain.

In 1865 the Stones estate was bought by Thomas Fielden. Shortly afterwards he sold it to his brother John, who proceeded to build Dobroyd Castle on part of it.

7

The Early Development of Textile Mills

When the new Halifax Piece Hall was opened on the 1st January 1779, all the cloth sold there from the upper Calder Valley was made, as far as records go, entirely by hand, except for the use of water power in fulling woollen cloth and gig mills (in which teasle-heads mounted on cylinders were used to raise the nap of the cloth). The new turnpike road along the valley bottom made it much easier for manufacturers, such as Joshua Fielden of Edge End and John Sutcliffe of Stansfield Hall, to transport their cloth to the hall for sale. The latter was one of the few owners who had purchased two of the 315 rooms, for £28 4s each, in which to carry on his trade, whilst in 1774 and 1775 the former was buying wool and yarn from a John Royds in Halifax, spending as much as £61 on parcels of wool and £56 on parcels of yarn.[1]

The invention of the flying shuttle by John Kay in 1733 speeded up the weaving process, thereby increasing the number of spinners needed to supply each loom with yarn. The response to this was a series of inventions in the 1760s and 1770s which mechanised the spinning process. The latter, whether done by hand or by the most complicated machinery, has three phases: drawing out a rope of fibres, putting in a twist, and winding the yarn on to a bobbin or similar device. The spinning jenny, devised by James Hargreaves about 1764, was based upon the 'great wheel'. A moveable carriage first drew out and twisted the yarn, and then reversed to wind it on to the bobbins. The roller frame, brought to a workable state by Richard Arkwright in 1769, copied the flyer-and-bobbin action of the Saxony wheel, which spun and wound simultaneously, and replaced the hands of the spinner drawing out the fibres by a set of rollers.

The roller frame, good for making warp yarn, was soon being driven by water wheels, hence its alternative name of 'water frame'. Jennies, more suited to weft, were normally hand-operated. By 1775 Arkwright had laid the foundations of the factory system by devising a series of machines for carding and spinning which could be tended by the cheap labour of women and children. A few years later, Samuel Crompton married the moveable carriage to the rollers to create the 'mule'.

Cotton fibres were easier to process mechanically than wool or flax, and because it had proved difficult to spin good warp yarn on hand-wheels, the inventions created what was for Britain virtually a new industry, making all-cotton cloth. The industry was centred on Manchester, to which Todmorden had easy access via the new turnpike road and so it could henceforth look west for cotton as well as east for wool and worsted. As cotton was the spearhead of the industrial revolution in textiles, this was to have a profound effect upon the industry of Todmorden.

The clothiers of Todmorden were not slow to move into the 'new' cotton industry. The foundations were laid by two members of the Fielden family, both of whom

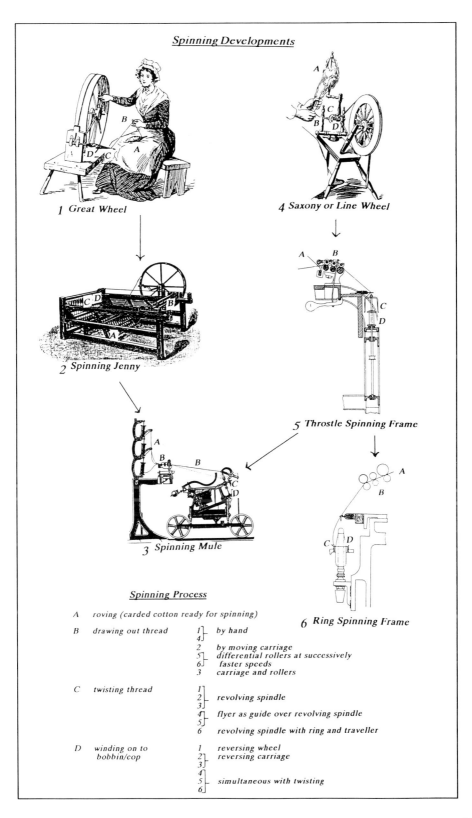

Spinning Developments

1 Great Wheel

4 Saxony or Line Wheel

2 Spinning Jenny

5 Throstle Spinning Frame

3 Spinning Mule

6 Ring Spinning Frame

Spinning Process

A	roving (carded cotton ready for spinning)		
B	drawing out thread	1 } 4	by hand
		2	by moving carriage
		5 } 6	differential rollers at successively faster speeds
		3	carriage and rollers
C	twisting thread	1 } 2 } 3	revolving spindle
		4 } 5	flyer as guide over revolving spindle
		6	revolving spindle with ring and traveller
D	winding on to bobbin/cop	1	reversing wheel
		2 } 3	reversing carriage
		4 } 5 } 6	simultaneous with twisting

came from the ranks of the yeoman clothiers and had been in business as worsted manufacturers. In 1782 Joshua Fielden, of Edge End Farm, began spinning with hand-operated 'jennies' in some converted cottages at Laneside. In 1784 he acquired the leasehold of property at Laneside together with the grant of a spring of water in Swineshead Clough. In two months he had mortgaged his properties for a total of £649 at five per cent interest, and so what became the Fielden enterprises of Waterside were born.[2]

In 1785 John Fielden, son of Samuel Fielden of Swineshead Farm in Langfield, employed another Fielden, William, a mason who may have been a relative, to build Clough Mill in Walsden. Completed in 1786, the mill was three stories high, containing carding and spinning machinery driven by a water wheel (the water being taken from the river at the bottom of Inchfield Fold meadow). At one end of the building was a dwelling house for one of the partners, and the whole was not unlike three or four dwellings of three stories in height.[3] The building was insured for £200 in 1797, the machinery for £200 and the stock for £100. The total insurance had doubled to £1,000 by 1801.[4]

In 1795 a contract, between John Helliwell of Hillhouse, John Ramsbottom of Todmorden and Robert Barker of Royd, was drawn up. Helliwell was to erect a three-storey mill for carding and roving cotton (roving was the first stage of spinning) at Houghstone Clough, otherwise Ratcher. Ramsbottom and Barker were to rent the premises at £22 per year as tenants in common for 21 years. The building was to be at least 12 yards long, and 10 yards wide, the latter being recommended by Arkwright as the width which could be safely spanned by a single beam without the hindrance of supporting pillars. The ground floor was to be made into two cottages, and the first and second floors were each to consist of a single room at least eight feet high to hold the machinery. The water wheel, eleven yards in diameter, was to be completely encased at the east end. This mill and Clough Mill were typical of the early purpose-built mills.[5]

In 1788 Patrick Colquhoun published *An account showing the different cotton mills erected in Great Britain within the last twenty years* [1768-88], *but chiefly within the last seven years* [1781-88]. The list included two local mills: Knowlwood Bottom Mill (Abraham Crossley), part of which survives as a pair of substantial semi-detached stone houses by the riverside, and was insured (including stock) for £400 in 1791 and in 1792 for £700; and Gauxholme Mill.[6] When Gauxholme Mill was offered for sale in 1787 it contained

Advertisement in the *Manchester Mercury* from the 18th September 1787, for the sale (including machinery) of Gauxholme Cotton Mill, one of the earliest in the district.

Oakfield or Yokefield Mill, on Oakhill Clough, Stansfield, was first referred to in 1790. It had four cottages built in pairs, back to back, on the ground floor, with chambers for carding, roving and spinning cotton above. It is now two cottages.

twelve roller frames. This mill was situated east of Walsden Water directly opposite the junction of the Bacup and Rochdale roads, which were not there in the 1780s (the turnpike road to Rochdale went from Shade over Guerning Dog Bridge and via Knowlwood, rejoining the modern line of road at Walsden Post Office), and neither were the railway nor canal constructed, so the landscape was quite different.

Lower down from Houghstone Mill at Oak Hill Clough were two other early mills, Holebottom and 'Oak' or 'Yoke' field. The *Leeds Intelligencer* on the 28th September 1790 advertised a sale by auction of the Royd, including ' ... a mill lately erected and now used as a cotton factory also two other sites for mills or machinery works with sufficient falls of water'. Prospective buyers could be shown round by Thomas Sutcliffe, the owner, or by George Stansfield of Holebottom Mill. Holebottom Mill developed

A reconstruction drawing of Houghstone Mill (right), above Holebottom in Stansfield. It
was built in 1795. Lawrence Wilson began his bobbin works here in 1823-5. The water
wheel was encased at the right-hand end, and the dam, now empty, is behind the mill.

into a much larger concern, but has now vanished, whereas 'Yoke' field remains today
as two substantial cottages.

Before building a water-powered mill, it was necessary to acquire, not only the site
of the mill, but also the land (or permission for its use) traversed by the mill goit and
tail goit (drainage channel from the wheel to the river), and also the right to build a
weir and divert the water. Christopher Rawdon, a substantial textile entrepreneur of
Underbank at Charlestown, in 1796 negotiated in detail with John Greenwood for
the water rights to guarantee an adequate supply for the mill which was planned at
Stoneswood on Bacup Road.[7]

Another to seize his opportunity was John Uttley of Lee near Lumbutts, who
between 1796 and 1802 sold or leased parts of his land near Lumbutts Clough, on
which three cotton mills were built. In 1796 he had leased, to his brothers Abraham
and William, a building 'formerly a Fulling Mill but more lately occupied as two
Cottage houses ... and afterwards used as a Cotton Mill ...'. It seems likely that at
this time the mill contained only hand-powered machines, as the indenture goes on
to grant the rights 'to divert and turn aside the water of Lumbutts Clough' to build a
reservoir 'for securing a Body of water necessary for driving a water wheel to be fixed
in the said mill ...'.

In 1801 he leased to Samuel Hollinrake of Heyhead in Stansfield, cotton manufacturer, and James Byfield of Manchester, merchant, land near to the above mill to
construct buildings on; land 'as was then staked marked or set out for that purpose

and to make use of the same when built as a Factory for Carding Roving and Spinning Sheeps Wool or Cotton or both the said purposes or for any other purpose whatsoever'. The site was as close to the first mill as possible without interfering with its operation by causing water from the second mill's weir to back up-stream and stop the earlier mill's water wheel.

In 1802 John Uttley sold, for £120, the next convenient site downstream to Samuel Hanson, who was a Quaker and innkeeper at the White Hart in Todmorden. Hanson had permission to build a weir to divert Lumbutts Clough 'for the use and benefit of any Mill or Mills hereafter to be erected ....', and also to get stone and lead it to the site. The mill to be built on this site was known at various times as Causeway, New or Midgehole Mill.

A reconstruction drawing of Knowlwood Bottom, Gauxholme. It is likely that a section of this building, now a pair of substantial houses, was part of the original Knowlwood Bottom Mill referred to as early as 1788.

Clough Hole Mill, an early water-powered cotton mill built across Rodwell End Clough in Stansfield.

Above these three mills was the original Lumbutts Mill, by now a cotton mill in the Fieldens' possession. So, in the space of seven or eight years the upper part of Lumbutts Clough was being intensively used as a power source, in addition to two other factories already established lower down, known as Causeway Wood/Folly and Old Royd Mills.

When looking at the sites of some early mills, it is obvious that water was the paramount consideration, ease of access being of secondary importance. Clough Hole Mill was one such small establishment. Little is known about it, although it is clearly marked on the maps of Stansfield Township for 1805 and 1816, and Travis states that amongst the early mills was 'one at Clough Hole above Cinderhill Mill in Stansfield'. It is now a cottage still straddling Rodwell End Clough, with the site of the mill dam clearly there

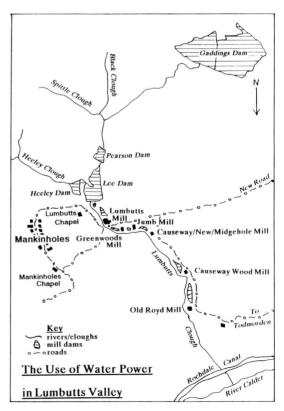

The Use of Water Power in Lumbutts Valley

A reconstruction drawing of Causeway Wood or Folly Mill on Lumbutts Clough, built in 1826 by Firth, Howarth and Firth.

A reconstruction drawing of Old Royd Mill, recorded in 1794 and demolished in 1912. It was next below Causeway Wood Mill on Lumbutts Clough.

behind it, and still has no recognisable road to it. Perhaps the most picturesque of all is Staups Mill, on Jumble Hole Clough, which marks the eastern boundary of the old borough of Todmorden. Now a beautiful ruin, it speaks eloquently of the early industrialists and workers, building, working, and moving goods to and from virtually inaccessible places.

Some of the very early mills, such as those at Castle Clough and Clough Hole, may have been used only for the carding and roving processes. In 1790 Samuel Uttley had a 'carding house' at Strines, Ramsden Wood Road, Walsden. By 1794, in conjunction with this, he was occupying James Hardman's Smithyholme Mill, which suggests that he was then in a position to mechanise the spinning side of his business as well as the carding.[8]

The rapid expansion of cotton spinning provided abundant work for handloom weavers, as it proved difficult to develop an efficient power loom, and new entrants flocked into the trade. Some manufacturers set up 'loomshops', containing handlooms, for more effective supervision. In a survey of Stansfield township in 1808, in the Middle and Upper Thirds, loomshops are recorded at Blind Lane, Millwood and New Gate Bottom in the valley, and at Upper Ashes (2), Fold, Bollingroyd West, Grey Stone (2), Hipperholme West, and Chapel House.[9]

A previous survey of the township in 1805 recorded only two loomshops, at Hipperholme West and Lower Eastlee, but two spinning rooms at Lower Eastwood and Howgate (above Ashenhurst), neither of which appear in 1808. Presumably the spinning rooms housed hand-operated machines, probably jennies which may have been obsolete by 1808.[10]

It is not possible in the scope of this book to describe each of the 'pioneer' mills in detail, but it is possible to map the positions of the mills known to be in existence by 1805, and to note the earliest reference found for each (see overleaf).

Some of the minor gentry found it profitable to build mills, or sell or lease land for building. Anthony Crossley of Todmorden Hall built Ridgefoot Mill (now the site of the Abraham Ormerod Day Centre) in the 1790s. He let it to John Buckley, who had wanted to build a steam-powered spinning mill in Manchester Road, Bradford, but was driven out by the hostility of the local inhabitants. The mill was water-powered at this time, the wheel receiving the water via an underground culvert leading from Hall Ings Dam, in the Salford area, just off Rochdale Road.

The Stoneswood mills in Dulegate were built on land sold by a member of the wealthy, landowning, Quaker, Greenwood family. Although the early mills in the Todmorden area were almost all cotton-spinning mills, at least one, Smithyholme Mill at Copperas House (now Milreed Lodge Residential Home), was, in 1794, a woollen mill,[11] whilst Lobb Mill was the pioneer worsted mill in the upper Calder Valley. A former fulling mill, it was bought in 1785 by Christopher Rawdon. It was still described as a fulling mill in 1786 but was being used for worsted spinning in 1790, when it was enlarged. In 1795, Rawdon was in partnership with William Ingham of Haugh (a house with beautiful Venetian windows just up the hillside from the site of Lobb Mill), and James Hollinrake of nearby Horsfall, worsted manufacturer. They insured the mill and contents for £2,500 in 1795 and 1797.[12]

Certainly before 1805 all the recorded textile and corn mills in what became the Borough of Todmorden were water-powered. They were situated by the river along the main Burnley, Walsden and Halifax valleys, as well as on the smaller, swift-flowing tributary streams such as Midgelden Brook (Bacup Road) and Lumbutts Clough.

The main river from Todmorden eastwards offered the advantage of a substantial

Staups Mill, Hippins/Jumble Hole Clough, Stansfield, as seen in the 1920s.

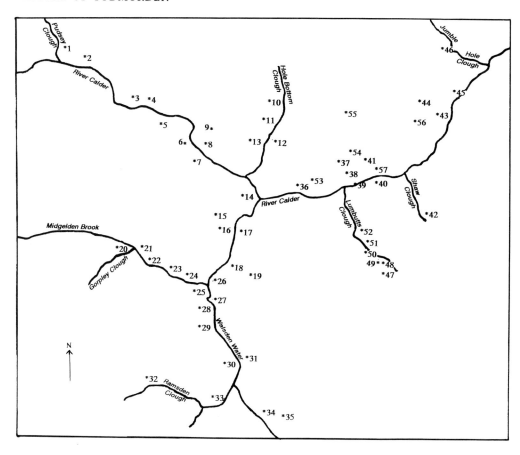

Map of water-powered mills/factories recorded by 1805.

No	Name		Earliest Reference Found
1	Pudsey Mill	1795	LTA Stansfseld
2	Frieldhurst Mill	1795	LTA Stansfield
3	Kitson Wood Mill	1804	LTA Stansfield
4	Lydgate Mill	1805	Stansfield Valuation
5	Lineholme Mill	1803	Fielden MSS
6	Scaitcliffe Corn Mill	1706	Will, Anthony Crossley
7	Ewood Mill	1801	LTA Todmorden with Walsden
8	Holme Mill	1795	LTA Stansfield
9	Cross Lee Mill	1804	LTA Stansfield
10	Greenhirst Hey Mill	1797	LTA Stansfield
11	Hough Stone Mill	1796	LTA Stansfield
12	Hole Bottom	1790	LTA Stansfield
13	Yoke Field Mill	1790	*Leeds Intelligencer*, 28/9/1790
14	Ridgefoot Mill	1801	LTA Todmorden with Walsden
15	Dobroyd Upper Mill	1800	Travis, *Notes on Todmorden & District*, 1896, pp 228-9
16	Dobroyd Lower Mill	1790	LTA Todmorden with Walsden
17	Waterside Mill	1782	Holden, p 159

18	Swineshead Lower Mill	1803	Langfield Constables Rate; CDA, Misc 165/18/4
19	Swineshead Mill	1790	Travis, *Notes on Todmorden & District*, 1896, p 25
20	Gorpley Mill	1626	Survey of the Manor of Rochdale (Fulling)
		1805	Fulling, Pearching or Raising Mill
21	Stoneswood Higher Mill	1797	LTA Todmorden with Walsden
22	Stoneswood Lower Mill	1803	LTA Todmorden with Walsden
23	Friths Mill	1795	Travis, *Chapters of Todmorden History*, 1901, p 57
24	Watty Corn Mill	1796	*Leeds Intelligencer*, 15/2/1796 (For Sale)
25	Gauxholme Corn Mill	1626	Survey of the Manor of Rochdale
26	Gauxholme New Mill	1786	LTA Todmorden with Walsden
27	Knowlwood Bottom Mill	1788	'Colquhoun's Enquiry'
28	Smithyholme Mill	1792—3	LTA Todmorden with Walsden
29	Clough Mill	1786	Travis, *Fielden Families of Walsden & Stansfield*, 1903, p 20
30	InchField/Travis Mill	1586	Travis, *Chapters of Todmorden History*, l9o1, p 126
31	Birks Mill	1801	Royal Exchange Policy Reg, Vol 32A, No 187267, 13/11/1801
32	Old Ragby Mill	1803	LTA Todmorden with Walsden
33	StrinesMill	1790	LTA Todmorden with Walsden
34	Bottomley Fold Mill	1800	Travis, *Notes on Todmorden & District*, 1896, p 25
35	Waterstalls Mill	1805	LTA Todmorden with Walsden
36	Stansfield Corn Mill	late 12th C	see page 17
37	Castle Clough Mill	1796	LTA Stansfield
38	Cinderhill Mill	1801	LTA Stansfield
39	Millsteads Mill	1805	Stansfield Valuation
40	Lobb Mill	1557	Halifax Wills II, No 193, Richard Horsfall, 14/10/1557
41	Clough Hole Mill	1805	Stansfield Valuation
42	Gut Royd Mill	1803	Langfield Constables' Rate
43	Cockden Mill	1797	LTA Stansfield
44	Eastwood Upper Mill	1789	LTA Stansfield
45	Wood Mill Corn	1627-8	YAS, Foster Greenwood, MSS DD99/B22/11
46	Staups Mill	1796	LTA Stansfield
47	Lumbutts Mill	1557	Feet of Fines Easter 1557 (Corn)
		1800	Cotton
48	Greenwood's Mill	1796-7	CRO FIE 27
49	Jumb Mill	1801-2	CRO FIE 26
50	Causey/New Midgehole Mill	1802-3	CRO FIE 51
51	Causeywood/Folly Mill (Causeway Wood)	1790s	Taken by Firth & Haworth on move from Midgehole Mill and redeveloped
52	Old Royd Mill	1794	*HAS* 1954, p 5
53	Priestwell Factory	1797	LTA Stansfield
54	Bean Hole Head Factory	1795	LTA Stansfield
55	Killup Factory	1796	LTA Stansficld
56	East Lee Factory	1796	LTA Stansfield
57	Horsfall	1796	LTA Stansfield

(NB: little is known about nos 54-57 other than the reference in the Land Tax Assessment.)

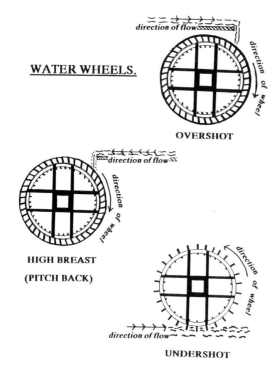

WATER WHEELS.

OVERSHOT

HIGH BREAST
(PITCH BACK)

UNDERSHOT

Three types of water wheel.

volume of water but, with a fall of only about fifteen feet per mile between Todmorden and Sowerby Bridge, limitations were placed on the number and height of mill weirs which could be constructed. From Calder Head in Cliviger the Calder falls 350 feet in 3½ miles to Todmorden, whilst Walsden Water falls about 300 feet to its confluence with the Calder. By comparison the tributary cloughs are narrower, with a much steeper gradient and hence a swifter flow, but they have a smaller volume of water. The broad, slow-flowing main river and the fast-flowing, steep, hill streams required different types of water wheel for optimum efficiency. Apart from differences in width, there are four main types of water wheel: overshot, turned by a flow of water over the head of the wheel; the high breast, also known as the pitch-back because the wheel revolves in the opposite direction to the flow of water; the low breast; and the undershot. The first three (sometimes called pelton wheels) have v-shaped buckets at intervals across the face of the wheel, and are turned by the weight of the water pouring into the buckets. The undershot is driven by the impulse of the water striking float boards.

We have no technical records of the wheels used by the medieval corn and fulling mills on the River Calder and its tributaries. Those on the main river were almost certainly undershot. Small overshot wheels may have been used on the tributaries. These early wheels probably generated only one or two horse-power each. It was, however, possible to increase the power by arranging two or three undershot wheels in a row. An arrangement such as this is suggested by descriptions of several seventeenth century fulling mills as 'two mills under one roof'. If this identification is correct, Lobb Mill (fulling) had three wheels when it was taken over in the 1780s for redevelopment as a worsted mill.

Some of the smaller spinning mills had wheels producing about 5 hp, which a stream, 3 feet wide and 6 inches deep moving at 3 miles per hour (walking speed), would generate turning an overshot or high-breast wheel of about 11 feet in diameter. In 1833 Causeway Wood Mill had a 5 hp wheel using water from Lumbutts Clough, plus a steam engine generating 8 hp.[13] In 1832 the Fieldens' Dobroyd Mill had a 1.5 hp wheel plus a steam engine; Lumbutts Mill had a 7 hp wheel; Causeway Mill a 6 hp wheel and Smithyholme a 3.5 hp wheel plus a steam engine.[14]

To drive the machinery of the larger mills, more power was needed. This could be achieved, where there was a good flow of water, by making the wheel wider. If there was an adequate head of water, as on the hill streams, the diameter of the wheel could

A reconstruction drawing of Greenhirst Hey Mill, a small cotton factory on Wickenberry Clough first mentioned in 1797. It had an encased water wheel at the right-hand end. The drawing shows the mill circa 1900, by which time it had been a dwelling for many years.

be increased, but there was a limit to this process. The larger the wheel, the slower must be its rim velocity to prevent centrifugal force throwing the water out of the buckets, and for this reason water wheels were rarely built above sixty feet in diameter.

The main problem in the use of water power was the variability of the flow. In flood, the water could back up the tail races of the mills on the Calder and stop the wheels turning. In drought, a mill might only be able to work intermittently. Severe frost could also freeze up the wheels, particularly those exposed to the elements. Mills on the steeper hill-streams had no problem with backwater but could be badly hit by drought, and so they built storage reservoirs — 'mill lodges' in local parlance. Mills higher up the stream had the advantage of first use of the available water; John and James Greenwood, Lumbutts, in their return to the 1833 Factories Inquiry Commission, state 'Work 6 a.m. to 7.30 p.m. if water holds out. Mill immediately above so cannot start work until they send water down.' Sometimes the mill lodges — albeit now empty — together with the weirs built across the river are the only surviving archaeological evidence that a mill ever existed. A good example of this is at Houghstone, where the reservoir was 'to be made capacious enough to contain all the water that shall run thereto in the course of one night in times of drought'.[15]

At Gorpley Mill, Bacup Road, where the mill race snakes spectacularly along the south hillside above the brook, attaining the height necessary to fall on the wheel, the storage reservoir was almost half a mile up the valley. It used water from a small tributary stream and was used only when Midgelden Brook was low in water. The water was released into the brook to supply the mill race further down.

One reservoir still in use is Folly Dam on Lumbutts Clough, which once supplied Causeway Wood Mill and is now used by Todmorden Angling Society for fishing.

The most spectacular arrangement of water wheels was found at Lumbutts Mill, where the tower housing them still stands. Water was piped from three reservoirs on the hillside above the mill

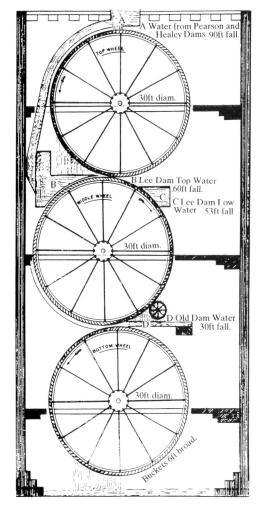

A Water from Pearson and Healey Dams 90ft fall.
TOP WHEEL
30ft diam.

B Lee Dam Top Water 60ft fall.
C Lee Dam Low Water 53ft fall
MIDDLE WHEEL
30ft diam.

D Old Dam Water 30ft fall.

BOTTOM WHEEL
30ft diam.

Buckets 6ft broad.

This diagram of the water wheel arrangement at Lumbutts Mill names the sources of water for each wheel, which was supplemented by the used water from the wheel above.

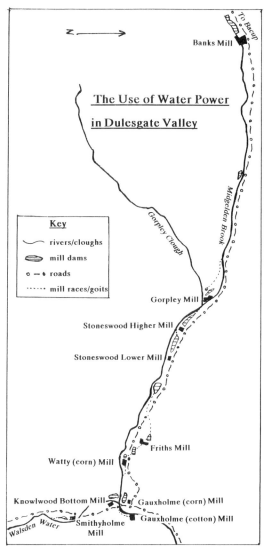

The Use of Water Power in Dulesgate Valley

Key
~~~ rivers/cloughs
⬭ mill dams
o — • roads
····· mill races/goits

Banks Mill
To Bacup
Midgelden Brook
Gorpley Clough
Gorpley Mill
Stoneswood Higher Mill
Stoneswood Lower Mill
Friths Mill
Watty (corn) Mill
Knowlwood Bottom Mill
Gauxholme (corn) Mill
Gauxholme (cotton) Mill
Walsden Water
Smithyholme Mill

and fed to four points on the wheels. In addition, water from the higher wheels fell on to the lower ones. Each wheel was thirty feet in diameter and six feet wide.

When the first mills were built, the only effective way of transporting goods in and out of the district was by horse and cart along the turnpike roads, but soon came the building of the Rochdale Canal to connect the Bridgewater Canal (1761) at Manchester, and the Calder and Hebble Navigation (1774) at Sowerby Bridge. This was to create a continuous waterway from Liverpool to Hull and had been proposed, without

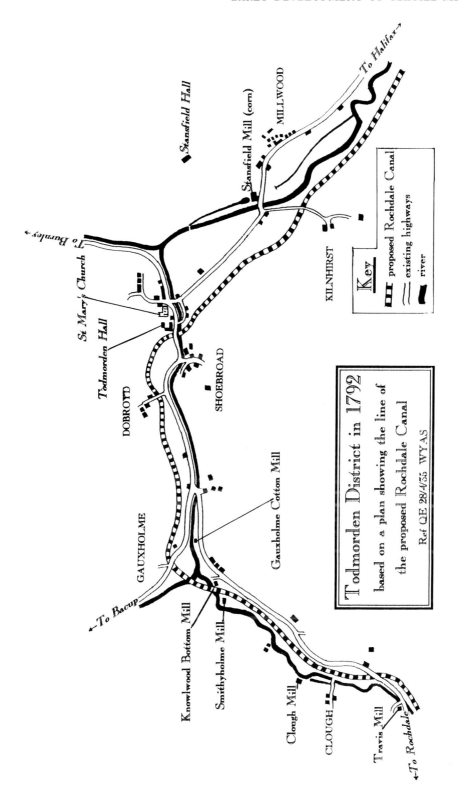

To Halifax →

Stansfield Hall

Stansfield Mill (corn)

MILLWOOD

← To Burnley

St Mary's Church

Todmorden Hall

DOBROYD

SHOEBROAD

KILNHIRST

Key

proposed Rochdale Canal

existing highways

river

Gauxholme Cotton Mill

GAUXHOLME

← To Bacup

Knowlwood Bottom Mill

Smithyholme Mill

Clough Mill

CLOUGH

Travis Mill

← To Rochdale

Todmorden District in 1792
based on a plan showing the line of
the proposed Rochdale Canal

Ref QE 28/4/55 WYAS

This view of the Rochdale Canal looks towards Todmorden. It shows the lower Gauxholme locks, crossed by the railway on Stephenson's skew bridge, and, in the distance, the Unitarian Church, the town hall pediment, the houses at Woodlands, and Stansfield Hall.

success, as early as 1766. The case for a trans-Pennine canal was powerful, yet it was only at the third attempt, in 1794, that Parliamentary approval was obtained.

Opposition came from the promoters of the Manchester, Bolton and Bury Canal, who proposed to extend their canal to Deanhead, near Littleborough, and thence by a tunnel under Blackstone Edge to the Ryburn Valley and down to Sowerby Bridge.[16] There were also objectors nearer home, in the form of the local millowners, who depended for their livelihood on a reliable supply of water, their only source of power. These owners and occupiers of the mills were dismayed at the prospect of the canal's promoters acquiring the rights to intercept and use all the streams, within one thousand yards of the line of the canal, and to build five small reservoirs near the canal's summit at Deanhead. Some local figures such as John Crossley of Scaitcliffe were in favour of the Rochdale Canal from the start, but millowners petitioned that, even without a canal, they suffered for want of water in a drought when 'many of them at these times are not able to work more than Twelve or Fourteen Hours in the Day'.

The Rochdale Canal promoters modified their proposals, which eventually persuaded the millowners of the upper Calder Valley to support them, although those lower down the valley (in and below Sowerby Bridge) continued in opposition. These new proposals confined the canal promoters to taking water from only twelve streams feeding the Calder, and then only to excess water from a gauge to be fitted at each clough. The extra water needed for the canal was to come from reservoirs to be built on Blackstone Edge Moor, and the canal company was 'to discharge from the said

This gauge on Stonehouse Clough, Walsden, was one of a series built on twelve of the cloughs between Sowerby Bridge and Summit under the terms of the Rochdale Canal Act, to ensure an adequate supply of water to the mills

Gauxholme wharf and warehouse (built in 1811), on the Rochdale Canal, are shown circa 1920 in this reconstruction drawing, when the canal was working. Note the water access to the warehouse. The wall in the background follows the line of the packhorse road, climbing Watty Scout to Stones, Sourhall and Burnley.

Canal and Reservoirs for and towards the Supply of the said Mills, a quantity of water equal to double the Quantity of Water which shall be intercepted and diverted'.[17] These conditions and obligations still hold today.

The canal needed all the water it could get because it climbed 316 feet from Sowerby Bridge to Summit, requiring 36 locks, and then fell 514 feet to Manchester, requiring another 56 locks. The estimated cost of £360,000 doubled by the time the canal was completed in 1804. The work was carried out by direct labour totalling about one thousand 'navigational workers' or 'navvies' (a word that has become part of our language), who must have made a considerable impact on the local society, living in their 'shanty' towns, which moved along the line of the canal as work progressed.

By August 1798, the ten and a half miles from Sowerby Bridge to Gauxholme was complete, and a few months later the next section to Rochdale was finished. As soon as a section was ready, it was put into use, and by May 1799, about £700 had been collected in dues according to the fifth annual report. In 1800 the canal was closed from July to October as, owing to drought, there was no water in Blackstone Edge Reservoir. Hollingworth Reservoir (Lake) was the only other source of water, but this had been built to supply water to the Lancashire side of the canal and its level was forty feet below Summit. To get water to Summit, a steam pump was installed to raise water from Hollingworth Reservoir, and a ditch or drain was constructed, following the 600 feet contour along the hillside, to the Summit Pool. This drain can

Ramsden Wood Upper or Spring Mill originally built for spinning in 1819 but shown here
circa 1870. Note the trough supported by pillars carrying water to the wheelhouse.

still be seen and, interestingly, was made without any fall, thus allowing water to be
directed either way.[18]

With the canal fully operative, income increased. At this time the canal company
did no carrying; it provided and maintained the canal, and its income came from the
dues paid by the users. The standard charge was two pence per ton per mile (240
pence=£1) but bulk loads such as stone and grain were allowed a reduced rate of 1½d
per mile.

In 1803, before the canal was fully operative, the millowners of the upper valley
joined together to monitor the stretch from Sowerby Bridge to Summit, to check that
the canal did not receive water to which it was not entitled by law. They checked the
culverts, which carried streams under the canal into the river, noting for instance that
'The Culvert on Studley Clough is Choaked up', and at 'Warland Clough here much
pains has been taken to divert one of the best feeders upon the line into the Canal,
there is a Culvert below made to collect several feeders but the Canal people have
scrued a piece of timber across the channel which prevents this water ever coming
into the Culvert'.

They identified seventeen areas of concern in a letter, signed by twenty-two millowners, to the canal company. The company replied that they were 'unacquainted
with the existence of any cause of complaint such as mentioned' and promised to
attend without delay to any specific complaints. The millowners continued to watch
jealously over their water supply for the rest of the century, believing, that as soon as
their vigilance wavered, the canal company would be up to something.[19]

The fortunes of the Fieldens' business is indicated by the records of the Millowners
Association. In 1803 Joshua Fielden paid a subscription of three guineas, whilst eleven
others, including John Buckley of Ridgefoot Mill, paid ten guineas. In 1813, however,
his son John Fielden became the association's chairman and subsequently the Fieldens
became its leaders.[20]

Forces for Change, 1800-1850

The Luddites

The industrial developments which brought fame and fortune to such as the Fieldens, and substantial profits from land transactions to the Crossleys, Greenwoods and other landowners, threatened the traditional way of life of the handicraftsmen. William Greenwood of Pudsey in Stansfield, a home-worker, left a diary for 1825. It shows clearly that, whilst having to work hard (in one week, the 21st-26th March, he wove 112 yards of cloth), he also had time for other things. He recorded the weather each day, eg 20th January, 'Rather coldish this morning some little snow lieth on the ground the sky looks heavy, 2 o'clock a snow shower'. He took time off on occasions: Friday 11th February, 'Eastwood Hounds was loosed this morning ... woven about ten yeards besides watching the Hunters at times'; Wednesday 16th February, 'Wm Greenwood John Law Robert Suthers and me have had a moderate walk this morning we went through Springwood through Obadiah wood up to witenstall up be Shar green bottom & came down Layfield oil'. Time was taken to notice and record the seasons: Wednesday 20th April, 'the larch fir begins to be a littel green'; Thursday 12th May, 'the Oak that carries yellow lef is leved I think to the bredth of a penny piece'.[1] Whereas the home-worker could take time off and make it up later (his only limitation being the daylight), the millworker was ruled by the rhythm and noise of the machine, from 6 am to 7.30 or 8 pm, on five days a week with marginally fewer hours on Saturdays. Allowing for meal breaks, the normal working week in the Calder Valley mills in 1833 was seventy-two hours.[2] Children aged eight or younger had to work from 6 am to 7.30 or 8 pm, doffing bobbins or piecing broken threads.

Handloom weavers had enjoyed relatively high wages from about 1788 to 1803, but then saw a steady decline in earnings, caused not by the power loom (the first recorded power looms in Todmorden were not installed until 1822 by the Fieldens at Waterside[3]) but by the sheer numbers coming into the trade. They and other weavers were at the mercy of trade fluctuations, accentuated by the French Wars (1793-1815). Wage rates were cut in depressions and only partly restored in the next boom.

Petitions to Parliament for the enforcement of ancient laws for the regulation of wages, bread prices and apprenticeship were answered by the repeal of the relevant Acts. The workers' discontent was expressed violently by croppers in the woollen trade, whose craft was threatened by new machines. In 1812 bands of Luddites, so called after a mythical leader Ned Ludd, attacked gig mills and shearing frames in the West Riding. Although the upper Calder Valley was relatively peaceful, detachments of troops were stationed at Halifax and Elland; when Stoodley Bridge Mill, near Eastwood, was burned down in the night (shortly after seventeen Luddites had been executed at York), the fire was investigated by the army officer in charge at Halifax.

William Sutcliffe of Stoodley, the millowner, was able to assure the officer that the fire was an accident, and the officer reported that amongst the lower classes 'the utmost tranquility prevails'. Shortly afterwards the withdrawal of the troops began.[4] Todmorden may well have been on the periphery of Luddism, but the 'age of agitation' had begun, and from then on Todmorden was at the very heart of the activity.

Political Reform

The agitation for parliamentary reform did not bear fruit for another twenty years. It was supported both by workers, who hoped that a reformed parliament would be responsive to their pleas for better conditions, and by the industrial and commercial middle classes, who argued that their interests were grossly under-represented. The Battle of Waterloo, which ended the French Wars in 1815, was followed by several years of distress and discontent. Unemployment rose, wages were depressed and a heavy burden of indirect taxation was loaded onto the necessities of life. The economic distress of 1819 fed the agitation for reform. Meetings in favour of reform were held in many towns, including Todmorden. In August a mass meeting in St Peter's Fields, Manchester, was attacked by the local yeomanry and a force of regular cavalry. In what became known as the Peterloo Massacre, eleven people were killed and over 400 wounded. The Government responded with new laws designed to suppress radical journals by imposing a heavy stamp duty, and restricting mass meetings.[5]

The most effective restraints on popular agitation were full employment and full stomachs. Tension declined through a gradual improvement in trade from 1820, which culminated in the boom of 1824-25. The year 1826, however, brought a severe depression; the plight of the handloom weavers was particularly hard. So much so that in April of that year, John Fielden chaired a meeting of cotton manufacturers, from Blackburn, Burnley, Colne, Todmorden and district, which resolved to fix a minimum piece-rate for handloom weavers. Fielden wrote to the churchwardens and overseers of the townships in the 'cotton belt' asking them to adopt the scheme, and to support, either from the poor rate or through voluntary subscriptions, any weaver who could not find work at a living wage. He was confident that this support would be needed only in the short term, whereas, the practice, adopted by some townships, of giving a bonus of 3d or more per piece to manufacturers as an inducement to employ the poor, would only hasten the pauperisation of the weavers.[6] Unfortunately, within a week of the Burnley meeting, the weavers around Blackburn and Haslingden rose in the most concerted outbreak of loom-breaking ever witnessed in the North. Fielden's initiative came to nothing; although condemning their machine breaking, his sympathy was still with them. If the rioters reached Waterside, he told his brothers, 'offer no resistance … something to eat and drink I fancy would do them more good than destroying the looms and I should offer it them'.[7]

Not surprisingly, Fielden became active in the campaign for parliamentary reform when it entered its decisive phase in 1830. He spoke at a reform meeting at Lumbutts, summoned by the constable of Langfield township at the request of fifty-two inhabitants in December 1830, when he was supported by Dr Hardman, a local doctor. Resolutions were passed in favour of parliamentary reform, annual parliamentary elections, votes for all adult men, vote by ballot, reductions of taxation and the repeal of the corn laws — a comprehensive radical programme.[8]

On the 13th January 1831, John Fielden chaired a meeting in the White Hart Inn, at which the Todmorden Political Union was formed. Similar unions were established

This view of Waterside Mill in the 1860s shows the cottages (centre) where Joshua Fielden began the enterprise in 1782. To their right is Waterside House, one of the Fielden family homes. Left of the cottages is the first small mill of 1804, with later extensions clearly discernible. Over the road is the clock-tower building, which housed the offices and, from 1827, the factory school.

in many other towns, including Hebden Bridge. The objects of the Todmorden Union, adopted at a meeting on the 15th February 1831, included a radical reform of the Commons; the abolition of slavery throughout the Empire (the slave trade had been banned in 1807, but slavery itself was not abolished until 1833); the repeal of all taxes on the press; 'the repeal of bad laws and the enactment of good laws'; and 'to take cognisance of all real local abuses'. The governing body of the union was the Political Council. John Fielden became a member of the latter and his brother James acted as treasurer.[9]

The rules of the Todmorden Political Union laid great stress on peaceful methods and internal discipline. Any member using or recommending 'intemperate or violent language or measures' was to be expelled. The Political Council was 'to devise means to preserve the peace and order of the town and neighbourhood during any disturbances arising from political excitement'. When the Whig government led by Earl Grey introduced the first Reform Bill in the House of Commons on the 1st March 1831, the Todmorden Union sent an address of support, which also urged the ministers to add to their measure shorter parliaments and voting by secret ballot. The bill was defeated in the committee stage and a general election followed. The new House of Commons had a substantial majority in favour of reform, and passed the second Reform Bill on the 22nd September 1831. The bill was then sent to the House of Lords, which had a substantial Tory majority.

A public meeting, convened by the Todmorden Political Union on the 29th September 1831, resolved to submit three petitions to the Lords, one from each of the three townships of Langfield, Stansfield, and Todmorden with Walsden. The House of Lords was urged to pass the Reform Bill and 'so avert those evils which would inevitably result from its rejection', a hint that peaceable organisations might lose control of their mass following if reform was denied them. Despite receiving wagon-loads of such petitions, the Lords rejected the bill on the 8th October.

A few days later a meeting in Todmorden, chaired by John Fielden, decided to publish an address, of which 500 copies were printed, to the people of the district. The address urged the people to remain disciplined and united. It warned them that the Tory peers hoped that 'the people will be irritated and urged on to deeds of riot and outrage', and so discredit the campaign for reform. 'Reform is only retarded, the King and his ministers are firm, and determined to carry the Measure by constitutional means attached to the Royal Prerogative', a reference to the reformers' hope that the king would agree to create enough new peers to overcome the opposition in the Lords.

The third Reform Bill was introduced in December 1831, and was approved by the Commons. When it went to the Lords the Todmorden Political Union again drew up an address to the government, which was supported by three separate township petitions, with a total of over 3,000 signatures. In this statement the threat that violence would follow the rejection of reform was made explicit. Any alteration in the qualifications for voting embodied in the bill:

> ... would inevitably produce great dissatisfaction in the manufacturing districts and consequences might follow which it is awful to contemplate. We form part of an extensive manufacturing district, the people of which have been long suffering from the pressure of the times, and thousands of families among the operatives are absolutely in a state of starvation ... they have hoped that the Reform Measure would lead to an amelioration of their conditions, and they now await in awful silence the results of the proceedings in the House of Lords.

The Lords passed the bill at its second reading by a very narrow majority, but then proceeded to tamper with it in committee. The king was unwilling to create new peers to override the opposition, and Grey resigned. A public meeting was called in Todmorden, and a new batch of petitions, carrying 2,300 signatures, was sent to the House of Commons and the king. The Tories failed to secure enough support to form a government and Grey came back into office, armed with a promise from the king to create as many new peers as were needed to carry the reform bill. The threat sufficed, however, and the bill became law on the 7th June 1832.

Todmorden celebrated the 1832 Reform Act with an open-air banquet for 350 guests, with John Fielden presiding, followed by a procession which included the Society of Whitesmiths, Independent Order of Oddfellows, Royal Foresters, Druids, Mechanics' Trade Society and Loyal Free Mechanics. Each society had its own band and banners. On a special flag appeared the words: 'The members of the Todmorden Political Union. Union has conquered and will conquer.'

The conquest did not amount to much. Industrial towns were given their own MPs — two each for Halifax and Oldham, one for Huddersfield — but the Todmorden townships had only a share of the two MPs to be elected for Lancashire and the West Riding respectively outside the boroughs. For the county vote there were property qualifications: freehold land worth £2 a year, copyhold or long leasehold of £10, or a tenancy of £50 a year, conditions which few members of the Todmorden Political Union could meet.[10]

The radicals of Todmorden and district had, however, three reasons to be pleased. First, the reform, however inadequate, was a step in what they regarded as the right direction. Secondly, their leader John Fielden and his friend William Cobbett were elected Radical MPs for Oldham at the General Election held in December 1832. Thirdly, they had tried out a powerful political weapon — an organised mass movement, the leaders of which could warn that discipline could give way to disorder if no concessions were made to the popular will. Earl Grey, who was not so much enthusiastic for reform as convinced that reform was essential to preserve the constitution, regarded the disciplined political unions as more dangerous to the established order than sporadic outbursts of violence. He argued, in writing to the king, that the only way to get rid of the unions was to pass the Reform Bill.[11]

Factory Reform

The political unions of Todmorden and Hebden Bridge did not dissolve themselves after the enactment of reform. They had become involved in a parallel campaign for a statutory limitation of working hours in textile mills. There was already some legislation on the statute book. An Act, passed in 1802, limited the hours of pauper apprentices working in factories to twelve a day and forbade their employment at night. The township of Todmorden and Walsden had resolved, in 1801, to apprentice pauper children only 'on condition that they are to work the usual hours and ... not in the night'.[12] It is unlikely that large numbers of pauper apprentices were used in the upper Calder Valley, where plenty of 'free' children — cheaper to employ, as the manufacturers did not have to house, feed and clothe them — could be drawn from the local population. In any event, the provisions for the enforcement of the 1802 Act were quite inadequate, making it totally ineffectual.

In 1819 an Act, which applied to cotton mills only, prohibited the employment of children under nine and limited those under sixteen to a working day of twelve hours, exclusive of mealtimes. Further legislation in 1825 reduced Saturday working for the under sixteens in cotton mills to nine hours. No special provisions were made for enforcement. The parents of children and adolescents working in a mill could hardly take the employer before a JP for a breach of these Acts and, when parents overstated the ages of their children to find them work, the law was powerless.[13]

A vigorous campaign for factory reform began early in 1830 with a letter from Richard Oastler to the *Leeds Mercury*, in which he argued that the conditions of the children in the textile mills were worse than those of negro slaves in the West Indies. The aim of the campaign was a reduction of working hours to ten a day. The battle was fought over the hours of children, but it was well known that most mills would find it difficult, if not impossible, to keep working for longer than ten hours a day without the essential input of their many young workers. Amongst Oastler's leading allies were John Fielden; Rev George S Bull, vicar of Bierley, near Bradford; and Michael Sadler MP.[14]

Sadler introduced the Ten Hours' Bill in the House of Commons in December 1831. A select committee, under his chairmanship, was appointed in the spring of 1832 to collect evidence. It interviewed many operatives, some of whom exhibited their deformities arising out of long hours of factory work from an early age. The select committee paid particular attention to stories of physical cruelty to children.[15]

Before the matter was settled in parliament, the 1832 Reform Act removed Sadler's constituency. He stood for Leeds in the election of December 1832 but was defeated. Lord Ashley (later the Earl of Shaftesbury) took the Ten Hours' Bill in hand, with support from the newly-elected John Fielden. The House of Commons resolved that a new investigation should be made, by a commission appointed for the purpose. The

'Ten Hours' campaigners denounced this move as a delaying tactic, but the minutes of evidence of the Factories Inquiry Commission served to build up, mainly out of the testimony of employers, an irrefutable case for new factory legislation.[16]

Twenty-nine mills in the upper Calder Valley, including five from Todmorden, answered the questionnaire sent round by the commission, or otherwise volunteered evidence.[17] The regular hours of work of the cotton mills in the sample ranged between 68 and 72 hours per week, with the under-eighteens working a total of 70 hours. Most of those who replied to the commission were ambivalent regarding the beating of children at work. Most were content to state that they did not sanction it. Only one set of employers, John and James Greenwood, who had a cotton carding and spinning mill at Lumbutts, said that corporal punishment was not forbidden by them, 'but would be if we saw cause'.

Some of the local millowners were resolutely opposed to any legislation which interfered with the hours of work in textile mills. Thomas Sutcliffe, cotton spinner of Stoodley Bridge Mill, considered that 'the earlier children begin to work, the more useful they become, both to their employer and themselves when they arrive at mature age'. Some of his workers in the 30 to 40 age group 'who began work when six or seven years of age … are the most robust and healthy hands that we have in the place'. Richard Ingham and Sons, who ran Millsteads and Cinderhill Mills, thought that factory children were better fed and healthier than those working in damp or cramped conditions in home employment.

One third of the millowners who replied to the commission were in favour of some kind of restriction on the hours of work of children. The view of Firth Howarth and Firth, cotton spinners of Causeway Wood Mill, was fairly representative; they did not 'object to the hours of children under fourteen being limited to eight or ten', but argued that older workers 'ought to be left at liberty in this business the same as in all others'.

In Hebden Bridge and Todmorden, the political unions took the lead in agitating for factory reform. The secretary of the Todmorden Political Union, James Suthers, was planning a meeting to be addressed by John Fielden during the 1833 Easter parliamentary recess.

John Fielden's main argument, expressed with the authority of a very successful businessman with forty years' experience of cotton mills, was that, even without any positive ill-treatment, long hours of work for children represented in themselves an intolerable cruelty. Fielden had started work at the age of ten in his father's mill, which was then in the 'jenny' and 'billy' stage, with much of the machinery hand-driven. The hours of work were only ten a day, but Fielden wrote that he would 'never forget the fatigue I often felt before the day ended and the anxiety of us all to be relieved from the unvarying and irksome toil …'. He considered that the burden upon factory children had increased since his own childhood, because machinery ran much faster and mills worked longer hours than ten a day. His father had lengthened the working week to seventy-one hours when he had 'introduced the machinery that is now used', presumably spinning mules. 'This he was obliged to do in his own defence', as other manufacturers with the same machinery were working their hands from 77 to 84 hours a week, until a check was imposed by the 1819 Act. Fielden was scornful of those who admitted the need for a restriction of children's hours, but were unwilling to achieve it by any means which would also limit the hours of adults, whom he considered also to be seriously overworked: '… they cannot interfere with the … "free labour" of the adult, because that is against sound principle! … their "principle" … is the principle of pelf against nature'.[18]

'Sound principle' triumphed, however, in the terms of the 1833 Factory Act, which followed closely the recommendations of the Factories Inquiry Commission. The employment of children under 9 years of age was prohibited in all textile mills except silk, for which the minimum working age was to be 8. Children under 13 were to work no more than 9 hours a day and 48 a week. 'Young persons' from 13 to 17 inclusive were restricted to 12 hours a day and 69 a week. Neither group was to work at night. The under-thirteens were to have two hours' schooling each day. Water mills were allowed to use children and young persons for a limited amount of overtime to make up for stoppages to the flow of water. Four inspectors were appointed to secure the observance of the Act nationally.[19]

The Sadler-Ashley Bill, which was the objective of most of the campaigners for factory reform, would have limited the hours of labour of all under 18 years to 58 a week. As most mills were heavily dependent upon the labour of children and adolescents, this limit would have applied in practice to all workers. Instead the children were limited to 48 hours, and by the employment of three children for every two jobs, the mills could keep running up to the limit of the young persons' hours, 69 a week. The Act involved, therefore, only a minimal interference with the hours of adults.

The restrictions of the 1833 Act were applied in stages: to children under eleven, on the 1st March 1834; eleven year olds a year later; and twelve year olds, on the 1st March 1836. The economy was, however, booming in 1836 and groups of millowners, anxious to maintain a full labour force, petitioned Parliament for the repeal or modification of the clauses of the 1833 Act relating to children under thirteen. A bill to repeal these clauses was introduced into the Commons but failed to pass. It was this campaign which moved John Fielden to write *The Curse of the Factory System*. The rival agitations for a Ten Hours' Act and for the modification of the 1833 Act continued for some time. A meeting of millowners of the parish of Halifax in August 1836 asked for a measure which would allow children over ten to work 11 hours a day or 66 per week.[20]

Resistance to the New Poor Law

John Fielden had been active on many radical fronts since his election in 1832. He joined with Robert Owen to form a 'Society for Promoting National Regeneration', which planned to secure an eight hour day without loss of pay, by the threat of strikes. After the collapse of this and other Owenite schemes in 1834, Fielden took up the cause of the handloom weavers, for whom he wanted a minimum wage.[21] The battle lines of a new campaign were laid down when the recommendations of the Poor Law Commission of 1832-34 were incorporated in the Poor Law Amendment Act of 1834. The commission was set up to investigate what were considered to be serious deficiencies in the administration of the poor laws, and particularly any form of relief to the able-bodied which might lessen the will to work. In the upper Calder Valley there had been no fundamental changes in the system of poor relief under the overseers of the poor, as described in Chapter 5.[22] All of the eight Yorkshire townships (Todmorden with Walsden made no return to the Poor Law Commission) had taken advantage of an Act of 1819 which allowed the establishment of a Select Vestry, which was a committee elected by the ratepayers to manage poor relief and, if desired, other township business.

The system of relief remained the same — allowances in money or kind, the occasional purchase of a loom for an unemployed man, assistance with the rent of paupers in most townships, and the use of township workhouses mainly for shelter and not as places where the poor were put to work. Some inmates of the workhouses lived there with their own furniture.[23]

Illegitimacy was a greater problem than formerly, but the main function of the poor law officers was to secure from magistrates orders for payment against the putative fathers. Stansfield had between 122 and 145 bastardy orders in force during the period 1827-32, but £2,150, of the total cost of £2,312, had been recovered from the fathers. A visitor to Todmorden in 1841 concluded from discussions with factory workers that the moral condition:

> of the people in the cotton mills here is very little better than in large towns. This is not to be wondered at, as the population is large and exposed to the same evils and temptations as at most other places. Many of the single women have had illegitimate children; some of them very early in life.[24]

The local townships made only limited use of the practice of supplementing inadequate earnings. As a general rule, allowances were made in such cases when there were three or more children in the family. Langfield, for example, had ten families whose weekly earnings were made up to 2s a head. Only Stansfield was in favour of the prohibition of the allowance system, and all of the townships were firmly opposed to relieving the children of the able-bodied poor only in the workhouse. The general opinion was that the townships could manage their own affairs well enough (except that Stansfield people had long wanted to subdivide their township for more efficient administration) and that the burden of poor relief was not excessive. The cost per head of the population averaged 3s 1d in the upper Calder Valley, compared with 5s 7d in the West Riding as a whole and 18s 3d in Suffolk.

The Poor Law Amendment Act transferred the responsibility for poor relief from individual townships to elected boards of guardians managing a 'Union' of townships. The overseers would now be merely rate collectors. Instead of outdoor relief in money or kind, the able-bodied were to choose between managing on their own or going into a Union workhouse, in which conditions would be worse — 'less eligible' — than those of the poorest employed workers. The whole system was to be supervised by a three-man Poor Law Commission set up in London.

By the time the officials of the commission came round to organising Unions in the industrial North, the boom of 1836 was giving way to a depression. John Fielden warned the House of Commons that the new poor law would be resisted in Oldham and Todmorden, 'and I do not mind telling you frankly that, if such resistance takes place, I would lead it'.[25]

The commission grouped six townships (Erringden, Heptonstall, Langfield, Stansfield, Todmorden with Walsden, and Wadsworth) into a Union based upon Todmorden.[26] Guardians were elected from four townships, but in Langfield and Todmorden with Walsden all the nominees withdrew, allegedly as a result of intimidation. A public meeting in Todmorden with Walsden resolved that the township would pay no poor rates to the Union but would continue to relieve its own poor, in defiance of the new law. The resolution spelled out the reasons for this resistance:

> We are resolved to make this stand ... against the attempt ... to place those poor whom we love and respect and who have been guilty of no crime in a workhouse and under a discipline and restraint more intolerable than is allotted to felons in a Gaol. We are well satisfied with the management of our own affairs in this

township, and pledge ourselves to resist union with any other township. If we be required to surrender ... that self-government which we have had handed down to us by our forefathers ... and live under a despotism consisting of three commissioners ... then to shrink from resistance would be a crime.[27]

These two considerations — opposition to the harshness of the new law and defence of local independence — were inseparably linked throughout the poor law controversy.

During its first year the board of guardians did very little apart from deciding to hold meetings at the Wood Mill Inn, Eastwood (halfway between Todmorden and Hebden Bridge), and making arrangements for the registration of births and deaths. The Union was divided into districts based on Todmorden and Hebden Bridge, each with a registrar and medical officer. At the second election, in March 1838, one nominee was chosen for Todmorden with Walsden, despite the tactics of the overseers who refused to receive the nomination. The new guardian was William Helliwell, a cotton spinner of Friths Mill, who was no lover of the new poor law but was opposed to unconstitutional action and resented John Fielden's domination of Todmorden and district. Two men were nominated for Langfield, but withdrew after receiving a petition signed by a large number of ratepayers.[28]

Helliwell's action provoked a speedy response. A Working Men's Association was formed at a meeting in Todmorden Unitarian Chapel (which belonged to John Fielden) on the 28th March 1838. There was probably a good deal of continuity of membership between the Todmorden Political Union and the Working Men's Association, but the adoption of a new name was significant. The London Working Men's Association, formed in 1836, which published demands for democratic reforms in *The People's Charter* in 1838, sent missionaries to the North of England in 1837-38, whose work

A reconstruction drawing of the original Friths Mill, Bacup Road, circa 1795.

led to the establishment of a large number of Working Men's Associations. The radical wing of the new movement, which was in favour of 'physical force if necessary', allied with the anti-poor law agitation then convulsing such towns as Oldham, Rochdale, Keighley, Huddersfield and Todmorden, gave a flying start to what became known as Chartism. The Todmorden WMA declared firmly that its principal object was 'to obtain the repeal of the Poor Law Amendment Act', although it later adopted the full Chartist programme. The membership fee was one penny per month, and weekly meetings were held in the schoolroom attached to Fielden Brothers' Waterside Mill.[29]

In an 'Address to the Inhabitants of Todmorden and the Neighbourhood', the association expressed its pained regret that 'there were some few individuals amongst you, so regardless of their own characters as to attempt, in direct opposition to the … wishes … of their neighbours … to bring that law into operation here'. It was determined to prevent 'any like attempts in future'. The thinly-veiled threats of this address, which were posted up all over the town, were quickly followed by a boycott of all tradesmen who showed any sympathy for the new law.[30] John Fielden replied with a letter to the guardians, which he also published as a poster. He condemned what he saw as the objectives of the new poor law:

> to subject the people of this country to work that shall be harder, and food that shall be coarser, than the already too hard work and too coarse food of the English Working People …
> The strict workhouse principle requires that all the members of a family claiming relief should enter the house … Each individual must put on the workhouse dress, the husband must be separated from his wife, their children from both, and the male children from the female children … . If you are willing to be made the instruments of the Poor Law Commissioners in reducing your neighbours to slavery, we will not become your instruments by employing the slaves of your making.

Fielden declared that unless the guardians resigned, the mills of Fielden Brothers would shut down on the fateful 6th July. His idea was that by throwing 3,000 workers out of employment and on to poor relief, he would make the new system unworkable, but no doubt he hoped that the threat would suffice.

Another poster, this time

John Fielden's anti-Poor Law poster of the 2nd July 1838.

coming from Stansfield township, summoned a public meeting in Todmorden Market Place for 8 am on the 6th July, to march, 'preceded by the Royal Juvenile Band and appropriate banners', to Kiln Field near the Wood Mill Inn. It was anticipated that Oastler, who was now using his invective in the anti-poor law campaign, would address the meeting. The guardians hurriedly met on the evening of the 5th July, in the White Hart Inn, Todmorden. Their chairman was James Taylor, of Todmorden Hall, a magistrate and a man of some standing in the neighbourhood. They passed a resolution, noting Fielden's letter and the threats of violence uttered at anti-poor law meetings, and expressing the opinion that:

> in the present defenceless state of the neighbourhood they would hazard their lives should they attend the Meeting of the Guardians intended to have been held tomorrow at the Wood Mill ... this meeting is of the opinion that the New Poor Law cannot be successfully introduced into this Union unless the local influence of Mr. Fielden can by some means be overcome by Government.

The guardians appealed for 'adequate protection, civil or military' and postponed the meeting scheduled for the 6th July. The Kiln Field gathering passed off peacefully.

At this point William Helliwell of Friths Mill, the sole guardian for Todmorden with Walsden, weighed in with a poster of his own. He was, he declared, 'by no means friendly' to the new poor law but was against illegal proceedings. He launched a bitter attack upon the Fieldens:

> I cannot understand the principles of action of the man ... agitating the Public on the subject of WAGES and pretending to be the Friends of the Poor Hand-Loom Weavers, Spinners and Factory Infants, when they have been for years back and now are introducing more and more Power Looms and Self-Acting Mules, which undoubtedly have had the direct effect of lowering such Wages ...

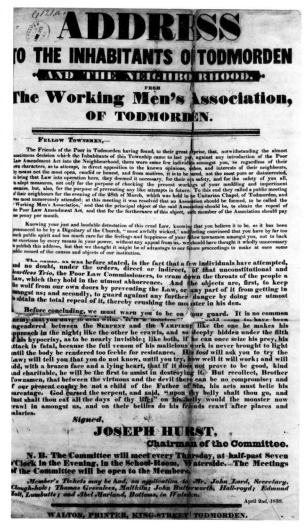

The address of the Working Men's Association of Todmorden, 2nd April 1838.

He described as 'disgusting and disgraceful' the system of 'exclusive dealing', ie boycotting of traders who favoured the new poor law, but was particularly incensed at John Fielden's threat to close his mills:

The idea itself — of a man raised in a comparatively short time to wealth and eminence, by the labours of thousands of his fellow creatures, many of whom have waxed old and hoary in his service, and the best part of whose days have been spent in administering ... to his comfort and luxuries ... arbitrarily Shutting his Doors against those workmen, and refusing them employ (without even the customary notice in the trade, without alleging that they had committed any fault ...) is one of the most grossly tyrannical and unjust acts that can be conceived.

Helliwell hinted that the real reason for the threatened closure was the slackness of trade, which would make a week or two's 'play' very convenient for the Fieldens.[31]

The Fielden mills closed on Friday the 6th July. A public meeting was called for the following Monday morning in Todmorden Market Place, with the intention of forcing all the guardians to resign. James Taylor and his fellow magistrate, John Crossley, who had been chairman of the board of guardians in 1837-38, replied by swearing in fifty special constables and calling in a squadron of cavalry from Burnley. The latter were quartered at Scaitcliffe, Crossley's home. These actions had the desired effect. The public meeting passed off quietly, with John Fielden urging the people 'to avoid tumult and riot'. The guardians refused to resign, and on the 16th July the Fielden mills reopened. The cavalry returned to Burnley Barracks.[32]

If the rebels had lost a battle, they had not yet lost the war. The board of guardians formally took over the administration of poor relief on the 12th August 1838, but both Todmorden with Walsden and Langfield refused to hand over their poor rates. They continued to pay outdoor relief to their paupers on the old system. The overseers were fined and, when they refused to pay, distress warrants were issued against them. Some cloth belonging to one of the Todmorden overseers, William Crossley, cotton manufacturer of Knowlwood Bottom Mill, was seized and offered for sale in Todmorden Market Place on the 21st October 1838. The millworkers poured out into the market place and their presence discouraged anyone from making a bid. The auctioneer asked the people around the stand to 'feel the quality', but the pieces of cloth soon began to travel across the square, and ended by being cut up and taken home by the local people. The auctioneer escaped, with difficulty, by promising never to sell any more distrained goods locally.[33]

Alfred Power, an Assistant Poor Law Commissioner, reported that two of the most active guardians, who were corn dealers, had lost a lot of custom as a result of the boycott, and one of them had resigned. He urged the commission 'to proceed at once against the parties who really influence and support this resistance in Todmorden', by which he presumably meant the Fieldens.[34]

On the 16th November 1838 two Halifax constables, James Feather and William King, went with a horse and cart to the Mankinholes home of William Ingham, a manufacturer and overseer of Langfield, to execute a distress warrant. The alarm was sounded by the bell at Fielden's Lumbutts Mill, and a messenger sent to Waterside Mill. Soon a large crowd of millworkers had gathered in front of Ingham's house. In James Feather's words:

The horse and cart were ... seized by the mob and thrown down, and I was thrown upon the horse. I then got up and was immediately struck on the side of my head with a large stone which again knocked me down. Stones were at this time flying in all directions and I was severely kicked ... I was seized by the crowd who said 'Hold him by his ears until he sees the cart burn ... '

William Ingham let Feather into his house, where he found King already hiding. The mob threatened to pull the house down but promised to spare the constables' lives if they left. According to Feather they said, 'We will spare your lives. Mr. Fielden said we must spare your lives.' The two constables set off for Halifax, twelve miles away, but were mauled, rolled in the mud, and had most of their clothes torn off. King managed to escape into a public house at Bottoms, and Feather took refuge in the house of Samuel Oliver (brother of Royston Oliver, a guardian) at Wood Mill. The mob broke the windows of Oliver's house and then did the same to the Wood Mill Inn on the other side of the road, where the guardians happened to be meeting. The latter escaped through the woods.

William Ingham had supported the anti-poor law movement but he was thoroughly alarmed by the ugly sight of mob violence. He wrote to the *Manchester Guardian* that he had been 'threatened after a most HORRIBLE and atrocious manner by three or four men upon Todmorden bridge ... that if I paid any money to the Bastile Guardians they would tear me to pieces ... it is high time that something should be done to prevent such disgraceful occurrences.' (The Bastille was the prison in Paris, stormed at the beginning of the French Revolution, to which the new Union workhouses were likened.)[35]

On the day that Ingham's letter appeared, Wednesday the 21st November, there was the most serious disturbance to date. A mob, or mobs, attacked the houses of several guardians, including William Helliwell, Royston Oliver and James Taylor. Windows were broken, and furniture and pictures destroyed. Taylor's new carriage was also wrecked. At 5 pm John Crossley sent this urgent note to the commanding officer at Burnley Barracks:

I do hereby request you to send here forthwith a squadron of Dragoons and some Infantry, as I have this moment received Information on oath of a large Mob which are now engaged in breaking windows and threatening the lives of the persons engaged in putting into force the New Poor Law here. I shall wait at Scaitcliffe till your arrival.

The speedy arrival of the cavalry restored peace and quiet, but it was thought necessary to quarter a force of infantry in the town.[36]

The local magistrates gathered the names of rioters from Feather, King, Helliwell and others. On the 23rd November five magistrates, 'a considerable body of constables', a troop of cavalry and 120 infantry surrounded Fielden's Lumbutts Mill and other mills, and made many arrests. After questioning, fourteen men were committed to York Gaol for the riot at Mankinholes, and two were sent to Kirkdale Gaol for the disturbances of the 21st November, some of which had taken place on the Lancashire side of the county boundary. The Todmorden Working Men's Association raised a subscription to help the accused men at their trial — 'Poor and innocent individuals ... dragged in chains of iron, from their affectionate Fathers, Mothers, Wives and Children' — and to support their dependants. The men were eventually bailed out by John Fielden and only one of them was sentenced to imprisonment, for nine months. The judge at the York Assizes commented that there were parties more deserving of punishment than the misguided men who stood before him for sentence.[37]

Now a youth hostel, this building in Mankinholes was the home of William Ingham, overseer of the poor for Langfield, in 1838 at the time of the Poor Law Riots.

A handloom weaving workshop on Salford was converted into temporary barracks at a cost of £325. Of this £118 was raised by subscription, and the rest advanced by John Crossley, who was eventually reimbursed by the Home Office. The presence of 100 infantry and 30 cavalry (who needed stabling and were billetted in four inns) kept the peace, but attempts to apprehend any more of the ringleaders of the 21st November riots were unsuccessful.[38]

The radicals now varied their tactics. The boycotts and intimidation were combined with legal proceedings on various technicalities. The overseers of the rebel townships were delighted to find that fines for breaches of the 1834 Act were to be paid over to — the overseers! The remaining guardians lost patience at the ineffectiveness of the law and began to evade or ignore the directives of the Poor Law Commission. It was decided in 1840 that, instead of having a relieving officer for the whole Union, one man would be appointed in each township to act as both relieving officer and rate collector, at a salary to be fixed by the township. This meant, in effect, restoring the old township system, but Assistant Commissioner Power had to advise that it would not be 'prudent to resist this under present circumstances', especially as the neighbouring Rochdale Union, where the guardians were also hostile, was about to be brought into operation. The Poor Law Commission was reduced to ineffectual protests but dare not press too hard, for fear that all the guardians would resign and destroy even the pretence of a Union.

By 1843 all the legal cases had been decided against the rebel townships, but there was no longer anything to rebel against. The guardians from Langfield and Todmorden with Walsden took their seats and co-operated happily with the new policy, which may be described as using the board of guardians as a shield, behind which the townships enjoyed their cherished independence.[39]

The commission persuaded the board that it was a bad thing to have rates collected and relief doled out by the same man, and the board admitted that 'the Officer in the course of his collection often found himself compelled to relieve dependants who were not actually destitute as the only means of quietly obtaining payment from some ratepayers'. The most that the board would do, however — and that not immediately — was to appoint separate relieving officers and assistant overseers (rate collectors) to cover pairs of townships. According to Assistant Commissioner Clements, Langfield was reluctant to be associated with Todmorden, 'a most litigious Township'.

In January 1844 Clements visited the six township workhouses, which he found to be generally dirty and neglected places used merely to lodge the homeless paupers. In Stansfield workhouse he found a lunatic pauper chained to a bed. There were nineteen inmates, and whilst 'the House is not crowded, every part of it is filthy — rags and lumber are scattered in every direction and altogether it is as disgusting a place as can well be imagined'.

Todmorden used the middle floor of a three-storey house, at the corner of Bacup Road and Pexwood Road, which was built into the side of the hill and could be entered directly at first-floor level. There were four rooms, one of which was a closet with no window. Two women, a girl, and a married couple with a child all slept in one room. Langfield had a small cottage at Croft Carr Green. There were nine inmates, including a woman with four bastard children who slept in one bed, 'the bedding of which was ... actually black with filth ... I could not have believed that in the country on the top of a hill with every facility for drying clothes, any woman could be found voluntarily to live in such a state of filth'.

Clements summed up the local workhouse conditions as 'one confused mass of squalid filth and wretchedness'. He told the commission that he had urged the guardians to take remedial action, 'but they think I am trying to induce them to build what they call "a regular Union workhouse"'. When the commission pointed out that all the workhouses in the Union were legally the responsibility of the guardians, the latter officially declared them closed. The townships continued to maintain them as before, the only difference being that as they did not officially exist, the workhouses could not be repaired out of the poor rate and were destined to grow worse rather than better.[40]

In the 1841 census, Gauxholme Workhouse had 17 inmates (11 male, 6 female), aged from 4 months to 80 years; all were classed as 'paupers', including one called James 'Awkard'! The 1851 census gives Gauxholme Workhouse as having 14 inmates (5 male, 9 female), aged from 5 to 73 years; one aged 71 was the head, the others were 'lodgers' as well as being paupers; 2 are given as former handloom weavers, 2 as former power-loom weavers, 3 as labourers, 2 as cotton piecers, 1 scholar, 1 NSO (no suitable occupation) and 3 (one aged 5) no job. The 1861 census states 'Gauxholme Workhouse no occupier each inmate paying a sum weekly'. There were 18 inmates (2 male, 16 female), aged from 3 to 83 years; 3 children, 3 NS (no suitable work), 1 disabled by epilepsy, 2 widows of labourers, 1 widow of lunatic, and 1 widow of a french polisher, the rest had jobs: 2 charwomen, 2 washerwomen, a hawker of earthenware, a needlewoman and a cotton frame tenter. By 1871 there were only 7 inmates (all female), aged from 12 to 76 years; jobs given were — 3 housework, 2 cotton spinners (1 former, with a lame hand), a dressmaker and a cotton operative out of employ; there was one orphan, and the others were unmarried or widowed.

Thus the workhouse inmates changed, on the census, from paupers in 1841 to lodgers in 1851, and by 1861 were 'equal contributors'. Two of the women who were

Lumbutts Mill, circa 1900 in this reconstruction painting, looking towards Mankinholes and Stoodley Moor. The Fieldens enlarged the mill and built the tower, which at first held two water wheels, a third being added prior to the final enlargement of the mill in 1845-47. The mill finally closed in 1926.

inmates for most of the period 1841-71 were described in the parochial accounts as 'simple' and 'idiot' respectively. In the 1861 census they were washerwomen. These subtle changes in the inmates' status concealed the fact that 'Gauxholme' remained a workhouse, despite its being officially declared closed following Clements's visit and report in 1844.

The people of the valley, confronted by the distress of 1842, regarded the workhouse solution as irrelevant as well as inhuman. The township relief committee compiled the following figures for Stansfield in the summer of 1842:

Total population 8,453 *(1841 census: 8,466)*

	Men	Women	Children over 12	Total
Capable of manual work	1,810	2,070	2,120	6,000
Fully employed	595	600	515	1,710
Partially employed	1,010	1,030	440	2,480
Unemployed	205	440	1,165	1,810

Only thirty per cent of the men were fully employed, but most of the remainder had some work, if only weaving an occasional piece of cloth at starvation wages. The normal condition of textile districts, when trade was depressed, was under-employment rather than massive unemployment. The theory behind the principle of 'less eligibility', that the threat of the workhouse would force the able-bodied to find work somewhere, made no sense in such communities.

Between the 29th August and the 31st October, 13,898 lbs of oatmeal (over six tons) were distributed to the needy in Stansfield. In December the following relief in kind was given, to 468 families containing 2,582 individuals: 230 pairs of cotton blankets, 140 coverlets, 1,856 yards of calico and 250 pairs of clogs. The minutes of the committee, recorded in the township order book, state: 'The committee regret that they have been reluctantly compelled to pass by many urgent cases in order to attend first the more destitute'.[41]

The Todmorden Board of Guardians continued to fight off the intermittent attacks of the Poor Law Board, which replaced the commission in 1847. They told the Poor Law Board, in February 1852, that they had decided, once again, not to build a workhouse. Later in the same year the Poor Law Board issued the Outdoor Relief Regulation Order, by which the boards of guardians were to refuse outdoor relief to men in work and were to set other able-bodied men to work and give half of the relief in kind. The board of guardians resolved that:

it was of the opinion that the said order is not well adapted for the manufacturing districts and that as regards this Union especially as all the relief ... therein is Outdoor Relief, and as there is no workhouse in this Union nor any probability of one being provided, the said order is wholly inapplicable to the Union; and this Board declares its total inability to carry out the provisions of such an order ...

The Poor Law Board rejected several demands that the order should be rescinded and the guardians refused to observe it. A compromise of sorts was reached whereby the board of guardians reported its cases of allowances to the employed and the Poor Law Board approved them, even to the extent of remitting certain sums, disallowed by the district auditor because more than half of the relief had been given in cash.

The relief being offered in such cases by the guardians was very modest, eg 1s a week in kind to a handloom weaver with a wife and six children, who was earning 9s a week. The largest payment was 4s a week in kind to a labourer (twenty-nine) earning 12s a week, with five children aged 6 years to 6 months but without a wife.

It could be argued that these allowances merely prolonged the agony of the declining trades like handloom weaving; but it was also necessary to assist power-loom weavers during periods of short time. In November 1853, a power-loom weaver in Stansfield, earning only 7s a week because the mill was running for only five hours a day, was granted 2s a week temporary relief. There are several other cases.[42]

The condition of the township workhouses was an intermittent cause of friction between the guardians and the Poor Law Board. In 1867 a deputation, including three of the Fieldens, told the president of the board, the Earl of Devon, that the decrepit condition of the cottages was the fault of the board, which had refused to allow repairs to be charged to the poor rate. As a last effort the Fieldens offered £3,000, either to convert the workhouses into cottage hospitals, or to build three new hospitals in different parts of the Union, on condition that they were used only for the sick, aged and infirm poor. The offer was refused.[43]

Eventually the Local Government Board, which took over the functions of the Poor Law Board in 1871, struck at the Achilles heel of local patriotism. It threatened to divide the Todmorden area between the Halifax and Rochdale Unions, which already had workhouses, unless a workhouse was built in Todmorden. The guardians reluctantly decided, in 1874, that a local workhouse was the lesser evil. It was opened in 1879.[44]

All was not lost, however: the Todmorden Board of Guardians knew that other Unions with workhouses had contrived to maintain selective outdoor relief to the able-bodied, including assistance to those in work. An inspector of the Poor Law Board told the *Manchester Guardian* in 1853: 'I can assure you that, to my knowledge,

TABLE I.—Dietary for the Able-Bodied.

		BREAKFAST		DINNER												SUPPER	
		Oatmeal Porridge.	Skimmed Milk.	Cooked Meat.	Potatoes.	Other Vegetables.	Bread.	Pea Soup.	Broth.	Rice Milk.	Potato Hash.	Cheese.	Butter.	Tea.	Coffee.	Oatmeal Porridge.	Skimmed Milk.
		pints.	pints.	oz.	oz.	oz.	oz.	pints.	pints.	pints.	oz.	oz	oz.	oz.	oz.	pints.	pints.
Sunday	Men	1½	1				8					2		1		1½	1
	Women	1½	1				8					2		1		1½	1
Monday	Men	1½	1	3	12	4	3		1							1½	1
	Women	1½	1	3	12	4	3		1							1½	1
Tuesday	Men	1½	1				4				1½					1½	1
	Women	1½	1				4				1½					1½	1
Wednesday	Men	1½	1				6						½		1	1½	1
	Women	1½	1				6						½		1	1½	1
Thursday	Men	1½	1	3	12	4	3		1							1½	1
	Women	1½	1	3	12	4	3		1							1½	1
Friday	Men	1½	1				6	1½								1½	1
	Women	1½	1				6	1½								1½	1
Saturday	Men	1½	1				6			1½						1½	1
	Women	1½	1				6			1½						1½	1

This is the weekly diet sheet for the able-bodied inmates at Stansfield View Workhouse, printed in the *Todmorden Union and Parochial Accounts* for March 1884.

Stansfield View Workhouse, Langfield, was completed in 1879 at a cost of £10,280.

wages are made up by rates in many places'. In 1881 the comment of the Local Government Board on the statistics of outdoor relief in England and Wales was that 'the old abuse of relief in aid of wages must largely prevail in some form or another'.[45]

The success of the anti-poor law campaign in the Todmorden area had three main causes: the bitterness of the workers, especially the handloom weavers at their condition; the solidarity which made possible an effective blend of threats, intimidation and occasional violence; and the reluctance of the guardians to become 'mere tools in carrying out rules and orders which we conscientiously believe to be illegal, impracticable and unjust', as they told the Poor Law Board in 1852. If the board did not like the way the Todmorden Guardians were operating, it could find someone else to do the job. But there was no one else. The centralised bureaucracy created by the 1834 Act depended upon the co-operation of local men of substance. In Todmorden only the two resident magistrates, John Crossley and James Taylor, were willing to resist violence, intimidation and the enormous influence of the Fieldens, but they received insufficient support. The Home Office expected the troops, stationed in the district, to be accommodated 'at the expense of those persons for whose protection a military force is stationed at Todmorden'. John Crossley commented: 'From the well known disaffection of this neighbourhood, you will readily believe that few will be found to contribute ... '.[46]

The Chartists
The printed address, in which the Working Men's Association thanked 'the inhabitants of Todmorden and its vicinity' for their 'very liberal support' of the rioters tried in March 1839, went on to announce a collection 'for the support of the National

Convention'. The latter was an assembly of fifty-four Chartist delegates, elected at public meetings all over the country, who met in London on the 4th February 1839 (in the words of the address of the Working Men's Association) 'to assist the people in getting a Parliament of their own choice to govern the country'.[47]

Historians have observed that, in the industrial West Riding, Chartism grew directly, both in spirit and in organisation, out of the anti-poor law movement.[48] In the upper Calder Valley this link was part of a greater continuity. The agitation for parliamentary reform, for the Ten Hours Bill, against the new Poor Law and for the People's Charter were phases of the same movement. Parliamentary reform was demanded, in 1830-32 and in the Chartist period, not as an end in itself but as a means to an end. It was taken for granted that a parliament representing the mass of the people would restrict the hours of work in factories, protect the workers in declining handicrafts such as wool combing and handloom weaving, and (after 1834) 'erase the infamous new Poor Law from the statute book' (Fielden).[49] According to the Todmorden Working Men's Association, 'We need only be true and united … . And then when the rights of all are restored and protected we shall behold smiling peace and plenty'.[50]

One of the dominant radical figures in Yorkshire was Feargus O'Connor. On the 18th November 1837 he launched the *Northern Star*, published weekly in Leeds, which became the chief organ of Chartism. It was avidly read (and read from, by the literate to the illiterate) and eagerly discussed by working men in the upper Calder Valley. In his autobiography, Samuel Fielden (a distant relative of John Fielden's family) remembers his father, a foreman at Waterside, saying 'that on the day the *Northern Star*, O'Connor's paper was due, the people used to line the roadside waiting for its arrival, which was paramount to everything else for the time being'.[51] The early reports in the *Northern Star* show that radical organisations were in existence in nearly every town and village of upper Calderdale. One of the problems of a radical association was finding somewhere to meet, and Todmorden Working Men's Association was fortunate in having the use of the schoolroom at Waterside Mill, by courtesy of the Fieldens.

The *People's Charter* was published in May 1838 by the London Working Men's Association. It set out the famous 'Six Points' of their cause: annual parliamentary elections; universal manhood suffrage; equal electoral districts; abolition of the property qualification for MPs; payment of MPs; and vote by ballot. Most of these points had been common aims amongst working class radicals for some time.

John Fielden was dedicated to political reform, seeing it as the way to the social reforms which were so dear to his heart. His speech at the Lancashire Chartist demonstration on Kersal Moor, near Manchester, on the 24th September 1838 shows this plainly:

> The argument … that because you have not property you ought not to have a vote, is, I contend altogether unsound, and the doctrine most mischievous, and knowing this I trust the people will continue to demand the elective franchise for the poor as well as the rich … But let me guard you gentlemen. All manner of devices will be resorted to in order to sow divisions amongst you. One will tell you that you should have a factory bill — a short time bill; another that you should have a repeal of the poor law; another will be for a repeal of the corn laws; and another for a minimum of wages for the handloom weavers; and another will promise you all you want, if you'll avoid asking for the suffrage. My advice is, to disregard all applications to you to divert you from your object. Keep to

the one single point ... The suffrage, and the suffrage only, should satisfy the working people of England.[52]

On the 15th October 1838 a great Chartist meeting was held on Hartshead Moor, roughly equidistant from Bradford, Halifax and Huddersfield. Contingents came from all over the West Riding, including the upper Calder Valley, each carrying banners with inscriptions such as 'Universal Suffrage', 'No New Poor Law' and 'No Bastille Punishment'. Among the main speakers were Feargus O'Connor and John Fielden.

The violent language of the Chartists, the sheer numbers gathering on Hartshead Moor and the riots in Todmorden in 1838 thoroughly alarmed the local magistrates. John Crossley of Scaitcliffe told the Home Secretary, Lord John Russell, that he had reason to believe that 'the Population is armed and desperate in their purpose to resist' the new poor law. The Home Office reacted cautiously, perhaps because there was already a military force at Todmorden, and asked for more evidence. However, following more unrest, a detachment of the 3rd Dragoon Guards arrived at Halifax on the 27th December. One of the JPs, J R Ralph, expressed the 'great satisfaction' of 'all the respectable inhabitants' and thought that the presence of the soldiers would 'give sufficient check to the ill-disposed'.[53]

In July 1839 the House of Commons declined to consider a Chartist petition, of which John Fielden was co-presenter, which was said to have 1,280,000 signatures. The National Chartist Convention, at first in favour of a general strike, broke up in dissension and left further action to local Chartist groups. The Todmorden Working Men's Association held a series of well-attended meetings, but adopted the practice of admitting members only, by ticket. John Crossley was frustrated at being no longer able to discover what was happening at the meetings.[54]

John Fielden was against those Chartists who advocated using physical force to gain their ends, arguing for the use of moral force instead. For a time the 'physical force' party held sway and locally the authorities were fearful of violence and bloodshed, swearing in large numbers of special constables and maintaining a military presence.[55] In May 1841, John Crossley was told that Lord Normanby, a Home Office minister, had 'received with great satisfaction your favourable report' of the military situation at Todmorden, and that it was not thought necessary to continue to station troops there. By October the temporary barracks had been abandoned.[56]

Meanwhile the Fieldens and their Todmorden supporters had opened up a second front against the established order. The Methodists, Baptists, Independents, Unitarians, Inghamites and Quakers, who together made up a substantial majority of the local population, resented paying church rates, especially, in the case of Todmorden and Walsden, the part which went to the parish church at Rochdale. The benefice there was very wealthy; by 1866 the income from glebe land exceeded £4,000 a year, largely as a result of the building upon it of hundreds of houses as the town of Rochdale expanded.

The appointment as vicar, in the middle of the first Chartist agitation, of Dr John Molesworth, a prominent Tory and campaigner against the reform bills, prompted the nonconformists and radicals to mobilise against the church rate. A placard, printed in Todmorden, offered a reward of £100 to anyone who would send the new vicar to hell and bring back the old one (who had died). The latter proposal is a little surprising, as Molesworth's predecessor was Rev William Robert Hay, an eighteen stone pluralist parson whose excellent social connections were not matched by his spiritual gifts. He had been the magistrate who read the Riot Act on the occasion of the Peterloo

Massacre, and as a reward for his fortitude was given the vicarage of Rochdale to add to his other benefices. According to cleric and historian Canon Raines, who knew him personally, 'he thoroughly disliked Rochdale' and kept his visits to a minimum. His neglect was partly responsible for the strength of nonconformity in and around Rochdale.

In July 1840 a proposed church rate was voted down by a majority of 66 in a poll of over 8,000 people, the balance being tilted by the large Todmorden contingent brought by the Fieldens by train and waggon. The church party called another meeting two weeks later, and won the subsequent poll by 6,594 votes to 6,481. On this occasion the voters of Todmorden and Walsden, who included women, eligible to vote if they were ratepayers, divided 146 for the rate, 1,340 against. The radical campaign, led by John Bright, MP for Rochdale, and John Fielden's brother James, continued and was victorious in 1843, when by a vote of 2,963 to 1,140 church rates in Rochdale were effectively abolished.[57]

In April 1842 the second Chartist National Convention met in London, and the following month Attwood and Fielden presented to Parliament a new petition which, it was claimed, had 3,300,000 signatures. It received no more support than the first one, but the rebuff was not followed by any militant action.

The Chartists were taken by surprise in August 1842 when the 'Plug Riots' erupted in Lancashire. Unemployment and wage cuts, in a severe trade depression, had caused great distress. Many families of the cotton handloom weavers, fighting a losing battle against the power loom, were starving. Early in August, millworkers began to come out on strike, against further wage cuts, and desperate mobs marched from mill to mill, forcing them to stop work and, if they refused to do so, pulling the plugs out of the boilers. This stopped work, by emptying the boilers of water, without which there could be no steam to power the machinery.

John Crossley and James Taylor, the Todmorden magistrates, were warned early on Friday the 12th August that a mob was approaching from Rochdale. They swore in 100 special constables and secured a troop of cavalry from Burnley, which was quartered in a 'large unoccupied loomshed' (according to Holden this was Buckley's Mill at Ridgefoot) at about 11 am. They offered protection to the leading manufacturers, 'but they all seemed disposed at once to give up working rather than run the risk of continuing their works in operation'. At about 1 pm, a crowd of people, estimated by Crossley and Taylor to number between 15,000 and 20,000, arrived, mainly along the Rochdale and Bacup roads. Many of them were carrying sticks.

The first mill in Todmorden to be visited by the strikers was Fieldens at Waterside. John Fielden declared his support, declined the offer of protection from the cavalry and closed the mill. On the following morning, according to Police Sergeant William Harrison (appointed under the 1839 Police Act), 'another large assemblage', apparently of local people, gathered under the new railway arches in Todmorden, and moved off towards Halifax, stopping any mills still working. On Monday and Tuesday, the 15th and 16th August, large crowds from upper Calderdale and Bradford became involved in clashes with the military in Halifax, resulting in some fatalities and many arrests.

The Chartists tried to identify with the strikers. Their posters, with the usual mixture of lurid language and religious imagery, claimed that the cotton workers had declared for the charter, and that every mill within forty miles of Manchester was stopped: '... rally round our sacred cause, and leave the rest to the God of Justice and of battles'.[58]

A royal proclamation, forbidding secret meetings, and a similar declaration from John Crossley and James Taylor were posted up in and around Todmorden on the 17th August.

On the following morning a meeting was held near the railway arches in Todmorden, attended by over 1,000 people. Robert Brook, secretary of the Todmorden WMA, urged the crowd to stay away from work 'until the Charter had become the law of the land', but to remain peaceful.

It proved impossible to sustain the strike and the operatives returned to work, after a lay-off lasting nearly a fortnight. On the 5th September Robert Brook was arrested on a warrant alleging unlawful conspiracy and riot. His correspondence and the books and other papers of the Todmorden WMA were seized, and James Newell Walton, the Todmorden printer, was brought before Crossley and Taylor to testify that most of the records were in Brook's handwriting.[59] Walton was biting the hand that had fed him, as he printed nearly all the anti-poor law and Chartist posters. Crossley and Taylor later told the Home Office that the books showed 'a very large number of regularly enrolled Chartists in this village and there are similar societies throughout the district'. Brook was committed for trial, along with O'Connor and fifty-seven others, at the next Lancaster assizes in March 1843, but an error in the indictment led to the acquittal of all the accused.[60]

The 'Plug Plot' was a hopeless move by workers driven to desperation. A general strike in the textile industry had no chance of success when trade was so depressed. The Chartists, who tried to harness the movement, were weakened by its collapse and the subsequent arrest of their leaders. In the upper Calder Valley, however, they remained in good heart, and if Crossley and Taylor hoped that their action against the Todmorden Chartists would subdue them, they were mistaken. They wrote to the Home Office on the 4th November 1842:

> In this district comprising a population of about 25,000 persons the Chartists are continually holding meetings, principally in the evenings after the hours of work, and have engaged lecture rooms in several places in which both on the Sabbath and on weekdays political sermons and lectures are delivered ... .

Despite the indictment of Robert Brook, the meetings seemed to be increasing in frequency. They usually broke up towards midnight, when 'they sing through the streets a Chartist song composed about Mr O'Connor as their leader, to the great annoyance of the peaceable inhabitants'.[61]

The Chartists and John Fielden saw the trade depression as a suitable opportunity for a new Ten Hours campaign. Three factory bills were debated in the House of Commons in 1843-44. The outcome was the 1844 Factory Act, which limited the hours of children under thirteen to six and a half per day, and raised their ration of schooling to fifteen hours a week. Henceforth these children were 'half-timers' at both mill and school. The restriction of hours was, however, taken as the justification for lowering the minimum age of employment to eight. Women were brought under the limit of sixty-nine hours a week previously applied to young persons. The fencing of all machinery was made compulsory. This measure fell far short of the aspirations of the radical movement, as it left all operatives over eighteen working a twelve-hour day.[62]

Two new attempts were made, in January and the autumn of 1846. Despite ill-health, Fielden worked tirelessly, making speeches, attending meetings, leading delegations and lobbying for support in parliament. An industrial recession weakened the manufacturers' opposition, and an alliance of Whigs and Protectionist Tories carried the bill, which provided for a ten hour day for women and young persons. It became law in June 1847, when there was great rejoicing in the textile districts, not least in

Todmorden. Paradoxically, partly because of his insistence on having John Cobbett, the son of his old colleague William Cobbett, as his running mate, Fielden lost his seat at Oldham in the election of July 1847.[63] He was not well but had sought election because there was still so much to be done in the field of social and political justice.

A new Chartist petition, enthusiastically supported by the upper Calder Valley, was presented to parliament in April 1848 but, despite its contemptuous rejection, the enthusiasm of the local Chartists was not diminished. At the same time the struggle for the Ten Hours' Act, which the reformers thought they had won, had been re-opened. The revival of trade in 1849 caused some millowners, led by John Bright, to look for loopholes in the factory laws. It had been the intention of the 1844 Act to prevent the working of women, young persons and children in shifts, but the wording was found by the courts to be ambiguous. Some millowners used children as assistants to men after the women and young persons had left work, so that the men, whose hours were not directly regulated, could be worked for more than ten hours.

John Fielden, ill though he was, came out of retirement to protect his Ten Hours' Act and addressed an audience of 3,000 at the Free Trade Hall in Manchester. He even began to consider a general strike to settle the issue once and for all, and advised at a

John Fielden's statue, originally at the town hall, was moved to Fielden Square in 1890 and then to Centre Vale Park

meeting in Oldham on the 29th August that adult workers, after giving notice, should refuse to work for more than ten hours. He advised the same course of action at a meeting in Warrington in October.[64]

In December, however, he was struck with his final illness and, although he was able to lead with Ashley a deputation to the Home Secretary in defence of his Act, he died a few days later on the 29th May 1849. He was described in the *Annual Register* as 'essentially the advocate of the labouring classes .... A member of the legislature, he was still in all his recollections and predilictions a member of the labouring multitude'. Many thousands of that multitude followed him, sorrowing, to his grave in the Unitarian chapel yard. His brothers James and Thomas, and his sons Samuel, John and Joshua, carried on his public work and organised 'Fielden Societies' to defend the Ten Hours' Act.[65]

In 1850 Ashley agreed to a compromise plan for a 10½ hour day for women and young persons — 6 am to 6 pm with 1½ hours for meals — but the loopholes were not all plugged and a new Act was required in 1853. The Fielden family never forgave Ashley (who became Earl of Shaftsbury in 1851) for his 'treachery'.[66]

Chartism in the upper Calder Valley did not fade out with the failure of the 1848 petition. It remained an active force for another ten years, before yielding place to new movements in which the Chartist veterans played a prominent part. The years 1848-49 may be taken, however, as the end of an epoch in local history. They saw, as well as the death of John Fielden, the last occasion on which the magistrates nervously watched the massed ranks of politically-conscious workers on the move, and wondered how many of them possessed guns and whether they would use them.

The 'Age of Agitation' in the Todmorden area is remarkable for a combination of strong group loyalties and a spirit of local independence. The roots of these attitudes lie deep in the history of a people struggling with a difficult environment. For those actively concerned — and they were many — it provided a profound political education, and also training in what the Co-operative movement later called 'the art of association'. These twin achievements should be placed alongside factory reform and the resistance to the new poor law, to balance the failure to protect the out-worker and gain the Charter.

The Town Develops, 1800-1850

Industrial and Urban Growth

By the early years of the nineteenth century Todmorden was confirmed as a 'cotton' area, with most of the tributary streams as well as the main rivers providing power for the mills carding and spinning cotton. The handlooms in the cottages, or the loomshops associated with some of the houses of the manufacturers, were busy weaving the cloth. There was still woollen and worsted manufacturing, and for many years to come there were more textile workers employed outside than inside factories. The district was still essentially rural and the population scattered, though set to grow dramatically as the century progressed.

POPULATION FIGURES

TOWN-SHIP	1801	1811	1821	1831	1841	1851	1861	1871	1881	1891	1901
Tod w Wal	2,515	3,652	4,985	6,054	7,311	7,699	9,146	9,333	9,237	8,904	9,085
Langfield	1,170	1,515	2,069	2,514	3,284	3,729	4,391	4,321	5,063	5,581	5,578
Stansfield	4,768	5,447	7,275	8,262	8,466	7,627	8,174	8,977	10,608	11,266	11,685
TOTAL	8,453	10,614	14,329	16,830	19,061	19,055	21,711	22,631	24,908	25,751	26,348

In the above figures, it must be remembered that the Lower Third of Stansfield (for administrative purposes Stansfield was divided into thirds, Upper, Middle and Lower), between Jumble Hole Clough at Eastwood and Colden Water at Mytholm near Hebden Bridge, is outside what became the Borough of Todmorden, and also that part of Cornholme in the township of Cliviger ought to be included. Nevertheless, the pattern of population growth can be clearly seen.

At the turn of the nineteenth century, however, the only signs of things to come were the many small spinning mills, the turnpike road and the Rochdale Canal. The latter's success mirrors the district's early industrial development. The canal's income from tolls or dues rose from £13,000 in 1807 to £41,000 in 1825. The annual tonnage carried reached 875,000 in 1839. The largest single item was coal.[1] In addition to the main warehouses at Manchester, Rochdale and Sowerby Bridge, smaller ones were built at Todmorden and Gauxholme.

The increased economic activity in the district led to a campaign for a regular postal service, which was orchestrated by John Crossley, treasurer of the turnpike trust. From 1791 a 'horse post' was provided on three days a week between Halifax and Burnley via Todmorden, but because the GPO was receiving only 1s per week for the Todmorden-Burnley section, the service was restricted to the Halifax-Todmorden road in 1799. The request for a mail coach was finally granted by 1824-25, after the line of the turnpike between Todmorden and Littleborough had been altered so as to

The building of the Golden Lion Inn in the eighteenth century followed the arrival of the turnpike road. Shown here in a reconstruction drawing, it became the town's coaching inn and the first post office.

provide an easier gradient. The coaches travelling between Rochdale and Halifax called at the Golden Lion Inn.[2]

The still essentially rural nature of the 'town centre' around 1820 can be gauged by the fact that observers standing on the canal bridge near the Golden Lion could see the stagecoach breast the brow at Castle Hill, which was the signal for the change horses to be warmed up along Church Lane.

The map of Todmorden, as surveyed in 1816 (see opposite), is worth looking at in detail. Notice the gardens, represented by the square, dotted areas, attached to most of the individual buildings. There were four places of worship: St Mary's Church in the centre; the Methodist Chapel, Doghouse, established in 1784, in which year John Wesley preached there;[3] Patmos Chapel, founded in 1816 by the New Connexion Methodists; and fourthly, the Friends (Quakers) Meeting House at Bank Top, built in 1808. The river still followed its natural course; Walsden Water ran in an open channel through the town and along the side of Burnley Road, before turning east (where Stansfield Road now is) and merging with the Burnley Valley Calder in meadows then belonging to Stansfield Hall. From here the Calder crossed the vale to join its present course near Stansfield Bridge at the bottom of Halifax Road.

The river was bridged at three points and the canal at one in their passage through the town centre: Pickles Bridge at Salford on Rochdale Road, where the sharp, left-hand bend in the river was made to accommodate the canal; Neddy Bridge over the canal (the original bridge is still underneath the present one); Royal Bridge at the top

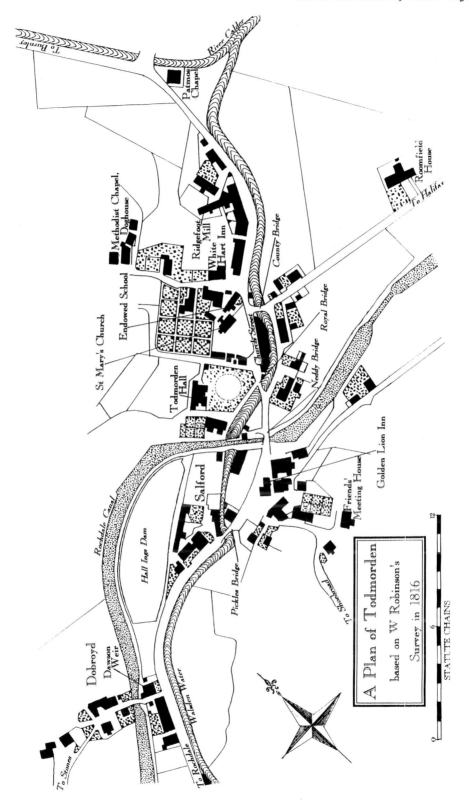

A Plan of Todmorden based on W Robinson's Survey in 1816

of Water Street (earlier known as Old Shop Lane); and County Bridge (the boundary between Lancashire and Yorkshire) at the junction with Halifax Road.

Near the church to the east were the Endowed School and old vicarage, and beyond these the White Hart Inn, originally called New Inn when it was built in 1728. Between the inn and its farm buildings, the old highway led out of Todmorden via Dog House Lane to Sourhall and forward to Burnley, with branches off to Bacup and Rochdale.

MARKET
AT
Todmorden.

——◦◦◦❦◦◦◦——

WHEREAS A MEETING
was held at the House of
MR. SAMUEL HANSON,

Known by the Sign of the White Hart Inn, in Todmorden aforesaid,
On FRIDAY, the 18th Day of December, 1801,
Pursuant to public Notice given, for the Purpose of taking into Consideration the Propriety of establishing

A MARKET

In the said Town, and for fixing the particular DAY on which the same should be held,

It was by the said Meeting unanimously resolved, That it would be of considerable Utility to the said Town and Neighbourhood for a Market to be held in Todmorden aforesaid, and that the most proper Day for holding the same, would be on Thursday in each Week; and that the First Market should be held on Thursday the Fourth Day of February next.

Notice is hereby given,

That in Pursuance of the above Resolutions,
A MARKET WILL BE HELD
In TODMORDEN aforesaid,
On Thursday the 4th Day of February next;
And on each succeeding THURSDAY;

when and where all Persons wishing to promote and encourage the same are requested to attend.
ANTHONY CROSSLEY, Chairman.
Todmorden, December 19, 1801.

Holden and Dowson, Printers, Halifax.

The open space in front of the White Hart was the site of the first market opened in 1802, following a decision by the township of Todmorden and Walsden. Market day was originally Thursday, then Saturday was added for meat, fish and greengroceries, Thursday being limited to corn and provisions. A cattle market was also held on the first Thursday of each month. The parish clerk was wont to act as town cryer after Sunday morning service, announcing at the church gate which local farmer or butcher would be killing a cow or sheep that week, so that fresh meat could be obtained.[4]

Turning left out of White Hart Fold along Burnley Road, there was a group of properties, fourteen in number, stretching about as far as the present Abraham Ormerod Centre, including two tailors' shops, two grocers' shops, the Patmos Inn and Ridgefoot Mill.[5] The mill at this time was water-powered, water being carried by an underground conduit under the canal and behind Todmorden Hall, from a large reservoir at Hall Ings (meadows originally belonging to Todmorden Hall) in the 'Salford' area of Todmorden.

The map shows very little development along Halifax Road. Immediately right after County Bridge was 'Old Shop Lane' (Water Street) containing the properties which are currently shops. Apart from one or two shops on the main road, the only other building was Roomfield House where the Rev Atkinson, curate at St Mary's and Cross Stone from 1795 to 1819, lived.

Along Rochdale Road, the first part of which is known as Church Street, was the present block of property including the Royal George Inn and some buildings, now demolished, including the Grapes Inn, which had a deed dated 1796.[6]

There were a few cottages and shops on Rise Lane and then Todmorden Hall, with gardens sloping down to the main road. More cottages were situated on Hall Street near the site of the present library, separating the hall from the canal. Over Neddy Bridge was the Golden Lion, the coaching inn referred to earlier. Beyond and behind the inn, in the areas named evocatively Cockpit, Hangingditch and Honey Hole, were some of the oldest properties in the district. The road passing through this part was the old highway leading via Shoebroad and Swineshead to either Rochdale or Halifax.

This 1820s letterhead of John Buckley, Ridgefoot Mill, shows the essentially rural nature of the pre-railway valley. St Mary's Church is on the left, with Todmorden Hall beyond.

Further along Rochdale Road and over Pickles Bridge, the area between the road and canal is known as Salford, which in 1816 was the most industrialised part of Todmorden, foreshadowing its future development. Here, fronting on to the main road, was the first steam-powered factory in Todmorden. Built by Henry Ramsbottom, it is recorded in Crompton's 1811 Spindle Enquiry as Todmorden Steam, having 2,592 mule spindles and 480 throstle spindles. It was next door to the Lord Nelson Tavern, and it is recorded that William Sutcliffe, the landlord, rigged up an attachment to the mill's power to rock the cradle of his son, who later in life claimed he 'shud be a sharp chap, for he wur rocked bi steeam'.[7] Behind the mill and abutting onto it was Jeremiah Jackson's mechanics' shop. Founded in 1796, it was one of the earliest of the ancilliary firms which served the textile industry. Next to this was Parkinson's size house, where warps were sized for Fieldens at Waterside, and then Stansfield's iron foundry. The power for all these enterprises, including the bellows of the foundry, came from Ramsbottom's engine. Also in the Salford area were James and William Chambers's dye works, and Richard Chaffer's wheelwright's shop.[8]

Beyond Salford, the next building along Rochdale Road was Dawson Weir, previously the 'Coach and Horses Inn' and later the home of John Fielden. The road over the canal next to Dawson Weir led to two small mills powered by water from Dobroyd Clough.[9] The upper mill, by 1816, was run by the Marland family, who made rollers for spinning machines; the other was a spinning mill occupied by Samuel Greenwood.[10]

On the opposite side of the main road was Laneside Mill, the home of the Fielden enterprise. By 1816 the premises had started to grow, but were nowhere near their ultimate size.

The map shows the river flowing openly through the town centre, which was at river level. Approaching from Rochdale the road climbed to cross the canal at Neddy Bridge, just east of the aqueduct which carried the canal over the river. Beginning in 1836 when the river, from this point to Royal Bridge, was arched over by Mrs Ann

Taylor of Todmorden Hall,[11] the whole of the town centre was gradually built up to its present level, leaving properties along Church Street, Water Street and the upper parts of Halifax Road with 'cellars' containing doors and windows which once opened at street level, a storey below the present-day pavement.

The industrial expansion of the first forty years of the nineteenth century more than doubled the population. Some mills changed their use: Pudsey Mill was taken by Laurence Wilson in 1825 for bobbin making; Frieldhurst Mill changed to corn milling in 1822, but by 1835 had reverted to cotton spinning.

New mills were built: Barewise Mill at Knotts in the Burnley Valley by 1808; Spring Mill circa 1819; and below it Ramsden Wood Lower Mill circa 1821. Gradually the best sites for water-powered mills were taken up, but the most dramatic innovation was the expansion of steam power, which Fieldens had introduced at Waterside by 1818.[12] Inghams had steam engines at Millsteads (10 hp) and Cinderhill (20 hp) installed in 1811 and 1824 respectively. Thomas Sutcliffe of Stoodley Bridge Mill had an 18 hp engine there by 1813, and Andrew Aspden of Harley House Mill one of 8 hp in 1823.[13] By the early 1830s several mills were using both water and steam, for example Causeway Wood Mill on Lumbutts Clough generated 5 hp by water and 8 hp by steam.[14]

There was a close connection between the expansion of steam power and the introduction of the power loom, which was sometimes referred to as the 'steam loom'. It had proved technically more difficult to mechanise weaving than spinning and, although a prototype power loom had been invented by Rev Edmund Cartwright in 1786, it was not until 1822 that a much-improved version, patented by Sharpe, Roberts and Company, led to its rapid spread. By 1822 Waterside was purchasing power looms.[15] Stoodley Bridge Mill included five power looms amongst sale items in 1825.[16] Another factor in the relatively slow spread of the power loom was the abundance of cheap labour available to work as handloom weavers (through the rapid growth in population), whose plight, as wages fell after 1815, became ever more desperate.

A return of power looms, made to the factory inspectorate in 1835 (which is probably incomplete), lists nine mills in the Todmorden area, eight of them in cotton with 1,284 power looms. Of these, Fielden Brothers had 810 looms at Waterside, powered by a 60 hp steam engine. At most mills each weaver tended two looms; Fieldens returned a figure of precisely 405 weavers. At the ninth mill, Ridgefoot, Buckleys were using 150 power looms to weave a worsted/cotton mixture known as 'gambroons', used for men's coats.[17]

At this time in the 1830s, there was still more cloth woven on handlooms by outworkers than in weaving sheds. Fieldens had 'takkin' in shops' in each of the three main valleys, collecting between 2,000 and 3,000 pieces a week. In July 1822 John Fielden requested £500 in sovereigns from Manchester to pay the weavers at Frieldhurst, Cornholme, where the takkin' in shop was 'John o' Susan's big chamber' (near Holme House railway arch).[18] Other manufacturers had similar arrangements or had cloth woven in 'loomshops'. Travis records that at 'Toad Hole' in 1820, James Stansfield had a number of handloom weavers working for Mr Ramsbottom (Ewood Mill) in a large room over a wheelwright and blacksmith's shop.[19]

The Fielden enterprises were moving inexorably onwards. Whilst expanding at Waterside they had acquired other mills in the district: Lumbutts Mill, circa 1794;[20] Causeway Mill (Midgehole), 1813;[21] Stoneswood Lower Mill, 1813/14;[22] Waterstalls Mill, 1820;[23] Smithyholme Mill, 1818/19;[24] and Dobroyd Mill certainly by 1832 and probably earlier.[25]

The cotton industry was liable to fluctuations in trade, and even a successful firm like the Fieldens was not immune from the effects of depressions. They had made their fortune during the good years of the 1820s, which helped them to weather the depression of 1831-32. John Fielden claimed that, from 1824, cotton manufacturing had ceased to be the main source of his family's income. By the end of 1836, Fielden Brothers' assets were £513,322, of which the Todmorden assets were £126,938 and included the mills, machinery, property belonging to the family, work in progress, plus stocks of cloth and raw cotton. The Manchester assets were £201,375, mainly stocks of woven cloth, cloth being finished, cloth in the process of being sold abroad, and money owing for cloth sold abroad. The sum of £199,215 had been invested in the financial house of Wildes Pickersgill, and it was this branch of their affairs which had to approach the Bank of England for assistance in the depression of 1837.[26]

The spinning process was improved by the development of Richard Roberts's self-acting mule in 1825, with patented improvements in 1830. It achieved a higher degree of automation than was previously available and, although a skilled male operative was still needed, production costs were considerably reduced. The Fieldens ordered improved self-actors from an American machinist in 1828.[27] When William Dodd visited Waterside works in 1841, he was told the mule frames of 1810 had 228 spindles on each, whereas the mules of 1841 had three times as many spindles and produced six times the output — presumably with the aid of two boy piecers instead of one.[28]

The improvements in the speed and complexity of textile machinery required similar advances of quality and performance in the engineering industry which supplied them. Two local firms in particular were very successful. Jeremiah Jackson, mentioned above at Salford, manufactured machines for every stage of cotton processing from opening the raw cotton to spinning, including carding engines, drawing and roving frames, and mules. In 1832, Buckleys bought a mule frame with 1,280 spindles (presumably self-acting) for £213 6s 8d. Jackson and his men also went round the mills maintaining and repairing machinery.[29]

One of the familiar routes to success in textile engineering was taken by John Lord and some of his sons. They had worked as mechanics at Waterside Mill, and moved out in the mid-1830s to set up their own machine-making business. At first they took a spare room-with-power at Clough Mill, but after a few years were able to build the Canal Street Works, where they prospered as one of the leading engineering firms of the area.

By 1801 Ramsbothams had a factory at Ewood, part of which was an iron foundry, making cotton machinery for Knott Mill, Deansgate, Manchester, the orders being shipped there by canal.[30] Ramsbothams had an interest in this firm, having come into the district from Manchester. In 1834, John Ramsbottom of Salford Steam Factory and Richard Holt, iron founder also of Salford, patented improvements to the power loom, including an automatic stop motion which operated if the weft threads broke. Two years later Ramsbottom patented a new arrangement of spindle and flyer for use in throstles, and similar spinning machinery to enable weft (finer than warp thread) to be spun on these as well as on mules.[31] The waterwheel for Ridgefoot Mill was made in 1790 by William and Robert Barker at Priestwell. Future generations of the family had foundries in the valley at Swan, Millwood, and Salford.[32]

The spinning machines required bobbins, flyers and spindles. Looms (especially as power looms increased) required shuttles, pickers, healds and reeds, so it is not surprising to find the development of works supplying these articles to the trade. The most celebrated of these was Laurence Wilson, who began his bobbin manufacturing at Houghstone Factory in 1823 with his savings plus £50 lent to him by John Fielden.[33] Two years later he took Pudsey Mill, and in 1831 moved to new works at Cornholme.

Bobbin making continued at Pudsey Mill after Wilson left, the works being taken over by John Helliwell of Shaws in Stansfield. Another bobbin-turning works was that of John Holt, who occupied the building known as 'Salford Barracks'. At Inchfield Fold, Robert Fielden began making pickers, the leather straps used for propelling the shuttle across the loom, as did his brother James at Clough Mill and Martin Holt at Sourhall. In 1936, Robert Fielden and Sons claimed to be the oldest picker-making firm in the world.[34]

The Railway Age

The first phase of the industrial revolution in the upper Calder Valley, dominated by the development of spinning mills, had been closely associated with improvements in transport — the turnpike road and the canal — which had transformed the Calder gorge from an obstacle to movement into a main channel of communication between Yorkshire and Lancashire. The Rochdale Canal, which linked waterway networks extending through the Lancashire and Yorkshire coalfields to the ports of Liverpool and Hull, had cut the transport costs of both raw materials and manufactured goods, and in particular had encouraged the use of steam power by supplying cheap coal. Yet within thirty years of its completion, the canal was potentially challenged by early moves to build a railway, an undertaking which was to change the physical appearance of the district more than any other human enterprise before or since.

The first trans-Pennine railway followed the same route as the Rochdale Canal.

The letterhead of Marlands, roller makers at Deanroyd, Walsden, shows the entrance to Summit Tunnel on the left.

On the Lancashire side, the Liverpool-Manchester line was opened in 1830, and by 1838 it had been linked by branch lines to Bolton, Warrington and several other industrial towns in South Lancashire. The first public railway in the West Riding was the Leeds-Selby, opened in 1834 and extended to Hull in 1840. Meanwhile, George Hudson's York and North Midland Railway was connecting Derby via Normanton with both Leeds and York. These lines opened on the 1st July 1840.[35]

In 1831 a parliamentary bill for the construction of the railway between Manchester and Sowerby Bridge via Todmorden was defeated through the opposition of the Rochdale Canal Company. In 1836, however, an Act approved a line from Manchester via the upper Calder Valley to Normanton, with running rights over the ten miles of the York and North Midland line between there and Leeds.[36]

The work began on the Manchester and Leeds railway in August 1837. The section from Manchester to Littleborough was opened on the 3rd July 1839, and in the opposite direction the line from Normanton had reached Hebden Bridge by the 5th October 1840.[37] On the 17th August 1838, to quote the directors' minutes, 'The Directors descended No 10 shaft, and the Chairman had the pleasure of laying the first brick for Summit Tunnel.'[38] Altogether fourteen shafts were sunk along the line of the tunnel, and work proceeded in both directions from the bottom of each shaft as well as from both ends of the tunnel.[39]

The work on the tunnel went slowly at first, and the original contractors were dismissed. It was completed by December 1840, at a cost of £251,000. At the time Summit Tunnel was the longest railway tunnel in the world, although with so much construction in progress it held this distinction for only a few months. It is 2,885 yards long, 21 feet 6 inches high and 23 feet wide. The brickwork lining the tunnel varies from five to ten rings in thickness, and is said to contain a total of 23,000,000 bricks.[40]

The highest point of the line is at the northern end of Summit Tunnel, 540 feet above sea level (60 feet below the level of Summit Pool on the Rochdale Canal). From there the level falls to 349 feet at Hebden Bridge station and 274 feet at Sowerby Bridge. At each end of the main tunnel, after a short gap, there is a further short tunnel. The crest of the Manchester and Leeds Railway, with the date 1839, is carved over the entrance to the short tunnel on the Littleborough side.

The narrowness of the Walsden and upper Calder valleys, already carrying the turnpike road and canal as well as the river, created engineering problems. Several more tunnels had to be driven, including Winterbutt Lee (306 yards), near Summit Tunnel. On its approach to Todmorden from the south, the line is carried by Gauxholme Viaduct, with nineteen spans across the river and canal, just beyond which the canal is re-crossed by another bridge. Beyond Todmorden Station the railway strides across the town centre on a fifty-five feet high viaduct. Between here and Hebden Bridge, a distance of four miles, there are a further two viaducts and four tunnels.[41]

There was originally a fifth tunnel, driven through a spur of the hill at Charlestown, but the instability of the strata defeated the engineers. The directors were informed in June 1840 that 'the masonry inside Charlestown Tunnel had given way from the extreme pressure of the hill. A diversion round the hill was being considered as a temporary expedient'. The 'temporary' curve is still in use. Trains are subject to a speed limit while taking this curve; on the 21st June 1912 the Liverpool to Leeds express was derailed at this point and eight people were killed.[42]

Todmorden had a temporary station until 1844. The station built then was replaced

One of Tait's series of railway prints published in 1840, which shows the newly-built railway viaduct straddling the valley. Through the arches can be seen Ridgefoot Mill and the eight year old Christ Church.

by the present building in 1865, and in 1881 the massive retaining wall for the goods yard was built.

The line was operational by the 4th January 1841, except for the Summit Tunnel section for which road coaches were used, and the whole sixty miles came into use on the 1st March 1841. There were eight or nine trains a day in each direction (four on Sundays), taking an average of three hours between Leeds and Manchester.[43]

There were three classes of accommodation, with basic fares of 3d, 2d and 1d a mile respectively. First class passengers travelled in carriages with a roof, seats and sliding shutters, which were later replaced by glass sash windows. Second class carriages had seats and a roof. These two classes corresponded to the 'inside' and 'outside' seats of the stage coach. Third class or 'waggon' passengers were considered to be of little importance and travelled, often packed like sardines, in open waggons, without roof or seats, known as 'stanhopes' after the open-road vehicle first made for the Honourable Fitzroy Stanhope. Early train travel was expensive. Taking the average weekly wage of men millworkers as 15s to £1, the 200 mile journey to London, even in waggons, would cost a week's wage. The return journey between Leeds and Manchester, travelling second class, cost £1.

Goods traffic on the Manchester and Leeds railway grew steadily in the early 1840s as the economy recovered from the depression of the 'hungry forties'. Between June 1842 and June 1844 the tonnage of goods carried per annum nearly doubled to 380,000 tons, whilst the number of passenger journeys rose from 1,127,297 to 1,337,475 per year.

In 1846-47 the Manchester and Leeds amalgamated with several smaller companies in both Yorkshire and Lancashire, and assumed the name Lancashire and Yorkshire Railway. This continued until its amalgamation with the London and Northwestern Railway created the London, Midland and Scottish Railway in 1922-23.[44]

One of the early employees of the Manchester and Leeds was Thomas Normington, who wrote a book after he retired. Here he describes a journey from Thornhill, near Dewsbury, to Manchester in 1845:

> I travelled in a passenger waggon train in a stand-up carriage. This carriage was simply a square wood box or waggon, without seats or roof, exposed to all sorts of weather, and the passengers all wedged in, like cattle in a truck. Of course, going to see my grandfather, I must go in my Sunday clothes, and had on a new top hat. To my surprise and sorrow, on emerging out of Summit Tunnel, I found my new hat entirely spoilt, the down being frizzled up by the small hot cinders emitted from the funnel of the engine.[45]

In November 1849 the railway line between Todmorden and Burnley was opened, and in the following year it was connected to the Preston-Colne line. A route for the branch had been surveyed in 1841, when the Manchester to Leeds railway via Todmorden was about to open. The surveyor, Henry Clarkson, was not impressed by the charm of the locals: 'The physical character of the inhabitants ... was for the most part uncouth and strange, in keeping with the roughness of their speech and manners.' He described how, when he was trying to list the occupiers of houses, 'a great rough-looking woman' would identify herself as the wife of 'Tom o' Dicks' or 'Bill o' Jacks', but disclaimed any knowledge of her husband's 'proper' surname. The temptation to have a little innocent fun at the expense of a stranger must have been too great.[46]

The construction began eventually in 1845. It was heavy work, involving tunnels at Kitson Wood, Holme and Towneley, and the spectacular North Wood Viaduct at Lydgate. The gradients on both sides of the summit are steep, being 1 in 65 on the three-mile climb from Stansfield Hall. To save money, only a single track was laid at first, but this proved inadequate as both commercial and holiday/excursion traffic increased. In 1859-60 the track was doubled.[47] There have been no trains between Todmorden and Burnley since the 1960s, but trains between Yorkshire and Blackpool still use the branch, turning off the main line at Hallroyd junction, just a few hundred yards east of Todmorden Station. At Hallroyd was Stansfield Hall Station, convenient for the Fieldens living at the hall.

The hours of work of railway employees in the mid-nineteenth century equalled or exceeded those of textile mill workers before the 1833 Factory Act. According to Normington, in 1852 guards worked shifts totalling 75 and 90 hours in alternate weeks. For a time the railway and canal were in competition, the latter cutting its tolls to stay in business. In 1855 a railway consortium leased the canal, at a rental which involved a subsidy for the canal shareholders but prevented competitive cost-cutting. This arrangement continued until 1890.[48]

Cotton Trade Fluctuations

The basis of the economy, which revolutionised communications, encouraged the spectacular growth in population with the attendant growth in education, churches and chapels, economic awareness and aspirations of ordinary people, was cotton. The industrial economy was subject to cycles of boom and slump, with major peaks

A reconstruction drawing of Gorpley Mill on Bacup Road, built by Madens of Bacup in 1805, on the the site of an older fulling mill. The drawing shows the mill circa 1894 just prior to its demolition. The notable features are the two water-wheel houses behind and to the left of the mill.

at intervals of six to eleven years — 1819, 1825, 1836, 1845 and so on. At the peak of a boom, speculation often developed both in get-rich-quick company promotions and in commodities. The latter caused a surge in imports and therefore a drain of gold. As a defensive measure the Bank of England raised interest rates and eventually the bubble burst, causing bankruptcies and, often, bank failures.

The boom of 1836 was followed by a depression in 1837 and early 1838. A partial recovery over the next twelve to eighteen months gave way to a severe and prolonged depression lasting from late 1839 to 1843, the period known as the 'hungry forties'. A contributory factor was a run of bad or poor harvests from 1836 to 1841, which also meant higher food prices, and increased distress to workers who were unemployed or on short time. Travis experienced the high price of bread in the lean years compared with normal times, noting that when he 'went to Ashton to work in 1842 his 4lb loaf was 8d, when he came back in 1848 it was 5d'.[49] Note has been made on page 140 of the massive operation by the township of Stansfield to relieve the distress.

The local textile firms weathered the storm of 1837 reasonably well. There was some new investment in 1838, including extensions to Gorpley Mill, Bacup Road, for Ormerod Brothers. The years 1839 to 1843 told a different story when, as well as some small firms, two cotton spinners, well established since the 1790s — Crossleys of Knowlwood Mill and Buckleys of Ridgefoot — both went bankrupt. Fieldens survived the depression. John Fielden's sons, Samuel and John, joined the firm, by now in its third generation and amongst the oldest and best established in England. In 1842 their eight spinning mills averaged 65,000 pounds of yarn each week — Lumbutts and Waterside spun both warp (twist) and weft, Causeway and Dobroyd only weft, Stoneswood, Smithyholme, Waterstalls and Mytholmroyd only warp. At the same time, the weaving sheds at Waterside were producing 3,000 pieces of cloth per week.[50]

The workers hardest hit in times of slump were the handloom weavers. In 1825 William Greenwood of Pudsey was receiving 2s 6d for weaving a piece of calico thirty yards long (1d per yard). Towards the end of the year he records in his diary 'Nov 24 Joseph Firth pooled [pulled] down 3d per calico yesterday'[51] (ie a ten per cent reduction in pay). Joseph Firth was the spinner for whom Greenwood wove, and was possibly of Firth and Howarth of Causeway Wood Mill on Lumbutts Clough.

By the 1840s the remaining handloom weavers were in direct competition with power looms, and were the hardest hit of all workers, being almost a labour reserve to be used as required — when trade was brisk.

The Rossendale historian, Thomas Newbigging, describing the conditions of the handloom weavers who lived on the moors between Bacup and Todmorden, quoted the account of an 'old dame' who told how she took her pieces of cloth across Langfield Moor to a 'taker-in' early in the morning before 'it wur gradely leet'. She earned about 5s a week. 'It wur hard wark i' thoose days, I con tell thi, to get porritch and skim milk twice a day, wi' happen a bit o' bacon on Sundays.'[52]

The 1851 census provides a detailed picture of the occupations of local people in the mid-nineteenth century, although it is not easy to reduce its data to reliable summaries. The enumerators were inconsistent in their use of occupational descriptions, often listing people as, say, cotton weavers without indicating whether they worked on hand or power looms, or as factory operatives without details of the type of factory. In handloom-weaving families the mothers, dividing their time between domestic duties and industrial work, might be arbitrarily described as 'handloom weaver', 'winder' or 'handloom weaver's wife'. Nevertheless, a valid picture can be obtained by using the information given in the census.

In 1851 the population was:

Langfield	3,729
Todmorden w Walsden	7,699
Upper two-thirds of Stansfield	5,937
TOTAL	17,365

Of these (excluding those doing unremunerative work at home, the retired, young children and scholars), the working population was 9,488, or nearly 55% of the total population. Of this working population, those recorded as weavers can be summarized thus:

Township	Handloom weaver	Powerloom weaver	*Weaver	Total
Todmorden with Walsden	106	713	111	930
Langfield	35	340	95	470
Upper & Middle Thirds of Stansfield	199	637	377	1,213
Total	340	1,690	583	2,613

*Weaver — loom not specified

The total number of weavers, 2,613, represents almost twenty-eight per cent of the total working population.

A detailed examination of the practice of the enumerators in Stansfield, correlated with the 1841 and 1861 census returns, suggests that a substantial proportion of the 377 'unspecified' weavers were in fact handloom weavers — some in wool, worsted or silk. It is safe to say that in 1851 at least twenty-five per cent of the weavers in the Middle and Upper Thirds of Stansfield were still handloom weavers. This is a significantly higher proportion than in either Todmorden with Walsden or Langfield.

What is immediately apparent from the 1851 census is the overwhelming proportion of workers involved directly in textiles, whether at home or in the factory. In addition to the 2,613 recorded weavers, there are another 2,671 occupied in the various textile processes, most of them in factories but some of them, such as 25 woolcombers, probably at home. These 5,284 textile workers represent nearly fifty-six per cent of the working population, and to them can be added the bobbin, picker, heald and shuttle makers as well as the machine makers and foundry workers — all ancilliary to the textile trade.

A glance at a map opposite of Todmorden as surveyed in 1850 shows how the town had developed since 1820. Most strikingly, the railway straddled the town centre and, to accommodate it, the rivers were diverted to their present courses, but Walsden Water was still open across the site of the present market place.

Along Burnley Road, Ridgefoot Mill had expanded with the addition of a weaving shed; Ridgefoot House (where Kwik Save is now) had been built; and Cobden (where Todmorden Community College and Ridgefoot Flats now stand) was being developed into streets of houses. There were properties fronting Burnley Road between Stansfield Road and Patmos Chapel, but little development between them and the railway, excepting West Lodge, which is now St Joseph's Priory.

Halifax Road was developed on the south side, back to the canal and eastwards beyond Stackhills Road, including Firth and Howarth's Albion Mill weaving shed, built in the 1830s. On the north side there was no development beyond Roomfield House, but between there and the town centre were York Street Chapel and Sunday School (now the Central Methodist); all the properties fronting Halifax Road; Bridge Street Chapel (now the site of Healds Supermarket); Brook Street houses (where Bramsche Square is now) and the Oddfellows' Hall.

More properties had been built on Water Street, and the first Unitarian chapel behind Cockpit near Longfield Road. Development had taken place in the Salford area, which was still the most industrialised area in Todmorden. The Fielden complex at Waterside had, by 1851, reached its fullest extent, stretching to the limit of the site.

The industrialisation, which created the valley town of Todmorden as we know it today, was well underway, sustaining a population which had increased $2^{1}/_{4}$ times between 1801 and 1841, but had been halted at that level until 1851 by the years of depression known as the 'hungry forties'.

Religious Life and Education

The first half of the nineteenth century was a period of diversification and competition in religion as well as industry. Four years after the death of John Wesley, the Methodist Conference adopted the Plan of Pacification (1795), which allowed each society to sever any connection it had with the Church of England. Some societies had tried to maintain the link, eg the Methodists at the Doghouse chapel used to walk the short distance to St Mary's Church in time to hear the sermon. Within Methodism, power was concentrated in the hands of the ordained ministry, which alienated those who wanted more lay participation and control. In 1797 the dissidents formed the Methodist

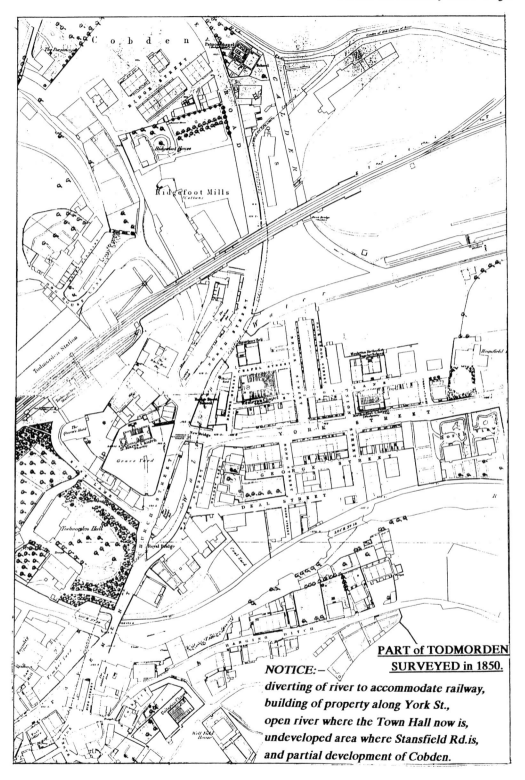

PART of TODMORDEN
SURVEYED in 1850.

NOTICE:—
diverting of river to accommodate railway,
building of property along York St.,
open river where the Town Hall now is,
undeveloped area where Stansfield Rd.is,
and partial development of Cobden.

This is the original Unitarian Chapel of 1824, which became a Sunday school after the new church was built in 1869, and was extended in 1899.

New Connection, which had a strong base in Halifax. Its first chapel in Todmorden was Patmos, opened in 1814.[53]

The next split to affect Todmorden began in 1806 when Joseph Cooke, a Wesleyan minister, was expelled for heresy — especially for teaching that someone could be saved without knowing it. After his death in 1811, some of the 'Cookite' groups formed themselves into the Methodist Unitarians. Cooke had preached in Todmorden and, one of his followers, Rev Richard Wright, preached several times in and around Todmorden in 1818. One of his converts was John Fielden who, as mentioned before, was instrumental in founding the Unitarian Society in Todmorden. In 1828 Fielden assumed ownership of the chapel in order to free the society from debts, which had burdened it since the erection of the building.[54]

A group expelled in 1811-12 adopted the name Primitive Methodists. In the early 1820s a Primitive congregation was formed at Bottoms, Walsden. The first purpose-built chapels were Salem at Knowlwood (1826) and Ebenezer at Castle Street (1832). The Primitive Methodists, like the New Connection, gave laymen a substantial share of power, and also used women preachers, a practice disavowed by the Wesleyan Conference in 1803. In places where the local Wesleyan societies were dominated by the millowners, the Primitives had a strong appeal to the working classes.[55]

The Wesleyan Methodists were not idle during these years, and in 1814 they established a congregation at Mankinholes, followed by others at Lanebottom in 1818, York Street in 1827, and Shade in 1848.[56]

A further dispute in Wesleyan Methodism in 1835-36 sundered some local congregations and led to the founding of the Wesleyan Methodist Association. Dissident members of Mankinholes Chapel were expelled in 1836, and set up their own chapel at nearby Lumbutts in the following year.[57] Other WMA congregations were formed

Wilson's bobbin mill at Cornholme in 1835. Wilson's house is attached to the mill, and the building on the right of the road has ground floor cottages with a chapel/schoolroom above.

in 1835-37 at Bridge Street; at Vicarage, Stansfield (which probably became Castle Grove); and at Lower Naze Bottom, Cornholme.

The last-named is of special interest, as it offers a fine example of millowner paternalism. When the Wilson family first moved to Cornholme they worshipped with a group of Methodists in rooms at Frieldhurst Mill, and later joined the WMA faction. They built Cornholme Bobbin Mills in the 1830s, and included, amongst the associated buildings, a meeting room which served as a chapel, day school and Sunday school. They also carried religion into the works. Joshua Wilson describes the daily routine of his parents:

> On their new works being opened for business, Mr and Mrs Wilson determined that God should be daily acknowledged and honoured in them. Accordingly every morning, fifteen minutes before breakfast time, the works were stopped, and the workmen called together, a few verses of a hymn sung, a portion of Scripture read, and prayer offered for the Divine blessing; Mrs Wilson taking part along with her husband, and all their Christian workmen, in praise and prayer. This practice was continued for about twenty years, until the works were remodelled after a fire, and became inconvenient for the purpose.[58]

Even after this, workers who had missed Sunday worship were questioned about it on Monday mornings.

The older dissenting sects had also expanded. The Particular Baptists were augmented when some members of the Inghamite Church were expelled about 1807, for arguing in favour of 'believer's baptism'. They met for a time in the old Baptist chapel at Rodhill (Rodwell) End, then sold that to the Wesleyans and built a new chapel at Millwood (now Leah's Feeds) in 1808.[59]

The General Baptists at Shore had an increasing membership drawn from the Burnley Valley at the bottom of the hill. From 1815 they hired a room for services at Naylor Mill, Lydgate, which resulted in the building of Bethel Chapel, Lineholme, in

1818-19. In 1845, a group withdrew from the Shore congregation to form a General Baptist cause in Todmorden itself.[60] They met first in the Mechanics Institute and later the Sobriety Hall until a chapel was built at Wellington Road in 1859.[61]

The Independents at Eastwood, who rebuilt their chapel in 1840 (the line of the railway claimed their previous site), expanded by building a chapel at Cloughfoot, Bacup Road, in 1830 and buying Patmos Chapel in 1841.[62]

Many of the local manufacturers were pillars of nonconformity, which embraced diligence, honesty, thrift and sobriety, desirable qualities valued in their employees. Mention has already been made of the Fielden and Wilson families. The application for a licence for the new Independent chapel at Eastwood in 1840 was signed by Christopher, James and Joshua Rawdon, members of a family of leading local textile industrialists. A similar application in 1842 to license the Oddfellows Hall, Todmorden, as a place of worship was signed by John Fielden (Clough Mill) and John Lord, both cotton spinners, and Thomas Lord, machine maker.[63]

Patterns in the distribution of some nonconformist chapels are worth noting. The Baptists were all in Stansfield; after the evangelical efforts of Dan Taylor, they colonised only those areas in which they already had some adherents. All branches of Methodism were widely spread in the Rochdale and Halifax valleys. Where two chapels were close together in the hillside settlements, they usually represented different branches. Along the Walsden Valley, within the space of about one mile, were the Wesleyan chapel at Shade (1842), the Primitive chapel at Knowlwood (1826) and the Wesleyan Methodist Association chapel at Inchfield Bottom (1847-48).

There was one Inghamite chapel — Stansfield New Chapel, built in 1798 at the bottom of Ferney Lee Road. For a time the minister was Norman Foulds. In his diary William Greenwood makes frequent mention of attending there:

> Feby 1825 21st Monday Churchel from Nottingham Preached at Norman fowls Chappel yesterday three times, Text I have no greater Joy than to see my children walking in the truth.
> March 1825 20th I went to Norman fowls chappel Norman Preached Text 23c 24v of Luke = Then said Jesus, Father forgive them; For they know not what they do.

The number of local Anglican churches remained the same until the 1830s. Alarmed by the growth of nonconformity in England, the Anglican interest secured parliamentary grants for church building of £1,000,000 in 1818 and £500,000 in 1824. With help from this source, Christ Church, built near to the new (1824) parsonage and cemetery, opened in 1832. St Mary's closed, but the rift — between parishioners loyal to St Mary's and the supporters of the much larger new church — remained for the next thirty years. St Paul's Church, Cross Stone, was rebuilt in 1834-35; a new church at Walsden, St Peter's, was opened in 1845, at a cost of £4,000, of which £2,900 came from subscriptions and £1,100 from the parliamentary grant. Additional service points were provided at some schools, including Longfield Church School, Oldroyd (1848) and Lydgate (1850), which was later replaced by Harley Wood Church.[64]

Educational provision was made by or in association with religious groups, or by the private enterprise of teachers who made a living from pupils' fees. The earliest recorded school in Todmorden was the 'endowed school', built in 1713 next to St Mary's Church. Of the £200 endowment, £150 was given by Richard Clegg, Vicar of Kirkham and grandson of Richard Clegg of Stonehouse in Walsden, and £50 was

Looking south-west from Rodwell End towards Todmorden, showing the river, canal, road and railway competing for space in the valley.

collected by him from various donors. The master, chosen by the freeholders of Todmorden and Walsden, was to teach 'free' four children: two poor children from Todmorden and Walsden chosen by the churchwardens; one child selected by the owners of Stone House; and the fourth by the owner of Eastwood (Richard Clegg's mother was daughter of John Eastwood, of Eastwood).[65] The schoolroom, holding 100 scholars, was on the ground floor, with the schoolmaster's living quarters above.[66]

A few years later a native of Cross Stone Chapelry (Stansfield and Langfield) named Pilling collected £65, mainly from friends in London, and, with some help

The original school at Cross Stone, founded in the early eighteenth century.

from the local people, built a schoolhouse near Cross Stone Church. The school was maintained by the chapelry and the interest on the money yielded £3 a year (in 1743), which paid for the free instruction of six poor children. In 1743 and in 1764 (when there were between 30 and 40 children in the school) the teacher was the chapelry clerk, who received fees from parents for teaching reading and writing to children other than the six.[67]

William Greenwood's diary discloses that he held a school on Sunday mornings at which up to twenty scholars attended. The fees were one penny per week. He does not say what he taught, but he kept accounts which record sales to his scholars of: 'Quils ½d'; 'Copy Books for 2d'; a 'reading easy' for 6d; and 'Rithmetic for 1s 8d'. He also held a night school on Wednesdays for at least part of the year. Greenwood himself attended a 'Grammer School' held at Shore Chapel where John Midgley, the minister, was the teacher.

Most children were busy from an early age at industrial tasks, either at home or in the mill, so that at best they could hope for only about three years of effective schooling, as distinct from attending a child-minding establishment (which was what many so-called infant schools effectively were). The answer to the problem was the Sunday school, which was seen as having the added advantage of keeping children out of mischief on their one free day in the week.

In 1816 John Fielden, with the support of the curate of St Mary's and a Methodist minister, started the non-denominational 'Union Sunday School' in a building where the town hall now stands. Holden records that the total cost, including 'letters and alphabet, spelling books, Catechisms, Testaments and Bibles, paper, quills and candles', was more than £50.[68]

A branch school was opened at Cloughfoot in 1817 and, at a meeting of subscribers and teachers in 1818, it was reported that the Sunday school at Doghouse had over 400 scholars, whilst the Union School and its Cloughfoot branch had 150 each.[69] The Union School met each Sunday from 9 to 11 o'clock in the morning and 1.30 to 3.30 in the afternoon. Beginning with singing and prayers, there followed forty minutes of reading, ten minutes spelling and thirty-five minutes religious instruction.[70]

In 1818 a school, built by public subscription, was opened at Lanebottom, Walsden, 'for teaching the children of the poor and indigent parents to read and write and the common rules of arithmetic upon each Sunday'.[71]

In 1825 the Unitarians, who had opened their chapel in the previous year, started a day school 'for 100 children of all denominations from the age of four years to the time of going to the factory'. This was one of the first non-denominational day schools in the country, and Fielden not only engaged a school mistress and two full-time teachers at his own expense, but familiarised himself with the current educational theories.[72]

By 1830 the Unitarians had a Sunday school, and in that year formulated a detailed set of rules in which Fielden's hand may be seen. Rule 5 states: 'The Teachers of Writing, Grammar, Arithmetic, History, Mathematics etc. are expected never to loose [sic] sight of Accuracy and Utility'. Below is a copy of the teaching plan for the school in 1834.[73] Anticipating the 1833 Factory Act by six years, Fielden had opened a factory school at Waterside for the child workers in 1827.[74]

In 1833 an enquiry was undertaken into the state of education in England and Wales.[75] The local returns (see Table A overleaf) may not be wholly reliable. There is no mention of the Fielden factory school or the Unitarian free school, but the Fieldens were notorious for failing to respond to official enquiries. The returns made show that of the 669 children enrolled at 21 day schools, only 10 received free instruction, and boys outnumbered girls by two to one.

Most children were in full-time work, either in a mill or in a domestic workshop by the age of nine — some earlier — and for them day schooling meant at best a few years between the ages of five and nine, subject to interruption when bad trade meant

TODMORDEN UNITARIAN SUNDAY SCHOOL.
TEACHERS' PLAN,
1834.

DATES.	MARCH.	APRIL.	MAY.	JUNE.	JULY.	AUGUST.	SEPTEMBER.	OCTOBER.	NOVEMBER.	DECEMBER.
	2	9	16	23	30		6	13	20	27		4	11	18	25		1	8	15	22	29		6	13	20	27		3	10	17	24	31		7	14	21	28		5	12	19	26		2	9	16	23	30		7	14	21	28
NOS.	1| 2| 3| 4|	1| 2| 3| 4|	1| 2| 3| 4|	1| 2| 3| 4|	1| 2| 3| 4|	1| 2| 3| 4|	1| 2| 3| 4|	1| 2| 3| 4|	1| 2| 3| 4|	1| 2| 3| 4

TEACHERS' NAMES.

BOYS.

First Desk, Bible Class.
No.
1 Jeremy Haworth,
2 William Taylor,
3 John Lord,
4 William Fielden.

2nd Desk, Introduction Class.
1 Henry Shepherd,
2 Thomas Dawson,
3 William Travis,
4 David Shepherd,

Third Desk, Testament Class.
No.
1 Joseph Greenwood,
2 John Fielden,
3 John Smith,
4 John Mitchel.

Fourth Desk, Spelling Class.
1 George Stell,
2 Thomas Stansfield,
3 George Haworth,
4 William Sutcliffe.

6th Desk, 2nd Spelling Class.
No
1 John Eastwood,
2 Robert Haworth,
3 James Pickup,
4 George White, jun.

6th Desk, Reading Easy Class.
1 John Ashworth
2 Abraham Crossley, jun.,
3 Samuel King,
4 William Greenwood.

GIRLS.

7th Desk, Reading Easy Class.
No.
1 Margaret Ashworth,
2 Esther Dawson,
3
4

Eighth Desk, Spelling Class.
1 Olive Suthers,
2
3
4

Ninth Desk, Testament Class.
No.
1 Betty Suthers,
2 Charlotte Dawson,
3 Mary Saville,
4 Elizabeth Haworth.

Tenth Desk, Bible Class.
1 Mary Taylor,
2 Elizabeth Dawson,
3 Grace Suthers,
4 Deborah Dawson.

that parents could not afford the weekly school pence. As a substitute or a supplement there was the free Sunday School. Table B below records 19 Sunday Schools in 1833: 3 Church of England; 3 Baptist; 1 Unitarian; 2 either undenominational or unspecified; and 10 one or other branch of Methodism. This analysis is also a comment on the spread of nonconformist chapels during the first half of the nineteenth century.

The first comprehensive picture of local educational and religious provision and distribution is found in March 1851, when an educational census (31st March) and religious census (30th March) were held to coincide with the population census.

There were within our local district 5 Church of England places of worship (one of which, Lydgate, had no service on census day and another, Christ Church, made no returns for reasons unknown); 14 belonging to the Methodists (5 Wesleyan, 6 Wesleyan Methodist Association and 3 Primitive); 4 to the Baptists (3 General and 1 Particular); 3 to the Independents and 1 each to the Inghamites, Unitarians and Quakers.[76]

The main problem involved in interpreting the census figures is translating attendances at two or more services in the same church or chapel into numbers of people actually attending on census day. How many people went twice or even three times?

TABLE A			
Numbers Enrolled at Day Schools, 1833 Education Enquiry			
	Endowed, Subscription and Boarding Schools	Private Enterprise Schools - Infants	Private Enterprise Schools - Other
Todmorden with Walsden	Clegg Church School 35 children, 4 free, endowment £6-15 yr.	-	8 schools - 276 children (all 9 schools had 178 boys and 133 girls)
Langfield	-	-	3 schools - 103 boys, 16 girls
Stansfield	Cross Stone School - 37 boys, 3 girls (6 free)	4 schools - 50 boys, 55 girls	4 schools - 75 boys, 19 girls
TOTALS	schools 2 children 75	schools 4 children 105	schools 15 children 489
TOTAL SCHOOLS 21, TOTAL SCHOLARS 669 (boys 443, girls 226)			

TABLE B									
Numbers Enrolled at Sunday Schools, 1833 Education Enquiry									
(figures in ( ) give number of schools where more than 1)									
	Church of England	Methodist (connexion not given)	Wes. Meth.	Prim. Meth.	Meth. New Con.	General Baptist	Part- icular Baptist	Unit- arian	Interdenomi -national unspec.
Todmorden with Walsden	(2) 350		(2) 382	530	132				26
Langfield			(2) 696					105	
Stansfield	109	(4) 569				(2) 297	280		240
TOTALS	(3) 459	(4) 569	(4) 1078	(1) 530	(1) 132	(2) 297	(1) 280	(1) 105	(2) 266
TOTAL SCHOOLS 19, TOTAL SCHOLARS 3716									

In an attempt to achieve a reasonable estimate, the following formula has been used for each place of worship: the number at the best-attended service, plus one third of the next best, plus one fifth of the next best, plus the highest number of Sunday scholars. To allow for the fact that Christ Church made no return, an estimated attendance of 500 has been made. This has to involve some guesswork, but there are certain factors which have been taken into account. Firstly, the opening of St Peter's, Walsden, in 1848 covered an area originally served by Christ Church. Secondly, the building of Christ Church and closing of St Mary's had alienated a section of the congregation. Thirdly, the opening of the 'outpost' at Lydgate would attract some of the congregation. Fourthly, Archdeacon Rushton, in his Visitation Returns in 1847, found that, of the two churches in Todmorden, one had been closed for fifteen years (St Mary's) and the other drew only forty worshippers. 'It is impossible to depict the religious ignorance prevailing in this locality' reported the archdeacon, finding the situation 'unparalleled in the whole English Church'. He considered the inhabitants to be 'a people deserted, dying in their sins'.[77] He meant of course that they were nonconformists. In 1857 the vicar, Mr Edwards, gave details which would indicate (using the above formula) an average attendance of about 450.[78]

The following table is the result of analysing the census by the above formula:

Denomination	People attending	Percentage of total
Church of England	1,483	18
Baptist	1,213	15
General (1,048)		
Particular (165)		
Methodist	3,777	47
Wesleyan (1,449)		
Wesleyan Association (1,237)		
Primitive (1,091)		
Inghamite	354	4
Independent	1,012	12
Unitarian	250	3
Friends (Quakers)	14	0.2
Total	*8,103*	

In view of the elements of uncertainty in the calculations it would be unwise to use precise figures, but the overall picture is quite clear. About four fifths (82%) of the local church/chapel-goers were nonconformists, compared to a national figure of just over half; about half (57%) of the nonconformists were Methodists (47% of total worshippers) and a fifth (18%) Baptists.

The three townships comprising modern Todmorden had a population of 19,055 in 1851. It has been suggested that in general a quarter of the population would be unable to attend church/chapel at any particular time — the aged, the infirm, young children and people at work at the times of the available services. This calculation would leave about 14,000 potential attenders in the area. To accommodate these there were about 10,000 seats, quite enough in total allowing for the frequency of second and third services. However, one half of the sittings were appropriated (some assigned to church officials and the remainder bought or rented). York St, then the large town centre chapel, had 300 free and 578 appropriated, whilst Lumbutts had no free seats. Amongst the major denominations, the Anglicans had the highest proportion of free seats, with St Peter's entirely free. The Baptists had between a third and a half free whilst the Independents had less than a quarter. The Inghamite, Unitarian and Quaker chapels were entirely free.

Even where the number of free seats was adequate, the system of appropriation would have increased the sense of alienation of poorer people, already inhibited by their shabby appearance. There was a major divide between the respectable working classes and the unfortunate or 'undeserving' poor, and one of the signs of belonging to the former was the possession of a decent set of Sunday clothes.

The picture produced by the census is clear. A substantial majority of people in the district who could attend religious worship did so, and in their ranks 'chapel' outnumbered 'church' by a ratio of about four to one.

The 1851 educational census gives an equally comprehensive picture.

A few years earlier, the 1844 Factory Act had reduced the work limit to six and a half hours a day, and raised the educational requirement to three hours, this time including silk mills which had previously been exempt. The age for starting work was reduced to eight. Henceforth the mill children under thirteen were half-timers, spending either the morning or the afternoon in school. This greatly increased the demand for school places. Three National (ie Church of England) schools were established locally at Todmorden (1845), Cross Stone (Priestwell, 1847) and Walsden (1848). The opening of the new school at Cross Stone led to the closure of the old chapelry school, which with its minuscule endowment found it impossible to compete.[79]

A school was founded at Cornholme under the auspices of the British and Foreign Schools Society, which was formally non-denominational but in practice non-conformist.

Some factory schools were maintained by the millowners, such as the Fieldens, whereas in the others an arrangement was made with a private-enterprise school teacher. The factory inspectors licensed the teachers of schools with half-time children so that the certificates of attendance which they issued, without which it was illegal to employ children under thirteen, would be recognised. In 1846 the inspector cancelled the licence of Sarah Greenbank, a teacher whose pupils all came from Gaukroger and Smith's mill at Ewood, Todmorden, for 'immoral conduct'.[80]

The schools recorded in the 1851 census can be classified into three broad groups. There were thirteen 'dame' schools, defined here not by the sex of the teacher (although all in fact were women) but by the curriculum. They taught reading and in some cases knitting and sewing, but not writing or arithmetic. (In fact three schools in this group included writing for a few pupils.)

Some of the teachers were incapable of teaching writing as they had not mastered the art themselves. Two, Esther Coopley who kept Milking Green Dame School, Bacup Road, and Hannah Greenwood, whose school was at Butcher Hill, Shade, both signed with a cross, whilst the husband of Mrs Stansfield of Millwood signed with a cross on her behalf. Most of the children attending dame schools were young — one third being under five — and the category probably includes both respectable if limited infant schools, and what were essentially child-minding establishments. The dame schools had 260 children in attendance on census day, almost equally divided between boys and girls.

The second category consisted of thirteen private elementary schools attended by 363 boys and 266 girls, an average of 48 children per school. All of these schools taught reading, writing and arithmetic, and in some, other subjects (eg grammar, geography, mathematics) were available at extra cost. The largest schools were:

In 1851 this building on Wellington Road was William and James Dewhirst's Classical and Commercial Academy.

Cockden Day School with 54 boys, 66 girls, two teachers and a monitor; and Line-holme, where 64 boys and 61 girls were taught by James Sunderland, assisted by his son and daughter.

The remaining 12 schools consisted of 4 church schools; 4 schools connected with nonconformist chapels (only 1 of them receiving financial support from the chapel); 2 factory schools; and 2 private academies with some post-elementary teaching.

Three Church/National schools had 248 boys and 122 girls in attendance on census day, an average of 123 per school. The numbers of half-timers are not given, but the factory inspector's reports show that in the 1850s a majority of the children worked in the mills. Walter Bell, assistant curate of Cross Stone, taught at the Oldroyd church school (44 pupils, about 18 half-timers).

The two factory schools were maintained by Fielden Brothers at Waterside (64 boys and 70 girls) and Lumbutts (15 boys and 25 girls). The latter was free to children from Lumbutts Mill, but there was a charge of 2d a week at Waterside, perhaps for subjects other than the 'three Rs'.

At Vale Houses on Wellington Road (then known as Pin Hall Lane), William and James Dewhirst, aged 28 and 27 years, kept their Classical and Commercial Academy, assisted by their two younger sisters Jane (23) and Betty (21), and a servant, George

173

	No of Sun. Schls.	Enrol ment	Attending				% of enrolment attending	% of total attendance
			Male	Female	Not stated	Total		
TABLE C — Sunday Schools, 1851 Educational Census.								
Church of England	5	897	289	369	20	678	75.5	20.9
Wesleyan	5	804	282	345		627	77.9	19.3
Wes.Meth.Assoc.	6	820	301	319		620	75.6	19.1
Primitive Meths.	3	493	227	233		460	93.3	14.2
TOTAL METHODISTS	14					1707		52.6
Gen.Baptists	3	480	164	186	60	410	85.4	12.6
Particular Baptists	1	93	38	34		72	77.4	2.2
TOTAL BAPTISTS	4					482		14.9
Independent	2	340	117	141		258	75.9	8.0
Inghamites	1	136	60	60		120	88.2	3.7
TOTALS	26	4063	1478	1687	80	3245	79.9	100.1

Laurence (19). The curriculum for their 132 pupils included French, German, Latin and Greek. They had four boarders as well as three described as 'day boarders'.

To summarize the figures of attendance recorded in the census:

	No of schools	Boys	Girls	Total attendance	No on register
Dame	13	120	140	260	281
Prvt Elementary	13	363	266	629	679*
Other	12	534	400	934	1,064
Total	38	1,017	806	1,823	2,024

* Including estimated number for 2 schools with no 'No on register'

The above figures show an attendance of 90%, which is high, especially for a Monday, and may be attributed partly to the compulsory element of the half-time system and partly to special efforts made to give a good impression on census day.

The estimated enrolment is 2,024, compared with 669 eighteen years earlier. The proportion of girls rose from 34% in 1833 (enrolment figures) to 44% in 1851 (attendance figures). The population of the district had increased by 13%. The earlier rapid growth had been checked by the decline of handloom weaving and the depression of the 'hungry forties'. The main cause of the 203% increase in enrolments, and the increased proportion of girls, was undoubtedly the half-time system.

Some schools gave details of the fees charged. The normal rate for dame schools was 2d per week. Todmorden and Cross Stone National Schools also charged 2d per week, whilst Walsden Parochial School charged 6d. The private schools usually had a sliding scale according to the curriculum.

There was one evening school provided by Walsden Church School, in the winter only, teaching writing and geography, the forty scholars all being factory operatives between the ages of ten and eighteen. With the mill working day finishing at 6 pm, instead of 7.30 pm or 8 pm as it did before 1833, it was possible to attend an evening school.

Over 4,000 pupils, no doubt nearly all children, were enrolled at 26 Sunday schools (see Table C opposite). There were seven more schools than in 1833, an increase of 37% but only an increase of 9% in enrolments, reflecting perhaps the relatively small increase in population and the schisms in the Methodist ranks. All of these Sunday schools taught both religious knowledge and reading. Four of them taught other subjects, mainly writing, on a weekday evening, apparently free of charge.

It is much more difficult to find out about the quality than the quantity of the education provided at this period, apart from such obvious clues as illiterate school dames. Occasionally a schoolmaster's reputation survived him, as in the case of James Sunderland of Linehome, who was described in a reminiscient letter to a local newspaper in 1904 as 'a rare man for getting the lads on', and who encouraged his pupils both in and out of class.[81] The accepted methods were very formal, aimed at teaching basic skills by repetitive drills. Where subjects other than the 'three Rs' were taught, the same methods were usually followed, so that historical dates and lists of rivers, capes and bays were committed to memory and never forgotten, if never used.

The schools which took half-timers received occasional financial support in the form of grants paid by the factory inspector out of the fines collected for breaches of the Factory Acts. In 1849-50 the National school at Cross Stone and Sunderland's school at Lineholme both received small grants of £5 to £8, to buy books.

The inspector's reports show the National schools steadily growing in size during the 1850s, probably at the expense of less effective or more costly private schools, but reflecting also the expansion of factory employment. The following figures come from 1858 and 1859.

National schools	Total children	Factory children	Grants from factory fine fund
Walsden	160	125	£10
Todmorden	229	145	£15
Cross Stone	124	92	£10

The National and British schools also had the benefit of an increasing national education grant, which was only £30,000 in 1839 but had risen to £837,000 a year by 1859.[82]

The factory inspectors operated, in effect, as inspectors of schools. For a time Rev Lindsay Taplin, Unitarian minister from 1856 to 1880, was the visiting inspector of the Fielden Factory schools, but when he complained that nothing came of his visits, he received the terse reply that the 'Fieldens had appointed him to make reports and not to carry them out without instructions to do so'.[83]

Economic Progress, 1850-1914

As employers built or extended their power-loom sheds, they no longer needed hand-loom weavers, except perhaps in boom periods. In April 1857, near the peak of a boom, Scholfield brothers of Eastwood advertised for about 200 handloom weavers 'to weave quiltings and other fancy cottons. Wages 6d per piece more than present rates. Constant employment.' (Could it also be that the mechanised loom was not sophisticated enough to deal with the more difficult 'fancy' cloths?) Such employment did not usually last long. When trade was stagnant, as it was in 1858, employers naturally laid off handloom weavers first, and kept their power looms running as long as possible to recover their capital investment. In 1861 Fielden Brothers pensioned off the last of their handloom weavers, two of whom were still drawing their pensions in 1884.

Industrial Expansion

By 1850 it was clear that the factory system had triumphed, but the amount of capital required to break into the system meant that it was difficult for an enterprising worker to become a 'small master'. However, the 1850s were, generally speaking, prosperous years, and it was possible for a working-class family to save some money, especially when their children were also wage earners and living at home.

A major change was also taking place in the political climate in the valley, as the radical agitations of the 1830s and 1840s gave way to amalgamation for mutual benefit in collective self-help through: Co-operative societies; savings banks; the temperance movement; and adult education. In the field of industrial enterprise, these trends produced both collective and individual opportunities with the formation of 'joint-stock' companies and the 'room-and-power' system.

Before the Companies Act of 1855 limited the liability of the individual to the amount of money he or she had invested in the company, the investor could lose the whole of his personal property if the venture failed. The first local company to take advantage of the Act, the Todmorden Commercial and Manufacturing Company Limited, was registered, in anticipation, in September 1854. It rented Shade Mill and filled it with looms, and then built Alma Mill at Hollins, Walsden, on land bought from John Crossley of Scaitcliffe. The nominal capital was £10,000 in £25 shares. They could be bought by instalments, paying a deposit and further 'calls', usually monthly, as capital was required. John Travis, who later put down his recollections of this period in a series of articles, published in 1901 as *Chapters in Todmorden History*, became secretary and manager of the company.

Some shareholders in the above company, who lived in the Burnley Valley, formed the Calder Vale Company, which by 1857 had built a weaving shed at Pudsey.

Meanwhile, the spinning and weaving departments at Alma Mill were in operation, and in 1859-60 the company paid a dividend of £10 per £25 share, a remarkable return. Soon afterwards the company bought Square Mill, further up the valley.

The 'Todmorden Joint-Stock Mill Company' was next on the scene. It was formed in 1857, with an initial capital of £5,000 in £1 shares, and built Crow Carr Ings Mill as a weaving shed for 726 looms. The shafting and gearing were installed by Jonathan Barker of Phoenix Ironworks, Millwood. By June 1858, when the two engines 'Unity' and 'Strength' were set to work, the shares were worth 23s 3d each. The chairman was Josiah Lord and the engineer Edward Lord, both of Lord Brothers, Canal Street engineering works. Less capital was needed for this venture as the company did not install or operate the looms, but let the mill in eleven sections, each capable of holding 66 looms.

The success of the companies and the favourable state of trade in 1860 encouraged similar ventures, including the Todmorden and Cornholme Bobbin Manufacturing Company, which made bobbins as well as spinning and weaving, in a mill on the site where St Michael's Church now stands. A company formed in Bacup leased Knowl-wood Bottom Mill, in 1860, using the existing water wheel and 40 hp steam engine to drive new spinning machinery. They then built a new spinning mill, a weaving shed for 300 looms, and some workers' cottages (Little Knowl Terrace).

The Derdale Cotton and Commercial Company had the most ambitious scheme — a spinning and weaving mill together with a small village of workers' houses — to be built on a site between Halifax Road and the canal at the eastern end of Todmorden.

The Rochdale Canal Company's boat *Daisy*, with Hoyle's Derdale Mill in the background, circa 1906. The cargo of grain for Stansfield Corn Mill has been loaded onto the the horse-drawn waggon.

The weaving shed at Ridgefoot Mill circa 1910. This mill was demolished in 1932-36 when, under the the will of Abraham Ormerod, a medical centre was built there and given to the town.

The company was incorporated on the 12th March 1861 with a nominal capital of £70,000 in £10 shares; the shares could be bought for a down payment of 2s 6d and a minimum monthly contribution of 5s. The founder members of the Derdale Company included two overlookers, who had forty-two shares between them, and a weaver, carder and clogger, with four or five shares each.[1]

In this way, small-scale investment was made easy, but as it could take over three years for a share to become fully paid up, and as it was common for only part of the nominal shareholding to be paid in the first instance, there was often a shortage of money to develop the enterprise. (In January 1862, the Derdale Company was advertising for loan capital at five per cent.) Another hazard was that a shareholder's financial circumstances could change before his shares were fully paid up. If he could not meet the call for the next instalment, he was still liable for the full cost of his shares, and stood to lose both them and the money already paid.[2]

A second development at this period was the 'room-and-power' system, which enabled enterprising workers to become small 'masters' of industry without involving them in heavy capital expenditure.

The practice of renting not only part of a mill but also a share of its power had been known for some decades, but the new system involved the building or conversion of mills specifically for the purpose of letting them in sections to manufacturers. The millowner provided the building, a steam engine or engines and the main gearing and shafting. The tenant put in his own machinery, in nearly every case power-looms.

An ambitious overlooker or weaver, who had saved up or could borrow enough money to buy, say, a dozen second-hand looms, could make a start in business with a very modest outlay, particularly if his family could provide all or part of the labour force. If successful, he could expand by taking more room-and-power and later have a mill of his own. If not, he could sell his machinery and return to the ranks, without a great loss of either face or capital.

Locally the forerunner in providing room-and-power was William Clegg, a shuttle-maker, who in 1854 built Vale Mill on Tip Side, Stansfield Road. The success of this led him to build three more sheds in the same location. Others followed suit. Jonathan Barker of Phoenix Ironworks, Millwood, built a weaving shed for room-and-power behind the Shannon and Chesapeake Inn, and John Helliwell and Sons, bobbin manufacturers of Pudsey Mill, Cornholme, one for 300 looms near their bobbin works. Other developers included warp-sizers and textile engineers.

It is noteworthy that most of these entrepreneurs were engaged in trades ancillary to textiles. They had the advantage of familiarity with the textile business and presumably the accumulated capital for which they could find no equally profitable outlets in their own line.

Some of the joint-stock companies went into the room-and-power business. The letting of Crow Carr Ings Mill in eleven sections has already been mentioned. The Calder Vale Mill Company let its mill on the same basis. Some of those, who began as hirers of room-and-power, were successful enough to take a mill themselves. Vale Mill was a launching pad for several, including Uriah Brook who bought and extended Frieldhurst Mill, and Barker Sutcliffe who built Nanholme Mill by the canal at Shaw Wood Road.

Other mills were constructed, to be used by the builders or let out as single units. The investors included grocers, drapers, a stonemason, and even a schoolmaster, William Dewhirst of Vale Academy. Established millowners expanded. From 1858 Abraham Ormerod of Gorpley and Ridgefoot mills had set up at Hollins Mill a spinning mill with 30,000 spindles and a weaving shed containing 600 looms.

It is apparent that in the 1850s Todmorden was a hive of industry, with numerous entrepreneurs, co-operative and private, speculating and investing in the expansion of the textile industry in the town centre and in every valley. Indicative of prosperous times were successful strikes for better pay at a number of mills. Increases of 1s and 1s 4d per week were won by the workpeople at Stoodley Bridge, Millsteads and Cinderhill Mills in 1853.[3]

One of Todmorden's longest-running family firms was established in the early 1850s when Henry Cockcroft, who appears in the 1851 census living at Lobb Mill and working as a cotton cloth manufacturer and draper, built Croft Mill, a weaving shed near the Rope and Anchor Inn, Halifax Road. He subsequently extended the mill to include warping and winding.

Meanwhile, throughout the 1850s Fielden Brothers continued to thrive and were running eleven mills. Their latest acquisitions, in 1841 at Mytholmroyd and in 1846 at Robinwood, were, after Waterside (where all the weaving was done), their largest concerns. A return of information in 1856 from all their mills shows a total of 69,128 throstle spindles, 33,224 mule spindles and 1,641 power looms. All the mills used a combination of steam and water power, except the two old mills Greenwood and Jumb, Lumbutts, which had only water wheels. The total workforce was 1,925, of which 1,134 worked at Waterside.[4]

The boom in the cotton trade in the later 1850s was caused by a very favourable set of circumstances. The Indian Mutiny and the war in China had ended, which led

This working boat from Runcorn, seen at Waterside about 1900, is unloading a cargo of stone. The gantry crossing the canal led directly from the Fieldens' warehousing at their railway siding to the mills.

to a big increase in exports to the Far East. An extension of the cotton plantations in the Southern States of America meant that cotton was plentiful and cheap, and the British economy, generally, was on the upturn. Some thought that this was all too good to be true. In January 1861 'Observer' wrote to the *Todmorden Advertiser*:

> I am very much surprised to see the blindness and infatuation of the public at the present time — one company after another is springing up to spin and weave cotton in the face of a short supply of cotton for those already at work. The consequences will be ruinous. The trade has become or is fast becoming unprofitable from a prospective short supply of the raw material.

When 'Observer' wrote, the main threat to the prosperity of the local industry was not a possible shortage of raw cotton but a combination of over-capacity and the unstable financial structure of some of the joint-stock companies. Within a matter of months, however, his forecast turned out to be tragically correct.[5]

The Cotton Famine and its Aftermath

In April 1861 the American Civil War broke out. A few months later the ships of the Northern States had blockaded the Southern ports, from which eighty per cent of Lancashire cotton came. By October 1861 the cotton towns were all too aware that the 'cotton famine' had begun.

The blockade was never completely successful, but raw cotton supplies in Britain soon dried up. Imports from the main alternative source, India, more than trebled

CAUSES OF POOR RELIEF

Langfield, Stansfield, Todmorden w Walsden (excluding vagrants)

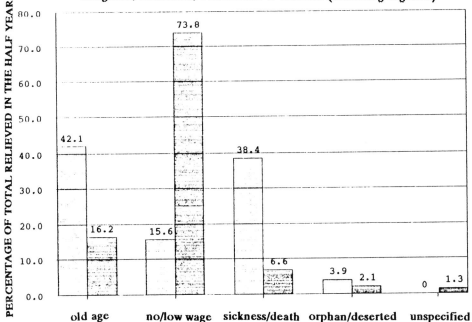

□ ½ year to March 1861 ▦ ½ year to September 1862

NUMBER OF PERSONS RELIEVED IN THE TODMORDEN UNION,

During the Half-Year ended 29th September, 1862.

1862
Cotton Famine

TOWNSHIPS.	Males.	females	children undr 16	Total.	vagrnts	Net Total.
TODMORDEN & WALSDEN..	167	255	449	871	..	871
LANGFIELD.............	50	90	109	249	2104	2353
STANSFIELD............	165	236	436	837	..	837
HEPTONSTALL..........	86	134	174	394	74	468
WADSWORTH........... ..	122	193	235	550	108	658
ERRINGDEN............	45	78	115	238	..	238
Total of Union.....	635	986	1518	3139	2286	5425
As compared with the corresponding half of last year Increase.	316	473	1081	1870	114	3012
Decrease.	..	..	..	..	..	..

Note, the main cause of relief Mar−Sep 1862 was no/low wage, whereas from Sep− Mar 1861 it was old age, sickness or death. (see graph)

The numbers (not vagrants) relieved Mar−Sep 1862 represent an increase of 147% on Mar−Sep 1961. (see table)

Information from 'Todmorden Union and Parochial Accounts'
half years ending the 25th March 1861 and the 29th September 1862.

between 1860 and 1866. Unfortunately, much of the Indian cotton was of poor quality and the very short-staple cotton from the Surat district, which was difficult to work, became symbolic of the miseries caused by the cotton famine. The uncertainty over supplies caused the price of cotton to fluctuate wildly and manufacturers faced tricky decisions about when to buy.

By January 1862 most of the mills in Todmorden were working from two to three and a half days only per week, and even Fieldens had commenced short-time working.[6] In the summer of 1862 the board of guardians reported that:

> Fieldens for some time past at Robinwood and more recently at Waterside have paid their hands three day's wages a week without a stroke of work in return and Ormerods and others left no stone unturned to find work three days a week and Surat.

By November the board of guardians (whose area included Erringden, Heptonstall and Wadsworth as well as the three Todmorden townships) was paying five times as much relief as a year earlier. Over 3,000 people (including the old and the sick) were being relieved, compared with an average of 500 in 1859-61. A relief committee was set up in Todmorden, which raised money locally, and also received allocations from funds established both nationally and abroad. During the last week of November 1862 it gave help, mainly in the form of flour, meal, blankets, coal, etc, to over 2,000 people. Local organisations offered support, eg the Todmorden Musical Union performed Haydn's *Creation* to raise money for 'the distressed poor'.[7]

In December 1862, to give it more impetus, the relief committee was reconstituted, with John Fielden of Dobroyd Castle as chairman. His firm immediately donated £500 towards the fund and promised a bonus of ten per cent on other subscriptions collected locally. In the first week of January 1863 the committee distributed £443 in coal, clothing and money.[8] As always there were those who tried to 'work the relief system', and there are apologies in the local press from those obtaining relief by false pretences. The relief committee did not prosecute them if they made a public apology and restitution.[9] In May 1863 the Todmorden Relief Committee reported on its educational efforts: 734 children under 13 years of age at school; 83 older boys and men at an adult school; and 419 women and girls at a sewing school; all paid for by the committee. The sewing class girls received 1s 6d to 2s 6d per week according to age.

Not even the cotton famine could suppress the sense of humour of the local people as can be seen in these two verses of the *Sewing Class Song*:

Sin th'war began an factories stopped
We're badly off its true,
But still we needn't grumble
For we'en noan so mitch to do.
We'er only here fro nine to four
An have an hour at noon;
We noather stop so vary late
Nor start so vary soin.

Its nice an easy sitting here
There's no mistak i'that;
We'd sooner do it a fine seet
Nor root amang th'Surat.
We'en ne'er no floats to unweave neaw,
We'er reet enough bi'th mass;
We couldn't have an easier loife
Nor goin to th' sewin class.[10]

Trade began to pick up in 1863, partly because of an improved supply of raw cotton, although the improvement was not dramatic. By early June nearly a quarter of the workforce of nearly 10,000 was in full work, with just over a quarter wholly unemployed. The others had two to four days work per week.[11]

Nevertheless, the worst of the distress was over. In October the Todmorden committee decided to suspend payments of relief 'for the present'. Clothing from its stock was distributed during the winter, and in April 1864 the committee, as its last recorded act, was preparing to make a final distribution of clothing to those with a weekly income of less than 3s per head.[12]

The main problem of 1864 was not the volume of raw cotton supplies but the unstable pattern of the trade. During the famine and afterwards, new sources of raw cotton were explored; as well as the notorious 'Surat', the Fielden Brothers' letter books mention 'China', 'Comptali', 'Smyrna', 'Margarole', 'Western Madras' (of which they were informed that 'though high coloured is a cotton that spins very well'), 'Japan' and 'Australian' (which was 'clean free from sand but not equal in staple to American cotton').

The letter books also illustrate the difficulties facing manufacturers, not only during the famine but afterwards. In January 1864 cotton at 28^1/$_2$d per pound was four times the pre-famine price, but a fall was expected, which made merchants reluctant to hold stocks. Fieldens' mills were closed, with no immediate expectation of re-opening. Throughout the year, uncertainty continued. In July Fieldens wrote to their agents, Messrs Colin Campbell and Son, asking them to buy 100 bales of Surat to keep the mills at work, 'but you must not pay too high a price or you will cause us to close our mills'. On the 3rd August they told Campbells: 'As we cannot dispose of our goods at anything like a price that will cover costs with present prices of cotton in your market, it is our intention to close our works in about a week. We must have either cotton down or goods up to induce us to go on working.'

That a firm the size of Fieldens' felt compelled to live from hand to mouth is a significant comment on the state of the market, yet this is the attitude expressed in their letters well into 1865. In January of that year they were reluctant to buy, expecting the price of cotton to fall, 'Still rather than keep our people in idleness we wish you to buy for us about 50 bales of Comptali cotton...'.[13]

It was estimated that in 1858-60 the average selling price of cotton cloth was ninety per cent more than the cost of the raw materials. By the same calculation the margin in 1862-65 was only twenty per cent. John Kelly, in his paper 'The End of the Famine', explains that the industry failed to liquidate its excess capacity because of the 'sophisticated network of credit allowing unprofitable manufacturers to stay in business'. Failed manufacturers were allowed to start up again after clearing only part of their debts, and marginal firms clung on in the hope that pre-famine prosperity would return.[14]

The traditional textile ups and downs continued. The boom of 1873-74 increased profits, but caused a wave of strikes because food prices were very high. Weavers at Adamroyd and Derdale Mills won increases through strikes in the April and May of 1874.[15]

Short-time working returned in 1876, and in the following summer several large firms were working only four days a week. These fluctuations gave way to a severe depression, beginning in 1879. During the next two decades, foreign competition became fiercer, profit margins were reduced and unemployment increased. In 1879 nineteen mills in Todmorden and Hebden Bridge were stopped altogether: eleven were working three days a week; twenty-one, four days; and three five days. Between 1877 and 1883 over twenty local firms went bankrupt.[16]

The problems of this period stimulated the development of trades unions. The Todmorden Weavers Association was formed in 1880 (there was already a union for spinners) and other unions were created for beamers, twisters and drawers, leather (picker) workers and various other trades. By 1894 there were enough union branches locally to form the Todmorden Trades and Labour Council.[17]

Expansion of Ancillary Trades

The textile industry, because it needed a variety of supplies and services, was responsible for the growth of ancillary trades which employed a considerable number of people.

Cotton warps needed sizing, with a mixture of flour and china clay, to strengthen them prior to weaving. The trade directories list fifteen sizing firms in Todmorden in the late nineteenth century. One of the largest was Gledhill, Ashworth and Co, of Crescent Size Works, which processed twelve million pounds weight of yarn in 1868, using 1,113 tons of flour and 780 of china clay.[18]

One of the oldest dyeing firms was that of James William Chambers of Salford. Bridge Royd Mill (Eastwood) was a dyeworks for many years before it was taken over around 1887 by Moss Brothers; as Brisbane Moss, it is still dyeing, and manufacturing corduroys. Cockden Mill, Eastwood, another very early cotton factory, was from circa 1867 until 1932 Dan Crabtree's dyeworks, eventually closing down in 1937. The Ramsden Wood Mills, built as spinning mills circa 1819-21, became a dyeworks from circa 1885 and are still functioning as Walsden Printing Company Ltd, textile printers.

Pudsey Mill became Lishman's dyeworks circa 1894, and is now BPT Polymers Ltd (previously known as Manchester Rubber Company), having been in continuous use since its founding in 1795.

The rise of the local textile engineering industry has already been described in the context of the development of steam engines and power-looms, the leading firms being Lord Brothers and Jeremiah Jackson. In 1844 Jeremiah Jackson set up the company of Jackson, Astin and Barker, machine makers and millwrights, in what became known as the Victoria Ironworks, on Salford. After a few years they separated into: Jackson, Sutcliffe and Jackson, machine makers; and Astin, Barker and Astin, millwrights; but continued to share the same steam engine. Jackson then founded the Derdale Ironworks on Der Street. By the end of the century the firm, run by five Jackson brothers in partnership, was in its third generation and still lives on by name at Alma Mill, Walsden.

Lord Brothers concentrated on the manufacture of textile machinery. An outstanding feature of their activities in the 1850s and 60s is the number of inventions and improvements which they patented, most of them in the name of Edward Lord. The inventions related to: opening, cleaning and blowing machinery; drawing, spinning and doubling frames; and the design of looms. The specifications of the patents are technical, usually long and difficult to summarize. By way of example, a patent of 1852 covered seven processes: a cotton-mixing machine which spread the raw cotton on a flexible feed (previously done by hand); two improvements to scutching and carding machinery, designed to leave the cotton cleaner; improved formation of laps at the end of the blowing machines, including automatic adjustments to the speed of the lap take-up roller to compensate for the increased diameter of the roller on filling; a new arrangement of rollers on the drawing-frame; improvements to the ring traveller throstle; and a better method of winding yarn on to the warp beam.

Some of the patents covered minor improvements to processes already patented. Twelve patents were registered by Edward Lord in the years 1861-65, some of them apparently designed to deal with technical problems created by the use of Indian

Waterstalls Mill, on the south side of the Walsden Valley beyond Bottomley, is drawn as it was in 1970. It was recorded as a factory in 1805, and in 1811 contained 1,200 spindles. Marlands, roller makers, were working the mill in 1817 and by 1820 it belonged to Joshua Fielden of Waterside. Water to power the wheel came from a system of dams, at differing levels on the moor behind, steam power being added later.

(including Surat) cotton in place of the more easily worked American fibre.[19] Some cotton manufacturers registered patents, eg for improvements to spinning mules.

The many local patents illustrate that invention is not a 'once for all' affair but a continuing process of adaptation and improvement; it demonstrates the spirit of enterprise in the constant race to find the quickest, cheapest and most reliable methods of manufacture.

The larger engineering firms put out work to local foundries and machine shops. John Marland and Sons, who had been in business in the district since early in the century at Dobroyd, Waterstalls, Strines and Sun Vale made rollers; at Sun Vale, they built an iron foundry and machine shop in 1855, and started making power looms and other textile machinery on their own account. Many firms, mostly small, made equipment and spare parts for looms, predominantly as replacements supplied to the mills. They included: reed and heald makers, who used flat, polished metal wire for the framework through which the warp threads were fed; at least ten shuttle makers, including William Clegg, the pioneer of room-and-power; and over twenty picker-makers.

Pickers were the leather straps which propelled the shuttles. In 1852 Robert Fielden and his brother James employed about fifty workers, and John Holt of Sourhall had twelve men and forty-three girls picker-making. Several other Holts were involved, including William, who developed a harder, machine-compressed leather picker for

An aerial view of Todmorden in 1990. The centre is dominated by the railway viaduct and the town hall. Beyond the viaduct, streets of industrial housing are crowded between the Burnley Valley railway line and the river. The Unitarian Church is prominent in the lower section, with the ancient highway via Shoebroad to Langfield, and thence on to Halifax or Rochdale, at the bottom.

An early 1980s aerial view looking along Halifax Road to the town centre, showing mills along the canal, and industrial housing between Halifax Road and the river. The cleared area, originally the site of older houses (some with cellar dwellings), is now occupied by the Rose Street Health Centre. The former Fielden's Waterside weaving shed can be seen top left.

This weaving shed at Joshua Smith's Frostholme Mill, Cornholme, is seen circa 1912.
Weaving ceased in 1967; the mill was subsequently used for making furniture.

power-looms. Martin Holt, from the same family, founded Perseverance Works at Eastwood
in 1854, a large red-brick building, which still has his name inscribed at the top.[20]

The largest in scale of the ancillary trades was bobbin-making. Every spindle needed
a stock of bobbins, and Fielden Brothers alone had 100,000 spindles, which could
well have required a stock of a million bobbins. As bobbins needed replacing about
once a year, the total yearly demand in Todmorden was numbered in millions, a
demand which could be met locally. The main concentration of bobbin firms was in
the Burnley Valley, with Wilson Brothers by far the largest. It was founded in 1823 by
Lawrence Wilson, who took Pudsey Mill in 1825 and then built the much larger
Cornholme Mills in 1830. There was considerable fire risk in the bobbin industry,
and the mills were burnt down in 1841, 1851, 1859 (when 200 men were said to be
out of work as a result) and 1888. The firm, however, continued to prosper and expand;
by 1874 there was a branch at Barnsley and a saw mill at Athlone in Ireland. In 1881
they patented a method of strengthening the ends of bobbins by stamping in a thin ring
of tinplate or brass. Licences were granted, for a fee, to other manufacturers who wished
to use this invention. They gave up the Athlone saw mills in 1893 and transferred activities
to Garston, near Liverpool, using their own ships to carry wood over from Ireland.[21]

The manufacture of chemicals was another ancillary industry, which developed to
satisfy the needs of the dyeing process. About half a dozen chemical businesses dev-

This is the winding room at Frostholme Mill circa 1912.

eloped in Todmorden, most of them in the Walsden Valley, at Steanor Bottom, Sun Vale Works, Copperas House (copperas or iron sulphate was used in dyeing black), Gauxholme, Knowlwood Quarry and Eastwood.

The mid-1880s in Todmorden saw a major new development in spinning technology. Ring spinning had been invented in the USA in 1828, but did not make much headway in Britain until improvements were made in the 1870s and 1880s. It was similar in principle to the throstle or roller frame described on pages 104 to 105, except that in place of the flyer the revolving part was a little hook of steel, called the traveller, which whirled around a metal ring surrounding the spindle and bobbin. The great advantage of the ring frame was its speed, 5,000 to 9,000 revolutions per minute according to the thickness of the yarn. It was seen as particularly suitable for integrated spinning and weaving firms.[22]

Fieldens installed 4,600 ring spindles at Stoneswood and 4,864 at Lumbutts in 1885, and had others on trial at both Robinwood and Waterside. From 1901 to 1905, William Barker, Wadsworth Mill, and Dugdales of Bottoms and Winterbutlee, largely changed from mule to ring spindles, and between 1908 and 1910 Fieldens introduced a further 16,000 ring spindles at Robinwood.[23] The change had important social consequences. Mule spinners were skilled men, with a good measure of operational autonomy, who were well paid by textile standards. Ring frames were tended by women, who were seen essentially as machine minders and paid much less.

Other leading firms at this time were Caleb Hoyle of Derdale and Walsden mills, with 60,000 spindles (type unspecified) and 1,600 looms, and Luke Barker, with

7,500 ring spindles and 1,406 looms. The largest of the weaving-only firms, of which there were about thirty, was Joshua Smith of Cornholme, with 1,760 looms.[24]

During the nineteenth century, the textile element of the dual economy came increasingly from younger members of the family working in the mills. In the earlier years of the century, these were the small carding and spinning mills, but later included the weaving sheds, which supplanted the handloom weaver. Meanwhile, the pattern of local farming and distribution of population was also changing radically.

Changes in Patterns of Agriculture and Population

In 1801 Stansfield and Langfield had, between them, 306 acres under oats, and the Parish of Rochdale, of which Todmorden and Walsden formed a part, 1,490 acres. Other arable crops in the two areas accounted for only a few acres.[25] By 1866, the first year for which agricultural returns are available, local arable farming had virtually ceased. Apart from 1898, when twenty-three and a half acres of oats were grown, and the odd acre of potatoes, turnips, swedes and cabbages, its almost total demise is confirmed by the returns for the rest of the century. This was partially counterbalanced by an increase in pastoral farming. The increase in population, mostly industrial workers, created a market for local dairy products and, between 1866 and 1905, an average of 1,600 milk cows was recorded annually within the local townships. Hay became the dominant crop as the farms concentrated on permanent grass and meadow. A feature of this was the summer hay-making scene, when itinerant labourers from Ireland and other parts of England were employed to help take in the harvest.[26]

Agriculture, in Britain generally, suffered continuing depression in the last quarter of the nineteenth century, not only from long spells of bad weather in the late 1870s, but also from cheap grain imports from North America and, from the mid-1880s, wool and refrigerated meat from Australia and Argentina. In this context it is significant that the numbers of sheep and lambs recorded locally peaked in 1881 at 2,347 and 1,475 respectively, but by 1891 had dropped to 1,161 and 666. Where figures are available for the separate townships, it is interesting that Todmorden and Walsden had considerably more sheep than Stansfield and Langfield, confirming the position in the seventeenth and eighteenth centuries (see pages 49 and 58). Pigs, which were unrecorded during these periods, showed a remarkable increase from 355 in 1866 to 1,001 in 1905; no doubt supplying the factory workers with bacon/pork.

The land, which in earlier centuries had been occupied by freeholders, was now mainly rented. In 1900 only 537 acres were owner occupied, whilst 5,538 acres were rented. The individual holdings were relatively small; of 303 occupiers who made returns in 1905, over 250 had between only five and fifty acres.[27]

Overall the population, in what became the borough of Todmorden, increased by just over forty per cent from 17,364 in 1851 to 24,369 in 1891, but within this increase lay significant changes in distribution. In the central part of the town, roughly bounded by Stansfield Bridge, Swineshead Clough (Shade) and Victoria Road, the population more than doubled from 3,754 to 7,540 and the number of houses increased by almost 1,000. From Lineholme to Portsmouth, south of the railway, there was an increase of almost 113% from 1,550 to 3,296, sequential to the building of several mills in the valley: Canteen, Robinwood, Vale, Vale Bobbin, Frostholme, Carrfield, Portsmouth, Springwood, Calder Vale; and the expansion of Wilson's Cornholme Bobbin Works.

In contrast, the outlying districts showed a steady decline. Moor-edge farms became increasingly uneconomic, as did the small mills in tributary valleys when faced with higher transport costs for coal to supplement their water power, and competition from the larger valley-bottom firms. In the Dulesgate Valley, above Gorpley Clough, Banks Mill burnt down in 1876, Italy Mill was used only intermittently after 1873, and Gorpley Mill ceased working from 1865. Consequently, the population declined by just over 70 per cent from 569 to 170, and the number of dwellings decreased by almost 20 per cent, with 50 of the remaining 99 houses empty.

In Stansfield, north of the road from Hippins Bridge (on Jumble Hole Clough) to Stiperden, an area always near the limits of cultivation, the population decreased from 541 to 245, almost 55 per cent, and the houses by 34 per cent from 122 to 80 between 1851 and 1891. In the south-east extremity of Walsden, east of the main road from Deanroyd to Warland, where Quarry Mill was empty by 1881, the decline from 304 to 111 was just over 63 per cent with a decrease in dwellings of more than 50 per cent from 66 to 31.[28]

11

Co-operation and Self-help

If the dominant social theme of the first half of the nineteenth century was 'Agitation', that of the second half was 'Co-operation and Self-help', as politically aware working men evolved other ways of achieving their ambitions. Many of the leaders of these new developments had served their time as active Chartists, thus bridging the overlapping movements. There are, however, records of societies in the early years of the century which show how people joined together for mutual benefit and protection.

Beginnings of 'Self-Help'

There were Friendly Societies, whose members paid regular subscriptions to a fund which could be drawn upon in times of illness or bereavement. One such was the United Free Mechanics, whose No 28 Lodge, 'Love', founded in 1821, met at the Bay Horse Inn, Cross Stone. They summed up their purpose thus:

> experience has taught us the useful lessons of reciprocal services and that this world is full of troubles and sorrows, for where is the man that can say:- 'I stand secure and fear not the approach of poverty and distress'. In this species of charity, the poverty of all becomes the wealth of all, since every man, who throws in his mite, does not only provide for his sick and needy Brother, but is laying up for himself a comfortable supply against the hours of distress.

The Oddfellows had several lodges: 'Shepherdess' Lodge, founded in 1825, met at the Roebuck Inn, Portsmouth; 'Humility' was founded in 1829; 'Perseverance' in 1829; 'Prudence' met at the Shoulder of Mutton; 'Mercy' at the Waggon and Horses, Walsden; 'Loyal Queen Victoria' at the Dog and Partridge, Lumbutts; and the 'Rose of Sharon' at the British Queen, Cloughfoot.

The Ancient Order of Foresters also used the local inns for lodge meetings: 'Goshen' met at the York Inn; 'Mt Hermon' at Shade, in the White Lion or Black Horse; the 'Royal Forester' used the Rose and Crown; 'Court Alexandra', the Roebuck; and 'Welcome Visitor' used Bottoms Inn, Eastwood.

Amongst other societies were the Royal Ancient Order of Buffaloes, 'St John's Lodge' met in Walsden, and the Ancient Order of Druids at the Greyhound Inn, Shade. One of the earliest of the societies was the Women's Friendly Society, 1816, which held meetings at the Royal George Inn. Their aim was the 'relieving, aiding and assisting the several members in sickness, blindness, old age and other infirmities, as well as granting certain sums of money to the widows, heirs and executors of deceased members'. Subscriptions were 10d per calendar month and age limits for joining were eighteen to thirty-five years.

Todmorden Old Building Society was founded in 1824, lasting for seventeen years before being wound up in 1841. It was apparently organised as a housing association, where members paid in regular subscriptions, and, as houses were built a 'draw' took place, the lucky winner being the next to occupy a house. All members continued to pay and eventually all the houses were built and all debts paid. The society's last recorded meeting was at the Golden Lion Inn in December 1851.

Early Adult Education

Other societies were concerned with adult education in its broadest sense. In 1828 the Todmorden Natural History Society started meeting at the White Hart Inn, and later at the Oddfellows Hall until its demise in 1843.[1] Its popularity suffered when the Todmorden Mechanics Institute was founded in 1836. The latter was part of a national movement which aimed to educate skilled workers in the scientific principles under-lying their craft. By 1851 there were nearly 700 Mechanics Institutes in Britain. In Todmorden there were two classes of members: those paying 12s per year; and those under eighteen years paying 6s but having no vote in the society's affairs. In 1839 the Todmorden president was John Fielden MP, and the membership was 212, an increase of 114 in twelve months. It seems that interest had been stimulated during the year by holding an exhibition of arts and sciences. The institute had a library containing 526 volumes. During the year, lectures were given on elocution, galvanism, electricity, pneumatics, geology, chemical nomenclature, atomic theory, chemical affinity and mechanics. There were also classes for chemistry, grammar, geometry, mathematics and vocal music. Plans were made for the erection of a building for the use of the 'Mechanics Institution and Literary and Scientific Association and other purposes', but unfortunately this came to nothing, owing to 'the depression in trade, and the apathy of those who profess to be the friends of popular institutions'.

The membership declined to 153 in 1839-40; the classes that year were 'not very active'; only nine lectures were held and they produced a deficit of £28, as very few non-subscribers had paid to attend. The institute was badly hit by the depression of the 1840s. By 1843 the membership was down to fifty-two, and soon afterwards the Mechanics Institute closed.

In 1846 it was replaced by the Todmorden Athenaeum which, like the Mechanics Institute, met in Bridge Street. Its membership of over 100 in 1847 had dwindled to 50 by 1850, and the Mechanics Institute's complaints of apathy were re-echoed. Finally, after only a few years, the Athenaeum folded. For the time being, attempts at popularising adult education had foundered.[2]

The Culture of Co-operation

One of the major movements towards improvement was the establishment of consumer Co-operative societies modelled on the Rochdale Society, which began in the Toad Lane shop in 1844. The idea of Co-operative trading had been tried earlier in Lancashire and the West Riding of Yorkshire. Todmorden had a society in 1832, which paid dividend in proportion to share capital, as was the common practice at the time, but it was with the spread of societies based on the Rochdale pattern that the movement really took off.[3] The Rochdale principle was to pay interest on share capital, but distribute profits in the form of a dividend on purchases, thus spreading the benefits more widely.

Todmorden Co-op, Dale St,
and (right) an early advert.

Many of the early local
'Co-operators' were also
active Chartists, such as
Thomas Mitchell, a Heb-
den Bridge man and active
Chartist, who was a leading
member of a Bacup society
formed in 1846. He kept
in touch with a group of
Chartists in the Todmorden/
Hebden Bridge area who
were planning to emigrate to
the United States and met
every Sunday morning in
the Chartist room at Dulesgate.[4]

Todmorden formed a
'Rochdale'-type society in
1847, and Walsden followed
suit in 1849. Two years later
the Bridge End Equitable
Progressionists Society,

based at Shade, separated from the Todmorden Society.[5] Operations were on a small scale in the early days. Todmorden's two shops, in Todmorden and Shade, opened only in the evenings after the mills closed (at about 6 pm), and were serviced by groups of members in turn. In 1851 Todmorden began to open its store during the day, and Bridge End followed in 1854, employing a shop man, who was paid 16s for an eighty-six hour week. Originally the societies dealt only in flour and oatmeal, and kept members informed by writing the accounts for the past week on a blackboard, which was hung up in the flour room not later than Wednesday night. By 1848 they had expanded into general groceries, and in 1850 butchering began at Todmorden, when they deputed 'five persons to purchase a cow for the use of the shops'.[6]

Another kind of Co-operative society was based on flour milling; one such was begun at Gauxholme and was supported by the Bridge End Co-op. Unfortunately, at this time it was usual, but illegal, to adulterate the flour by adding a small amount of alum to make it white, aesthetically more popular than the darker natural colour. When the Gauxholme miller was sacked, he reported this practice to the law, the premises were inspected and the alum found. Although the society reverted to milling pure flour, their reputation was damaged and they went bankrupt.[7]

The spirit of Co-operation spread and the societies in Todmorden expanded, both by building branch shops in every area of the district, and by extending their range of operations into drapery, millinery, tailoring, dressmaking, clogging, boots and shoes, coal delivering, etc.

The sales of the Todmorden Society in 1891/92 were in excess of £130,000 a year and, by 1900, 3,717 members were receiving dividends averaging 3s in the pound. Bridge End, sandwiched between the Todmorden and Walsden Societies, ceased to grow in either membership or sales after 1882, but retained a membership of nearly 700 and sales averaging £22,000 a year, until the end of the century. By this time, dividends in excess of 3s in the pound were quite usual; Walsden paid 3s 8d and Bridge End 3s 4d in 1900.

The average annual purchases per member in the local societies at the turn of the century were as follows:[8]

	1897-98	1902-03	1903-04
Todmorden	£35 3s 9d	£36 15s 6d	£36 3s 5d
Bridge End		£34 15s 3d	
Walsden		£37 13s 10d	£36 10s 4d

The average Co-operative family was therefore receiving dividends in the range of £5 to £7 a year, substantial sums when related to the average weaver's wage at this period (taking men and women together) of about £1 per week.[9] The well-remembered 'divi' was invaluable in tiding families over slack times in the mills or providing an extra treat if times were good.

The dividend could be used towards purchasing a house, whereby, after saving a certain amount, a member could secure a housing loan. Societies also bought or built cottages (rented to members) as a society investment. In 1883 the Bridge End Society built a new branch, which included eighteen cottages in the development at Co-operative Street, opposite Walsden Station.[10]

The Women's Co-operative Guild was founded in 1883 and a branch started in Todmorden a few years later, followed by one at Bridge End in 1888. It gave women a taste of responsibility at a time when most important positions in the movement were held by men.[11]

This view, from Neddy Bridge towards the town centre, is drawn with a certain amount of artistic licence. It was published circa 1870 as an advertisement for London House, one of the shops on the Strand.

The societies also organised social activities, concerts, galas, sports days for children, and excursions. Bridge End loaned £40 to the Education Committee in 1876 towards 'getting up a trip for Easter'.[12] Walsden's gala in 1900 attracted 600 children, the accompaniment being provided by Walsden Temperance Band.[13]

Educational Extension

The local Co-operative societies were slow to follow Rochdale's practice of allocating two and a half per cent of net profits to an educational fund. However, in 1892/93 Todmorden gave £527, Bridge End £66 and Walsden £57 to educational funds. These donations were used for a variety of purposes, including the provision of libraries and reading rooms, lectures, classes and social activities.[14]

Included in the educational programme were University Extension Lectures provided by the University of Oxford, normally in the form of six lectures and discussions at fortnightly intervals. The three Co-operative societies provided the financial and moral support which made Todmorden (with Hebden Bridge) one of the few places in the country where the extension movement had any lasting success in attracting working-class students. The subjects in Todmorden included history, literature and science. In the winter of 1889-90 Rev Hudson Shaw, a popular Oxford lecturer, had an average attendance of 400 for his course on 'The Age of Elizabeth'.[15]

The lecture, which was seen as a form of high-minded entertainment, was followed by a discussion class for the benefit of the more serious students, who could also write essays and take a certificate examination. One of the most dedicated students was Robert Halstead, a weaver. Born in Walsden and left an orphan, he went into the mill at the age of eight as a half-timer. He attended evening classes and extension courses in both Todmorden and Hebden Bridge, distinguishing himself in the examinations and winning a succession of essay prizes which took him to most of the extension summer meetings held in Oxford and Cambridge in the 1890s. He was an ardent and eloquent supporter of the 'Co-operative' ethic, becoming a prominent figure in the Co-operative movement nationally. He gave evidence, on behalf of the Co-operative Union, to the Royal Commission on Secondary Education (1894-1897).[16]

A link was forged between the extension programme and the twenty or so mutual improvement societies attached to churches and chapels in Todmorden. Members of the latter attended extension courses to feed back the knowledge to their own societies, and ministers of religion conducted discussion classes on the subject of the current extension series. An attempt was made in the winter of 1890-91 to federate all the local societies into an educational association to underpin the contribution of Oxford. It was not successful, but the idea was sound, and a similar movement was started on a national basis in 1903, when Robert Halstead helped to found the Workers Educational Association.[17]

The first local branch of the WEA was formed in Todmorden in 1907. It displayed a labelled collection of wild flowers in the public library, and organised a series of lectures on the use of the library, some natural history rambles, and an extension course on 'The Study of Animal Life'. Tutorial classes in Todmorden began in 1912 with a three year course on English Literature, which attracted thirty-six students.

The mutual improvement societies were part of a complex pattern of organisations created in the second half of the nineteenth century by churches and chapels to cater for the intellectual, recreational and sporting, as well as spiritual, needs of their members. Sunday schools diversified their roles. The Unitarian Sunday School Circular for 1869-70 shows that they: espoused the 'temperance' ethic by having a Band of Hope; had a burial club which served part of the aims of a 'friendly society'; ran a book club, the beginnings of a library; and encouraged thrift through their savings bank. The school also had a choir and band, which amongst other activities performed, from 1868, an ambitious 'Annual Concert'. In addition to the weekly Sunday morning and afternoon sessions, the school organised classes on every other night of the week. Similar

Todmorden Unitarian Sunday School

CHOIR & STRING BAND.

THE SECOND

ANNUAL CONCERT

Of the Choir and Instrumental Band connected with the Unitarian Sunday School, Todmorden, will be given

In WATERSIDE SCHOOL-ROOM,

(Kindly lent by Messrs. Fielden Bros.,)

ON SATURDAY EVENING, APRIL 3RD, 1869.

The First Part of the Programme will comprise

SELECTIONS FROM

Handel's "Dettingen Te Deum,"

&c.;

The Second Part will consist of a

Selection of Songs, Duetts, Part-songs, &c.

Conductor - Mr. ROBT. LORD; Pianist - Mr. W. S. HOLLINRAKE.

Tickets : Reserved Seats 2s. ; First Seats 1s ; Second Seats 6d. ;
May be had of Mr. Thos. Law, Music-seller, North-street ; Mr. John Lee, Cheapside ; Mr. William Sutcliffe, Lock-street, Shade ; and at the Door.

Doors open at 7-30, the Concert to commence at 8 o'clock.

TODMORDEN

UNITARIAN CHURCH.

ADMIT THE BEARER

TO

THE OPENING SERVICE

On Wednesday, 7th April, 1869,

AT TWO O'CLOCK IN THE AFTERNOON.

activities would be found in most of the other twenty or so Sunday schools throughout the district. In 1879 there were twenty-three libraries in association with local
Sunday schools containing a total of 11,279 books.

At the Unitarian 'Men's Mutual Improvement Society', the chairman drew lots to
decide which member would introduce a discussion on his chosen topic at the weekly
meeting. Some of the subjects were dear to members' hearts, such as 'What are the
best means of improving the conditions of the working class?' Others were more
philosophical, eg 'Does morality increase with civilisation?' There was little discussion
after a paper on the French Revolution, as 'the class was not sufficiently read' in the
subject. It was agreed to try again a fortnight later, in the meantime filling in with a
short discussion on 'Are bachelors a nuisance?', which, the members concluded, was
more in their line.

Religious Life and the Temperance Movement

After virtual stagnation during the 1860s, population growth resumed, albeit modestly,
for the rest of the century. This, together with a general rise in prosperity and the
continuing influence of Sunday school and chapel, led to the last era of chapel building
in the district. As part of this, substantial provision was made for what were called
Sunday schools but were, in fact, used throughout the week for religious, educational
and recreational activities. Between 1870 and 1880 no fewer than eleven chapels were
enlarged or rebuilt: Shore, 1871; Knowlwood, 1870-71; Bridge Street and Lanebottom,
1875; Lumbutts, York Street and Shade, 1877; and Patmos in 1878. The Baptists at
Millwood rebuilt at Roomfield in 1876, whilst the Methodists at Rodhill End did
likewise at Springside in 1873. An Independent Methodist Chapel was built at Old
Royd in 1880.[18]

The Roman Catholics first met for mass in 1864 in a room over the iron foundry at
Salford, before renting a room at Back Ridge Street, Cobden, and by 1876 opened a
purpose-built school and church, also on Cobden, where Todmorden Community
College now stands.[19]

During this period the controversy caused by the building of Christ Church was,
at least legally, resolved. Strenuous efforts had been made to re-open St Mary's Church.
Churchwardens were elected and, in 1860, a Sunday school begun. Services were
conducted by lay members and the Rev Verity of Habergham Eaves, Burnley, the
only local clergyman willing to associate with the 'old church party' as the St Mary's
supporters were known. When the Rev Plow became vicar in 1864, he refused to
allow the 'old church party' use of St Mary's, whereupon they used the Oddfellows'
Hall and some upper rooms in Oxford Street. Attempts to solve the problem revealed
that — the legal rights and privileges belonging to St Mary's had never been transferred
to Christ Church, which, for thirty years had been conducting illegal marriages and
baptisms! It required the Rochdale Vicarage Bill (1866) to regularise the situation,
and, at the same time make Todmorden a parish in its own right. Christ Church
became the parish church and St Mary's re-opened as a chapel-of-ease.

Sadly the Rev Plow was a victim of the vicarage murders of 1878 when Miles
Weatherill, who lived at Brook Street, took terrible revenge because the vicar refused
permission for Weatherill to court a servant, Sarah Bell. When Jane Smith, another
servant, betrayed their illicit meetings, Sarah was sent home to York. Weatherill entered
the vicarage with pistols and a hatchet: in the ensuing struggle he killed Jane Smith
and wounded Mrs Plow, her husband and baby daughter, the last two fatally. Found

Knowlwood Chapel, rebuilt in 1870, is typical of the more ostentatious designs of nonconformist chapels during the last great rebuilding period from the late 1860s to the 1880s.

guilty, Weatherill was hanged at Manchester on the 4th April 1869 — the last public execution in that city.[20]

The continued growth of Cornholme as an industrial village was reflected in the building of St Michael's Church in 1904. It was built on the site of, and with the stone from, the former Cornholme bobbin works, Bridge End, and provided by the generosity of Mrs Master-Whitaker of the Holme in Cliviger.

In the late Victorian period, temperance became almost inseparable from nonconformity. Earlier in the century the Todmorden Teetotal Society, founded in 1834, had a short albeit lively existence, but it was the Band of Hope movement which drew the chapels into the temperance camp.

Culture and Entertainment

Not all of the 'improvement' organisations were offshoots of Co-op or chapel. In the musical sphere were the Todmorden Musical Union, the Todmorden Amateur Brass Band, and bands at Walsden, Lobmill, Gauxholme and Cornholme. The Todmorden Literary Society had an in-and-out existence. The Todmorden Botanical Society was inaugurated in 1852, its two leading members being Abraham Stansfield and John Nowell. Both born in 1802, the former lived as a youth at Fast Ends, a house built

Members of the Band of Hope at Castle Grove Methodist Chapel, Millwood, prepare for a procession, circa 1910.

into the rocks at Bride Stones, before following his interest in botany by becoming a gardener and nurseryman at Vale Nurseries in Wellington Road. He compiled a *Flora of Todmorden* in conjunction with Nowell, whose own special interest was mosses, on which he acquired an international reputation, whilst still continuing work, first as a weaver then as a twister-in. He turned down the offer of a post at Kew Gardens, preferring to remain in Todmorden, where he died in 1867. An obelisk to his memory stands in St Mary's churchyard.

The Todmorden Mechanics Institute was revived in 1859, mainly owing to the efforts of the Unitarian minister, Rev L Taplin, meeting first at the Sobriety Hall and later at the Strand. During the thirteen years of its existence, it instituted classes in connection with the Science and Art Department at South Kensington, resulting in a number of local students being awarded courses of study at the Royal College of Science. Similar South Kensington classes were held at the Walsden Institute and the Working Men's Club (founded in 1864). They met in rooms over the Hollins Branch of the Walsden Co-operative Society, and many of the students gained scholarships at South Kensington. The local classes continued until the passing of the Technical Instruction Act in 1889, when they were transferred to the county council.

The interest aroused locally in science led to the formation of the Todmorden Scientific Association in 1876, which for twenty years organised meetings, discussions, and rambles.[21]

As well as educational activities, chess clubs, and dramatic societies, the churches and chapels spawned cricket, football and rugby teams. The impressive Todmorden and District Cricket League's trophy was competed for from 1890 to 1959, with breaks during the two world wars. In the early 1880s, football in Todmorden was just

Parr's All England XI versus Todmorden and District XXII, played at Centre Vale on the 23rd, 24th and 25th July 1868.

as likely to mean rugby union football, when teams such as Todmorden Wanderers, Todmorden Juniors, Swan Rangers, Millwood Dodgers, Ditch Rovers, Castle Street Rangers, Swan Hornets, Toad Carr and Meadow Bottom Ramblers played at various places, including Longfield, Sandholme and Tipside.

At the apex of the sporting scene were two cricket clubs: Walsden, founded in 1870 and captained for a time by the Rev J R Napier, vicar of Walsden; and the much older Todmorden CC, which was in existence by 1835. Travis in his notes relates that the three sons of John Fielden were keen cricketers, who would call upon some of their workers to make up a team to play with them in a field at Shoebroad (Longfield), 'their wages at the mill going on all the offtime', ie they were paid for time off work to play cricket.

After the Fieldens acquired the Centre Vale estate, Samuel Fielden bought the field and the 'Ridge' hillside behind it, and the Todmorden club has played there ever since. Samuel was a keen cricketer, and an early scorebook of 1839 shows him playing. As owner of the ground and president of the club, he kept a firm grip on affairs. At

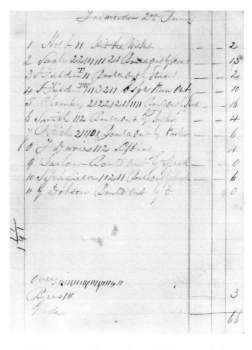

This extract from the earliest surviving scorebook of Todmorden Cricket Club shows the Todmorden innings against Littleborough in 1839. Batting at number four was Samuel Fielden, son of John Fielden MP, identified by the title 'Esqr' and the initials 'DW' for Dawson Weir where he lived. He was run out for ten. Note that 'not out' was then 'left in'.

the same time, he was generous in financing improvements to the ground and premises. Two memorable matches played at Centre Vale were Parr's All England XI versus twenty-two from Todmorden and District, played over three days in July 1868, and, a South v North match, when W G Grace and his brother G F Grace played, in July 1874.

With the spread of cricket in the manufacturing towns of Lancashire, the two town clubs were founder members of the leagues. Todmorden joined the North-East Lancashire Cricket League in 1890, but withdrew to join the South-East Lancashire Cricket League, along with Walsden, in 1892. Walsden has remained in this league, which became the Central Lancashire League, whilst Todmorden resigned in 1896 to rejoin their earlier league, which was renamed the Lancashire League in 1892.

The fortunes of commercial entertainment were as varied as those of the 'improving' societies. A music hall on Salford was opened in 1873 as the Victorian Theatre, for a brief period it became a roller-skating rink, but then reverted to its original role, as the Theatre Royal. A typical weekly bill offered by a Mr Dornton and his company was *The Two Orphans*, *The Enemy Drink*, *Little Emily* (taken from *David Copperfield*), *East Lynne* and Shakespeare's *Richard III*. In November 1883, *Uncle Tom's Cabin* included in the cast freed American slaves as real negroes. By 1885 the theatre had closed, and the building was taken over by the Salvation Army.

For a few years, travelling theatres operated on the market ground (now the bus station), the town hall was used by visiting companies, and regular visits by Sanger's Circus were the highlights of the year. The town had a permanent theatre again when the Hippodrome Theatre, Halifax Road, opened in 1908.

Above and Left: A visit by Sanger's Circus attracted large crowds to watch the colourful procession of animals and performers, seen here along Rochdale Road, at Salford circa 1901. Performances were held in an enormous marquee erected on the Hare and Hounds (Holme) field, now the site of Mons Mill.

Management of Community Affairs

As industry developed in the valley bottom, houses for workers were built, and Todmorden became the town recognisable to anyone who has known it during the last 140 years. The old system of township government was not suited to deal with the new situation; practices which were adequate for small scattered rural settlements were not viable in the urban context.

In 1858 the Public Health Act allowed local boards to be set up, with powers to provide for and look after new buildings, sewerage, roads, street lighting, and public health. Todmorden adopted the Act in 1860, when the Todmorden Urban Sanitary Board was formed, taking responsibility for the area as far as: Knotts Road, in the Burnley Road Valley; Lobb Mill, in the Halifax Road Valley; and Inchfield Fold along the Walsden Valley. This, it will be seen, comprised those parts of the local townships which could be described as 'urban'. The initiative in persuading the local districts to adopt the act was taken by the Fieldens, John as chairman being joined on the board by brother Joshua.

In 1868 Cornholme (from Knotts Road to Portsmouth) became an Urban Sanitary District, which merged with Todmorden in 1875. At the same time the outlying parts of Langfield and Stansfield (except the Hebden Bridge end) and a small part of Cliviger, including Portsmouth, were added.

In 1862 the Todmorden Board began widening and paving the footpaths in the town, at an eventual cost of £3,000. The public health problem was highlighted by the investigation of the Rivers Pollution Commission in 1866. The questions asked relating to the river prompted answers which confirmed the actual words of two witnesses that 'the watercourse here is a common receptacle for everything'. All the manufacturers interviewed turned the liquid waste from their works into the river; the majority tipped the ashes from their boiler fires into the river and the excrement from their privies (toilets) also went, untreated, either directly or via sewers into the river. Houses built near a stream/river had privies emptying directly into it, and waste material, dug out when preparing the foundations, was thrown into the river.

A few days prior to the commissioners' visit, the town had been flooded. Mr Thomas Priestley, whose draper's shop was at Cheapside, Rochdale Road, said to them: 'I wish you would take a walk round and see the misery and desolation which has been occasioned by the last flood'. Todmorden is naturally prone to flooding, and was even more so when the river was treated disrespectfully.

Mr James Byrom Bamford, a surveyor living in Todmorden for twelve years, detailed nine occasions, between October 1855 and June 1863, when there had been flooding. On seven occasions, his own house at Patmos had been flooded between two and twelve inches deep, but houses below, which included those on Cobden, were always flooded three to four feet deeper than his. There were also cellar dwellings which always suffered badly.

John Fielden, chairman of the local board, admitted that drainage in Todmorden was poor, that there was a sewer down York Street (Halifax Road), but not a good one, and that the local board intended to call in an engineer to give an estimate.

Mr Frederick Rodley, surveyor and inspector of nuisances to the local board for the past three years, said the board had been talking about a system of drainage for the whole place, 'ever since I have been here', but he added, 'We only go slowly in Todmorden'. He said that about 300 houses had been flooded recently up to three feet six inches deep; that the tenants had the expense of cleaning up afterwards; that many of the houses were not fit to live in, being built on low-lying land; that the local

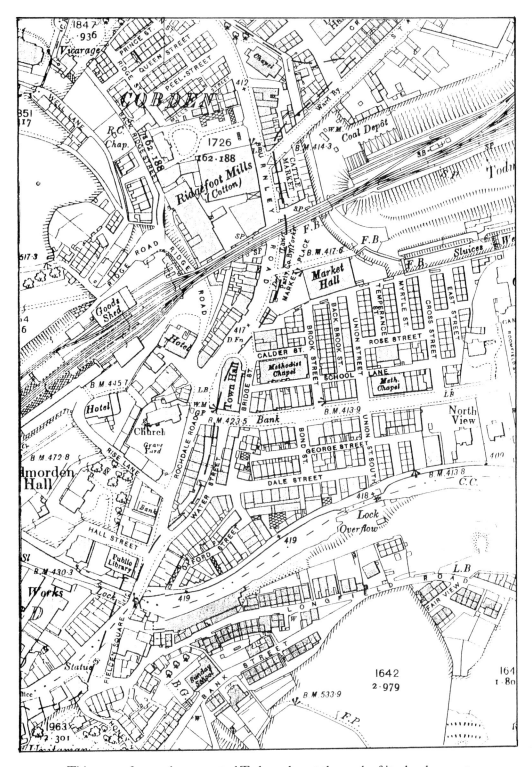

This map of 1907 shows central Todmorden at the peak of its development.

The town hall (below) and (above) the ornamental detail of the stonework supporting the triangular pediment. At the time of its building in 1875, the county boundary (the river) flowed underneath the hall, and the statuary reflects, on the left, Lancashire's cotton trade, and, on the right, Yorkshire's engineering industry and agriculture.

board now prevented houses being built in such places; but that, 'the local board came 10 years too late as regards Todmorden'.

It is obvious that, as the town developed rapidly from about 1850 onwards, unregulated building had taken place, resulting in poor dwellings on unsuitable sites. Excrement from toilets had traditionally been used as fertiliser on the land but, with the increase in population, this was no longer viable and, as there was no alternative, the river was used.[22]

Work started on a drainage scheme in 1868. A sewer over a mile long was laid from Lobb Mill to Bond Street at a cost of £12,000. The serious smallpox outbreak in October 1874 highlighted the unsanitary conditions in the town. An isolation hospital was hurriedly acquired, a building which had formerly housed Holt's picker works at Sourhall. Samuel Fielden initially paid for the staff and equipment. By 1875 all the streets were lit by gas, which was provided by three private undertakings, the Todmorden Gas Company, Fieldens' gasworks, and Wilson Brothers' gasworks. In 1878 the riverbed was cleaned out at a cost of £1,800, £1,500 of which was donated by Samuel Fielden. The market hall was opened in the following year.

The stretches of the turnpike roads to Halifax, Rochdale and Burnley, within the area of the local board, became the responsibility of the latter when the turnpike trust was wound up in 1878. The board decided in 1887 to buy the three local gas undertakings, a process concluded in 1892-93 at a cost of just over £100,000.

Under the terms of the 1870 Education Act, a school board was formed for the six townships of the Todmorden Poor Law Union, ie, the area from Walsden to Mytholmroyd. The first election in 1874 was contested on sectarian lines. Only two 'Church Conservatives' were elected, the other seven seats going to nonconformists and/or Liberals, including a Wesleyan Liberal, a United Methodist Free Church Liberal, and two Unitarians, Rev Lindsey Taplin and Mrs Sarah Jane Fielden, the only woman member. The latter had a keen interest in education, having opened a school on Cobden before moving, in 1872, to her newly-built school at Centre Vale. She taught there for a time, expounding her well-researched educational theories and maintained direct control until it closed in 1896 to become the Fielden School of Art under the local board. She founded the Fielden Chair of Education at Manchester University, receiving the honorary degree of doctor of literature in 1906.[23]

Board schools provided undenominational Bible teaching, which suited the nonconformist majority in the district. By 1878 board schools had been built at Roomfield and Cloughfoot. In the following year the board took over Lanebottom School, until it could be replaced by Walsden Board School in 1879. By 1881 further board schools had been opened at Eastwood and Vale, and in 1895 Cornholme Methodist School was taken over until a board school was built there in 1899. To meet the costs of building and running the schools, a separate education rate was levied.

The Charter of Incorporation

The growth of the town — nearly 700 houses were built between 1876 and 1886 — encouraged the Todmorden Local Board, in the latter year, to try to secure a charter of incorporation as a municipal borough, a status achieved by nearby Bacup in 1882. Besides the enhanced status from having a mayor, councillors and aldermen, the town would increase its autonomy with greater powers of self-government. Public meetings were overwhelmingly in favour, a petition for incorporation attracted 2,400 signatures within a few weeks, and most of the leading manufacturers gave their support. However, the opposition included Samuel Fielden, who argued that the trappings of mayoralty would be expensive, and that improved amenities, mainly serving the urban part of the borough and being of minimal benefit to the rural parts, would mean a sharp increase in rates for all. His faction used paid canvassers to collect signatures for a counter-petition, and won support from farmers in outlying areas, who would gain little from urban improvements. Less than one seventh of the local board's area comprised the actual town of Todmorden; the rest was farmland or open moorland. A public enquiry was held, and the request for incorporation rejected.

Samuel Fielden died in 1889, the year after the first step in the restructuring of local government was taken by the creation of county councils. Having a county boundary running through the middle of the town was now even more inconvenient, and so in 1888 the whole of the town was placed within the West Riding. In 1894, local boards of the Todmorden type became urban district councils, only a step away from borough status. Todmorden already had a splendid town hall, built in 1875 by the three sons of John Fielden, and given to trustees for the use of the community. It was formally handed over to the local board in 1891. Even 'Mr Sam' would not have been able, had he so wished, to block incorporation, which was secured in 1896.[24]

Todmorden determined to celebrate Charter Day, Saturday the 22nd August 1896, in unforgettable style. The Todmorden Co-operative Society, to commemorate the day and its own jubilee, presented its library of 8,000 books and a building in which to house them to the town. The foundation stone of the new library was laid with great ceremony on the morning of Charter Day.

The town was decked out for the occasion. Across the roads there were triumphal arches, each with its appropriate motto: at Gandy Bridge 'May peace and prosperity reign', Stansfield Bridge, Church Street and Waterside 'Welcome to our Infant Borough'. Banners with mottos, such as 'Success to our Town and Trade', 'May our rates be small, prosperity great and happiness for all' and at Salford 'The cradle of Todmorden Industries', festooned the main streets, twenty-eight from the market to Gandy Bridge, nineteen from County Bridge to Stansfield Bridge, and nineteen from County Bridge to Gauxholme, put there by the shop- and inn-keepers. These covered the route of the procession, which went from the town hall to the Holme via Burnley Road, returning via Garden Street, Wellington Road, White Platt Street and Stansfield Road to Burnley Road, then continuing down Halifax Road to Stansfield Bridge and returning to the town hall, before processing to Gauxholme Arches and back to the field at Waterside. On the market ground was a giant fountain with a basin forty-five feet in diameter containing thirty water jets, with one in the centre 150 feet high at full pressure.

The procession began at 2.30 pm. There were cyclists in a variety of costumes, mounted police, Sunday schools (whose order was chosen by ballot) with the younger scholars on waggonettes, a company of the Lancashire Fusiliers with their band, a long string of carriages with guests, the Todmorden Fire Brigade and those of neighbouring towns, Todmorden Cricket and Football Clubs, Todmorden Post Office staff, the Trades Council, Cloughfoot branch of Burnley Miners' Association, St John's Ambulance Brigade, Todmorden, Walsden and Bridge End Co-operative Societies, the various Friendly Societies of the town with Walsden and Nazebottom Brass Bands, and finally the local tradespeople with exhibits of their trades on various lorries and waggonettes, of which there were seventy-five separate vehicles. That of Messrs Gledhill, Ashworth and Company of Crescent Mill carried a working loom powered by an

Stoodley Pike is a well-known landmark in upper Calderdale. An earlier pike was built to
commemorate the surrender of Paris to the allies in 1814, although there is evidence to
suggest some earlier structures. Following its collapse, the pike was rebuilt in 1854, to the
design of local architect James Green. It is likely that the obelisk shape reflects the
freemasonry of Samuel Fielden, who not only subscribed £50 towards the project
but cleared the final debt of £212.

The Charter Day procession under the viaduct on its way up Burnley Road.

oil engine. A local fishmonger, Mr Robert Gibson, had a large block of ice into which were frozen a salmon, lobster, conger-eel and bream.

When all were assembled in the field at Waterside, there was singing to massed bands; the reading of extracts from, and acceptance of, the charter, and an announcement that the first election for the council would be on the 2nd November — followed by the first meeting a week later. There was a banquet in the town hall that evening, whilst the scholars had the traditional buns and coffee or tea at their own schools.

During the evening there was a firework display on Longfield Hill by James Pain and Sons of London. It was estimated that, during the day, over 12,000 people came into the town by train.[25]

The borough council had three councillors for each of six wards, plus six aldermen, a structure retained throughout its life. The long-serving clerk to the local board, Dan Sutcliffe, became town clerk, and the first mayor was Caleb Hoyle, a prominent cotton manufacturer who had supported the incorporation move in 1886. The council busied itself with essential services. The only water supply, apart from wells and springs, was provided by the private Todmorden Waterworks Company, established in 1882, which built a reservoir in Ramsden Clough between 1885 and 1888. The logical step was for the borough council to buy out the company, but Rochdale Borough Council, wanting to extend its own gathering grounds, bought it first in 1898. In the same year Todmorden secured authority to build reservoirs in Gorpley Clough, and one was constructed there between 1900 and 1905. It was arranged that in the meantime Todmorden would still be supplied from Ramsden Clough.

Between 1901 and 1908 a new sewage system, with works at Sandbed, was developed. Improved sanitation caused a marked drop in the incidence of water-borne diseases. Electricity works were built at Millwood in 1905. A tramway system was considered, but the council decided instead in favour of a municipal bus service, which began in 1907. The initial costs of these developments caused the rates to rise, from 4s 8d in the £ in 1896 to 8s 2d in 1912, but the bus account moved into surplus in 1914. By 1916 the bus undertaking was saving the ratepayers nearly £2,000 a year.

When the borough was formed, Todmorden was given a separate school board. It bought the Fielden Brothers' factory school at Waterside, and turned it into the Waterside Technical Institute. Under the 1902 Education Act, school boards were abolished, and their powers transferred to local councils. The borough of Todmorden became responsible for elementary education, and the West Riding County Council for secondary education. A new elementary school, which had been planned by the school board, opened at Shade in 1904. The Todmorden County Secondary School at Ferney Lee was completed in 1912.

All schools, including church schools, were now supported from the rates. Some nonconformists objected to paying rates towards church schools — they formed the Todmorden (mostly Cornholme) branch of the Passive Resistance Movement — withholding the 'education' element of their rates. Consequently, personal goods (commonly watches) were distrained in lieu and retrieved later at auction at Vale Street Police Station. This echo of past protests continued until the outbreak of war in 1914.[26]

12

Todmorden Between the Wars

By 1911 Todmorden had grown into a town of over 25,000 people, but a town with a distinctive shape. Most of the working-class housing was simultaneously congested and dispersed, squeezed into the narrow valley bottom, but strung out along the three main roads as far as Portsmouth, Eastwood and Walsden Bottoms. Recreational facilities were similarly dispersed, to a considerable degree divided between the churches and chapels, with their societies and sports teams, and their rivals, the numerous public houses and working men's clubs.

The first major recreational facility for the town as a whole, and an important step towards its maturity as an urban community, was acquired in 1910, after the death of Mrs Sarah Jane Fielden. Her son John Ashton Fielden sold Centre Vale estate, comprising the parkland, cricket field, Centre Vale Mansion, Ewood Hall and farms at Carr Laithe and Platts, to the council for £10,000.[1] The estate was opened as a public park in 1912, with bowling greens created in 1915, followed by tennis courts, a miniature golf course and, for the children, a play ground, paddling pool and boating pond. The bowling greens became the focus for the sport in the town. Many other crown greens were attached to public houses, and a thriving league developed which is still popular. The mansion was converted into a hospital for wounded and convalescent soldiers from November 1914 to February 1919. It later became a museum until dry rot forced its closure in 1947, and demolition in 1953.

On the industrial front, trade looked deceptively good. Raw cotton consumption in Britain reached its all-time peak in 1913. Over eighty per cent of cotton cloth woven was exported, Britain having two-thirds of the world's trade. Epitomising this success, the Weavers Institute, with union offices and function/recreational facilities, was opened on Burnley Road in 1914. Cotton products made up a quarter of all British exports. It could not last. A large proportion of the exports went to low-wage markets, nearly forty per cent to India alone, where modern textile industries were bound to develop.[2] Todmorden assisted this process. Joshua Holden, in 1912, noted that of the cotton-spinning machinery made by Lord Brothers, 'a very large quantity [is] sent abroad'.[3] What would otherwise have been gradual developments were, however, hastened by the effects of the First World War.

Thousands of Todmorden men served in the armed forces, as volunteers or, after March 1916, as conscripts. In September 1914, led amongst others by Captain R H Barker (son of Luke of Friths Mill), local volunteers gathered at Dalton Street Drill Hall to join the 6th battalion of Lancashire Fusiliers. The regiments in which Todmorden men served took heavy casualties at Gallipoli and in the trenches.[4] Amongst those who lied about being under-age in their eagerness to enlist was William 'Billy' Holt, who echoed their sentiments: 'I left my looms without regret … a heaven sent

This view of industrial Cornholme circa 1908 is dominated by Wilson Brothers' Bobbin Works. The mill chimneys on the right belong to Caldervale and Springwood mills. In the background is the Shore hillside.

opportunity of climbing out of the valley!'[5] The engineering and metallurgical firms in the town made munitions, and by 1915 most of the leading textile firms were dealing with government orders. The German submarine campaign in 1917 led to the rationing not only of food, but also, under the Cotton Control Board, of raw cotton. In June 1918, for example, spinning mills using American cotton and not on essential government work, were restricted to using half of their spindles, and for 40 hours a week instead of 55½.[6] Meanwhile the Japanese cotton industry was racing ahead, quadrupling its exports between 1913 and 1918, and making serious inroads into Britain's Far Eastern markets.[7]

After the Armistice in November 1918, the general obsession was with 'getting back to normal'. In 1919, by the threat of strikes, the cotton workers won a cut in working hours from 55½ to 48 hours per week without loss of pay. The negotiations were industry-wide except that, characteristically, the Todmorden employers kept their own association. They were more willing to grant this concession because of boom conditions which lasted until late 1920. Prices soared and wages chased them upwards. In the spring of 1920, by means of strikes and the threat of strikes, the Todmorden cotton workers won wage increases of 25% to 28½%.[8]

R H Barker, who ended the war as a major, won the Sowerby Bridge Division in the 'Khaki Election' of December 1918, as the candidate of the Discharged Sailors and Soldiers Association. He stood down in 1922 because of the needs of the family textile business. In the general election of that year, the split between Coalition (Lloyd George) Liberals and Independent (Asquith) Liberals, together with the presence of a Labour candidate, gave the Conservatives the chance to take a constituency which had been Liberal from 1885 to 1918. W A Simpson Hinchcliffe of Cragg Hall, an unsuccessful candidate on three previous occasions, topped the poll. The Liberals, reunited, regained the seat in 1923, but for the last time. It was subsequently Conservative, except between 1929 and 1931 when it was held for Labour by W J Tout, secretary of the Todmorden Weavers Association.[9]

Cornholme was a hive of political activity. Until 1922 three parliamentary divisions, Middleton, Clitheroe and Sowerby, all met at Cornholme. Elections were diverting occasions, as candidates from all three constituencies held packed meetings in the Methodist Schoolroom — to much local heckling/cheering from the voters seeking entertainment as much as enlightenment. Cornholme had its own Liberal Club (appropriately at the bottom of Rosebery and opposite Gladstone streets), which later became the Labour Club.

During 1920, memorials to the fallen were unveiled at many churches and chapels, and in October 1921 the borough's war memorial, bearing 659 names, was opened in Centre Vale Park. One consequence of the wartime losses was seen in the 1921 census, when there were nearly 1,600 more females than males in the population.[10]

There was more leisure time, and the town's cultural organisations re-formed. The Todmorden Musical Society, which had given its fiftieth performance of Handel's *Messiah* in 1905, separated into the Todmorden Orchestra and Todmorden Operatic Society. Both are still in existence, their continuity broken only by the Second World War. Amongst those who graduated from the orchestra was Ben Horsfall, violinist. He studied at the Manchester College of Music in 1926 and played with the Hallé, the BBC Northern and other premier orchestras. He took a degree and doctorate in music, before retiring, when he returned to conduct the Todmorden Orchestra from 1962 for the next twenty years.[11]

Pursuing a career in popular music was Geoff Love, the well-known band leader, who took his first trombone lesson from Dr J de Ville Mather, a founder member of the orchestra. Geoff presented a trombone to the orchestra in 1959 in recognition of the opportunities it had opened to him.

Many received their first taste for music in church/chapel choirs and in the musical concerts presented in the various Sunday schools. This was certainly true of Todmorden Male Voice Choir, formed as a competition choir in 1906, and achieving an enviable reputation between 1907 and 1914, being placed in the first three in thirty-six competitions and winning two firsts at the prestigious Blackpool Festival under the conductor T H Lees. Also active was the Glee and Madrigal Society, winner at Wigan and District Musical Festival in 1936. These societies formed the core of the still-thriving Choral Society, founded in 1938. The Operatic Society presented a Gilbert and Sullivan opera annually from 1917 to 1925, before entering the wider field of musical comedy. Their production of *Desert Song* in 1935, with the Male Voice Choir as the 'riff's' chorus, was the highlight of their shows between the wars.

For about five years prior to 1927, there was an excellent boys' choir under Mr Ronald Cunliffe. It broadcast four times, and its operas for 1925 included *The Magic Flute*, *The Golden Cockerel* and *Pagliacci*. Over 150 boys, including Geoff Love, were members during its existence. It won acclaim from the *Manchester Guardian* and Sidney Nicholson, Westminster Abbey organist.

The Todmorden, Cornholme and Walsden brass bands continued to thrive between the wars as they had done throughout the last half of the nineteenth century. As ballroom dancing became fashionable, local dance bands developed. Ellis Wood, violinist and saxophonist, was a popular musician with the Belvedere dance band, formed in 1922 and still active, before starting his own Astorians band around 1930. Several of the churches and chapels had dramatic societies, with ambitious productions such as Oscar Strauss's *The Waltz Dream* (Cornholme Methodist) and Shaw's *You Never Can Tell* (Eastwood Congregational) in 1936. Todmorden Little Theatre, founded in 1934, performed at the Co-operative Hall, and in 1936 had 183 members.[12]

Amongst other societies were: the Photographic Society, formed in 1907 and still in existence; the Cycling Club, inaugurated in 1892 and continuing into the 1960s; and the present Natural History Society which dates from the 1920s. The WEA had a membership of 132 in 1936, when it ran tutorial classes in modern history, geology and psychology, as well as arranging public lectures and rambles.[13]

In the 1920s Todmorden's public affairs were still managed mainly by the alliance between Co-operative nonconformist Liberals and the mill-owning nonconformist Liberals. The first group was personified by Alderman Robert Jackson (died 1922), mayor from 1911 to 1918, who received the OBE and was made a freeman of the borough for his wartime services. He was branch manager then secretary of Walsden Co-op, president of Todmorden Co-op, a United Methodist and active temperance worker. Representative of the second group was Edward Lord (1850-1924), cotton manufacturer at Gauxholme Mill, who served on the borough council, county council and board of guardians, and was a Wesleyan Methodist and lifelong teetotaller. It is not surprising that no alcohol was sold in the Todmorden Liberal Club.[14]

Todmorden elected its first Labour mayors in 1920 and 1922, both from Cornholme, a Labour stronghold.[15] However, the process whereby the working-class vote switched to Labour, and Conservatism became more acceptable among the employers, developed only gradually. Of the first 24 mayors, 14 were Liberal. The elections of November 1927 produced a council of 10 Liberal, 8 Conservative and 6 Labour members. Ten years later there were 7 Liberal, 7 Labour, 5 Independent and 4 Conservative members, plus 1 'trade unionist'.[16]

The boom in the cotton trade collapsed at the end of November 1920. In May 1921, over 7,000 people in Todmorden were unemployed or on short time, and by the end of the year the industry was suffering what *Todmorden Advertiser* called the worst depression since the cotton famine. During 1921 cotton-spinners' wage rates were cut by 30% and clothing trade rates by 12%. In 1922 there was a fifteen week strike by engineering workers against a wage cut. The union eventually gave in, but the Todmorden men voted 62 to 38 against acceptance.[17]

The cotton trade gradually recovered, but by 1925 Todmorden had lost ground relative to the Lancashire industry as a whole.[18] It should be explained that Worrall's textile directories, a major source of information, included Todmorden in their Lancashire statistics on the grounds of economic affinity. In 1916, when the number of looms in Lancashire reached its maximum, Todmorden had forty-two spinning and/or weaving firms, with a total of about 340,000 spindles and nearly 18,000 looms. It had lost about 12% of its capacity by 1925, although there had been very little contraction in Lancashire as a whole.

In 1916 Todmorden had thirty weaving-only firms, with an average of 391 looms each. The largest was Joshua Smith of Frostholme Mill, Cornholme (1,723 looms), the smallest A Y Schofield of Spring Mill (80 looms). By 1925 there had been a net loss of two firms and over 1,500 looms.

The largest of the six spinning-only firms in 1916 was Mons Mill, built in 1908-10 as Hare Mill and taken over by the Mons Mill Company in 1914, with nearly 98,000 mule spindles. By 1925 its capacity had increased to 123,000 spindles, including 17,000 ring spindles and 5,952 spindles (on eighteen ring-frames)[19] used for doubling, ie

The Lancashire and Yorkshire Railway Atlantic engine *Highflyer*, number 1413, crossing Gauxholme Viaduct in 1924 *en route* to Manchester.

twisting together two or more yarns, in this case to produce wool/cotton mixtures. The firm also specialised in hosiery yarns. This group had, thanks to Mons, almost exactly the same number of spindles as in 1916.

In 1916 six firms combined spinning and weaving. The largest was Fielden Brothers, who had about 1,450 looms and 56,000 spindles (although they continued to report to Worrall the figure of 100,000 spindles, which they had not had for many years). By 1925 they had 33,000 ring and 10,000 mule spindles, but still 1,450 looms. Hoyles had split into two companies, at Derdale and Hollins mills, and cut their spinning capacity by eighteen per cent. Only Luke Barker, of Friths, Dancroft and Crow Carr Ings mills had expanded. The integrated firms favoured ring spinning, the spinning-only firms generally preferred mules. Both groups were producing mainly coarse and medium yarns.

By 1928 there had been further contraction. Fieldens had closed Lumbutts, concentrating all their spinning at Robinwood on 31,000 ring spindles. Unemployment was stubbornly high, and under-employment was endemic: a three- or four-day week; three looms running instead of four; and extended (unpaid) holiday stoppages. At Christmas 1928, for example, eighty per cent of the firms extended the holiday break by up to eight days, and two months later many of the four-loom weavers had one loom idle. Throughout the interwar period, it was rare for a textile worker to be able to look back on twelve months' continuous and full employment, and weavers who were the sole earners in a family often took home much less than a living wage.[20]

The borough council organised some unemployment relief schemes, mainly road-widening. Its utilities — gas, electricity and buses — expanded, and from 1923 all were making profits. A small housing scheme was abandoned in 1924 as too costly. The council was cautious about expenditure, not only from instinct, but also because of economic depression and a declining population — from 25,404 in 1911 to an estimated 21,210 in 1935. In 1935-36 Todmorden had a birth rate of 10.42 per thousand, compared to an average of 14.7 for England and Wales, and a death rate of 16.3 compared to 11.7.[21]

The housing problem was one of quality rather than quantity. Over 2,000 of the 7,000 houses in the borough were back-to-back, some of which were suffering from damp and decay. In 1933 the council began its first major housing programme with the development of the Ashenhurst estate, and, by the end of 1939, 232 houses had been built.[22]

The council extended the provision of maternity and child welfare clinics in the 1920s. It was responsible for elementary education, and in 1936 built an Open Air School at Stile, for delicate children, to replace a wooden structure at Ferney Lee in use since 1920. The Abraham Ormerod Medical Centre (1938) was a gift to the town from the old textile family, which operated at Gorpley and Frith mills, Bacup Road; built Hollins Mill, Walsden; and in 1843 took over Ridgefoot Mill. The 'clinic' was built on the site of Ridgefoot.[23]

The 1929 Local Government Act abolished boards of guardians. From April 1930 the responsibility for poor relief in Todmorden was transferred to the West Riding County Council. In a faint echo of past struggles, voices were raised in the town protesting against the loss of local control.[24]

Another major area of public life experiencing a decline was religious worship. Local nonconformist activity had peaked even before the First World War, and soon afterwards, perhaps because the carnage of war had undermined religious belief, it was clear that a downward trend had set in. Between 1922 and 1929, Sunday school enrolments fell by twenty per cent; some of the thirty Bands of Hope existing in 1924 had folded by 1931; and increasingly the preachers' theme was 'the empty church'. It was a decline, and not yet a collapse, but congregations were beginning to feel lost in some of the huge chapels, eg York Street Methodist with over 1,200 seats had little need for the gallery by 1930 and in 1942 it closed in a merger with Bridge Street Chapel.

SYLLABUS--1939-40.

1939
Oct. 9—Presidential Address ... ...
Rev. W. S. Davies.

23—"Parasites of Man ' ... ...
Dr. T. Southwell, D.Sc., F.R.S.E.

Nov. 6—"Some Glimpses of Indian Life" ...
Mr. Peter Greenwood, Burnley.

20—"An Hour in a French Library" ...
Mr. J. Sagar, Bacup.

Dec. 4—"Caste and Christianity" ... ...
Mr. W. Wilcock, Todmorden.

18—"Will Democracy Survive" ... ...
Mr. H. R, Sutcliffe, Todmorden.

30—Social Evening.

1940
Jan. 8—"Democracy and the Press" ... ...
Mr. H. V. Wiseman, M.A., B.Sc.,
Rochdale.

**Shore Young Men's
Mutual Improvement Society.**

ESTABLISHED 1868.

List of Officers--1939-40.

President—Rev. W. S. DAVIES.

Vice-Presidents—
Coun. J. E. Webster, Mr. Mark Greenwood.

Secretary—Mr. W. J Heywood.

Ass. Secretary—Mr. James Sagar.

Treasurer—
Mr. James Earnshaw Greenwood.

Lanternists—Messrs. H. & E. Clegg.

Committee—
Messrs H Horsfall, E. Clegg, W Greenwood (Pudsey Road), J. Johnson, J. H. Greenwood Frank Helliwell, W. Robinson, Walter Greenwood, H. Earnshaw, H Clegg.

Auditors—Messrs. F. Shackleton and James Ed. Greenwood.

Member's Fee for Session—1/6.

All Subscriptions to be paid on or before December 31st, 1939.

Jan.22—"Happiness" ... Mr. P. Bairstow.

Feb. 5—"Light and Shade in a Minister's
Life" ... ...
Rev. J. R. Brightman, B A., Todn.

19—Open Date.

Mar.4—Selected ... ... Rev. P. Flanders.

18—Selected ... ... Mr. W. Robinson.

Apl 15—Annual Meeting and Statement of Accounts.

Meetings are held on alternate Monday Evenings (unless otherwise stated) in Shore Baptist Sunday School (Primary Room), commencing at 7-30 p.m.

The Society's Annual "Week-End" will be held on Saturday and Sunday, April 6th and 7th, 1940.

Cunliffe Brothers, Todmorden.

The syllabus of meetings for the Shore Young Men's Mutual
Improvement Society, 1939-40.

In 1932 the three local Methodist connexions — Wesleyan, Primitive and United — came together in the Methodist Union. (The New Connexion had merged with the United Methodists in 1907; the Particular and General Baptists had united in 1891.) There was no immediate rationalisation of chapels because of local loyalties. One new church was built, on Wellington Road in 1929, by the Roman Catholics, who had outgrown the 250-seat church in Back Ridge Street, Cobden, used since 1876.[25]

Some preachers blamed radio and cinema for filling the leisure time previously devoted to chapel-related activities. Films were shown in the Hippodrome Theatre, which was primarily a cinema from 1917. By 1932 there were three venues for the

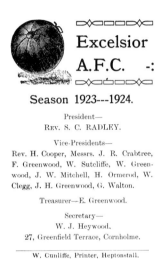

Excelsior A.F.C.

Season 1923---1924.

President—
Rev. S. C. RADLEY.

Vice-Presidents—
Rev. H. Cooper, Messrs. J. R. Crabtree, F. Greenwood, W. Sutcliffe, W. Greenwood, J. W. Mitchell, H. Ormerod, W. Clegg, J. H. Greenwood, G. Walton.

Treasurer—E. Greenwood.

Secretary—
W. J. Heywood,
27, Greenfield Terrace, Cornholme.

W. Cunliffe, Printer, Heptonstall.

Excelsior A.F.C.   Fixtures 1923--24.

1923	Name of Club	Grnd Rslt
Sep. 22	Cup Tie.	
,, 29	Walsden United Res...H......	
Oct. 6	York Street ....H......	
,, 13	Dulesgate ....A......	
,, 20	Cup Tie.	
,, 27	B.V.Y.M.C.A. ....H......	
Nov. 3	Walsden United Res...A......	
,, 10	Bourillion ....A......	
,, 17	Cup Tie.	
,, 24	Bourillion ....H......	
Dec. 1	Cornholme B.W. ....A......	
,, 8	Cross Stone ....A......	
,, 15	Cup Tie.	
,, 22	Knotts Celtic............H......	
,, 29		

1924	Name of Club	Grnd Rslt
Jan. 5	Shamrocks ....A......	
,, 12		
,, 19	Cross Stone ....H......	
,, 26		
Feb. 2	B.V.Y.M.C.A. ....A......	
,, 9	Shamrocks ....H......	
,, 16	Knotts Celtic............A......	
,, 23		
Mch. 1	Knowlwood United Rs.H......	
,, 8	Dulesgate ....H......	
,, 15		
,, 22	York Street ....A......	
,, 29	Knowlwood United Rs.A......	
Apr. 5	Cornholme B.W. ......H......	

Football and cricket fixture lists from the 1920s, for the Excelsior Club (Shore and Vale Baptists) in the Todmorden and District League.

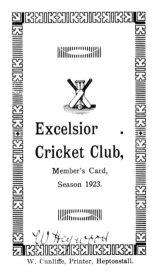

**Excelsior .
Cricket Club,**

Member's Card,
Season 1923.

W. Heywood

W. Cunliffe, Printer, Heptonstall.

List of Fixtures.
First Eleven.

Date	Name of Club	Grnd Rslt
April 14	Lydgate ....H......	
,, 21	Walsden Wesleyans ......A..... .	
,, 28	York Street ....H......	
May 5	Roomfield ....A......	
,, 12	Oldroyd ....H......	
,, 19	Mankinholes.................A......	
,, 26	Unitarians ....H......	
June 2	Patmos ....H......	
,, 9	Parish Church ....A......	
,, 16	Wellington Road ....H......	
,, 23	Bridge Street ....H......	
,, 30	Lydgate ....A......	
July 7	Walsden Wesleyans ......H......	
,, 14	York Street ....A......	
,, 21	Roomfield.....................H......	
,, 28	Oldroyd ....A......	
Aug. 4	Mankinholes ....H......	
,, 11	Unitarians ....A......	
,, 18	Patmos ....A......	
,, 25	Parish Church ....H......	
Sept. 1	Wellington Road............A......	
,, 8	Bridge Street ....A......	

List of Fixtures.
Second Eleven.

Date	Name of Club	Grnd Rslt
April 21	Parish Church ....H......	
,, 28		
May 5	Dobroyd ....H......	
,, 12		
,, 19	West End ....H......	
,, 26	Unitarians ....A......	
June 2		
,, 9	Dobroyd ....A......	
,, 16		
,, 23	Bridge Street ....A......	
,, 30		
July 7	Walsden Wesleyans ......A......	
,, 14		
,, 21		
,, 28	Walsden Wesleyans ......H......	
Aug. 4	West End ....A......	
,, 11	Unitarians ....H......	
,, 18	Bridge Street ....H......	
,, 25	Parish Church ....A......	

Fred Root, Todmorden cricket club professional, responding after the presentation of the
Worsley Cup to Todmorden in 1933

'talkies': the Hippodrome; the Gem, Cornholme, known as the BOS from its opening
in 1915 to 1931; and the Olympia, originally a corrugated iron building which opened
for skating in 1909 but converted to a picture palace in 1910, showing silent movies
along with live entertainment, until replaced in 1931. It was still not unknown to have
live entertainment in the new building, and Mary Midgley's dancing pupils performed
between feature films for a week in 1938.[26]

Some churches, for example Mount Zion and St Michael's in Cornholme, had
their own tennis courts, but the most flourishing form of activity created by the competitive social endeavours of churches and chapels was the Todmorden and District
Cricket League. Most of the teams were attached to places of worship. The headline
'Exciting clash between the Church and the Spiritualists' meant nothing more
disturbing than a cricket match at Dobroyd.[27] Their cricket grounds were all on the
farming 'shelf' and an 'away' fixture might only be two fields distant. Some of the
players graduated to the town's leading clubs, Walsden and Todmorden. Walsden's
resources were limited, and it was not unusual for them to finish a season in the
bottom half of the table. Todmorden, however, were a force to be reckoned with,
having the third-best record in the league in the period 1897-1937. They had an
excellent spell from 1933 to 1937, when Fred Root of Worcestershire was the
professional, winning the league in 1933, and the Worsley Cup in 1935 and 1937. In the
following year they achieved the 'double'. For an attractive fixture involving a visiting
world-class professional (Constantine was the most famous), the Centre Vale ground,
one of the finest anywhere, would be packed, with spectators numbered in thousands.[28]

When Root came to Todmorden, he found as many people watching the pre-season
net practice as would have made a good gate for a county match at Worcester:

Everybody seems to be a member of their respective Lancashire League club.
They would rather miss joining the Co-op than the cricket club, and when bad

Portsmouth Rovers AFC, 1919-20; one of their most successful seasons.

times make money scarce their sacrifices to enable them to pay their annual subscription are almost pitiful.[29]

In the absence of any professional football team, there was good support in the 1920s for the three leading amateur clubs, Portsmouth Rovers, Walsden United and Knowlwood, all competing at that time in the Northeast Lancashire Combination. Operating at a lower level was the Todmorden and District Football League. Perhaps because some of the clubs were associated with industrial firms, the football league fared worse than its cricket counterpart during the interwar period, and closed down at least twice.[30]

'They would rather miss joining the Co-op ...', but of all the major elements in the economic and social life of the town, the one which best withstood the stresses of the 1920s and 1930s was the Co-operative movement. The three local societies — Todmorden, Bridge End and Walsden — could only manage dividends in the range of 1s 4d to 1s 8d in the £ in the turbulent conditions of 1920-22, but in 1928-29 Todmorden paid 2s 6d (a rate maintained for nearly all of the next decade) and Bridge End 2s 9d and 3s. Membership of the Todmorden society rose steadily, from 4,927 in 1920 to 5,833 in 1939. Bridge End absorbed Walsden in 1935-36, at which time the two societies had about 1,800 members.

In October 1928 the Todmorden society paid out, for a half-year, over £12,000 in dividend and over £3,000 in interest on share capital. £50,000 of its capital fund was out on loan to members for house purchases. In 1936 it opened its first new branch since before the First World War, to serve the new Ashenhurst housing estate, and then had a total of fifteen branches from Walkmill in Cliviger to Eastwood. Co-operative trading covered a wide range: groceries, butchery, clothing, footwear, hardware, furniture, coal, a cafe and a funeral service. The Todmorden society closed down its ten reading rooms in 1921, hoping that the Free Library service, which was virtually a Co-operative creation, would fill the gap. Otherwise it remained socially active, with: an annual treat for upwards of 2,000 children on 'Co-operators' Day' in early July; a winter programme of public lectures; and, from 1922, an annual music festival.[31]

It was as well that many local families had the dividend, as the cotton trade plunged into a deep depression from 1929. Unemployment nationally in cotton, including those temporarily stopped, rose from 9 per cent in February 1928 to 46 per cent in August 1930. In that year, local Communist William Holt led a demonstration of Todmorden women carrying empty shopping baskets, as a symbol of their plight, and was arrested for his pains. Again in 1932, for leading a demonstration by the Todmorden branch of the National Unemployed Workers Movement against the Means Test, he was arrested and committed to Wakefield Prison for nine months by Leeds Assizes. On his release he was elected Communist councillor for Stansfield ward until the local branch closed in 1934.

Regarded locally as eccentric, Holt was an accomplished author, best known for: *Under a Japanese Parasol* (1933); *I Was a Prisoner* (1934); *I Haven't Unpacked* (1939), recalled by Alan Bennett as one of his mother's favourite books because it was 'the story of someone brought up … in a mill town … had bought a horse and gone on his travels';[32] and *I Still Haven't Unpacked* (1953). His novels, apart from *The Weaver's Knot* (1958), were less successful. During the Second World War he joined a team, which included J B Priestley, in 'Britain Speaks', broadcasting regularly to America. In the early 1960s he toured Europe with his horse Trigger, publishing his last book *Trigger in Europe* in 1966. Weaver, author, broadcaster, traveller, teacher and artist, his varied life was captured by Yorkshire Television in *The All or Nothing Man* in 1969. His home for thirty years was at Kilnhurst.[33]

In July 1929 the cotton employers decided to reduce earnings by nearly thirteen per cent, but ninety-two per cent of the members of the Todmorden unions voted for strike action in defence. After a stoppage of two weeks, the dispute was referred to arbitration, the outcome of which was a wage cut of six and a half per cent.[34]

Soon afterwards came the first of three severe blows inflicted on the local economy. The largest spinning concern, Mons Mill, failed and its assets were sold for knockdown prices. The doubling mill went for £1,400; its frames were soon removed, possibly for use elsewhere. The main mill and machinery were bought for £27,000, to be sold on quickly to the Lancashire Cotton Corporation in 1930.[35] (This was a conglomerate set up under pressure from the banks in an attempt to rationalise a highly-fragmented industry.)[36]

Since 1920 the leading textile machine makers in Todmorden, Lord Brothers, had been owned by the Manchester firm of Brooks and Doxey. In September 1929 the Canal Street works in Todmorden, employing 250 men, were closed, and the business transferred to Manchester.[37]

Wilson Brothers, the bobbin manufacturers who had been the main progenitors of the industrial village of Cornholme, had for many years concentrated most of their production at Garston, Liverpool, convenient for the importation of timber. In 1925 there were 1,400 workers at Garston and upwards of 300 at Cornholme. In September 1930 it was decided to close the Cornholme works and move the equipment, and a few of the workers, to Garston. It was, according to the *Todmorden Advertiser*, 'the biggest industrial blow ever experienced in Todmorden and in Cornholme in particular'. One side effect was the disbanding in mid-season of the Wilson Brothers' football team.[38]

The worrying feature of the Lords/Wilsons experience was that Todmorden enterprises, owned by companies which had their principal centre of interest elsewhere, were particularly vulnerable during periods of contraction. Todmorden's geographical location was emerging as a serious liability for the first time since the sixteenth century. Whether the same factor was partly responsible for the decline of the Todmorden cotton industry in the early 1920s is uncertain.

At the time of the 1931 census: 1,561 people, 12% of the workforce, were completely unemployed; 6,000 people (60% female) were employed, in fact, often under-employed, in the cotton industry; about 600 (75% female) in clothing; 900 men in the engineering and metal trades; and about 600 men in various kinds of wood working and manufacture.[39] The last two figures would have been higher before the closure of Lords and the bobbin works.

Cotton export markets were shrinking, partly as a result of the growth of local industries, and protectionist policies. Between 1929 and 1937, British exports of cotton cloth to India fell by three-quarters. By 1936-38, Japan was exporting fifty per cent more cloth than Britain. Most of the Japanese cotton industry was owned by a few large firms which had invested heavily in the latest technology. The threat to Todmorden and the Lancashire industry in general no longer arose simply from low-wage competition.[40]

Trade picked up late in 1931, and by the following spring most of the larger firms in Todmorden were working full-time, except for extended holidays. 1933 was a little better, 1934 a little worse, and so the fluctuations continued. The Hoyle family went out of business. In 1929 Joshua Hoyle died suddenly, and his brother-in-law, William Albion Barker, whose family ran mills in Todmorden and Littleborough, took over the running of Hollins Mill; but by 1936, when it was taken over by Neuss Hesslein Kempton Ltd (NEHESCO), cotton spinners and manufacturers, it had been closed for a period. Meanwhile, Philip Hoyle at Derdale had taken the decision to close by 1935, prompted by a dwindling market for their plain calico and a lack of support for double-shift working, the necessary price for re-equipping with modern machinery. Consequently in 1936 he sold the firm for a nominal £5 to Cockcroft Brothers, Leo (his son-in-law), Eric and Keith, who were in business at Birks Mill, Walsden, as John Cockcroft and Sons. The Derdale spinning section was sub-let to T Hill and Co, bedspread printers.[41]

In 1934 Luke Barker and Sons went out of business, leaving Friths Mill idle for a year, until it was purchased by Temperleys Ltd, sanitary pipe makers.[42] In the same year, Alma and Jubilee mills, Walsden, both owned by Lancashire Cotton Corporation, closed, leaving 185 unemployed. Unemployment amongst the insured population in June 1934 was twenty-two per cent.[43] By 1935 the town had 23 textile firms, 216,690 spindles and 11,169 looms, which represented decreases of 4 firms, 40,788 spindles and 915 looms since 1934.[44] There was a mini-boom in 1936-37, and the cotton wages in the town rose for the first time since 1920, by about 6-7%. 'At long last we have turned the corner', commented the report of the Todmorden Weavers Association in April 1937.[45]

In 1936-37 Fieldens installed 240 Northrop automatic looms, which fed the weft cops automatically to the shuttle. The improvement in trade, however, did not last. 1938 was generally a bad year, with extensive under-employment. The numbers of spindles and looms in the town were now little more than half of the 1916 figures.[46]

Within these general ups and downs, the fortunes of different weaving firms could vary a great deal, as this side of the industry was highly differentiated and specialised.

In 1938, for example, Joshua Smith (1,450 looms) produced, in widths between 27 and 66 inches, umbrella cloths, gaberdines, satteens, venetians, poplins and cambrics, and also wove rayon cloth. W L Sandbach of Hope Street Mill (800 looms) made 'bedspreads, all classes of cotton and waste sheetings, sized and pure ducks, stripes, dobbies, etc, from single and double yarns, 36-112 in'. With so many different potential outlets, one weaving shed could be working full-time while another was on short time or stopped.[47]

There were so many involuntary holidays in the interwar period that cotton workers often had mixed feelings about the annual 'wakes week' in early July. A family with more than one earner which had had a reasonably good year could have a tidy sum to spend, often accumulated through a savings club. To the less fortunate, the wakes week was simply another spell of unemployment. William Tout, secretary of the Todmorden Weavers Association, told the Trades Union Congress in 1937: 'There must be hundreds and thousands of workers to whom the prospect of a holiday is one that fills them with feelings almost of horror.' The textile unions had been campaigning intermittently for holidays with pay since 1920. They were finally successful in 1939 when agreement was reached on one week's paid holiday.[48]

In the autumn of 1939 Jubilee Mill, Walsden, was re-opened by Messrs J W Greaves, cotton wadding manufacturers of Rochdale, after being closed for four years. The other mills were busy and, by November, shortages of skilled weavers and juveniles for the spinning firms were reported. The explanation was simple. Another war had broken out.[49] By 1941 Jubilee Mill was producing cocoa for the troops. Rowntrees took it over to fulfil their government contract, as it was in a less vulnerable area than York. They also used Bottoms and Lumbutts mills for storage throughout the war years.[50]

13

Postwar Todmorden:
The End of the Culture of 'Cotton, Co-op and Chapel'

The *Todmorden Advertiser* reported on the 30th September 1938 that 30,000 gas masks were expected to arrive shortly in the town. During the following summer air-raid precautions were rehearsed, although Todmorden was expected to be in less danger than the large industrial towns and was designated as a reception area for refugees. The outbreak of war on the 3rd September 1939 came as no surprise. The Todmorden Food Control Committee was appointed within a few days, to manage the rationing system locally, and by November a 'Cotton Control' system was in operation.[1]

The word 'cotton' was normally associated with the 'gaberdines, satteens, cambrics, sheetings, bedspreads', mentioned at the end of the previous chapter. In wartime it meant canvas, parachutes, hosepipes, tyres, insulation fabrics and many other require-ments of the armed forces. The Todmorden spinners, dealing mainly with the heavier yarns, found themselves economically in the front line. Four concerns were identified as important to the war effort: Fieldens; Mons; S & A Barker at Adamroyd Mill; and Nehesco.

By the end of 1941 the shortage of both labour and raw cotton led the government to close nearly forty per cent of the mills and weaving sheds in Lancashire as a whole (a geographical designation which, for the cotton industry, included Todmorden). Most of the Todmorden producers, however, were kept busy with government orders. Prices were controlled and profits virtually guaranteed. Cotton workers were subject to 'essential work orders', preventing their moving without permission to other employment.[2]

Like other, towns Todmorden became involved in special money-raising schemes: War Weapons, Warships, Wings for Victory weeks, and National Savings targets. Regarded as a safe haven, Todmorden became a refuge for evacuees from Bradford, Manchester, Liverpool, London and Brighton; mothers with small children, and older children alone, were billeted with families in the district. Anyone with a spare bed/room was expected to take someone and received a weekly allowance from 10s 6d for a ten year old to 15s for those over sixteen.

School dinners at 5d were introduced, and 'British Restaurants' opened for adults at Cornholme, Walsden, Castle Street, Roomfield and the Weavers' Institute. This ensured a balanced midday meal for 10d (soup and bread 1d; main course 6d; sweet 2d; tea 1d;) and released women to fill the jobs vacated by the serving men or created by the demands of war.[3]

At the end of the war, the cotton industry faced an unusual situation, called upon to make a major contribution to the export drive — 'Britain's bread hangs by Lancashire's thread' — and respond to what Worrall's *Directory* for 1946 called 'an instant and insatiable demand from the home market'. At this time the Todmorden industry was about half the size it had been at the end of the First World War. The weaving-only firms were fewer but larger: fifteen companies with an average of 527 looms, only two having fewer than 300 looms. There were three integrated spinning/ weaving firms: Fieldens, Nehesco and Bottoms Mill, Walsden; and the same number of spinning mills: Mons, Barkers at Adamroyd, and Cinderhill in Castle Street. Altogether, Todmorden had nearly 10,000 looms and 210,000 spindles, just over half of them on mules.[4]

It is not clear how fully this capacity was used. In Lancashire as a whole, thirty per cent of the spindles were idle in 1950, mainly through a shortage of labour. For the latter reason the Cinderhills Mill began an evening shift in November 1946. Memories of the interwar years made people reluctant to work in cotton mills if alternative employment was available. In Todmorden there was not much alternative manual employment available outside textiles and the ancillary industries, other than in service trades such as transport and shops. However, some of the 1,600 looms which had been scrapped by 1950 (700 out of 1,450 went at Joshua Smiths) may have gone because they could not be regularly used.[5]

As part of its consideration of postwar needs, the Todmorden Borough Council commissioned a report by the distinguished town planner Thomas Sharp, which was published as *A Plan for Todmorden* in 1946. He made the obvious point that for the town to continue to be overwhelmingly dependent upon cotton was to court disaster. New industries, especially medium and heavy industry which provided work for men, should be encouraged.

Turning to housing, Sharp noted that 2,335 houses, a third of the total, were back-to-back, with only twenty to thirty feet between blocks. 'The extreme cleanliness and neatness of the majority of these houses is astonishing, when the congested and unsatisfactory conditions under which people live in them is taken into account.' He recommended selective conversion to through houses, and the demolition of the rest. Some areas should be deliberately run down: Portsmouth, Cornholme, Lydgate and Eastwood because they were too far out to be effectively part of the town as a social unit; and Shade because the land was more suited to industrial use.[6]

There was a good deal of industrial dereliction on the outskirts of the town, especially in the Cornholme area. The men's discussion group of the Todmorden Co-op was reported in the local newspaper in January 1946 as saying: 'Every approach to the town reveals derelict mills and disused shops. The chief eyesores are the corn mill, the bobbin works and the semi-demolished mill at Copperas-house' (near Shade).[7]

Where to locate new houses was a problem, as Todmorden had grown up as a kind of ribbon development along the bottom of the three valleys. Sharpe's main solution was a 'neighbourhood unit' of 5,670 people at Dobroyd, in a bowl-shaped depression, 'the only suitable site above the valley bottom'. A new road would be needed, with a 1 in 8 gradient, but the slope would not worry Todmorden people.

While the council and interested citizens were debating the Sharp plan, urgent housing needs had to be met. In May 1946 the first prefabricated houses were placed on the Ferney Lee recreation ground. More followed on five other sites, at Portsmouth, Lineholme, Dineley Avenue (Ashenhurst) where they were 'double deckers', Wadsworth Avenue (Shade), and Lacy Avenue (Walsden). The last two are still in use. The council completed the Carr House estate, begun before the war, but when a more ambitious housing programme became possible they preferred relatively small-scale developments to the Dobroyd scheme. These included flats and houses at Hallroyd (on the site of Stansfield corn mill), flats on the site of Shade Mill, flats and houses on the Cornholme bobbin works site, and a relatively large estate at Harley Wood, where

Working at Mons Mill in 1949.
Above: beaming — from the
bobbins, parallel threads are
wound onto the large beam and
will form the warp threads in the
loom. *Below:* ring-spinning
frames producing thread for use
as warp or weft in the loom.

Looking towards Todmorden along the Walsden Valley from the Warland hillside, showing the main road and Rochdale Canal, which when fully restored will aid regeneration.

two blocks of flats are named Cockcroft House and Wilkinson House after local Nobel Prize winners.[8]

In 1946 the freedom of the borough was conferred on the Todmorden man best known in the outside world, Dr J D Cockcroft. He worked with Lord Rutherford at Cambridge, where they first 'split the atom' and was the first head of Harwell atomic research establishment. He was awarded the Nobel prize for physics in 1951, the KCB in 1953, OM in 1957, and was the first Master of Churchill College, Cambridge, from 1959-67, when he died. In the 1950s he was a director of the family textile firm which ran Birks and Derdale mills. The other Nobel Prize, for chemistry, was awarded to Sir Geoffrey Wilkinson in 1973.[9]

From about 1950 the local cotton industry began to contract again. The main cause at first was declining exports, in the face of competition not only from the restored Japanese industry, but also from high wage/high technology producers in Western Europe. By 1960 Belgium and the Netherlands together were exporting fifty per cent more cloth than Britain. In the late 1950s, much to the chagrin of the Lancashire cotton manufacturers, the home market was flooded with imports from India, Pakistan and Hong Kong, which under Commonwealth trading arrangements had free access to the British, as well as colonial, markets. A quota system was negotiated, but it had little effect.[10]

In 1959, for the first time, cotton cloth imports exceeded exports. In that year the Cotton Industry Act offered a package for contraction and re-equipping. Firms scrapping spindles and looms could claim compensation, two-thirds of which was paid by government, one third by a levy on the continuing operations of the industry. For the purchase of new equipment, a 25% grant was offered. A redundancy agreement was reached between employers and unions which compensated displaced workers according to length of service, up to a maximum of thirty weeks' pay.[11]

Many cotton firms had been staying in business only because they had long since written off the cost of their pre-1914 looms or mules. Some of the plant was already standing idle. The Act offered a way out. Todmorden was hit by a wave of closures, including Crow Carr Ings Mill (which had been recently re-equipped), Crescent and Nanholme mills. In the weaving section, ten firms were left, with fewer than thirty per cent of the looms which the town had had in 1946. The 'end of an era' feeling was emphasised by the closure of Fieldens under the above Act, although the company continued in a much-reduced manner as Waterside Plastics, until bought out by its management in 1972 — and finally closed in 1990.[12]

A few local firms took advantage of the re-equipment grant. Charles Crabtree Ltd of Ferney Mill, which had also taken over Adamroyd spinning mill, bought 180 automatic looms to replace 584 'Lancashire looms' (the name used to describe the older power looms) and ran them in conjunction with 14,400 ring spindles. They bought Crow Carr Ings Mill to house the looms, ceasing production at Ferney Mill. This was the last firm in Todmorden to process cotton from its raw state to finished cloth. Crabtrees finally sold out to Kagan Textiles in 1971-2. Northfield Mills in Der Street scrapped 180 Lancashire looms and installed 112 automatics. John Dawson of Albion Mill put in 72 automatics in place of 588 old looms, but did not stay long in business. An automatic loom cost three times as much as a Lancashire loom, but one weaver could tend a large number (20 to 30) of them.[13]

The 'merger mania' of 1963-64 brought the Carrington Viyella Group into the town as owners of W L Sandbach Ltd, Hope Street Mill. This mill was purchased in 1993 by P J Flowers & Co Ltd, Berkhamstead, who have invested £1,000,000 in it. They employ over 100 machinists in making up home textiles (bedding etc), mostly for department stores. Courtaulds swallowed up the Lancashire Cotton Corporation and thereby acquired Mons Mill, which they closed in 1968. Plans to demolish it were averted when two prominent councillors, Leo Cockcroft and Alfred King, held it overnight until the council met and agreed to purchase it. In 1971 it was bought by Ward and Goldstone Ltd, currently trading as part of the Volex group.[14]

Councillor K Cockcroft summed up the developments of the 1960s in an account written for the borough's seventy-fifth anniversary:

> By 1962 there were eleven firms, in 1964 there were ten, then in 1969 there were seven. Modern machinery installed by some of the remaining mills has made highly efficient production possible with a high level of wages, multi-shift working being involved. The industry is no longer a cotton industry; man-made fibres and blends of these fibres with cotton and wool have opened up new horizons.[15]

In 1968, 2,570 people (almost equal numbers of men and women) still worked in textiles in Todmorden, out of a total industrial workforce of 4,569. Engineering and electrical workers numbered 540, and the clothing trade employed about 350. Services (transport, shops, administration etc) employed 6,663 people. There was a similar ratio between industry and services in Halifax and other local towns.[16]

Todmorden had lost 20% of its jobs between 1953 and 1966, Hebden Bridge only 9% in the same period. In the spring of 1959, unemployment in Todmorden was 8.6%, three times the national average. Increasing numbers worked outside the town. In 1966 the annual average number of train journeys per hundred of the population

The interior of the Unitarian Church, built by the three sons of John Fielden MP, and opened in 1869 at a cost of over £35,000.

was 453, compared with 277 for Hebden Bridge and 87 for Halifax. The main movement was towards Manchester; the fastest train took only twenty-five minutes.[17]

In 1968 the Yorkshire and Humberside Economic Planning Council published a report on the Halifax-Calder Valley area, in which it took a gloomy view of Todmorden's economic prospects. The members admired 'the efforts which have been made to foster industry, but are not able to envisage any major new development'.[18]

The planning council noted that Todmorden still had a large number of sub-standard houses. Only 3.6% of the dwellings still lacked a water closet, but over 20% had no hot water on tap, and nearly 40% no fixed bath. Between 1961 and 1966, 366 houses had been demolished, mainly through the borough council's clearance programme, but about 1,900 back-to-back houses, over a quarter of the total stock, remained. The borough council pressed on with its programme of clearance and improvement, and by 1971 had made over 1,000 improvement grants. Between 1961 and 1971, the population had fallen from 17,428 to 15,140.[19]

If the people of the town wanted spiritual consolation for the decline of industry and population, they did not seek it in the churches and chapels. A dwindling minority was committed to regular attendance, and chapels built for several hundreds had to be maintained by a handful of supporters. Of the six Baptist chapels in Todmorden, Vale, Lydgate, Lineholme and Wellington Road were demolished between 1953 and 1967. Roomfield Chapel, pulled down in 1959 because of dry rot which plagued several chapels, was replaced in 1962 by a small prefabricated building, which became

Lumbutts Chapel (Wesleyan Methodist Association), built single-storey in 1837,
and rebuilt in 1877.

the schoolroom when a permanent chapel was added. Shore has closed, but the shell of the building, with its once-thriving Sunday school, still stands. At Vale, services are held in the schoolroom, the only surviving place of nonconformist worship in the Burnley Valley.[20] The once numerous Methodist chapels are reduced to three: Central Methodist (now using the former York Street Sunday School); Trinity Methodist at Walsden; and Lumbutts. The two Congregational chapels at Eastwood and Patmos were demolished, and Cloughfoot is a private dwelling. The last to retreat was the Church of England: All Saints, Harleywood, was demolished and private houses built on the site; St Aidan's mission (on Bacup Road) is now 'Aidan's Arts', an artists' co-operative workshop; and Christ Church closed following the re-ordering of St Mary's which became the parish church for the first time in its 500 year existence in 1992. Cross Stone retracted to Priestwell, which became a chapel of rest when Cross Stone and Todmorden parishes merged in 1994.

In 1969 the Todmorden Unitarians celebrated the centenary of their splendid Gothic church. However, they could no longer afford a minister of their own, and launched an appeal for £5,000 to pay for essential repairs. Later the small congregation retreated to the church lodge, but in April 1992 they disbanded.[21]

Cotton, chapel ... the third great 'C' of local economic and social life was Co-operation. As the cotton mills closed around them, the Todmorden and Bridge End Co-ops began to feel the chill winds of competition from multiple stores and discount supermarkets. Dividends of 2s 6d or 3s, which had made so much difference to working-class living standards, had been created out of the large profit margins of retailing. As these contracted, dividends dwindled, were temporarily replaced by

The interior of St Mary's Church was re-ordered prior to its reopening as Todmorden's parish church in 1992, following the closure of Christ Church. It retains features from various periods of its history, including the Georgian staircase and gallery.

Walsden Cricket Club, winners of the Central Lancashire League's Wood Cup in 1954.

stamps, and then vanished. Although, to a minority of activists, Co-operation was a movement for moral regeneration, a key element in the process of building a better society from the bottom upwards, to the majority of members it meant the 'divi' and the annual children's treat.

Between 1958 and 1994 the Co-operative share of the retail market nationally fell from 11% to 4%, and the number of stores from 30,000 to 4,500 (although, on average, the remaining stores are much larger in size). The Todmorden Co-op, now part of Norwest Co-operative Ltd, abandoned its Dale Street premises (except the electrical department) in November 1995 and opened a new 'Food Market' (employing eighty-five people) on the site of the former Albion Mill, Halifax Road. Bridge End Co-op closed in the mid-1960s. The Co-op has survived as a trading organisation, but the days are gone when, as part of its centenary celebrations in 1946, it served mountains of buns to 3,000 children. It is no longer an active social movement.[22]

The two leading cricket clubs had an *annus mirabilis* in 1954, when Todmorden won the Lancashire League championship and the Worsley Cup, and Walsden won the Wood Cup. However, by 1959 the Lancashire League was talking in terms of a crisis, with membership of its clubs declining — affected, of course, by the contraction of the cotton industry.

A decade later, it was clear that the days when the Lancashire League grounds were bustling before the start of the season, the boys eager for a practice game in the outfield, the young men in keen competition for team places working hard in the nets, and the older members strolling around comparing the present first team unfavourably with the giants of their youth, had gone for ever. A decline in playing standards was more than matched by a fall in attendances, crowds even on the best days being measured in hundreds not thousands. Todmorden and Walsden had memberships of around 1,000 and 750 respectively in the 1950s; now numbers have dropped to about 500 at each club. Since the war, six of the town's cricketers have played at county level — Richard Horsfall (Essex), Harold Dawson and Derek Shackleton (Hampshire), Kenneth Fiddling (Northants), Peter Greenwood and Peter Lever (Lancashire) — whilst both Shackleton and Lever have played for England.

Although the local cricket league functioned with postwar enthusiasm through the late 1940s and 1950s, few if any of the teams had chapel connections. In his account of local sport written in 1971, R Wild noted that the local cricket league had gone the same way as its football counterpart. They 'faded through diminishing facilities but mainly through lack of interest'.[24] Apart from the competition of other leisure pursuits, the cricket league could not have survived the closure of the chapels.

Sport on the uplands was left to the golf club, which formed at Todmorden Edge in 1894 with 66 men and 38 lady playing members. E B Fielden, Dobroyd, was president until 1942. In 1907, after a new farmer put the rent up and 'would not allow us to cut, and himself kept the field insufficiently stocked, so there were loud complaints about bad lies', the club moved to its present home at Rive Rocks, above Cross Stone, where it now has about 200 playing members.[25]

Amateur dramatic societies picked up the threads again. Todmorden Players grew out of the Regnal Circle and, from 1951, have presented plays at the Hippodrome, which initially suspended films for productions. The first season of four plays attracted a total audience of 9,000. In 1954 the Operatic Society reformed, leasing the Hippodrome when it closed as a cinema in 1956. The Gem closed in 1957 and the Olympia in the early 1960s, leaving the town without a cinema. In 1986 the operatic and dramatic societies merged and in 1990 purchased the Hippodrome, ensuring that Todmorden has its own permanent theatre. With the Todmorden Brass Band having competitive success at the Royal Albert Hall in 1995, and the Choral Society and orchestra going strongly, the town's cultural life is in good hands.

Following the 1944 Education Act, the secondary school at Ferney Lee became a secondary grammar school, and a secondary modern school was created using the first floor at Roomfield, with annexes at Castle Hill, Cornholme, Lumbutts, Fielden School of Art and in the 1950s Calder College. The other schools in the town became primary schools, teaching children up to the age of eleven. In 1957 a new secondary modern school was built at Scaitcliffe which, with the grammar school, served the town until 1978, when they combined to form Todmorden High School, initially on two sites until Scaitcliffe was extended. Ferney Lee became a primary school — replacing Roomfield which was demolished. Mirroring the town's contraction, the schools at Vale and Robinwood were closed, later becoming a community centre and an activity centre respectively. A further education centre opened in 1955 at Cobden. Originally known as Calder College, it was renamed Todmorden Community College in 1994.

Sheltered housing has replaced Roomfield School, and nearby a new medical centre opened at Rose Street. Further developments of sheltered housing are at Stanley Cryer Court (British Legion) off Halifax Road, and Ridgefoot (local authority). A residential home stands on the site of the former prefabs/open-air school at Ferney Lee.

In 1974, as part of local government reorganisation, the borough of Todmorden was merged with eight other authorities to form the borough of Calderdale, technically a metropolitan district. Under the same legislation, localities were given the opportunity to form new-style parish councils, known in urban areas as town councils. One was established in Todmorden, but has limited powers apart from acting as the voice of the town in civic affairs. It does, however, make recommendations to the Calderdale Planning Authority, was instrumental in starting the Tourist Information Centre, and was involved in the early stages of the Regeneration Initiative.

Despite the negative comments of the regional planning council in 1966, the strategy of attracting new industries to the town, pursued first by Todmorden Borough Council and then by Calderdale, has had some success. In 1996 the Volex Group employ 450 people in Mons Mill, making wiring harnesses for the motor industry. Warman International produce heavy-duty pumps in the premises of the former Sandholme Iron Company, with a workforce of 267. Charles Openshaw and Sons (supplying the printing trade here and exporting to over 100 countries) have 219 workers at Todmorden, and recently acquired two more companies. There are few firms employing 50 to 100, people but a lot of companies in various manufacturing industries, eg plastics, electrical and stainless steel, with between 20 and 50 (inclusive) employees. There is also a larger number of small firms with fewer than 20 employees making a variety of goods, from a moulded fibre-glass church spire to shuttles (60% for export worldwide). In November 1995, forty-six firms were asked whether their trading trends over the last five years were up, static or down:

No of workers	Up		Static		Down		Total		
	firms	wkrs	firms	wkrs	firms	wkrs	firms	wkrs	
100 or more	6	1,284	0	0	1	200	7	1,484	(69%)
20-50 incl	5	133	9	322	1	21	15	476	(22%)
fewer than 20	11	92	4	26	9	78	24	196	(9%)
TOTAL	22	1509	13	348	11	299	46	2,156	
	48%	70%	28%	16%	24%	14%			

Note: some of these would be part-time.

Only one textile firm reported an upward trend (1 up, 5 static, 6 down) and 6 of the 7 firms with 100 or more workers were 'up' (some only recently — in the last one or two years), the only down (slightly) being in textiles. The textile printing firm, Walsden Printing Company of Ramsden Wood, is one of the largest survivors of the once-dominant textile industry, employing about 200 people. Bottoms Mill, Walsden, is still weaving sheetings, but with only about twenty-six workers. Cinderhill (still a family firm) is scutching, carding and spinning, employing thirty. Brisbane Moss, Bridgeroyd Works, has thirty employees and is the sole remaining corduroy manufacturer in the United Kingdom. Derdale Mill, once part of John Cockcroft and Sons Ltd (of Birks Mill), is now JCS Textiles, with twelve employees warping and weaving on dornier (shuttleless) looms, producing blazer, duffle, uniform and equine cloths. The last new textile factory, Heatherdale, opened in 1975 at Woodhouse with new dornier looms producing furnishing fabrics. Unfortunately an unfavourable combination of recession, adverse exchange rates and high interest resulted in closure in 1980. Machine manufacturers are all 'up', except one making agricultural equipment. There are many small firms in engineering, clothing, plastics, etc, some in industrial units developed on the sites of former cotton mills. It is encouraging that 70% of the workforce is with manufacturing firms where the trend is 'up'.

Following the war, Todmorden became home to a number of 'displaced persons' from Eastern Europe who, whilst having their own Ukrainian Club in the Mons Mill office building, integrated fully with the community, which is enriched by their cultural

The sign above the present Bear Wholefoods on the Strand is a reminder of the days when the Co-op had a substantial influence: this was its drapery store.

The interior of the Hippodrome Theatre, 1996. The theatre opened in 1908, but was a cinema from 1917 to 1956. The Todmorden Operatic and Dramatic Society bought the theatre in 1990. It is one of only a few surviving theatres of its kind in the country.

contribution. From the late 1960s and the 1970s an increasing number of Pakistani families have settled in the town, establishing themselves as traders with shops in the town centre, Cornholme and Walsden. Talented in sports, the cricket ground is one place where they join in the town's activities. They meet at the former Spiritualist Church at Eagle Street. Dobroyd Castle, former home of the Fieldens, is now a Buddhist retreat. The Jehovah's Witnesses gather at Kingdom Hall on Stansfield Road.

In 1989 a tourist information bureau was opened in Todmorden, to cater for an increasing number of visitors. The full development of the town's tourist potential is quite a challenge. Four miles away, people can potter about the compact town of Hebden Bridge, then drive up to Heptonstall on the hill above, scramble down to Hardcastle Crags, and see a great deal in a day. Todmorden's urban development has been linear, and its outlying attractions are widely dispersed. It would be a very energetic daytripper who would visit Centre Vale Park with its swimming pool; take the picturesque town-centre walk from the Golden Lion to the White Hart, passing on the way a canal lock, Todmorden Hall (now a restaurant) and St Mary's Church; have a look at Gauxholme Locks; and then explore Lumbutts, Mankinholes, Stoodley Glen and Pike, and the Stansfield hillside with its yeomen-clothiers' houses.

It is, however, on the uplands that regeneration is taking place. Houses which had become derelict or neglected have been restored and outbuildings converted into dwellings. Rodwell End, whose fifty or more inhabitants in 1851 had reduced to fifteen by 1891, became totally derelict but is now being restored. On the Stoodley hillside is the modern estate of Harvelin Park; the nearby Fielden Hospital is converted into houses and the former workhouse at Stansfield View is due to follow suit. Many attractive 'up-market' residences nestle in the folds of the lower slopes below the golf course, and a costly 'repair' development has transformed the council's Dineley estate from prefabricated to brick houses.

The Todmorden Boundary Walk attracts many visitors to the district, as do the Agricultural Show and Carnival. Paths have been cleared and stiles repaired, and walking and horse riding are becoming increasingly popular. A further attraction is the market, which is active on five days a week.

The culture of 'cotton, chapel and Co-op', which once defined the economic and social character of Todmorden, is dead. The question of what survives of its traditional combination of solidarity and independence — or comradeship and cussedness — is one for sociologists rather than historians. Thomas Sharp, writing in 1946, described Todmorden as 'a well-settled community. They and their fathers for some generations have made this town. ... Their lives... their spiritual and emotional attachments ... are centred in it.' But Sharp was talking about a town of 20,000 people; the population had dropped to around 14,000 by 1995. He anticipated the decline of the cotton industry, but not the decay of other parts of Todmorden's cultural inheritance.[26]

A suitable theme for a concluding reflection is provided by the canal. It was the canal, bringing cheap coal to feed the steam engines, which drew industry and housing into the valley bottom. After long being derelict, most of the Rochdale Canal, including all of the Yorkshire section, has been restored by the Rochdale Canal Trust, using voluntary labour and with financial support from local councils and central government. In October 1995 the Millenium Commission allocated almost £12 million from the National Lottery to complete the remaining work. The fully-restored canal may have some potential for carrying goods, but it is — and will be — primarily recreational, for pleasure boats and for fishermen, with the towpath providing a long-distance walk.

Commenting on the Millenium Commission's award, the northern editor of the *Guardian* wrote that it 'also invokes the New North of spruced-up Victorian warehouses, hi-tech industry and tourist attractions'.[27] If people and organisations dealing with either information technology or high-value products choose to locate themselves amongst the rugged scenery in the heart of the Pennines, the hills surrounding Todmorden, so long seen as presenting obstacles to be overcome, may prove to be the town's greatest asset.

Glossary of Medieval Terms

Assart	Virgin land cleared for cultivation.
Berewick	Outlying part of a manor.
Bondage	Restrictions on personal freedom, the nature of which varied from manor to manor, exceptionally within the same manor. A bondman could not take legal action against his lord over matters relating to rents, tenure and services. In the manor of Wakefield he could not hold freehold land.
Bondhold land	Land held by the rules, relating to rents, tenure and obligations which applied to tenants in bondage, but which could be held by freemen.
Bovate	see oxgang.
Carucate	Eight bovates.
Customary tenure	A system of landholding, which in many places evolved from bondhold, whereby the rents, inheritance arrangements and entry fines were governed by the custom of the manor. As the title deeds consisted of copies of entries in the manor court roll, this tenure became known as copyhold. In Todmorden and Walsden, by the seventeenth century, rents and fines were regarded as fixed, and the rights of inheritance as secure.
Demesne	Land used directly by the lord, and not occupied permanently by tenants.
Entry fines	Payments for entry to land on clearance, purchase, leasing or inheritance.
Heriot	A death duty/inheritance payment in respect of bondhold land.
Oxgang	The basic peasant holding, ranging locally between 10 and 18 acres in size. Bovate is the equivalent term of Latin origin which appears in written records; *bos*, genitive *bovis* = ox.
Ploughland	Eight oxgangs.
Relief	A death duty/inheritance payment in respect of freehold land.
Royd land	The vernacular term for assart, ie virgin land cleared for cultivation, in active use until about 1400.
Tourn	Major meeting of the court of the manor of Wakefield, held twice yearly.

Bibliography and References

Sources and Abbreviations

Newspapers and Periodicals

CN	*Co-operative News*
CS	*Chetham Society*
EcHR	*Economic History Review*
HAS	*Transactions of the Halifax Antiquarian Society*
HC	*Halifax Courier*
HG	*Halifax Guardian*
HBT	*Hebden Bridge Times*
NS	*New Series*
TA	*Todmorden Advertiser, otherwise Todmorden News and Advertiser, Todmorden and Hebden Bridge Advertiser, Todmorden and District News*
THBHA	*Todmorden and Hebden Bridge Historical Almanac*
YAJ	*Yorkshire Archaeological Journal*

Other Publications

Cal PR	*Calendar of Patent Rolls*
EYC	*Early Yorkshire Charters (YASRS)*
FIC	*Factories Inquiry Commission, 1833, PP* 1834, Vol XX, pp 26-75
PP	*Parliamentary Papers*
Pennine Valley	B Jennings (ed), *Pennine Valley: A History of Upper Calderdale*, by the Hebden Bridge WEA Local History Group, Smith Settle, Otley, 1992; reprinted with corrections, 1994
PLC	*Report of the Poor Law Commission, 1832-34*
VCH	*Victoria County History*
WCR	The first five volumes of *Wakefield Court Rolls, 1274-1331*, in *YASRS*, cited as *WCR I-V*
WCR(NS)	*New Series of Wakefield Court Rolls, Yorkshire Archaeological Society*
YASRS	Yorkshire Archaeological Society Record Series

Manuscript Sources

BIHR	— Borthwick Institute of Historical Research, University of York Wills and inventories, Langfield and Stansfield

Archbishop Drummond's Visitation Returns
Dissenting certificates, Yorkshire

CDA — Calderdale District Archives, Halifax
Township records, Langfield and Stansfield
School board records
Rochdale-Halifax Turnpike Trust minutes 1827-48

LCRO — Lancashire County Record Office, Preston
The following relating to Todmorden and Walsden:
Wills and inventories; township records; Land Tax assessments
(LTA); church terriers

London Guildhall
RE — Royal Exchange Insurance Policy Register

Nottinghamshire County Record Office
SR — Saville/Rufford MSS, class DDSR

Public Record Office
Classes DL, E, HO, MAF, MH, PL, SC

TPL — Todmorden Public Library

WYAS — West Yorkshire Archive Service, Wakefield
West Yorkshire Quarter Sessions records
Calendars of Wakefield House of Correction
Land Tax assessments (LTA) for Langfield and Stansfield
Todmorden churchwardens' accounts
Fielden Brothers MSS

Yorkshire Archaeological Society, Leeds
WCR MS — Wakefield Court Rolls, MS 759

Other MSS locations are given in the references.

References

The place of publication is London unless otherwise stated

Chapter 1

Information for this chapter is taken from:
Joshua Holden, *A Short History of Todmorden* (Manchester, 1912), pp25-27; P F Kendall and H E Wroot, *The Geology of Yorkshire* (1924); *The Geology of the Rossendale Anticline*, Geological Survey 1927 (HMSO); Geoffrey G Watson, *Early Man in the Halifax District*, Halifax Scientific Society 1952.

To the late Mr W Cross of Todmorden for advice and help — grateful thanks.

Chapter 2

1   The Yorkshire *Domesday* material is taken from Margaret Faull and Marie Stimson (eds), *Domesday Book Yorkshire* (Chichester, 1986), no page numbers; *HAS Record Series II*, 1914, Extent of Sowerby Graveship 1309.

2   For a review of the evidence, see B Jennings, 'The Study of Local History in the Pennines: the Comparative Dimension', *HAS NS*, Vol 3, 1995, pp13-30.

3   *VCH Lancs I*, pp273, 286-7; M Faull and S A Moorhouse (eds), *West Yorkshire: An Archaeological Survey to AD 1500* (Wakefield, 1981), p542.

4   *VCH Lancs I*, pp291, 312-3; *EYC III*, pp149, 185; *Pennine Valley*, pp18-19.

5   *EYC III*, p197.

6   C T Clay, 'The Family of Thornhill', *YAJ* Vol 29, pp286-321; Richard Holmes, 'Asolf or Essolf : A Yorkshire Minor Lord of the Twelfth Century', Thoresby Society 9, *Miscellanea*, pp23-62; David Michelmore, 'Subinfeudation of Sowerbyshire', in Faull and Moorhouse, p278; YASRS 50, *Yorkshire Deeds II*, p180.

7   J Watson, *History of Halifax* (1775), p87; SR 26/25; YASRS 12, *Yorkshire Inquisitions I*, p103.

8   SR 26/31, 44, 45, 53, 55, 67, 76, 79, 30/5, 6.

9   Clay, 'Family of Thornhill', p307; Watson, p211; SR 26/108.

10 Extent of Sowerby Graveship 1309; Watson, pp144-5; *WCRV*, p163; SC 6/1145/21.

11 Record Commission, *Rotuli Hundredorum I*, p127; *EYC VIII*, pp234-6; *WCR I*, ppxi-xiv, 171; *WCRV*, p163; *Cal PR 1301-7*, p277; *Pennine Valley*, pp28-31.

12 Watson, pp106-7.

13 *VCH Lancs V*, pp187-99, 227; CS NS 71, *Survey of the Manor of Rochdale 1626*, pp138-45, 150-3.

14 Record Society of Lancashire and Cheshire, Vols *48 Lancashire Inquests 1205-1307*, p157, *51 Some Court Rolls of the Lordships of Thomas Earl of Lancaster*, pp20, 145; SR 28/1/37, 209/10.

15 *Survey of the Manor of Rochdale*; Christopher Towneley's MSS, British Library Add MS 32104.

16 *VCH Lancs VI*, pp478-82; Thoresby Society 8, *Coucher Book of Kirkstall Abbey*, pp193-9, 202; Thoresby Society *Miscellanea, Vol IV*, p196; Thoresby Society 58, G D Barnes, *Kirkstall Abbey 1147-1539* (1982), pp6, 10, 16-18, 33, 35, 44; CS 112, *Two Compoti of the Lancashire and Cheshire Manors of Henry de Lacy, Earl of Lincoln*, pp124, 181.

17 WCR MS, 28th April 1337; *WCR (NS) 1350-52*, p43.

18 WCR MS, 6th Dec 1336, 1st Oct 1337.

19 Holden, p70.

20 *WCR I*, pp136, 167, 246, *II*, pp77, 89, 186; *WCR (NS) 1331-33*, p159, *1350-52*, p71; WCR MS, 1st Oct 1337.

21 *Pennine Valley*, pp25-7.

22 Place-name references are from A H Smith, *The Place-names of the West Riding of Yorkshire* (Cambridge, 1961-62), Vols 3, 7.

23 *Bradford City Art Gallery and Museum Archaeology Group Bulletin*, Vol 12, No 2, Feb 1967.

24 *Two Compoti of … Henry de Lacy*, pp129-38, 156-65.

25 SR 26/7, 8, 66, 28/1/14.

26 *TA* 18th June 1926.

27 Smith, *Place-names*, Vol 3, p183.

28 CDA, PHM 3.

29 Towneley's MSS; *Survey of the Manor of Rochdale*.

30 *Lancashire Inquests 1205-1307*, pp38-40.

31 *Some Court Rolls of the Lordships of Thomas Earl of Lancaster*, pp16, 144.

32 SR 26/6, 44, 45.

33 CDA, PHM 3.

34 *Pennine Valley*, pp31-6.

35 Ibid, p34; SC 6/1145/21, 1148/6.

36 *Pennine Valley*, pp35-7; *VCH Lancs II*, p29.

37 *Pennine Valley*, p37; *WCR (NS) 1350-52*, pp91-2.

38 DL 29/76/1498.

39 SR 26/67; YASRS 3, *Yorkshire Fines I*; *Survey of the Manor of Rochdale*.

40 *Pennine Valley*, pp40-1.

41 SR 1/21/1; E W Crossley (ed), *Halifax Wills* (Halifax, nd), Vol II, p158; J Travis, *Chapters of Todmorden History* (Todmorden, 1901), p126; *Survey of the Manor of Rochdale*.

42 *Lancashire Inquests 1205-1307*, pp38-40; J Holden, *Short History of Todmorden*, pp10, 23; Watson, pp144-5; John Aitken, 'On the discovery of an Ancient Ironmine in Cliviger', *Trans Manchester Geographical Society 1878-80*.

43 Ibid; *Two Compoti …*, pp119, 181.

44 *Pennine Valley*, p42; *VCH Lancs V*, p193, *VI*, p442.

45 Faull and Moorhouse, pp210-2; Watson, pp334, 339, 295-6, 412.

46 G C Ramshaw, *Concerning Todmorden Parish* (Todmorden, 1911), p4; *VCH Lancs II*, p34, *VI*, pp442, 450; CS 60, *History of the Chantries, Lancashire*, Vol II, p277.

47 *Pennine Valley*, p64; *VCH Lancs II*, p14.

48 E 179/17, 30, 37.

49 *YAJ* Vol VI, p296; M W Beresford, *The Lay Subsidies, the Poll Taxes of 1377-81* (Chichester, 1963).

Chapter 3

1   SR 1/14/6; *Pennine Valley*, p52.

2   YASRS 101, *Wakefield Manor Book 1709*, pp2-3; R Somerville, *History of the Duchy of Lancaster Vol I, 1265-1603* (1953), pp302, 506, 519, 523; *VCH Lancs V*, pp190-1.

3   SR 1/15/1-26, Box 10 243-7, 250-4, 26/109.

4   CS NS 71, *Survey of the Manor of Rochdale 1626*, pp138-45, 150-3.

5   DL 4/20/42.

6   DL 4/49/53, 5/27, 44/973.

7   *Survey of the Manor of Rochdale*; DL 44/1178.

8　SR 30/48.

9　SR 26/120-1, 127-130A, 134-40, Box 10 264-9; *Survey of the Manor of Rochdale*.

10　The next three paragraphs are based upon the MSS Wakefield Court Rolls (YAS MS 759). The specific examples can be identified by the date.

11　*Pennine Valley*, pp64-7.

12　DL 4/20/42.

13　E W Crossley (ed), *Halifax Wills I* (Halifax, nd), pp60, 108-9.

14　*Pennine Valley*, pp55, 67.

15　CS 60, *History of the Chantries, Lancashire*, Vol II, p277.

16　DL 4/20/42; CS NS I, *The Vicars of Rochdale I*, p37.

17　A G Dickens, *The English Reformation* (1967), pp401-17.

18　W Aveling, 'Catholic Recusants of the West Riding of Yorkshire' (*Leeds Phil & Lit Soc Proc*, Sept 1963), Vol X, Part VI.

19　Holden, pp91-2.

20　Deed in possession of Mr J Chadwick.

21　J T Cliffe, *The Yorkshire Gentry from the Reformation to the Civil War* (1969), pp266-7.

22　Holden, p94; H Heaton, *Yorkshire Woollen and Worsted Industries*, (2nd edn, Oxford, 1965) pp183-4, 201-2.

23　Holden, pp95-6.

24　H Fishwick, *History of the Parish of Rochdale* (1889), p471.

25　Cliffe, pp291-2; T W Hanson, *The Story of Old Halifax* (Halifax, 1920), pp138-9.

26　H P Kendall, 'Local Incidents in the Civil War', *HAS 1909*, p19.

27　Kendall, 'The Civil War', *HAS 1910*, p46; Holden, p103.

28　W A Shaw (ed), *Minutes of Bury Presbyterian Classis 1645-57* (1898), CS NS Vol 36, p53.

29　Ibid, p79.

30　Ibid, pp105, 106, 107, 109, 119; Ramshaw, pp20-21.

31　Ramshaw, pp21-22.

32　A G Matthews, *Calamy Revised* (Oxford, 1934), pp70-71.

33　J H Turner (ed), *Oliver Heywood's Diaries* (Brighouse, 1881-5), Vol 4, pp89-91.

34　Ibid, Vol 3, pp340-1.

35　J H Turner (ed), *Northowram Register* (Brighouse, 1881), pp138, 141, 149, 153-4.

36　H Wood, *Congregationalism at Eastwood* (Todmorden, 1940), pp13-16.

37　N Penny (ed), *The First Publishers of Truth* (1907), pp191-2.

38　W P Thistlethwaite, *Yorkshire Quarterly Meeting 1665-1966* (Harrogate, 1979).

39　Cornholme WEA, *Shore in Stansfield, a Pennine Weaving Community, 1660-1750* (Cornholme, Todmorden, 1986), pp47-49.

40　Ibid, pp54-55.

41　*Oliver Heywood's Diaries*, Vol 2, pp260-1.

42　Holden, pp126 and passim.

43　*Northowram Register*, pp144-5, 152.

44　C E Shipley (ed), *The Baptists of Yorkshire* (Bradford, 1912), pp73-86.

45　Lambeth Palace MSS, 'Notitia Parochialis', 748, 908.

46　Rt Rev Francis Gastrell DD, *Notitia Cestriensis* CS, Vol XIX, p147.

47　Ramshaw, pp26-27.

48　Holden, pp118-120; Ramshaw, pp22-24; D Wilson (ed), *Register of the Parish Church of St Mary Todmorden 1666-1780*, Lancashire Parish Registers Society, 1978.

Chapter 4

The wills and inventories referred to in this chapter are either from the Deanery of Pontefract, BIHR or the LCRO, Preston, with the following exceptions:

John Rodes 1564　Fishwick, *Rochdale*, pp111-2
James Ffielding 1587　Ibid, pp465-6
James Gibson 1735　held privately

1　H Heaton, *Yorkshire Woollen and Worsted Industries*, pp94, 120.

2　Heaton, p118; N Lowe, *The Lancashire Textile Industry in the Sixteenth Century* (CS, Manchester, 1972), chapters 1-4.

3　B Jennings, 'The study of local history in the Pennines: the comparative dimension', *HAS NS* Vol 3, 1995, pp13-30.

4　*Pennine Valley*, p49.

5　Heaton, p201.

Chapter 5

For additional information and illustrations, see *John Fielden's Todmorden* (Todmorden, 1994), by Linda Croft, who has worked independently of the authors of *Pennine Valley* and the present book, using many of the same sources.

1　S W Waters, *History of Wakefield in the Seventeenth Century* (Wakefield, 1933), p28; Constables' Accounts, Sowerby, 1636-37, 1688-89, Todmorden and Walsden; S S Tollit, 'The First House of Correction for the County of Lancaster', *Transactions of the Lancashire and Cheshire Historical Society*, Vol 105, pp69-90.

2　Holden, p232.

3　A Newell, 'Cross Stone', *HAS 1928*.

4　Township Constables' Accounts, passim; *Leeds Mercury*, 5th December 1769; S and B Webb, *The History of English Local Government*, Vol I (1963), p583 n.

5　WCR MS, passim, in particular the paper drafts (latest 1737-78).

6　W E Tate, *The Parish Chest* (Cambridge, 1960), p241; WCR MS, 1737-38.

7　Constables' Accounts, Todmorden and Walsden.

8　Relevant Local Township Records, for the rest of this chapter, unless otherwise stated.

9　Tate, p210-11; C P Ketchley, 'Vagrancy', *Amateur Historian*, Vol II, No 10 (1956), p309-10.

10　Todmorden Terrier, 1778 (LCRO).

11 Tate, Pt 1, Ch II.
12 C G Ramshaw, *Concerning Todmorden Parish*, p31.
13 Ibid, p12.
14 Ibid, p79.
15 Todmorden Terriers, 1747, 1778, 1780.
16 E W Watson and B Gledhill, 'Wadsworth Township Accounts', *HAS 1951-55*.
17 J L Hanson, 'Transport Development in West Yorkshire from the Industrial Revolution to the Present Day', (London PhD, 1949), pp22-41.
18 Minute Books of the Turnpike Trust, for the account of the turnpike roads, unless otherwise stated.
19 Tate, pp11, 190.
20 Charity Commission *Report*, Vol 18 (1828), pp560-92.
21 Holden, pp140-1.
22 Tate, pp191-3, 197-9.
23 Holden, p151.

Chapter 6

Unless otherwise stated, the information about the Quaker influences comes from deeds in the possession of J S Chadwick, formerly of Todmorden, now of Whalley.

1 A C Underwood, *A History of the English Baptists* (1947), pp134-5.
2 YASRS 71, 72, 75, 77, *Archbishop Herring's Visitation Returns* 1743, Vol 1, pp131-2, Vol 2, pp31-9, 149-50, Vol 3, pp49-51, Vol 4, pp226-9.
3 F Baker, *William Grimshaw 1708-1763* (1963), p29.
4 W B Wilson and W S Davies, *A History of the Halifax and Calder Valley District of Baptist Churches* (Halifax, 1968), p10.
5 H Wheeler Robinson, *The Life and Faith of the Baptists* (1927), p49.
6 Baker, pp29, 35-6, 39, 49-50, 54-5, 61.
7 Jacob Stanley, 'Memoir of Mr Edward Stanley', *Methodist Magazine* (1826), pp796-7.
8 W Darney, *A Collection of Hymns* (Leeds, 1751), p270; Baker, p97.
9 W Jessop, *An Account of Methodism in Rossendale and the Neighbourhood* (London, 1880), pp40-3.
10 Baker, pp95-101.
11 N Curnock (ed), *Journal of John Wesley* (1936), Vol 3, p293.
12 J Telford (ed), *The Letters of John Wesley* (1931), Vol 4, p160; L Tyerman, *The Life and Times of John Wesley* (1875), Vol 1, p545, Vol 2, p13; W J Townsend, H B Workman and G Eayrs, *A New History of Methodism* (1909), Vol 1, pp317-8.
13 *Journal of John Wesley*, Vol 3, p372.
14 M Edwards, *John Wesley and the Eighteenth Century* (1955), p180.
15 Baker, p149; Townsend and others, Vol 1, p299.
16 Tyerman, Vol 2, pp126-9.

17 J Jackson (ed), *Lives of Early Methodist Preachers* (1866), Vol 6, pp43-6.
18 *Letters of John Wesley*, Vol 2, p171.
19 F Baker, *Charles Wesley*, (1948) pp86-7; Baker, *William Grimshaw*, p159; Tyerman, Vol 2, p128.
20 Darney, *A Collection of Hymns*, ppiii, iv, 9-16, 26, 81.
21 *Journal of John Wesley*, Vol 4, pp17, 31-2; Baker, *William Grimshaw*, pp51, 107; Archbishop Drummond's Visitation Returns 1764.
22 *Journal of John Wesley*, Vol 4, pp68, 113.
23 Townsend and others, Vol 1, pp566-7; Baker, *Charles Wesley*, pp97-103.
24 Archbishop Drummond's Visitation Returns.
25 A Taylor, *Memoirs of Rev Dan Taylor* (London, 1820), pp2-9; Tyerman, Vol 2, p199.
26 Taylor, pp10-17.
27 Underwood, pp152-4; Taylor, pp76-8.
28 *Journal of John Wesley*, Vol 5, pp179-80; Baker, *William Grimshaw*, p244.
29 *Journal of John Wesley*, Vol 4, pp212, 332; Tyerman, Vol 2, p275.
30 *Journal of John Wesley*, Vol 5, pp373-4, 475-6, Vol 6, pp16, 228, 275, 350; *Lives of Early Methodist Preachers*, Vol 3, p334.
31 A Taylor, *Dan Taylor*, pp87-100.
32 *Archbishop Herring's Visitation Returns*; Watson, *History of Halifax*, p452.
33 J H Turner, *Halifax Books and Authors* (Brighouse, 1906), pp106-8.
34 Ibid, p256.
35 Tyerman, Vol 3, pp362-3; Baker, *Charles Wesley*, pp134-7.
36 *Journal of John Wesley*, Vol 7, pp157-8.
37 Ibid, Vol 8, p61; Tyerman, Vol 3, pp655, 658.
38 Baker, *Charles Wesley*, p150.
39 Edwards, *John Wesley and the Eighteenth Century*, pp150-61, 180-2.
40 Henry Fishwick, *Family of Fielden* (1884), p8, App F, p89.
41 LCRO, Ref WCW 1602, James Fylden.
42 *VCH Lancs V*, p231; *Family of Fielden*, pp3, 4.
43 *Survey of the Manor of Rochdale 1626*.
44 Cornholme WEA, *Shore in Stansfield* (Cornholme, 1986).
45 *Family of Fielden*, p90, quoting Duchy of Lancaster Pleadings, Eliz Vol 81, F2.
46 *Family of Fielden*, p42, will proved at York, 1645.
47 Ibid, p87 (extracts from Marsden Monthly Meeting Minutes).
48 Ibid, p83 (ibid).
49 Ibid, p86, App E (extracts from Brighouse Monthly Meeting Minutes).
50 Titus Thornber, *A Pre Industrial Blast Furness*, Lancashire Industrial Histories, No 1 (Burnley, 1994).
51 Will of Nicholas Fielden of Edge End, 1714.

Chapter 7

Some of the material on the firm of Fielden Brothers, used in Chapters 7, 9, and 10, has been supplied through the generosity of Brian R Law, in the course of preparing his book *Fieldens of Todmorden, A Nineteenth Century Business Dynasty* (George Kelsall, Littleborough, 1995). As Mr Law's book was published just as the present book was going to press, it has not been possible to provide page references for the material supplied to us.

1   B R Law, 'Fielden Brothers Todmorden: The Rise to Prominence 1782-1832', *HAS NS* Vol 3, 1995, pp91-112.
2   R G Wilson, *Gentlemen Merchants* (Manchester, 1971), pp20, 245; CDA, RP932; RE 157243; Holden pp158-60.
3   Travis, *Chapters of Todmorden History*.
4   RE 7253.
5   Mrs J Cockroft, Oakhill, MSS.
6   Land tax returns 1786, 1790; 'The Arkwright Mills', Colquhoun's Census of 1788; archaeological evidence; S D Chapman, *Industrial Archaeological Review*, Vol VI, No 1, 1981-82.
7   Deeds belonging to Fern Cottage, Bacup Road, Todmorden.
8   Land tax returns, 1790-94.
9   Calderdale Archives, MIC 17.
10 Ibid.
11 B R Law, 'The Calder Millowners and the Rochdale Canal', *HAS* Jan 1954.
12 RE 7253.
13 FIC.
14 Machinery Valuation 1832, WYAS C353/132.
15 Mrs J Cockroft, MSS.
16 *HAS* Jan 1954.
17 Ibid.
18 Newspaper report quoted in James Beckett, 'A History of the Rochdale Canal' (1956), Rochdale Library.
19 Minute book of Calder millowners, Fielden MSS.
20 B R Law, Fielden MSS.

Chapter 8

1   'William Greenwood's Diary, 1825' (held privately).
2   FIC.
3   B R Law, 'Fielden Brothers Todmorden: The Rise to Prominence 1782-1832' *HAS NS* Vol 3, 1995, pp91-112.
4   HO 40/2/3 and 9.
5   A Briggs, *The Age of Improvement* (1959), pp207-10; Thompson, *The Making of the English Working Class* (1963), pp718-9; Holden, *History of Todmorden*, p184.
6   Fielden MSS, Letter, 18th Apr 1826.
7   Fielden MSS, J F to Fielden Bros, 15th Apr 1826, quoted in S A Weaver, *John Fielden and the Politics of Popular Radicalism* (Oxford, 1987), p48.
8   J Fielden, *The Curse of the Factory System* (1836, 2nd edn 1969), ppxiv-xviii; Holden, p184.
9   All references to Todmorden Political Union in this section are from their printed minutes, TPL.

10 C Seymour, *Electoral Reform in England and Wales* (1915, reprinted Newton Abbot 1970), Chapter II.
11 Briggs, pp239-53.
12 Holden, p161.
13 J T Ward, *The Factory Movement 1830-1855* (1962).
14 'Sketch of the Life of Richard Oastler' (Bradford, nd, c1861/2) in *British Labour Pamphlets*; W W Bean, *Parliamentary Representation of the Six Northern Counties of England* (Hull, 1890), pp727, 928.
15 House of Commons Committee on Factories Bill, *Report*, p455 and passim.
16 Ward.
17 FIC.
18 Fielden, *Curse of the Factory System*, pp31-35; W Dodd, *The Factory System Illustrated* (1842, reprinted 1968), p145.
19 Ward.
20 Fielden, p4; R Oastler, *A Letter to the Owners and Occupiers of Mills in the Town and Parish of Halifax* (Leeds, 1836); R H Greg, 'The Factory Question' (1837), *British Labour Pamphlets*.
21 Fielden, ppxxii-v.
22 Information about poor law administration in 1831-32 comes, unless otherwise stated, from the *PLC Report*, App A1, *PP* 1834, Vol 28/1, pp797-9; App B1, *PP* 1834, Vols 31-34, pp614-633 in each volume.
23 Langfield Overseer to the PLC, 13th Jun 1836, MH 12/6272.
24 Dodd, p144.
25 Fielden, pxxiv.
26 J and J P Sutcliffe to PLC, 28th Jan 1837; reply, 3rd Feb 1838, MH 12/6272.
27 W Ormerod to PLC, 31st Mar, 9th Apr 1838, MH 12/6272.
28 Correspondence, Apr 1838, ibid.
29 J Stansfield to PLC, 18th Apr 1838, ibid; A W Fox, *The Todmorden Unitarian Congregation* (Todmorden, 1924), p31; J T Ward, *Chartism* (1973), pp72-89.
30 Printed poster, MH 12/6272.
31 Correspondence Jun-Jul, and posters, MH 12/6272.
32 A Power to PLC, 14th and 17th Jul 1838, MH 12/6272; HO 40/38, 41/13.
33 Correspondence, Jul to Oct 1838, MH 12/6272
34 A Power to PLC, 2nd Sept, 19th Oct 1838, ibid.
35 Correspondence, Nov 1838, Ibid, HO 40/38.
36 G Pollard to A Power, 22nd Nov 1838, MH 12/6272, HO 40/38.
37 A Power to PLC, 24th Nov 1838, MH 12/6272, HO 40/37, 38, 41/13.
38 HO 40/37, 41/13.
39 Correspondence, 1840-42, MH 12/6272; 1843, MH 12/6273.
40 Correspondence, 1843-44, MH 12/6272.
41 Stansfield Township Order Book, 1842.
42 MH 12/6272.
43 *TA*, 18th July 1867.

44 *TA*, 4th Apr 1879.
45 M E Rose, 'The Allowance System under the New Poor Law', *EcHR 2nd Series*, Vol xix, pp607-20.
46 MH 12/6274; HO 41/14, 40/37.
47 HO 40/37; Ward, *Chartism*, pp105-13.
48 Ward, *Chartism*, pp87-91.
48 Fielden, *The Curse of the Factory System*, pxxxv.
49 HO 40/37.
50 Samuel Fielden, *The Autobiography of Samuel Fielden* (ed P Foner), in *The Autobiography of the Haymarket Martyrs* (New York, 1969), p132.
51 Ibid.
52 Weaver, p12.
53 HO 41/13; G R Dalby, 'The Chartist Movement in Halifax and District', *HAS 1956*, p106.
54 Ward, pp129-132; HO 40/37, 41/14.
55 HO 40/51, 53; *Northern Star*, 18th May 1839.
56 HO 41/16, 45/43.
57 CS NS 2, *The Vicars of Rochdale II*, pp184-328.
58 HO 45/249; PL 27/11, Pt.2/ERD 1418; *HG*, 13th Aug 1842; *MG*, 17th Aug 1842; Ashworth, *An Account 16*, quoted Weaver, p241; PL 27/11, Pt 2/ERD 1418; T E Ashworth, *The Plug Plot at Todmorden* (1901).
59 PL 27/11, Pt 2/ERD 1418.
60 HO 45/249; Ward, *Chartism*, pp164-9.
61 HO 45/249; *Northern Star* 1843-44, passim.
62 Briggs, *Age of Improvement*, p336; Ward, *The Factory Movement 1830-1855*, p292.
63 Fielden, *Curse of the Factory System*, ppxxxiv-vi; *HG* 14th Nov 1846.
64 Weaver, pp126-128.
65 Ward, *Factory Movement*, pp346, 389; Fielden, ppxxxvi-ix.
66 Ibid, pxxxviii.

Chapter 9

1 Hadfield and Biddle, *The Canals of North-West England* (Newton Abbot, 1970), Vol 2, p280.
2 B Gledhill, 'A Pennine Turnpike', TPL; To Mr Eric Hebdon, Burnley and District Philatelic Society, for this information, grateful thanks; *THBHA*, 1866.
3 Roger Birch, *Todmorden Album* (Todmorden, 1993), Vol 3, p14.
4 Holden, p174.
5 E M Savage, *Development of Todmorden 1700-1896* (Todmorden, 1971), pp8-9.
6 Ibid, p8.
7 *TA* Dec 1895.
8 Ibid.
9 Travis, *Notes on Todmorden and District* (Todmorden, 1896), pp228-9.
10 LTA, 1816.
11 Holden, p171.
12 B R Law, 'Fielden Brothers, Todmorden: The Rise to Prominence 1782-1832', *HAS NS 1995*, Vol 3, p100.
13 *FIC*.
14 Ibid.

15 *HAS NS 1995*, Vol 3, p101.
16 *Bradford Courier* 1825.
17 Factory Inspectorate Return of Power Looms 1835, *PP* 1836, Vol XLV, pp148-57.
18 *HAS NS 1995*, Vol 3, p106.
19 Travis, *Historical Sketches of Some People and Events* (Todmorden, 1901), p10.
20 Langfield Church Lay Assessment 1794.
21 Langfield Poor Rate Assessment 1813/14.
22 LTA, 1814.
23 LTA, 1820.
24 Ibid.
25 WYAS c353/132 Machinery Valuation.
26 *HAS NS 1995*. Vol 3, pp91-112.
27 Weaver, p24.
28 W Dodd, *The Factory System Illustrated* (1842, reprinted 1968), p 145.
29 Jeremiah Jackson, Account Books (held privately).
30 Travis, *Handbook of Cornholme 1908* (Todmorden, 1908), pp11-12.
31 Denis Griffiths, *Locomotive Engineers of the LMS* (Somerset, 1991).
32 Travis, *Memorial of the Barker Family* (Todmorden, 1901), pp10 and passim.
33 Holden, p173.
34 *TA* 19th Jun 1936.
35 J Marshall, *The Lancashire and Yorkshire Railway* (Newton Abbot, 1968), Vol I, pp24-34; E G Barnes, *The Rise of the Midland Railway 1844-1924* (1966), pp51-55.
36 Marshall, Vol I, pp38-39; *A Companion to the Manchester & Leeds Railway* (Halifax, 1841).
37 Marshall, Vol I, pp41-48.
38 Directors' Minutes, Manchester and Leeds Railway, Rochdale Reference Library.
39 F Whishaw, *Railways of Great Britain and Ireland* (1842, reprinted Newton Abbot 1969), p318.
40 Marshall, Vol I, p42; Whishaw, pp317-8.
41 Marshall, Vol I, p45.
42 *HC* 22nd Jun 1912.
43 *A Companion to the Manchester and Leeds Railway*.
44 Ibid; Whishaw, pp320-1.
45 T Normington, *The Lancashire and Yorkshire Railway* (Heywood, 1898), p7.
46 H Clarkson, *Memories of Merry Wakefield* (Wakefield, 1889), pp134-6.
47 Marshall, Vol I, pp117-9.
48 T Normington, p53.
49 Travis, *Historical Sketches of Some People and Events*.
50 Fielden MSS, Account of yarn production and wages paid, Jul–Sept 1842.
51 William Greenwood's diary.
52 C Aspin, *Lancashire, the First Industrial Society* (Helmshore, 1969).
53 Townsend and others, *A New History of Methodism*, Vol I, pp386-8, 405, 499-502; R Currie, *Methodism Divided* (1968), pp58-9; Horsfall Turner, *Halifax Books and Authors*, p238.
54 Townsend and others, Vol I, p415; Fox, pp1-9, 18-29; Jessop, *Methodism in Rossendale*, pp186-90.

55 Religious and Educational Censuses 1851, HO 129/495-6.
56 *THBHA* 1900.
57 *TA* 13th Aug 1937.
58 Joshua Wilson, *A Short Memoir of the late Mrs Alice Wilson* (Manchester, 1877), pp14-16.
59 Wilson and Davies, *History of Halifax and Calder Valley District of Baptist Churches*, p35.
60 Ibid, pp17, 30-38.
61 A Taylor, *History of English General Baptists* (1818), Vol II, pp286-7; Wilson and Davies, p30.
62 *THBHA* 1900.
63 BIHR, Dissenting Certificates.
64 G Lawton, *Collections relative to the Dioceses of York and Ripon* (1842), pp129-30; HO 129/495-6.
65 Rt Rev Francis Gastrell DD, footnotes by Rev F R Raines, *Notitia Cestriensis*, Vol II, Pt I, p153.
66 Holden, p136.
67 Charity Commission, *Reports*, Vol 18, 1828, pp586-7; Vol 19, 1828, pp291-2.
68 A W Fox, *The Todmorden Unitarian Congregation, a centennial sketch* (Todmorden 1924), p11; Holden, p197.
69 Holden, p198.
70 Ibid, p198.
71 Ibid, p199.
72 Ibid, p199; Weaver, p32.
73 Fox, pp32, 35.
74 Fox, p25.
75 *1833 Education Enquiry Abstract* (1835).
76 HO 129/495-6.
77 Weaver, pp31-2.
78 Ramshaw, p88.
79 *PP* 1846, Vol xx, p631; 1849, Vol xxii, p326; Ramshaw, pp117-20; Holden, p200.
80 Greenbank, *PP* 1846, Vol xx, p631.
81 Sunderland, *TA* 30th Sept 1904.
82 *Factory Inspectors reports* (*PP*), Apr 1858, p38, May 1859, pp24-5; S J Curtis, *A History of Education in Great Britain* (4th edn, 1957), pp230-1, 254.
83 Fox, p51.

Chapter 10

Throughout this chapter, information on the fortunes of individual firms and mills, unless specifically referenced, comes from John Travis, *Chapters on Todmorden Industry* (Todmorden, 1901) and/or from the files of the *Halifax Courier*, *Halifax Guardian* and *Todmorden and Hebden Bridge Advertiser*.

1 *Memorandum and Articles of Association*, Derdale Cotton and Commercial Company, 4th Mar 1861 (TPL).
2 *TA* 25th Jan 1862.
3 *HG* 13th, 20th Aug 1853.
4 Fielden MSS, Return from Mills, 14th May 1856, kindly supplied by B R Law.
5 *TA* 26th Jun 1901.
6 *TA* 25th Jun 1862.
7 *TA* 13th Sept, 18th Oct, 29th Nov, 13th Dec 1862.
8 *TA* 10th Jan 1863.
9 *TA* 24th Jan 1863.
10 *TA* 7th Mar 1863.
11 *HC* May/Jun 1863.
12 *TA* 17th Oct 1863, 2nd Apr 1864.
13 Fielden MSS, 1864-7.
14 J Kelly, N B Harte and K G Ponting (eds), *Textile History and Economic History* (Manchester, 1973), pp354-86.
15 *HG* 16th May 1974.
16 *HG* 20th May 1876; *HC* 19th, 30th Jun, 28th Jul, 11th, 25th Aug 1877.
17 *TA* 9th, 16th Jan, 6th Feb, 16th Apr, 29th Oct, 5th Nov 1880, 4th Feb 1881, 20th, 27th Jan 1882, 21th Feb 1930, 22th Sept 1939.
18 *Rivers Pollution Commission, 3rd Report*, Vol ii, Pt 2, *PP* 1871, Vol xxvi, p148.
19 Patent Office, 27 patents in the names of the Lord family, 1847-70.
20 1851 Census; *Directories*: Pigot 1834; Jones 1863-4; Kelly 1893; Travis, pp47-8, 80, 101-2.
21 Holden p173; Wilson Bros, *One Hundred Years 1823-1923* (Todmorden, 1923); *HG* 26th Nov 1859.
22 W S Murphy, *The Textile Industries* (1910), Vol 3, Ch 6.
23 B R Law, *Fieldens of Todmorden: A Nineteenth Century Business Dynasty* (Littleborough, 1995), pp135, 138, 243.
24 Worrall, *Lancashire* 1901-12.
25 HO 67/6/93 and 26/116.
26 *The Autobiography of Samuel Fielden* (P Foner, ed), in *The Autobiographies of the Haymarket Martyrs*, p136.
27 MAF 68/ 37, 38, 81, 82, 361, 383, 760, 782, 1330, 1352, 1523, 1751, 1865, 1922, 2150.
28 Population statistics from census returns on microfilm, TPL.

Chapter 11

References to Friendly Societies and the Unitarian Mutual Improvement Society and Sunday school are from original pamphlets, notes, minute books etc, in the possession of Mrs E M Savage, Todmorden.

1 *The TPL Journal 1934*, 'Science in Todmorden, A Brief Historical Survey'.
2 Based on the Yorkshire Union of Mechanics Institutes, *Annual Reports 1840-48*.
3 *CN* 30th Jan 1937.
4 N H Gregory, *A Century's Progress; 100 Years of Co-operation in Hebden Bridge* (Hebden Bridge, 1948), pp3-4; *CN* 16th May 1903.
5 F Pickles, *Jubilee History of the Bridge End Equitable Progressionists' Society Ltd* (Todmorden, 1901).
6 Ibid.
7 Ibid, p34-35.
8 *Annual Reports of the Co-operative Congress 1878, 1903, 1904*.
9 S C Moore, 'An Industrial Study of Hebden Bridge' in *The Economic Journal*, Vol XXI, 1911, pp613-24, and Vol XXIII, 1913, pp442-7

(a copy of Moore's paper is in the library of the Hebden Bridge Local History Section).

10 Pickles, p80.

11 Gregory, p21; Pickles, p143.

12 Pickles, p107.

13 *CN* 26th Jul 1900.

14 P Thomas, 'The Origin and Early Ideals of the Hebden Bridge WEA' (Leeds MA dissertation, 1974), p26.

15 B Jennings, *Albert Mansbridge* (Leeds, 1973), pp1-3; Oxford Delegacy, Annual Reports; *HBT* 8th Mar 1889.

16 *CN* 18th Oct 1930; B Jennings, 'Robert Halstead', J M Bellamy and J Savile (eds), *Dictionary of Labour Biography* Vol 2 (1974), pp154-9.

17 B Jennings, *Knowledge is Power, A Short History of the WEA 1903-78* (Hull, 1979), pp1-7.

18 Information for the rest of this chapter, except where otherwise stated, has come from *TA*; *THBHA*; Travis; letters belonging to Todmorden Cricket Club; Mrs E M Savage, *The Development of Todmorden 1700-1896*; and Mrs S Cockcroft's research on local fairs and theatres.

19 *Centenary Booklet of Roman Catholicism in Todmorden* (Todmorden, 1968).

20 Ramshaw, pp80-95; E M Savage, *Murder at the Vicarage*, Todmorden Antiquarian Society Publication, no 3.

21 *The TPL Journal 1934*, 'Science in Todmorden'.

22 Much of the material comes from the *Rivers Pollution Commission*, Minutes of Evidence, pp387-399, and Evidence—Answer to Queries, pp146-149.

23 Holden, pp201-2.

24 Transcripts of the Todmorden Charter Opposition Official Inquiry, 5th-14th Oct 1886, held at Todmorden Town Hall before Hon T H W Pelham (TPL).

25 *THBHA* 1897.

26 Cornholme WEA, *Gold Under the Hammer. Passive Resistance in Cornholme 1902-14* (Todmorden, 1982).

Chapter 12

In this chapter, information about the equipment and products of the local textile firms comes from Worrall's annual *Cotton Spinners and Manufacturers Directory for Lancashire*, continued from 1931 as *The Lancashire Textile Industry* (Oldham), cited here as Worrall, *Lancashire*. The returns to Worrall from Fielden Brothers have been corrected by reference to Brian R Law, *Fieldens of Todmorden*, pp135, 248, and the totals given have been adjusted accordingly.

1 *Todmorden Trail* (Todmorden, 1975).

2 R Robson, *The Cotton Industry in Britain* (1957), pp331-8; J H Bamberg, 'The Rationalization of the British Cotton Industry in the Inter-war Years', *Textile History*, Vol 19 (1), 1988, p83; M Dupree,

'Fighting against Fate: the Cotton Industry and the Government during the 1930s', Ibid, Vol 21 (1), 1990, p102.

3 Holden, p207.

4 R Birch, *Todmorden Album* (Todmorden, 1983), p60.

5 *William Holt 1897-1977* (Todmorden, 1980), p9.

6 J A Lee, *Todmorden and the Great War 1914-18* (Todmorden, 1922), pp7-47, 87, 135-42, 163; *Ministry of Labour Gazette*, Feb-Jun 1918.

7 A J Robertson, 'Lancashire and the Rise of Japan 1910-1937', *Business History*, Vol 32 (4), Oct 1990, pp87-9.

8 Lee, pp138-9; *TA* 31st Dec 1920. 9 *TA* Dec 1918, 1922, 1923, Oct 1924, Jun 1929, 1931, 1985.

10 *TA* 31st Dec 1920, 14th Oct 1921; 1921 Census, *Population Tables*.

11 This and the next four paragraphs were researched by Mr Jack Bednall.

12 *TA* 27th Mar, 29th May 1936.

13 *TA* 29th May 1936; R Birch, *Todmorden Album*, p45, Vol 2, p123.

14 *TA* passim 1920-21, 1st Feb, 14th Mar 1924.

15 *TA* 12th Nov 1920, 26th Dec 1924.

16 *TA* 2nd Nov 1928, 5th Nov 1937.

17 *TA* Dec 1920 — Jun 1922.

18 The next four paragraphs are based, unless otherwise stated, on Worrall, *Lancashire*, 1916, 1925, 1928.

19 *TA* 26th Sept 1930.

20 *Ministry of Labour Gazette*, Jan, Mar 1928; *TA* 26th Apr 1929; B R Law, *Fieldens of Todmorden*, pp246, 248.

21 Borough of Todmorden, *Abstract of Accounts* (Todmorden, annual).

22 *TA* 10th Jul 1936, 29th Dec 1939.

23 *TA* 7th Aug, 2nd Oct 1936, 9th Dec 1938.

24 *TA* 3rd Jan 1930.

25 *TA* 12th Dec 1920, 18th Jan, 1st Feb 1924, 12th Apr, 20th Dec 1929, 17th Jan 1930, 16th Jan 1931 and passim.

26 Borough of Todmorden, *75th Anniversary Booklet* (Todmorden, 1971), pp54-5; *TA* 21st Feb 1930; R Birch, *Todmorden Album*, Vol 3, p46.

27 *TA* 10th Jun 1927, 6th Jun 1930 and passim.

28 *TA* 26th Jun 1936, 10th Sept 1937, 2nd Sept 1938 and passim.

29 Fred Root, *A Cricket Pro's Lot* (1937), pp186-7.

30 *TA* 26th Dec 1924 and passim.

31 *TA* 1st Apr 1921, 24th Mar 1922, 5th Oct 1928, 15th Mar, 20th Sept 1929, 3rd Jul, 19th Sept 1936, 29th Sept 1939 and passim.

32 Alan Bennett, *Writing Home* (1995), p7.

33 *William Holt 1897-1977*.

34 *TA* Aug 1929 — Jan 1930; *Ministry of Labour Gazette*, Aug, Sept 1929.

35 *TA* 6th Jun 1930

36 *TA* 2nd, 9th Aug 1929, 13th Jun, 16th Jul, 26th Sept, 5th Dec 1930; Bamberg, pp87-94; Worrall, *Lancashire 1931*.

37 *TA* 6th Sept 1929, 3rd Jan 1930.

38 *TA* 22th Aug, 26th Sept, 3rd Oct, 26th Dec 1930.
39 1931 Census, *Occupational Tables.*
40 Robson, p22; Robertson, pp96-7; W Mass and W Lazonick, 'The British Cotton Industry and International Competitive Advantage: The State of the Debates', *Business History*, Vol XXXII (4), Oct 1990, p50.
41 *Ministry of Labour Gazette*, passim; *TA* 6th Mar 1936; Cockcroft family records.
42 *TA* 26th Jul 1935.
43 *TA* 4th Jan 1935, 27th Jul 1934.
44 *TA* 24th Apr 1936.
45 *Ministry of Labour Gazette*, Jan 1937; *TA* 1st Jan, 24th Apr 1937.
46 *Ministry of Labour Gazette*, Jan-Dec 1938; Worrall, *Lancashire* 1938; A Fowler, 'Lancashire Cotton Trade Unions in the Inter-war Years', in J A Jowett and A J McIvor (eds), *Employers and Labour in the English Textile Industries 1850-1939* (1988), p121.
47 Worrall, *Lancashire* 1938.
48 S G Jones, 'Work, Leisure and the Political Economy of the Cotton Districts Between the Wars', *Textile History*, Vol 18 (1), 1987, p44.
49 *TA* 29th Dec 1939; *Ministry of Labour Gazette*, Oct-Dec 1939.
50 'Cocoa Works in Wartime 1939-45', Rowntree magazine in the possession of Mrs E Marshall, Todmorden.

Chapter 13

1 *TA* 1st to 15th Sept, 29th Dec 1939; R W Lacey, 'Cotton's War Effort', *Manchester School of Economic and Social Studies*, Vol 15, 1947, pp26-69; J Singleton, 'Planning for Cotton 1945-1951', *EcHR 2nd series*, Vol 43(1), Feb 1990, p63.
2 Lacey, pp31, 56; Worrall, *Lancashire* 1938.
3 *TA* 12th Sept 1941.
4 Worrall, *Lancashire* 1946.
5 Singleton, p76; *TA* 15th Nov 1946; Worrall, *Lancashire* 1950.
6 T Sharp, *A Plan for Todmorden* (Todmorden, 1946).
7 *TA* 18th Jan 1946.
8 *TA* 24th May 1946; Borough of Todmorden, *75th Anniversary Booklet*, p13.
9 *TA* 21st Jan 1946, 3rd Jan 1947; *Whitaker's Almanack.*
10 L Briscoe, *The Textile and Clothing Industries of the UK* (Manchester, 1971), pp86-9; J Tomlinson, 'Planning for Cotton 1945-1951', *EcHR 2nd series*, Vol 44(3), Aug 1991, p524.
11 J Singleton, *Lancashire on the Scrapheap: The Cotton Industry 1945-1970* (Oxford, 1991), pp154-9; *TA* 1st, 22nd May 1959.
12 *TA* 8th May 1959; Worrall, *Lancashire* 1960; B R Law, *Fieldens of Todmorden* (Littleborough, 1995), p282.
13 Ibid, 1965, 1970; W Mass and W Lazonick, 'The British Cotton Industry and International Competitive Advantage: the State of the Debates', p23.
14 Singleton, *Lancashire on the Scrapheap*, pp221-30; The Royal Commission on the Historical Monuments of England: Yorkshire Textile Mills Survey, Mons Mill, CD 9D, Jul 1988.
15 *75th Anniversary Booklet*, p58.
16 *HC* 24th Jan 1968.
17 *TA* 6th Mar 1959; Yorkshire and Humberside Economic Planning Council, *Halifax and the Calder Valley: An Area Study* (HMSO 1968), pp84-5, 145.
18 Ibid, pp5-29.
19 Ibid, pp142-4; *75th Anniversary Booklet*, p13.
20 W B Wilson and W S Davies, *A History of the Halifax and Calder Valley District of Baptist Churches*, pp12-22.
21 Todmorden Unitarian Church, *Centenary Booklet* (Todmorden, 1969).
22 J Burchall, *Co-op: the People's Business* (Manchester, 1994), pp154-64.
23 *TA* 13th Mar 1959.
24 *75th Anniversary Booklet*, p63.
25 H G Stevenson, *A History of Todmorden Golf Club* (Todmorden, 1983).
26 Sharp, p8.
27 *Guardian* 31st Oct 1995.

Index

Note: The township names — Langfield, Stansfield, Todmorden and Walsden — have been excluded, as the references would be too numerous to be useful. Otherwise this is a comprehensive index of topics and major place-names in and near upper Calderdale. Houses, mills and chapels have been indexed selectively, to facilitate cross-referencing. Names of people mentioned only once in illustrative extracts from documents have in most cases been omitted.